JOURNEYS IN THE NIGHT

JOURNEYS
IN THE
NIGHT

CREATING A NEW
AMERICAN THEATRE WITH
CIRCLE IN THE SQUARE

a memoir

THEODORE MANN

APPLAUSE THEATRE & CINEMA BOOKS ■ NEW YORK
AN IMPRINT OF HAL LEONARD CORPORATION

Applause Theatre & Cinema Books
An Imprint of Hal Leonard Corporation
7777 West Bluemound Road
Milwaukee, WI 53213

Trade Book Division Editorial Offices
19 West 21st Street, New York, NY 10010

Paperback edition published in 2009. Originally published in hardcover in 2007 by Applause Theatre & Cinema Books.

Printed in the United States of America

Editor: Glenn Young
Co-editor: Greg Collins
Book designer: Mark Lerner

ISBN 978-1-4234-8155-3

The Library of Congress has cataloged the hardcover edition as follows:

Mann, Theodore.
  Journeys in the night : creating a new American theatre : Circle in the Square : a memoir / by Theodore Mann.
      p. cm.
  ISBN-13: 978-1-55783-645-8
  ISBN-10: 1-55783-645-0
  1. Mann, Theodore. 2. Theatrical producers and directors—United States—Biography. 3. Circle in the Square (Theater) I. Title.
  PN2287.M298A3 2007
  792.02'33092—dc22
  [B]
                                                           2007010310

www.applausepub.com

DEDICATION

This book's genesis was a transatlantic phone call from my son Andrew, who out of the blue asked why I wasn't writing a history of Circle in the Square. My answer: "Because I don't think a publisher would find two people to buy it." Andrew, who now lives in France, said he could think of three off the bat—Samuel, Clementine, and Benjamin Theodore, my three grandchildren. The bad news for my publishers is that I intend to give those three copies away.

So, I dedicate "Papoo's" book to my grandchildren named above, and to Jackson and Dakota, the children of my son Jonathan and his wife Chandra. Here's to discovering new worlds and while I'm at it, I hope a French edition of this book.

CONTENTS

CONTENTS

JOURNEYS IN THE NIGHT

CHAPTER 1

A BOY GROWS IN BROOKLYN

I remember the very first shows I staged—family gatherings at which I'd put on dad's derby, grab his cane and sing songs "a cappella." If my voice quality was anything like it is now, that was real parental love! Over at P.S. 161 in Brooklyn, we'd all sing for Mrs. Ott, a broad-chested teacher who wore her red hair in a roll. Mrs. Ott would say, "Someone is flat here. Who is it? Raise your hand." That would be me.

I remember going around the corner from our apartment on Eastern Parkway to St. John's Place to see vaudeville at the Riviera. Its walls were bare but there was a stage and lights and an orchestra pit with eleven men. To this day, my spine tingles at the memory (if my youthful memory serves me correctly) of seeing Harry Houdini's brother, "Hardeen," perform there. He was inside a trunk, totally locked and chained. He then magically unlocked the trunk and was revealed to be chained and locked to a chair, which he also got free of. It would be many years before I'd hear the equal of the collective gasp emitted as he tumbled his way back to the stage before us.

It turns out I also saw Henny Youngman in one of his virgin engagements at the Riviera. Of course, to me he looked and sounded like a veteran jokester. Many years later, in a booth at the Carnegie Deli—that New York comic hangout immortalized in Woody Allen's *Broadway Danny Rose*—I met Henny and he confessed to me he had been scared to death up there during his big break. Until then his act had been limited to the Borscht Belt in the Catskills.

I remember going to the roof of Loew's Kameo movie palace with my parents. Potted palms encircled the audience. Two large standing electric fans cooled us and the air passing through the palms supplied a Mediterranean Brooklyn breeze. The racket of the trolley cars and automobiles three floors below were a world away.

Stepping out of the darkness came Jackie Coogan, Johnny Weismuller, King Kong, Leslie Howard—the best heroes ten cents could buy. What an adventure! The next day I'd gather some friends and we'd play in the alleyway of our apartment building. The setting was clothes lines stretching from one building to the other, which in my mind became the trees that Tarzan swung from. Gunga Din in the Sahara desert was in the sandbox of the Jewish Center next door. My imagination was so stimulated by these movies—prompting me to grunt and howl like King Kong, or carry a water bucket like Gunga Din, or stride elegantly about like the Scarlet Pimpernel, or practice walking bowlegged so folks would think I'd just rode in from Dodge.

Funny how character is formed—usually when you're not looking, or in my case, while I was looking at *Snow White and the Seven Dwarfs*. Until I was eleven I unthinkingly accepted cartoons as part of the entertainment world. But sitting in the balcony of the Savoy movie house one Saturday morning, watching the dark witch and Snow White eating poisoned apples, something in my little gut rebelled against that manipulation of my brain. I knew my palms were sweaty at the same time I knew I really didn't care one way or the other what happened to these sentimental splotches of pigment. I couldn't accept fear as entertainment. From that day forth I've never watched a cartoon, nor science fiction films for the same reason. This is much to the chagrin of my three French grandchildren, though I've convinced my American grandchildren to shun cartoons too.

My father encouraged a modicum of controlled rebellion. Sunday mornings he'd take my brother and me out of our strict kosher home into the verboten world of Irish ham and eggs at Murphy's. I don't think there was an Irishman who enjoyed his breakfast with so lusty an appetite. Other days, Dad would treat us to the savory delights of Chinese cuisine. The dumplings were very similar to the food we ate at home. I think the Chinese must have lulled their Jewish clientele into thinking they were eating kreplach. My mother, who would only cook and eat kosher food, was appalled by both of these exotic cuisines. We were anchored in a comfortable conformity at home but were expected to show independence and initiative when we crossed its threshold.

"Independence Within Limits" was my father's motto. But he was none too proud when his youngest son declined to study for his Bar Mitzvah. I'd gone too far and at the age of 14 was dragged to the Temple to become a man.

I grew up surrounded by my mother's family and my father's. I come from a political family with immigrant grandparents from Herson in Russia and Poland. My father's mother, Ida, was short and feisty. Many of the family Seders were at her home. She came over from Poland as a young girl and immediately had to go to work. The family spoke Yiddish at home so she never learned to read or write English—which she regretted. She was always advising me, "Study, learn." She had six children and they all had the print of her face.

Seders in later years were spent at my parent's apartment on Eastern Parkway and other Seders in the apartment of relations on my mother's side of the family. Visits to my father's relatives were usually preceded by a tempestuous scene from my mother refusing to go and expressing a multitude of reasons why. This finally led her to tears and my father would spend the next hour consoling and coaxing her to make the visit. Finally, we would wearily get in the car and go to my father's family. Once arrived, mother was sweetness and good humor and on the way home promised never to do it again.

My mother was the most wonderful, warm, friendly woman in all her other relationships, whether it be the tailor around the corner, the next door neighbor, the iceman bringing his large blocks of ice, the superintendent, the ragman who would shout up the alleyway, "Any rags today" (people would toss them out their windows and they'd float down like birds coming to rest), the butcher, my friends, their parents, and dad's friends. My mother was also very beautiful. Through her entire life she retained her Victorian coquettishness. She was about the best-dressed woman in the neighborhood and she made sure that my father, brother and I were very well attired. She loved the finer things in life and surrounded herself with them in the house: Paintings, furniture and carpets. She was an avid book reader. I learned a great deal from my mother—how to be friendly and nice to people. She was a very loving mother, ministering to my colds with mustard packs on my chest, treating hives on my legs (which required salves and wrappings several times a day), and repairing all my other cuts and bruises. I remember when I had a bump on my forehead, my mother would press a cold butter knife on the bruise. Coming back from the movies once my mother and I danced and sang in the street, "the bells are ringing for me and my gal." I loved my mother.

I was perplexed, though, by her different and exaggerated affections when it came to relatives. Mother was at silent war with my dad's side and at beautiful peace with her own. My mother loved anybody in her family that was her blood and was suspicious of any newcomers. Consequently, I guess my father gave up fighting for visits to his relatives and spent most Sundays with my mother's sisters or brothers. Whom he genuinely loved. As my dad would say, "If you can't beat 'em, join 'em."

One summer my mother's two sisters and their families rented a two-story house in Long Beach, Long Island. I had a warm happy time as I always did with my mother's side and felt somewhat alien towards my father's, which I think was a result of her discomfort with them.

My brother was always told that he looked like my mother's family, while I was delegated to looking like my dad's. So my growing up was lopsided and I was confused. I didn't like being identified with the side my mother disliked. This might be the seed of why I changed my name from Goldman to Mann when I was in my early 20s. Of course, another factor was the strong anti-Semitism prevalent in the United States well into the 1950s.

Artson was my mother's maiden name. The family had its origins in a seaport town on the Black Sea in Russia. When they came through customs at Ellis Island the immigration officer obviously misunderstood when my grandfather announced his name and the city he was from. So Herson became Artson—the sound is similar. An instant WASP name! And to top it, my cousins from my mother's side were blond-haired and blue-eyed while the Goldmans were all black-haired and brown-eyed like me. Mother was always exclaiming how beautiful these blue-eyed, blond-haired children were. The Artson name for us took on a significance as a non-Jewish name, and therefore "better" than Goldman.

Several times a week my mother and I would ride the trolley from Eastern Parkway to Flatbush to spend the day with my grandmother, Molly, who lived with her daughter Anna's family. She was a slender, beautiful woman with her hair tied into a bun at the back of her neck—very simple like a ballet dancer. Maybe that's why I've always loved dancers and have always encouraged my women to wear their hair in that style. Which they do—in the initial, short-lived thralls of enchantment.

I would run from the trolley stop to Molly's house, up the front stoop, back into the kitchen. Molly would pick me up and twirl me around and make me laugh. Her kitchen smelled wondrous. I loved my Grandma Molly. She's always been in my life watching me—this beautiful woman. Her oldest daughter Anna and my mother Gwen both looked like her, as do a few grandnieces and my grandson Samuel —with the same bone structuring, coloring and skin tone.

One day when I was about eight years old we were walking from the trolley towards Molly's house and saw a fire engine go by and I said excitedly, "Maybe they're going to Grandma." My mother said, "Shush, don't say that." As we rounded the corner the truck was in fact in front of Grandma's and as we ran up I saw Grandma lying on the ground wrapped in a gray blanket. She was taken away in an ambulance and it was explained to us by Aunt Anna that Grandma had been washing clothes to give to poor people. She was using kerosene in a large tin bucket to disinfect the clothes. Her rubbing the clothes caused friction which ignited into flames. Mother and I and the family rushed to Coney Island Hospital.

I was told to wait in the lobby on the second floor. The marble staircase railing was cold as I leaned on it. I prayed to God as hard as I could, pleading over and over, "Please save my Grandma! Please, please." I kept repeating the phrase over and over until it was dark in the hospital lobby and my mother came and stood by me, tears streaming down her face. She didn't say anything—but I knew. God had not helped my Grandma. At that moment, at age eight, I became a non-believer and didn't want to follow the Jewish religion's synagogue services or Bar Mitzvahs—I resisted it all.

As I have matured I have come to believe that God is within each one of us when we do good things for the world—that love and creativity within us is a sign of God. My sense of spirituality has grown over the years and I believe now in each man's connection to the universe, but we have to seek out the power of the universe and channel it into ourselves.

Many years later when my beloved wife, Patricia, was very sick with multiple sclerosis, I prayed again to God to help her to get better. But the disease just kept getting worse. I believe now you must help yourself and your loved ones with every means spiritual and medicinal that you can find.

When I was nine, it was one of my relatives, my Aunt Ruthie (pronounced "Fufu" by the children), who first revealed to me the wonders of Manhattan. Until that day, I'd never seen a building higher then three stories. "Extra! Extra!" was shouted from every street corner. But everything seemed "extra" on this trip to the big city. Extra automobiles, extra hawkers, extra crowds, extra frankfurters, more of anything than I'd ever beheld in my life. And this was my conclusion before we'd even reached our destination: the Roxy on 50th Street and 7th Avenue.

The Roxy had as many seats as I thought there were people in the world. Well, 2,750 seats was three times greater a capacity than any theatre I'd known in Brooklyn. Sure, I'd been to the movies hundreds of times but I'd never been anyplace like this. The interior was a masterpiece of movie palace kitsch with high ceilings, dazzling lights and soft seats. There were side boxes for the audience—the walls of the Roxy were decorated with gorgeous crimson drapery, marble columns and crystal chandeliers. The movie hadn't started yet but this day was already a showstopper. When my Aunt Ruthie and I traveled back to Brooklyn, this little boy left his heart on 50th Street, amazingly, about a half block from where I now work for my mistress, Circle in the Square.

We'd come to Manhattan to see the new movie *42nd Street*, starring Ruby Keeler and with choreography by Busby Berkeley. For this novitiate who'd yet to see a Broadway play, I was transfixed by what went on behind the scenes. Was I destined to become my own version of Julian Marsh, the hard-nosed but romantic producer/director? Wait a second, I've never sported a pencil-thin moustache! But there is some irony in that one of the leading actors in my first New York "theatre" experience was a producer—played by Warner Baxter. Ginger Rogers was the tough talkin' "Anytime Annie," and who in that audience that day will ever forget Ruby and Dick Powell singing "You're Getting to Be a Habit With Me"? There followed innumerable living room performances by yours truly of "Shuffle Off to Buffalo."

It was a short time later that I got my first taste of professional theatre when I was taken to see *Tobacco Road*, which ran from 1933 to 1941. Brooks Atkinson, the theatre reviewer for *The New York Times*, wrote a very interesting review: "The Theatre has never sheltered a fouler or more degenerate parcel of folks than the hardscrabble family of Jeeter Lester." Although Atkinson did go on to admire the "blunt truth of the characters." He also said that Erskine Caldwell, the playwright, is "a demonic genius—brutal, grimly comic and clairvoyant."

Atkinson greatly admired Henry Hull's performance and wrote that, "he creates a character portrait as mordant and brilliant as you can imagine." Later in the lengthy run, I saw James Barton in the same role—Jeeter, a Georgia cracker, bearded, dressed in dirty rags and heavily wrinkled face. He covered the whole range of emotions and passions. These people were sad, dirty but wonderfully funny.

I vividly remember the brother, Dude, throwing a ball against the wall of the shack continuously throughout the show. And Jeeter's daughter Ellie May, dressed in her pa's overalls—cut off to expose her thighs.

The *Tobacco Road* people—the Jeeter Lester family—were depicted as the lowest element of our population. In a way they are similar to the characters in another important American play that was to play a huge part in my theatrical career, Eugene O'Neill's *The Iceman Cometh*. In both dramas the people are at the bottom of our society and ignored.

I think my family thought it was important for me to see an aspect of life I was not exposed to in Brooklyn. They wanted us to live comfortably but not if it meant we were blinded to the injustice and cruelty in the world.

This was the first play I'd seen and I was in awe. My father was a longtime Democrat whose party has always fought for the rights of poor people. Some notes of synergy—James Barton played Hickey in the 1946 production of *The Iceman Cometh*, which we later produced in

1956. The theatre I saw *Tobacco Road* in, the 48th Street Theatre, was the same one that in 1954 we moved our off-Broadway production of *The Girl on the Via Flaminia* to. At the time of that move I *thought* there was something familiar about that theatre. Only now have I made the connection.

On Saturday afternoons I'd sneak away with my friends up Eastern Parkway to Bedford Avenue, all of us laughingly tripping each other as we went along. We were heading for the weekly cowboy serials with Tom Mix, Ken Maynard, and Harry Carey, plus a feature film at the Savoy movie theatre. I still wanted to be a cowboy.

I worked as an usher after high school at a nearby movie theatre and on the weekends. Around the corner from Erasmus High was the Flatbush Theatre, where I also worked and saw Canada Lee in *Native Son*. I still remember his intensity, his anguish and frustrations with his burning eyes filled with tears and sweat beads rolling down from his high forehead. There were a few more forays into the theatrical realm. On my second trip to Broadway, I saw Ray Bolger in *On Your Toes*, and today when I sing a few lines of "There's a small hotel by a wishing well," I still hear Bolger's rich, warm, playful voice. In my mind, at least.

CHAPTER 2

A WORLD OF CULTURE

After Erasmus High School, I entered New York University's School of Commerce at the eastern end of Washington Square Park. Bored with my subjects, I would go out and sit on a bench in the park, looking west, not knowing I was staring at my future. My brother had told me stories about a place with a funny name, Greenwich Village, where he saw comedians such as B.S. Pulley and Zero Mostel. Sitting on my bench I had no idea I was a few blocks away from where my theatre career would bloom.

I was taking accounting courses at NYU in preparation to become a tax lawyer—my father's wish. I tried out for NYU's Junior Varsity basketball team whose practices and games were at the campus of NYU in Washington Heights. Miracle of miracles, I made the team, along with Reggie Austin and Lionel Malamed. Reggie was the first black basketball player I'd ever played on the same team with, though I'd competed against black teams in Harlem when I played for the Brooklyn Jewish Center Varsity. Being selected as a member of the team was a great personal victory for me because, at Erasmus High, Coach Al Bedain had failed to see my ball-handling talents.

This was the day of 5'8" and 5'9" ball players. We practiced every day after school at the NYU Washington Heights Campus. Many days we scrimmaged against the varsity, which included Jerry Fleishman, Sam Mele, and Dolph Schayes. They all became professionals, Jerry with the

Knicks, Dolph with Syracuse and Sam as centerfielder for the Boston Red Sox.

After practice, I had a long subway ride from Washington Heights Campus to Brooklyn. I slept most of the way—I was exhausted from the warm ups, workouts, and no-timeout scrimmages that Coach Howard Caan drove us through. Coach Caan was a benevolent dictator, a big man who rarely raised his voice, never smiling but definite. He believed that you had to run, run and run. In the winter months we ran outdoors. Whistle in mouth, he punctuated the practice with that shrill sound. And just when you couldn't run any more you had to run some more. The payoff for all the work was playing some of our games in Madison Square Garden.

But the cold abstract numbers required in the tax course couldn't relate to my exhilaration for life. My mind wouldn't digest it. So I just took liberal arts courses at the university instead. My career choice became moot in June of 1943 when I was drafted into the Army. My transfer to the South Pacific was then interrupted when the Army found out I could type and take shorthand. So I was kept in Monterey in the medical corps, at Fort Ord, as a private.

Like the Boy Scouts before, when I was pushed ahead to be an Eagle Scout, the Army saw promise in me and elevated me to Sergeant at the dispensary there. I devised a weekly schedule as follows: one week you worked four days and were off three, and the next week you worked three days and were off four. Part of my reasoning was to carve out enough time to attend classes at Hollister Junior College in Salinas. I hitchhiked the twenty miles from the base three nights a week. The teachers were overjoyed. Out of a base of 50,000 I was the only GI who'd come to study. Was there a particular degree I wanted to pursue? Nope. I just wanted to stimulate my mind. It had fallen dormant with army routine and I was elated to feel it working again.

There was very little after-hours fun at Ft. Ord. The USO was cavernous and dreary. It was a place where GIs could hang out, play the juke box, buy candy and soda pop, and maybe get a dance with one of the few local girls who showed up. I decided to hitchhike over to Carmel where I'd heard the USO was smaller but couldn't possibly be any duller.

As it turned out, the Carmel USO had a lot of girls and very few

GIs. This was the place for me. As I walked toward the club I saw this girl playing ping-pong outside with a GI. She was very agile, laughing brightly, and I was instantly attracted to her. She had long straight black hair, blue eyes, an olive complexion, and a beautiful shape. Her name was Kraig Short. We danced, and afterwards we talked as I walked her home through the charming tree-lined streets of Carmel. Kraig had a wild streak running through her; she was full of ideas with the life bursting inside of her. She introduced me to her mother, Marie, who also had black hair, though dyed. Marie was extremely energetic, with darting eyes, an inquisitive strong personality, and a Pall Mall cigarette always dangling from her lips. As she talked her hands would fly like birds let out of a cage.

Marie would invite her friends over for a regular cookout every Sunday. They would go to the beach and search for abalone in the low tide. Afterwards they would all gather at the house. Amongst them were local artists Robinson Jeffers, Edward Weston, and John Steinbeck's ex-wife. Langston Hughes would also sometimes drop in. Young officers joined in from the Presidio in Monterey, many of whom were New York writers and journalists. They all brought vivacity, fun, camaraderie, and ethnic mix to the household. I felt, somewhat to my amazement, comfortable being with them. It was probably because I was treated as an adult and not a child. More importantly, these adults were not my relatives, who previously had been my main social exposure. The other wonderful thing about them was that they weren't related to one another. They never wore ties or socks and many of the artists had beards. This was like being in a new country and proved a riotous stimulus to my young 19-year-old mind. I stumbled on an oasis of culture in Carmel that would resonate throughout the rest of my life. You do get some benefits from being in the U.S. Army—not necessarily those they advertise.

Their ideas were like sparks. I realized how bored I'd been. My relatives' conversations seemed to be on an endless loop. Please don't misunderstand. I loved my family, but I was 19 and ready to burst. Fate smacked me into the world of art. Except, I couldn't write. I couldn't paint. But I knew I wanted to be in the world of art in some way.

I had a furlough and decided to bring Kraig back to New York to meet my family. We wanted to get married. Kraig's mother was a friend of Anne Morrow Lindbergh's sister, who was heading back east and wanted her car driven there. It was a Chevrolet with the driver's window missing. I agreed to drive the car back with Kraig. So one day late in the afternoon we started on our cross-country trip.

As we proceeded, the light dimmed and rain started to fall. I had very little experience driving under such conditions and was following the yellow line. Suddenly, there was no yellow line. The next thing I knew I was sitting in a car that was standing still, the horn blowing, the headlights beaming straight ahead. I got out of the car. As I did, two GIs who'd been coming in the opposite direction came to help me. I couldn't see them because blood had run into my eyes. Fortunately, an ambulance from King City that had driven north to pick up an emergency patient that had proven to be a false alarm, was on its way back to King City hospital empty. The two GIs waved the ambulance down and it took me to the hospital. Kraig had fallen out of the car and was perfectly all right. She came along with me to the hospital.

The next morning a state trooper came into my room carrying my shoes and told me the car had landed ten feet from a ravine and how fortunate I was. The glass that had cut my face and broken my nose had come from the front windshield. The trooper said that all the glass in the car had been shattered. The car had been totaled. A couple of hours later, a couple came in to see me. They had been driving on the road and had seen the accident and were anxious to know if I'd survived. They told me my car, which had been traveling at 60 mph, had turned over four times. I had missed a curve and shot off the highway. When I looked at my face in the mirror, I was stunned and cried. It was bandaged with dried blood all over. Every day Kraig would come and see me in the hospital. Her love helped me to get through this terrible experience. It helped me to believe that my ravaged face was not ugly. If those GIs and the ambulance after them hadn't come along, I would have died. I would not be writing this book and sharing all my other somewhat less hazardous adventures with you.

Two weeks after the accident I was transferred to the hospital at Fort Ord, where I recovered for the next two months. When I was released from the hospital, I stayed at Kraig's house for another month. Kraig never got her chance to visit New York City, which she had wanted very much to do.

Eventually the stitches and bandages on my face were removed and my nose was reset. The doctor asked me which way my nose had been before. Fortunately or not, it snapped back on the other side. That snap was the most painful thing I'd ever experienced. After another month, I was discharged from the Army and went back home, with Kraig and I agreeing to speak daily. The war had ended a couple of months before. When I returned home I applied to Brooklyn Law School. The credits I'd earned at Salinas Junior College and my earlier year and a half at NYU qualified me. On one of my calls to Kraig, she informed me she'd fallen in love with another man, Edward Weston's son Neal. (I knew Neal; he was a wonderful carpenter, a handsome, sturdy young man.) On the phone I tried to persuade Kraig otherwise, but to no avail.

When I hung up, within a minute or two the phone rang. It was the phone operator, who said, in a Brooklyn accent, that she'd heard the whole conversation. She said, "I think it's just aww-ful the way she treated you." It was nice to get any positive feminine vibrations at that dire moment. The operator wanted to further express her sympathies, so we agreed to meet at Grand Central Station the following week. As I approached the information booth, I saw a fat, squat lady, about 30, and I turned on my heels and went in the opposite direction. I knew that that person could not assuage my emotional pain. We did speak over the next few months, and she would send me birthday cards for several years.

Just two years ago, I was in a health food store in Carmel. There was a young lady there whose chin line reminded me of Kraig. I asked, "Are you Kraig Short's daughter?" She replied, "Yes." I said, "I'm Ted Mann." And she said, "Oh, my God! My mother talked about you for years." (Kraig had since passed away.) I invited her to meet Jonathan and his family. She brought with her a silver bracelet. My silver bracelet. Kraig had kept it, as well as photographs of her and myself, in a special box all these years. I invited the daughter to come to New York to fulfill her mother's long ago thwarted trip. Which she did and I was so happy that "Kraig" in the person of her daughter Jana had finally come to New York.

CHAPTER 3

BEATNIK

I was living in my family's apartment in Brooklyn. My brother had married and I was alone in our bedroom feeling totally out of place. I missed Carmel. I kept talking about it, how beautiful it was, and the artistic atmosphere.

It was through my dad that I found my way back to the world of Art. One day he said, "Let's take a drive." Unbeknownst to me he'd done research and found an artist community in New York State—Woodstock. As soon as we drove down the road towards town, my senses were alive by what I was seeing, painters with easels working on the side of the road. Beatniks filling the streets. People everywhere were dressed casually, racially intermixing. There were art galleries, bookstores, cafes, theatres, and a jazz bar. It was a beautiful thing my Dad did—he helped change my life.

My parents rented a house in Woodstock that summer. This too was real parental love because my mom, a city bred girl, was afraid of the country—the bugs and especially the dark. When my mother would get out of the car to walk up to the house, my father preceded her and put newspaper down all along the path so she wouldn't step on any insects.

Every Friday I'd leave Brooklyn Law School as soon as class was over. I dropped my books and hitchhiked up to Woodstock where I immediately began to meet artists and make more and more friends. Early Monday morning, I'd hitchhike back to school and arrive unshaven

Maverick Theatre exterior, Woodstock, N.Y.

with no socks on. I was in rebellion even though I was still living at home in Brooklyn.

One night, at The Seahorse jazz bar I met the artist Ed Mann (no relation), with his mischievous sweet, bright smile. He wanted me to meet a friend who was staying at his house. When we reached his family's house on top of Ohai Mountain, I met José Quintero. When he came to the door he was clutching a book to his chest and had this beautiful warm welcoming smile, sparkling eyes, and shiny teeth. He was a touch under six feet with startling wavy black hair. We sat around drinking red wine—this is where I learned how to tilt the jug by balancing it on my arm. José was writing the "Great Panamanian Novel." That night he read poetry and Ed played his guitar and sang songs. José had a magnetic power and I felt drawn to him. José from Panama and me from Brooklyn, yet we both belonged to the same country, one that has never appeared on any map. As the sun started to rise I went to sleep on their couch. The next morning, I walked back into town feeling enriched by two new friends.

José became my tour guide into art. He loved poetry, painting, and dance—he particularly loved Martha Graham. I don't remember his talking of theatre in those early days.

At the end of the summer he and Ed moved back to their apartment at 52 MacDougal Street. I still lived in Brooklyn. Sometimes José and I would ride the subway together to raid my family's refrigerator. The IRT was my artistic lifeline but it also served as José's gastronomical one.

At the time, I was working in the stacks of the NYU library gathering books, a full square block under the library. The wooden floor space was so vast that we used roller skates to retrieve the books. José needed a job so I got him one there—after he assured me he could skate. Well, it turns out he'd never even been on skates. As a matter of fact, no one in Panama had ever skated or had even heard of them. It was quite a sight to see José hurtling down the library rows clutching on to the shelves. Each time a request came down the chute, off he went and when he finally returned with books in hand, there was a big victorious smile on his face. He'd made a successful skating trip in the library's labyrinth and hadn't fallen down.

One hot night in Woodstock, I went skinnydipping with a group of girls and boys. We drove to a secluded lake outside of Woodstock and when we were stripped and frolicking in the water a bunch of towns-people gathered on the bank to taunt us—particularly the women. Arms angrily folded they shouted obscenities at us, urging their boyfriends to take action. I told my friends to swim over to the opposite bank. I would gather everyone's clothes and drive the car over the bridge. When I got out of the water naked, the townies surrounded me. They clutched my throat, pushed me up against the car and rocked me and the car. One townie shouted, "We can't damage the car, it's personal property." So they stopped rocking it and gave me a shove. I was so scared for my life, if I'd had a gun I'd have pulled the trigger. I got our clothes and jumped in the car—thank God it started and sped off to the other side of the bridge. My friends piled in and we shot out of there, all of us naked. Everyone was quiet and shivering as they pulled on their clothes. After about two miles, I stopped the car and we all howled with laughter, which brought relief from the terror we'd just escaped. It was like we'd just survived a lynching.

That first summer in Woodstock on my way to the bookstore, there on the lawn I beheld June, a stunning young woman performing modern dance. June and I sat around on the lawn drinking and talking. Within days we were living together in her Woodstock studio. In October I found a brownstone in Manhattan for her on Perry Street and I moved around the corner on Charles Street. A below-level passageway between the two buildings proved a very useful quick exit whenever a relative of hers dropped by.

I talked to her constantly about Carmel. We decided to go for a visit after I finished taking the bar exams. June went ahead to visit her aunt who lived in the area. When my exams were over, I followed and within a few days after my arrival her aunt died. June stayed to settle the estate and I helped her through this difficult time. It's funny how fate steps into your life because we ended up staying a year in Carmel.

I rented a little cottage—a converted chicken coup on the ocean— from the Reilly family. They owned everything on the ocean side from Point Lobos to the Carmel River. What a fantastic, peaceful spot. We could wander the whole length of the property—a half mile wide and five miles long—without seeing a single homo sapien. This kid from teeming Brooklyn loved the isolation. I was following my father's thwarted desire to live in the country, a desire to which my mom always replied to him, "Well, maybe next summer."

June began doing pencil sketches of seaweed, seashells, and all the flotsam and jetsam we found on the beach. I collected seaweed that had curled into fanciful shapes and hung them as mobiles on the frames of our full-length picture windows facing the Pacific. One day, a bearded guy knocked at our screen door to ask permission to drive closer to the water. Something about the way the man looked made me think he was okay. But the first time I looked out I saw him standing on top of his station wagon roof and setting up an enormous camera with tripod. I watched with anxious curiosity as he pulled a black cloak over his head and looked into the camera. As a dutiful "Lord of the Manor," I strode out and demanded he leave. I suddenly felt an atavistic threat. I didn't want "my" property invaded. He pleaded with me to allow him to make just a few exposures. He was a heavyset man—bald with a cheery manner. He invited me to look in the camera to see what he was photographing. I saw gorgeous rock formations with waves of sea salt crashing high above them. Each formation was so unique it told a different story. I was in awe. All the images I was seeing were upside down. But that didn't affect my appreciation of the potential photograph. Of course, I acquiesced.

When he finished, I invited him to tea with June and myself and he introduced himself as Ansel Adams! Not a household name in 1949. He admired June's fine pencil drawings and my mobiles which hung in various shapes. He said they reminded him of Alexander Calder's work. We talked for about an hour—he was curious about our life in New York and then he left. Over the years I would see Ansel many times in the town, in galleries, cocktail parties and exhibits. He always referred to me as "the kid from Brooklyn."

Kraig's new husband, Neal Weston, introduced me to his brothers Brett and Cole, both serious photographers. We'd all been recently discharged from military service at the end of World War II. Through Brett, I met Robinson Jeffers' son, who showed me the wonderful maze of bushes he'd built on his father's property near the ocean in Carmel. And through Brett and Cole I met the photographer Morley Baer and his wife, Frances. I found myself interested in the world of photography. Morley lent me an old 4 x 5 Ansco view camera and tripod and I began shooting landscapes, houses, horses, cows, and June.

I also visited Edward Weston—whom I'd met in my earlier Carmel days at Kraig's house—at his Wildcat Canyon studio down the coast. Edward was a short man with a gentle manner, deep blue eyes and thinning hair. When I expressed a desire to see his photographs, he sat me

down at the table in his studio and stood beside me as he carefully removed the onion skin paper that protected each one of his photographs.
Then he'd patiently wait for a comment from me and only then would
show me the next photograph. These viewing sessions generally lasted
an hour. I was so overwhelmed by their simple beauty I asked if I could
buy some. After I made my selections, we'd sit around with a glass of
wine, bread and cheese, and talk about art, literature and the beginnings
of his career in photography. His companion, Dody Goodman, also a
photographer and writer, would join us as did his dozens of cats that
wandered in and out of the cabin. I didn't have much money—earning about $150 a week working as a ranch hand, gardener, or house
painter—but I had to own some of his work. His photos were wondrous.
There were many hundreds to choose from. I chose—as I have done all
my life—works that moved me, those that I wanted to live amongst.

Edward never enlarged his work; what he saw through his camera
lens was the size he printed. At one point in Willard Van Dyke's documentary about Edward, Willard's camera was directed at Edward's famous cyprus tree on Point Lobos. Talking about the photograph that
Edward took—Willard moved his camera right and said "not there." He
moved the camera left and again said "not here" and then he moved to
the exact position of Edward's frame and said "right here." As they say,
art is in the details. Edward's photos now sell for many thousands of
dollars but at that time his work went for $50 a piece. This was a hefty
sum for me but I loved them and in my innocence I bought six prints
signed by Edward during that year. These prints still live with me and
have become invaluable as Edward's fame has grown. Edward was yet
to achieve vogue status and I am proud that the first print I ever sold of
my own work was to Edward—three horses grazing near the ocean—for
which he paid me $10. Edward's appreciation of my photograph made
me feel that I might have the eye of an artist.

During that year, 1949, I also worked as a census enumerator. In my
wanderings through this wonderful country, a woman I came upon was
cutting flowers. Spotting this young bearded fellow walking towards her,
she clasped her hands, dropped to her knees and raised her head to the sky
exclaiming! "Jesus has come!" I gently took her by the elbow and helped
her up saying, "The good news is that I am Jewish, but not Jesus!"

During that summer, Kraig and I saw each other again, returning to an old trysting spot under a giant cyprus tree overlooking the Pacific. The years fell away and the past wrapped us in its arms. We were as close as we had been, once again in love. We walked back to her house hand in hand. Neal was there and the dream evaporated. But it had been a delicious interlude.

One day, when I was working as a gardener, I came home after a grueling stretch of field work and told June I had to use my brain in some challenging way. I was frustrated and stagnated and wanted to go back to New York. That was fine with her. Her family had been agitating for her to join them on a trip to Paris—a very good way for them to get rid of me.

CHAPTER 4

BLUEBELL MEETS THE NATIVE AMERICANS

June and I drove cross country on old Route 66 through the desert, in "Bluebell," my newly bought, used 1935 old blue coupe—a two-seater, with a shelf behind us large enough to allow Geno, my black lab, to rest comfortably in.

Anyone who has traveled that route knows it's rich in multivaried desert vegetation. We tied a burlap water bag to a headlight. The desert temperature was 110 degrees and when the radiator dried up we were so grateful for that bag of water. It was a great adventure. Every day we stopped for a picnic lunch and slept in little motels with cooking facilities where we made our nightly dinner, washing the dishes and pots so as to be ready for the sunrise departure.

One day, just before the sun came up we arrived at the Petrified Forest. No one was there—not even Humphrey Bogart, Bette Davis, or her protector Leslie Howard. June and I felt we were back in prehistoric times as we wandered and tripped through the darkness. As the sun came up we became aware that we were standing among rock formations that had been a verdant forest eons ago. Despite my lifelong aversion to science fiction, I couldn't help feeling like I was Buck Rogers in an extraterrestrial adventure—a visit to an unknown planet.

Canyon de Chelly (pronounced "Chey"), friends in Carmel told us, was a required next stop. June and I asked the way from a group of Indians at a grocery store off the main road. Remembering my Brooklyn boyhood cowboy aspirations, I asked them what tribe they were from. They grunted "Oot Oot," sounding like owls. They had to grunt several times before I understood that they meant U-T-E. They eagerly gave me the directions. Pointing northwest they told me, "Road much bumpy" and smiled quietly.

They had, clean, weathered features, set against their bronze skin with beautiful straight jet black hair. The men were much more color-fully dressed than the women and were taller than me at 5'10". They carried themselves like prized roosters with their hand-wrought jewelry on their wrists, fingers and necks. As we stood amongst them I thought the Indians were thinking, "It's all right, we'll still be here when all of you white people are gone. This earth will some day be ours again."

When I bought Bluebell I asked the mechanic if it would get me cross country and he said, "Yes if you go forty miles an hour." This was a blessing in disguise because all of the other cars sped ahead of us. We enjoyed the scenery with the road to ourselves at our horse and carriage pace. We'd agreed that 250 miles was the most we'd try to cover in a day so that we could have a swim, if we were lucky, and see the wondrous sites.

We proceeded on the "road much bumpy" and boy was that an un-derstatement—the road from the main highway was all dirt and rocks— the dry dust billowing around our coupe which had no side windows. I looked down toward the dried riverbed of the canyon. A group of Indi-ans riding on horseback were going in the same direction, and then sud-denly they stopped, turned around, stood still and pulled their blankets over their heads. As we continued to drive I wondered, "What's going on?" Then, in a minute or two a sandstorm out of nowhere whipped up. We tried to deflect by putting shirts and sweaters at the broken windows, but to no avail. Geno was yelping and we were hysterical with laughter! Just as quickly as it had started it stopped. God jammed the brakes on. Every inch of our bodies was coated with sand. We wiped our eyes, our hair, and when I looked down into the riverbed I saw that the Indians had turned around and resumed their journey. We continued to bump along.

It was getting dark and we needed a place to sleep. Suddenly a trad-ing post appeared out of the dust like a movie set. A trader there who looked like Wallace Beery told us about a Christian mission with sleeping accommodations about twelve miles ahead.

As we drove into the mission, night had fallen and we were amazed to see lit street lamps, paved streets, and grass growing in front of the buildings down to the sidewalks. The mission looked like a small New England town. The entire surrounding area was desert and canyons. It was an extraordinary change of scenery. There were canyons on one side of the entrance and Salem, Massachusetts, on the other. Inside the mission, were Indian women dressed in Victorian servant outfits — stockings, shoes, white caps, and aprons. They served us delicious roast beef and potatoes and green vegetables prepared New England style and later took us to our room with a large four-poster bed with perfectly ironed white sheets, soft covers, and pillows. The next morning we had a big New England breakfast of bacon, eggs, ham, potatoes, and biscuits. The food was served by the Indian women on a table with beautiful white linen cloths. I offered to pay for the sleeping accommodations and the food but they refused. As we left, I looked back at the archway we'd driven through on our way in. It read: "Tradition is the enemy of progress." We got a big laugh out of the hypocrisy of the missionaries and their message to these beautiful people and their tradition.

The next morning June and I went to Canyon de Chelly to witness those legendary orange, red, and yellow canyon walls. Recessed into the walls were cave dwellings carved out thousands of years before. They looked down on a dried river bed which had been the sight of a Spanish invasion in the 16th century. The Spaniards had come to slaughter the Indians because they were infidels, but that night the riverbeds miraculously swelled up with rainwater and drowned most of the invaders. By the time the riverbed was again passable, the Indians had climbed to the canyon's inaccessible highest point.

As we resumed our trip east on Route 66, we stopped at an Indian's roadside lean-to where they were selling beautiful handmade jewelry. We didn't have any money to buy their necklaces, rings, or bracelets. But when I opened my trunk, they were astonished to see shells from the Pacific Ocean in shapes and colors they'd never seen before. They asked for permission to touch them and then in awe they passed them around to each other and raised them to the sun to revel in their transparency and reflections. I had starfish, abalone, and a dozen other variety of shells. Ancestral tales had told them of their existence but this was the first time that they'd actually seen and felt them in their hands, felt their spiritual powers. The Indians eagerly offered me any of their jewelry in trade and I accepted their generosity. We gave them the shells and they in turn honored us with their jewelry.

Once we got out of the desert the trip was about passing around and through cities as expediently as possible. We drove through the Holland Tunnel into New York City. As I turned onto Canal Street, Bluebell died. I mean died! The axle gave out and hit the pavement, the rear wheels splayed out like a spent horse. She was towed away to her happy hunting grounds.

That afternoon I took June home in the train to South Orange and told her mother that I wanted to marry her daughter. She said, "That would be nice if you were Polish, German, but not ah ah ah …" She hesitated, but never got to "Jewish."

CHAPTER 5

DISCOVERING A TREASURE

Dejected, depressed, and unwanted, I went to Woodstock to see my old friends. José had written to me that he and Ed had started a theatre and invited me to visit. I arrived in a new old secondhand car with my dog Geno, my view camera, and one book. José took me on a walking tour and showed me the shacks real estate agents advertised as "cottages" where the actors were living—sans running water and electricity. Only one of the buildings had cooking facilities. I said, "Where does everybody shower?" José said, "At the creek about two miles away." "That is quite a walk," I responded. "Not when you're dirty," he said.

My first visit to the new theatre was like entering a scene out of Bruegel. Outside the theatre, the actors were making masks, painting and building scenery, vocalizing, and trying on costumes as the music was playing on the windup Victrola. It was a scene of joy. After my somber meeting with June's mother it showed me that there was still life and it made me a little more sanguine.

The work that the company was doing was for the Loft Players' first production, Lewis Carroll's *Alice in Wonderland*. Ed Mann designed the set, masks, and costumes, and painted most of the scenery, after the drawings of John Tenniel. Ed was a man of many talents. Everything he touched he did well—very well—but, unfortunately, he never could settle on which discipline he especially wanted to do.

The Maverick was one of the oldest summer stock theatres in Amer-

Alice in Wonderland (1950), Maverick Theatre

ica, rumored to have been designed by Stanford White. It was a large structure built with local wood with long benches capable of seating 600 patrons. The audience area was raked; the floor was dirt and gravel. The proscenium stage was twenty-five feet wide by twenty feet deep. The Maverick Theatre unfortunately burned down in the seventies. When I last visited Woodstock, the recital Hall which had been built around the same time as the theatre was still standing, as was an old sign down at the crossroad which read "Maverick Theatre" and whose arrow pointed in the direction of our old theatre.

José told me his dreams for this theatre and added that they were existing on a shoestring. I told him about the manual work I had done in Carmel: gardening, ranch hand, carpentry, and how I loved photography. José gave me a skeptical look, which I was to see on his face many times in future years. I then told him that June and I had broken up and explained how desolate I felt. José gently took me by the shoulders and asked, "What are you going to do now?" I said, "I don't know. I just came to visit for a couple of days." José then asked, "Would you like to be our business manager?" I said to myself, "What is a business manager?" I'd never worked in an office before. On the other hand, I didn't have anything else to do that summer. I thought this would be a nice place to use my view camera to take photographs and to read that sole book, Henry James' *Turn of the Screw*. There was a lot of space for Geno, who'd already made friends with the actors. So I said yes, not fully comprehending what I was getting into.

José took me into a room at the back of the theatre where foliage was growing in through the window; there was an old wooden desk that shook a lot. On it was a large writing pad, a pen, and a telephone. José asked me to wait while he talked to the board of directors about my officially joining them as their manager.

I sat down at the wobbly desk and started to make a list of what I thought a business manager did. The list included: theatre parties, posters, audience, tickets and discounts, and food for the actors.

Before José returned I was dialing local hotels and country clubs to interest them in a theatre party and, while I was at it, would they let me put some posters in their windows? Next, I called printers about having flyers made because we didn't have the money to advertise in newspapers. I also asked the printer if I could buy a roll of blank tickets—the kind you used to get as a kid to pretend you were selling admission at the movie theatre. I called the police department and asked them what the largest food market was in the area. They told me of one in Kingston, New York. I had obviously picked up more business savvy from my father than I'd realized.

Later that afternoon, I had a meeting with the board members—Aileen Cramer, Jason Wingreen, Emily Stevens, and Edward Mann. They all welcomed me as their business manager. *Alice in Wonderland* opened—we got a nice notice in the Kingston newspaper. Our ticket price was only 50 cents but we still had great difficulty in attracting audiences. The acoustics were very good except that when it rained it was difficult to hear the actors. Those audiences that did come huddled down together close to the stage in this vast wooden structure. Amongst them were artists Jack and Sophie Fenton, who became my lifelong friends.

To help pull in audiences, Aileen came up with the idea of having a barter night once a week. I distributed flyers around Woodstock offering free tickets for food. The size of the audience increased, but unfortunately, those people who came brought mostly canned food—predominately baked beans, which have their well-documented undesirable side effects.

The kitchen shack had electricity, running water, and a stove. The company had fifteen actors and each week one was assigned as housemother to prepare meals on a single burner. I went to that store in Kingston, the biggest nearby city, to buy the large quantities of discount foods. When I returned I was playfully accused of buying dog food; "Here comes 'Woof-woof!'" they used to say. It was canned corned beef hash and pretty tasty to our groaning stomachs—especially when potatoes, rice, and ketchup were added for flavoring. On some rare barter nights we received fresh vegetables.

I threw myself completely into the theatre's needs. I sold the tickets at the box office and worked the concession at intermission. As the first act curtain was ready to go up, I ran backstage with coins jingling, the entire box office take in my pocket. The actors were already in their beautiful costumes, jewelry, fancy hairstyles, and in makeup sitting at the table waiting for the curtain to go up. I crawled under the table to say my one line as the "Leg of Mutton." As I sat there awaiting my cue, I looked around and saw the actors' legs. Some were dirty, some were hairy, some had torn stockings, and some were shoeless. Those that did wear shoes wore the same ones that they wore in the streets of Woodstock. At that very moment I thought: This is exciting! *This* is what I want to do! I want to be in the theatre! I felt like I was looking at heaven. Finally, the art form I'd long been searching for presented itself. The contrast between their beautiful costumes and their dirty feet was tailor-made to what I'd been discovering about the dichotomy of life. The glamour above and the squalor below.

From that moment, I knew I was locked into a life in the theatre. It's funny how little things become so meaningful. Years later, nothing has happened to dim that passionate love of theatre that I felt under the *Alice in Wonderland* table at The Maverick.

At night, after the performances, I'd retreat into my little cabin next to the theatre and read a page or two of Henry James' *Turn of the Screw* by my kerosene lamplight and doze off with the thoughts of a new life in the theatre. Years later, Julius Rudel, head of the New York City Opera, invited me to direct Benjamin Britten's opera *Turn of the Screw* with Marilyn Niska as the Governess. The production was very successful and it remained in the repertoire for ten seasons.

I was still doing photography every day with my wooden tripod and heavy 4 x 5 Ansco view camera—a smaller version than that of Ansel's: a daisy bursting out through the wooden dilapidated steps, an old rock sitting on an abandoned road and another of strips of daylight photographed from inside the theatre, and a large roll of hemp in dark recesses of the theatre. In the early days of the Circle, some of my photographs of the production were used for a display in the lobby.

After *Alice in Wonderland* we did Tennessee Williams' *The Glass Menagerie* with Emily Stevens playing Laura directed by Ed Mann, a double bill of Edna St. Vincent Millay's *Aria de Capo* with Federico Garcia Lorca's *The Love of Don Perlimplin for Belisa in his Garden*, directed by José, then William Saroyan's *The Beautiful People* with Aileen Kramer, and finally J.M Synge's *Riders to the Sea*.

As our summer season came to an end, Aileen had the brilliant idea to auction off all our sets, costumes, and props to pay off our debts. We also went to local artists Fletcher Martin, Herman Cherry, Jack and Sophie Fenton, Aileen's father Hilton, and many others who contributed their works for auction. After the event we were left with a surplus of $383. We were the first theatre company in twenty years not to be run out of town by the Woodstock merchants for monies owed. I'd been having nightmares of falling victim to the same fate as Huck Finn's dubious thespians, the King and the Duke, that of being tarred and feathered and run out of town on a rail. Feeling victorious, we decided to stay on and do more plays.

In October the cold winter started to blow in from Canada through our nonheated shacks and thin summer clothing. At our next meeting we all agreed we wanted to start a theatre in New York City. The board dispatched me to find a suitable site in the big town. One of our main motivations was as clear as the ice forming on our windowpanes—to get out of the cold—but our real one was our passion to do theatre.

CHAPTER 6

GIVING BIRTH

We had the auction money—which, in my naïvete, I hoped we might start a theatre with. I gravitated to Greenwich Village. The Cherry Lane Theatre and Provincetown Playhouse on MacDougal Street had been empty for several years. I went to see them and they both made me feel like the old woman who lived in that shoe. They had only 99 seats with tiny stages. They felt cramped and wrong. After the summer experience, where we performed on a big stage these two theatres seemed very limiting.

During the late forties, there was no activity known as "off-Broadway." There had been movements in the late thirties and early forties in which classic plays were performed but it quickly disappeared because rumor has it they were done poorly. In 1950, when I was looking, off-Broadway was like a ghost town with the wind blowing though the empty rows of seats at the Cherry Lane and The Provincetown.

My father suggested I look at an abandoned nightclub at 5 Sheridan Square across from Café Society Downtown. The New York State liquor authority had closed it down for violations. To its right was Louie's Tavern; to the left was Chemical Bank. I felt very cozy sitting between the money and the booze. Many nights in our coming stressful financial times I would think of drilling a hole to get at their vault. When I went inside the nightclub, what I saw was a typical 1930s hotspot, though empty. There was a semicircular dance floor with three supporting pillars running up the center, surrounded by tables and chairs. The bandstand sat at the far end of the semicircle. The walls were plastered with painted murals of pseudo-South Pacific scenes—an excuse for naked ladies, naked palm trees and naked animals. The building was two four-story brownstones joined together. The parlors became the entertainment area. When I walked up the rickety wooden staircase to the floors above the nightclub I found ten rooms. Their former glory had faded—discarded G-strings, broken roulette wheels, dice tables, and cots decorated with every kind of stain. The place looked like it hadn't been occupied for years. The rooms were a nice size and I thought—cleaned up—they would be perfect for us to live in—certainly better than the shacks. There was heat and running water. There was even one shower on the second floor. We could all bunk out here in these rooms and cook our meals in the old nightclub kitchen—with its big restaurant stove and mammoth refrigerators still in place. The kitchen was equipped with silverware, pots, and plates up the kazoo. There were even breadbaskets—ahhh! those infamous baskets—more on them later.

At that time, there'd been several stories in *The New York Times* about a theatre in the round run by a Professor Hughes at a university out west

Ernie Martin in the kitchen at Sheridan Square Arena Theatre (1950)

in Washington. I thought this space would make a perfect three-sided theatre similar to the Greek and Roman amphitheatres and also like Shakespeare's Globe Theatre. This was pretty grandiose thinking for a "tap dancer" from Brooklyn. I liked the idea of us doing plays in a new and different format. Something New York had never seen. The dance floor was sixteen feet wide by thirty feet deep. There was room for the actors to breathe. It would be so much more thrilling than those teeny "old woman in the shoe" theatres.

I was so charged up, I drove back to Woodstock in less than an hour. I told the board what I'd found. My adrenaline was pumping. I felt like a kid stumbling over hidden treasures. The board members got excited too and that night nobody slept. The next day we closed down the Maverick Theatre and drove to New York. By the time we got there it was dark. We went into the club holding up matches and everyone moving very slowly, taking in the space. When I found the light switch, there was José, standing center stage, beaming.

The Board authorized me to lease the premises at the best possible terms. The next day I paid a visit to the real estate agent, Jay D. Robilotto, who asked for a lot of money. Three thousand a month—ten times what we had in the bank. I explained to him that we were a new theatre group and didn't have that kind of money. He finally agreed to accept $1,000 per month, which we also didn't have. I didn't know where we would get it but I just kept pushing forward. I told my dad about the meeting and he said, "Rent the space . . . I'll give you the one thousand dollars. Try it for a month and see how you like it." I promptly took the check to Jay D. who said "Fine! But the landlord wants a seven-year lease with a security deposit of $7,000!"

I was stumped. The $383 which seemed so enormous in Woodstock shrunk to nothing in the Big City. My Dad suggested, "Go back to Jay D. and ask him if you can put up the security by paying it off on a monthly basis, over the term of the lease." Jay D., who was a very elegant and well-dressed man in his 60s who'd seen and known everything that happened in the Village, finally agreed to the deal.

A number of the Maverick actors came with us to the city—Ernie Martin, Frank McDonald, Claire Michaels, Miriam Green, and of course, the Board, Jason Wingreen, Aileen Cramer, Ed Mann, and

Emily Stevens. All of us set to cleaning the theatre, the kitchen, and the rooms upstairs. We took down the naked murals and piles of dirt followed. We removed the tables and arranged the chairs in rows. We removed the canvas and wood frames from the murals and stored them along with the nightclub tables for possible future productions. These tables, with their beautifully carved Victorian wrought iron bases, were eventually used six years later to help create Harry Hope's saloon in *The Iceman Cometh*.

Days later we were as clean as we needed to be to start life. We wanted to build a repertory company of twenty actors and we knew we had to audition, so now we began the process of finding more actors. We put a notice in *The Villager* and the theatre trade paper *Show Business* about what we were doing. The board all sat behind three tables with notepads, trying to look very officious as actors auditioned. This went on for a week—then the board convened and decided on their selection of actors. The pay for actors and all the rest of us was to be $25 per week. Those who wished to could live upstairs in the rooms. Ed, José and Emily continued to live on MacDougal Street. Aileen lived in her apartment on West Fourth Street. Geno and I lived in one of the second floor rooms, right behind my new office.

If you lived in one of the studios you had to take a turn serving as the weekly housemother. In addition, all of us, whether we lived there or not shared in all the chores that needed to be done to maintain the theatre. These included making costumes, building sets, sweeping, and shoveling the snow on the sidewalk in front of the theatre, keeping the mens and ladies rooms clean and maintaining the coal-burning furnace in the basement.

We named our new home the Sheridan Square Arena Theatre. In late October, 1950 we started to rehearse *Dark of the Moon* by Howard Richardson and Richard Berney, directed by José. I was busy doing business affairs so I only saw bits of rehearsals as I passed through the theatre. They were going quite well. The actors were telling stories to get the southern rural environment and language that was so important for the play. Emily was responsible for the building of the sets and Aileen hired somebody that she wanted to do costumes. I can only remember her first name which I think was Nastie—which she wasn't. She was a delightful person and a hard worker. Finally, after four weeks of rehearsals, we began to perform.

Dark of the Moon featured a new addition to the company: James Ray as the witchboy. Jimmy was Southern and brought a lot of wonder to the role, an authentic nature boy. The play is based on "The Ballad of Barbara Allen" and it begins with John, the witchboy, asking the Conjur Man if he can become a human. Later in the scene, John falls in love with a human, Barbara Allen. Eventually, the Conjur Woman, played by Nadine Murray agrees to change him into a human and tells him he'll be able to stay human forever if he is able to marry Barbara Allen—and if she remains faithful to him for one year. Through John's arrival in the town and the consequences of his bargain, the play explores the hypocrisy and unconscious prejudice of the townspeople and the town's moral figurehead, Preacher Haggler, played by Jason Wingreen.

Aileen was doing public relations for us and tried but couldn't get any critics to come from either the large or small newspapers. The only newspaper that did come was *The Villager* and they gave us a nice review. But very few people came to buy tickets. We had thought that in a city of 5 million we would at least have five hundred per week. But we were drawing about five to ten people a performance at $1.50 per person. Most performances the cast of twenty was larger than the audience. We were in trouble.

On top of that the police department declared us illegal. The captain said, "This space is zoned as a cabaret and you can't operate here. You have the wrong license. You need a theatre license." The word theatre in our name drew attention to us. If we'd just called ourselves the Sheridan Square they would have thought it was another nightclub and not bothered us. I pleaded, "Can we continue to perform, if we don't charge admission?" Begrudgingly the captain agreed. So we took down the name of the theatre and continued to perform.

Remember those bread baskets? After every performance, José gave a speech and asked for money and then we'd pass the baskets around. People were stingy—very little money came in. We needed it so desperately. My heart sank when I saw the pennies, nickels, and dimes. But somehow we kept going. José was so nervous making that pitch each night that he'd have a drink beforehand next door at Louie's Tavern to calm himself. As far as I know José had never touched hard liquor before and I remember the expression on his face was one of disgust with its taste.

When we started the theatre, I'd also been working in my father's law office on Broad Street. His associate had been my teacher at Brooklyn Law School, in Contracts, Professor Block. I consulted with him on our problem with the police. He said, "Look at the New York City code for nightclubs. There is a section which defines a cabaret." When I looked at the code, it read that a cabaret is (and I'm quoting from memory) "A place of public assembly in which there is entertainment and food and/or drink served." I thought wow this is a description of what we do! What does drink mean? The code did not define "drink" therefore it could be a grape drink or orange juice. If so, that meant that we didn't have to serve "liquor," and that "food" could be something as simple as a brownie, and "entertainment" could be a play. "That's it! We're home free!" I felt like Sherlock Holmes having discovered the missing clue. Sherlock was always very nonchalant about his accomplishments, but I was smiling big and was overjoyed that what we were doing was allowed by the city code, with some adjustments.

Brownies, etc., were provided by the wonderful bakery of Mrs. Douglas. When I'd come in to pick up the "food" she always had the look one often sees on a baker's face—contentment and fulfillment as she wiped the flour she had been baking with off of her hands onto her apron.

We could in effect satisfy the wording of the New York City code. We had met these three requirements. We forged ahead to get a license to operate a nightclub. But there was still something we had to do—come up with a new a name for our space. We board members, Aileen, Ed, José, Emily, Jason, and myself, sat in my office on the second floor overlooking Sheridan Square and threw alternative names around and around. We couldn't use the word theatre but we needed to convey that we were a theatre in the round without actually saying it. This was the dilemma. Our old name Sheridan Square Arena Theatre had been a dead giveaway. We sat for hours struggling to find a name. Many variations were suggested but rejected. We had run out of ideas completely. We were sitting in silence, exhausted, when someone said, "How about circle in the basket?" (Chicken in the basket was a popular fast food joint at the time.) Somebody jokingly said, "How about chicken in the square?" We were laughing and playing a word game now. Finally, after many variations someone, I think Ed, said, "how about circle in the square?" That was fantastic! The word circle would convey theatre in the round and square would indicate our location. Best of all, Circle in the Square is offbeat and presents a unique, memorable visual image. You have to think before you say it. This was the time that offbeat names for music groups began to appear on the scene.

We still had to tackle the whole process of transforming this nightclub into a theatre. We always were a theatre and now we were pretending to be a nightclub . . . we were play acting. The casts of characters in this drama were the inspectors from the New York City Municipal Building, the Police Department, and myself. As every good theatre student knows every play has to have an obstacle and an objective. In this case, the obstacle was securing the license to operate and our objective was to become a theatre by looking like a nightclub.

In order to get the cabaret license I had to obtain permits from the Fire Department, Health Department, Building and Housing Department, etc. So, I entered the dark, murky, mysterious and secretive world of municipal bureaucracy and spent many days at the Municipal Building on Chambers Street trying to find the right person to guide me and tell me what had to be done to satisfy all the departments. I felt like a Kafka character wearing a long raincoat. One of the most helpful persons in this bureaucratic nightmare was Commissioner Henry Finkelstein who guided me through this maze step by step, like a saint helping me to circumvent disaster.

Our task was to build the make-believe nightclub. Miraculously, a wandering young German named Otto came by and offered to do carpentry in exchange for a place to sleep. He was stocky with blond wavy hair and very thick eyeglasses. I wondered— could this guy hit a nail? We desperately needed somebody to do the work, so I readily agreed to the swap. He became our carpenter for the special tables we had to have built, as well as the elevated wooden bench bleacher section at the far ends of the theatre. The wood required for the job came from abandoned shipping crates which I found in the streets of the meat packing district near 14th Street.

These new small wooden tables were three feet in height and nailed to the floor. The face of the table was the size of today's medium pizza—just large enough to hold a soft drink and a brownie. They were spaced in between every two customers. The Fate known as "necessity," from the song of the same name was helping to shape our amphitheatre. When I introduced this idea of serving brownies, there was a lot of kidding that marijuana was being hidden in each cake. The admission tickets were the same size as a theatre ticket, however the language was cabaret. It read "COVER CHARGE," and under that "$1.50" and under that "TWO DRINK MINIMUM." They were designed to look exactly like a cabaret cover-charge card. All of this was done so that we could fulfill our part of the script entitled "nightclub disguised as a theatre." If the authorities accepted this "facade" we'd be legit.

Police regulations also required all cabaret personnel to be fingerprinted and photographed (known as a mug shot), so that each employee could be issued a cabaret identification card. The cabaret world had a tendency to attract the criminal element—bootleggers, drug dealers and ladies of the evening—and the police needed these cards to help weed them out. I had some familiarity with these cards. My dad had a financial interest in several jazz clubs on 52nd Street and I had worked at these places from time to time. This part of my own and my father's New York entertainment world escapades deserves its own chapter which will be coming along shortly, along with a story I have to tell about Billie Holiday.

All the young actors, not yet famous, who would come to us over the next few years, had to have these cabaret cards, including Jason Robards, George C. Scott, Colleen Dewhurst, Geraldine Page, and Peter Falk. José and all the rest of us also had to trudge downtown to the main building of the Police Department for this glorious initiation into the world of cabaret. I kept all of those cards in my office for safe-keeping and they are still in our archives.

Forty-five years later Jason Robards and I were at a seminar on O'Neill and he showed me his *Iceman* script, which had in it the last remaining nightclub cover-charge card. When he revealed the card, he chortled with devilish glee. "Four and a half hours for a buck fifty! They got a hell of a bargain."

Still lacking a license, we plunged on, performing *Dark of the Moon* and José still making a pitch for money before each performance. Jason W., Emily, Aileen, and I also joined in making the pitches. Finally in February after passing inspections of all of the city departments, the police approved us for a cabaret license. Hallelujah! This meant we could charge admission again and stop making the bread basket speeches! We hung our cabaret license right up next to the front door for the convenience of the first policeman or inspector that showed up looking for trouble. As an actor might say we had overcome our obstacle and achieved our objective. I didn't realize it at the time but, in through a side door of my life, my exasperating, seductive, glorious mistress, Circle in the Square, had walked in to take up permanent residence.

We continued on with *Moon*, at eight performances per week still attracting only small audiences. Understandably, there was a lot of unhappiness amongst the company about us having to play to so few people. But I pleaded, "We've got to perform the schedule we announced, audiences have to learn to trust what we advertise." So we slogged our way ahead fulfilling the announced schedule of performances. In the lobby at our desk box office, I'd hear couples walking by and the women asking, "what kind of club act is *Dark of the Moon?*" And the other would respond, "probably a fan dancer covering her you know what." But after a few weeks of continued bad business, we decided we had to let the *Moon* finally set.

Next we did a new play, *Amata* by Eugene Raskin, a professor at Columbia. He and his wife Francesca loved to perform. He played the guitar and she sang. I think that's how they came into our lives—through Ed Mann, also a guitar player. Now the conversations of passers-by were "Hey Ralphy, *Amata* must be a new snake charmer let's go in . . . nahhh let's go across the street and listen to Josh White and have a beer."

Amata wasn't much of a play and the business wasn't any better than *Dark of the Moon*. After five weeks we closed it.

Things were hard and getting harder. Salaries had to be reduced to $15 per week! The level of disgust and disenchantment was rising. The actors were getting fed up with the extra work they were required to do on so meager a salary—it was grueling. And besides everything else, we had to kowtow to our temperamental coal-burning furnace. It's a very delicate skill to bank a furnace to let it rest overnight and yet still produce heat. None of us ever perfected it; it was pretty much luck when it worked. When there was no heat, those of us lacking knowledge about furnaces (like me at 4:30 A.M.) would try to restart it by throwing on shovels full of coal and fail. Then I would make a frantic call to the plumber, Tony, a sweet short and chubby Italian man, to help. He was local—as nice as can be, but oh so hard to find (the days before cell phones). When he finally came and got our temperamental grandfather—the furnace—working, I would pay him immediately, and all other expenses had to wait. It came out of one of my pockets, instead of the other. That furnace must have dated back to the Civil War.

While all this was going on, Aileen, Jason, and I were trying and succeeding on occasion to get money from relatives and friends. Getting money for the company was a daily chore for me. A few bucks came in. After those sources dried up, I'd flip open the Manhattan Telephone Directory and shut my eyes and wherever my finger landed, that's the number I called seeking money, almost always getting rejected. One time I called a woman and she invited me over. It turns out she was an Orgon Therapist, Alice Kahn. When I came to her Westside apartment, I immediately started to tell her about the theatre and all its troubles. I was very nervous. She said, "Slow down. You have to relax. Go and sit in my Orgon box for a half hour—then we will talk." She told me about her 86-year-old grandmother who'd been cured from some disease by years of sitting in the box. The box which was the size of a super-large, walk-in refrigerator, had a bare light bulb and a wooden bench, the walls were lined with steel wool, which she assured me would draw the tension out of my body. She repeated, "Sit in there for half an hour to relax. You'll feel better. Then we can talk of why you called." After a torturous, claustrophobic half-hour without a telephone, I came out and said, "Oh, I feel so much better," and calmly continued to make my pitch for her to help the theatre. I told her what we were trying to do, about the plays we were putting on, and the unusual performance space. It worked; she contributed $250! What a wonderful thing an Orgon box can do! Those seeking to raise money should be required to use the box—$250 was a substantial amount in 1951, probably the equivalent of $2000 today.

Our next play was Jean Anouilh's *Antigone* with company member Miriam Green playing the lead. With every play we gave company members the important roles. This was one of the sad shortcomings in the early days. We were choosing plays based on company members rather than doing the best play we could find.

Anouilh adapted Sophocles into modern day France during WWII. The actors wore costumes of that period. The play had been Anouilh's statement of support for French resistance during the German occupation. This was our third play and we still were not getting critics and didn't have money for advertising and the hole of troubles was getting deeper.

Next was Giraudoux's *The Enchanted*, with Kathleen Murray directed by José, which ended our first season. It was a beautiful play but once again no major critics, no advertising, and no business. It was now June and the theatre was not air conditioned and we were nearly broke. Fortunately our good friend Fate stepped in and someone came along who rented the theatre and put on a new play for the summer. One day I came back to pick up papers and I saw the producer sitting with his feet up at my desk. I got so upset that someone was invading my territory. And this time the intruder was no Ansel Adams! But Patricia, the woman I was living with and soon to be my wife, said, "It's only a desk, dear!" How right she was!

Having the theatre rented took care of our weekly costs, so I was able to plan something else for us to do in the summer. I thought of the Borscht Belt in the Catskills where I thought the hotel patrons must be theatre lovers. I was soon to learn the error of that long held maxim—that all Jews love the theatre. So I began to make calls to see if I could get bookings. Mostly their entertainment was stand-up comics and dance bands. Rarely did they present a play. Famous comics such as Danny Kaye, Sid Caesar, Mel Brooks and many others all came out of that Borscht Belt training. So I drove up Route 17 to see if I could convince them of the wonder of putting on a play. I told the hotel owners, "How unusual this would be for your patrons. Good theatre from New York City. Your guests would love it, especially the great play by Tennessee Williams, *The Glass Menagerie*." I didn't dare mention Christopher Fry's A *Phoenix Too Frequent*, the other play that we were preparing, until I could find the right hotel that wouldn't be intimidated by its ancient Greek setting. Several of the hotels agreed to book *Menagerie*. Boy was I happy! We were gonna get paid $150 for each performance! I hoped to get three bookings a week. That would be $450 a week for the company. And no furnace to worry about!

So suddenly we had a tour with seven or eight hotels lined up for *Menagerie*. With my broken down stationwagon, I transported the actors and props to each hotel. At least we always got a free dinner in the kitchen.

One hotel in New Hampshire was advertising every Sunday in *The New York Times* about their cultural weekend—Arthur Miller, Lillian Hellman, etc.—I thought that would be a perfect place for *A Phoenix Too Frequent*—an intelligent audience would really appreciate this esoteric play.

At many of the *Menagerie* stops the audience would be talking or shouting out across the tables during the performance: "Minna, what did you have for an appetizer?" And Sammy would respond, "I love the chopped chicken liver!" Needless to say it was theatre chaos. They weren't interested. We were performing in their dining area at the far end of the room without the benefits of stage lights or a platform—so there was no theatrical separation. They must have thought we were somebody's kids pushed into the corner to play so we wouldn't bother the adults.

The New Hampshire Hotel, where we brought *A Phoenix Too Frequent*, had a small theatre with a stage and lighting equipment. It had one exit for the audience. The performance was packed, two hundred people filling every seat. Before the show, Ed Mann, the director, stood up at the front of the stage and began to explain the meaning of the title. He said, "Phoenix is a mythological bird that . . . " Before he could finish someone in the audience shouted, "Phoenix Shmenix get on with the play." Ed quickly departed. The lights came up on stage and Aileen dressed as an ancient Greek nurse appeared; her first words were, "Oh Zeus, oh some god or other." At this point the audience got up and began to leave through the one exit. The play was forty-five minutes long and it took that amount of time for all to escape, except in the front row where six waiters from the kitchen staff were seated. When the play ended they stood up and applauded. They had a great time.

The next morning I went to the owners office to collect the $150 check. He said, "I'm not paying you. Nobody stayed, they all walked out." I replied, "But the waiters stayed" and he said, "they don't count." I went and got the cast and brought them into his office and sat down on his floor. I think that this was one of the first sit-down strikes in America. Certainly it was the first one that this owner had ever experienced. We stared at each other for ten minutes until he relented and said, "All right here's your check." He underestimated the starving stomachs he was up against.

Back in New York City, the summer tour over, we started our second season. We chose *Burning Bright* by John Steinbeck which had failed on Broadway several seasons earlier. Jason Wingreen and Emily Stevens played the husband and wife acrobats, with Felice Orlandi as another acrobat and a new company member, Joe Beruh, as a clown. *Burning Bright* is about a group of circus performers. As the play develops the setting cleverly changes from the circus to a farm and then to a ship. We follow the main character, Saul, played by Jason, in his desperate attempts to have a child to carry on his bloodline.

Next came *Bonds of Interest* by Jacinto Benevente, directed by Ed Mann. Still there was no major critical coverage. Small audiences and money shortages were popping up all over the place. For me it was like trying to keep an ocean liner afloat in rough seas with gaping holes in its sides.

Other than drama critics from *Show Business* and *The Villager*, we just couldn't get the major newspaper critics to attend. The big newspapers weren't interested, I guess, because they thought their readership wasn't interested. But Brooks Atkinson of *The New York Times*, an adventuresome man and the most important critic in the country came to see *Bonds of Interest* in November. I thought "oh boy this is our big break." His entire review was about five lines long. He gave the name of the play and its author and some further information about the location of the theatre and a brief remark about the play and concluded by saying, "The theatre was hot." You could imagine how our hearts dropped on reading that review. I took an advertisement out in *The New York Times* and I used the quote, "'It's Hot!' Brooks Atkinson, *New York Times*." It ran several days until the *Times* called to say "Your

Geraldine Page in Garcia Lorca's *Yerma* (1951), directed by José Quintero

add is incorrect." I reluctantly withdrew the ad.

Just before our production of *Yerma*, which opened in May of 1952, Aileen Cramer resigned as a member of the board of directors for personal reasons. Aileen was in love with a young man doing construction work for us, Jan Marisack. Jan was a charmer, tall, blond with a smile like summertime, and I think she thought she could have a more peaceful life away from our disorders. She was probably right, because I've seen her recently and she looked healthy and happy. She was the first board member to leave. Shortly thereafter Ed also left. I don't know what his reasons were but I would have to assume that it had to do with his deteriorating relationship with José.

As I write about the past it's strange how people keep popping up. Maurice, the scenic designer for *Burning Bright* and *Yerma*, came to see *Metamorphoses* in 2002 at the Circle on Broadway and stopped in to say hello to me. I asked him how much he'd gotten paid for designing those early shows and he replied, happily, "Nothing. I built some of the set in my apartment and carried them down on the subway."

It's interesting that José, who's Spanish, had the least directorial success with the two Spanish plays we'd done, *Don Perlimplin in the Garden*, in Woodstock, and *Yerma*, both by Federico Garcia Lorca. It was hard for him to galvanize these plays into meaningful theatre. Why this was so, I can only guess. Perhaps he needed a new world which he had never experienced but which had similarities to his own life as he would find later in the plays of O'Neill and Williams, both subtly religious playwrights.

A friend of José's from the Goodman School in Chicago had been hanging around the theatre. She was long and slender, fair-haired with a beguiling manner and face. Beautiful hands, beautiful arm movements, with gawky pigeon-toed feet and a smile that could raise the moon. Our repertory company was starting to break up so we began casting some actors from outside and José decided to cast this schoolmate in *Yerma*. She played an 80-year-old pagan crone. She entered upstage left in the second act wearing what she called "my schmatta." Around her head she wrapped a shawl, and wore a decrepit moth-eaten long woolen dress and a burlap bag slung over her left shoulder. She walked barefoot in silence — looked around at the countryside and squinted her eyes at the glaring sun. She then wiped the sweat from her forehead with the back of her hand and slid down the center pole with her butt on the floor and knee raised to her chest, and began to tell us her story. After a few minutes she took an apple out of her bag. She wiped it on her sleeve and took a bite. Anybody who ever saw her in that play can still hear that crack of her bite and remember the humor and pain she brought to that five-minute monologue, as she continuously wiped her mouth with the back of her sleeve. Her name was Geraldine Page.

Gerry had the extraordinary ability to transform her body, and as she chewed that apple, it was as if her face and the apple became one for a moment. Her sparkling eyes roved around the audience, and then she'd take another breath and continue her story. After the scene she got up and walked out and there was a hushed silence because clearly something extraordinary had just happened on the stage.

Before the performance she'd put some dark streaks of makeup on her face and hands to age herself and look dirty. She was in her late 20s but as an actress, it was her body and her voice that told us her age and her pain. In other plays which I saw Gerry in over the years, there was always this physical transformation she achieved. You'd swear she was short, tall, fat or thin, just as the character was supposed to be. Of course, she didn't change physically but this was the art of her acting. All of this came out of her unrelenting journey for the truth of the character. I once asked her about her craft and she said, "Well, I think I come to the role as an empty vase and little by little I put buds in this vase and they bloom." She was one of the rare ones that I was so fortunate to work with.

We were so excited by Gerry that we wanted to find a play for her. This would be the first time we had ever tried to find a play for a particular actor. Previously, as I said, we would select a play and then cast the company members in a leading role. But we were now looking for a play for somebody very special, who glowed on stage.

Many members had left and we were no longer a repertory company but we were in a deep quandary over which play would be best for Gerry. So, with *Yerma* still running, I and the rest of the board all went off to read plays.

Because of our looming financial crisis, I was desperate to get people into the theatre. I had some tickets run off on a mimeograph machine as giveaways and actors went up and down the streets in the Village and over to NYU to distribute them. One night I went with a bunch of tickets in my pocket, walking up Seventh Avenue. It started to rain—to pour. I found shelter under the canopy of Max Gordon's Village Vanguard. As people opened the door to get in I heard laughter. So, I steeled myself and walked down the stairs, opened the door and found myself on the stage dripping with water. Professor Irwin Corey was holding forth and immediately stopped his routine and said to me, "Whatta you got to say, whatta you gotta tell?" I froze and then my mind said, "It's now or never to get people into the theatre." So I went into a spiel as I moved around the room distributing the tickets. I told a brief story about the play, the unusual theatre and the admission was only $1.50. I urged them, almost begging them, and acting up a storm to come to any performance except Sunday or Monday (dark days) and then thanked them. By this time, I was center stage. For a minute—and probably for the first and only time in his career—Professor Corey was speechless. I bowed to the Professor and said, "Thank you for the free advertising," and quickly made my exit. As I turned and walked up the stairs, I heard them laughing and applauding. I was so proud I'd had the courage to lift up the gauntlet Professor Corey had thrown at my feet.

During the early years all the actors knew about our money problems and Harry, one of our young actors in his early 20s, told me he'd talked to a Chinese man in Louie's Tavern about our problem. The man offered to give us $1,000 if we'd match it. I told Harry that I had come to a dead end in asking for money and that I couldn't even get $50 from anyone, let alone another $1,000.

I thought that was the end of it, but the next day Harry, who was irresistibly persistent, came back and said he talked to the man and explained that I could not raise money to match his offer. The man, whose name was not disclosed to me, told Harry to have me meet him at the Chemical Bank on Sheridan Square right next to the theatre the following morning at 11 A.M. The next morning, I was waiting at the bank. I was surprised to see a very young, short oriental man, tieless and jacketless, walk into the bank and come right up to me. He smiled and said, "Hello, are you Ted Mann?" I nodded. We shook hands and he reached into the little watch pocket we all used to have in the front of our trousers and pulled out a neatly folded green paper, put it in my palm and before I could say thank you he walked away. I unfolded what appeared to be a stamp, but glory be to heaven it was a $1000 bill! I'd finally broken through the wall into that bank vault! I went right onto the teller's line and deposited it into our account. Harry had told me never to acknowledge or reveal the source of the money. Occasionally the young Chinese man would come to the theatre to use the men's room—Louie's next door, where he spent his evenings, was always over-crowded. I don't think he ever came to see any shows. I have respected his request for anonymity for over fifty years. This is the first time this story has ever seen print.

In the '50s Louie's Tavern was the most popular bar in the Village. It was owned by Louie and his brother. Friendly Italians. When they were confronted with a problem they played off of each other like low keyed Abbott and Costello. Their bartender was named "Red" whose hair had turned gray but to one and all he was always "Red." He was the sole bartender on a twenty-foot-long bar. Quite an accomplishment since Louie's Tavern was always mobbed with just enough room to stand up and hold your drink. All three were great guys. They probably were one of the influences that helped us to get our cabaret license. They must have told the cops to ease up on us. The tavern had a low ceiling and was about twenty feet wide and thirty feet deep. Every night it was packed with young people "in the scene" and those trying to be in it. The "in" people wore the authentic garb—boots, leather jackets and jeans, frayed and worn out. Those trying to be "in the scene" wore the same clothing, but new and had an expensive look to them standing out like the shiny coins they were. Unknowns like Steve McQueen, with his motorcycle parked outside, Jack Kerouac, and Bob Dylan were regulars.

These were fervent times—1952. Truman was president and Eisenhower was preparing to take office. Seven years after the end of WWII the country had changed dramatically and there were many veterans back from the war who were now trying to find their way in life. The old rules didn't apply anymore, the youngsters were about to make their own.

While I was writing this, one night, I had an anxiety dream—God, how those front doors of the Circle and Louie's side steps are in my dreams! I'm in my car and I see that the front doors are wide open and I have to get to them and close them, but there's no place to park. The theatre is unprotected and then I wake up. The moments pop forth as though they are happening right now. I am reliving and experiencing the stressful situations anew—but, luckily, also the happy ones.

CHAPTER 7

52ND STREET SAID IT ALL

Some of my readers may remark upon my producing talents that seemed to come out of nowhere. In fact, they came from a place quite close to home, from my father. My dad was an attorney, but he also was financially involved in a number of jazz clubs on 52nd Street. Some of my instincts for innovation in tough situations came from watching him in action. The clubs were perpetually in trouble. There's a view today that the clubs were jammed with customers. But anyone who was there running and performing knows better. All the clubs were hanging on by their fingernails. Except for weekends, these "rooms," as they were lovingly referred to by the musicians and owners, were very thinly attended. My dad could have bought any one of their buildings outright for $15,000, but he didn't think it was a good investment because of the weak club business. Still, if 52nd Street were thriving today, the Rockefellers who I think bought that whole block would have had to find another part of the city to tear down in order to put up their own investment "playground."

To give you some idea of how thinly frequented these clubs were, my father was involved in three but they had only one doorman. Pinkus was a short, fat man dressed in an elaborate Sid Caesar–type doorman's outfit that reminded me of the character in the silent German film *M*. Pinkus held a cigar in his mouth like a little torpedo and would run on his stubby legs from one entranceway to the next, opening cab doors and greeting customers. He wore that big coat and hat in the heat of summer, in rain and in snow, but he always made sure I had transportation and didn't get knocked around in the street. He continued as my friend, in fact, and when Eddie Condon's Jazz club moved to 54th Street, right around the corner from my apartment, while walking my black Labrador Geno, I would stop and talk to him about our jazz heroes. He was now the doorman for the last surviving jazz club in midtown as jazz interest was in serious decline from the heydays of 52nd Street (and now two blocks removed).

Fifty-second Street as a music mecca started in the forties after World War II and lasted into the early fifties. Jazz was synonymous with 52nd Street; it meant the best in jazz. We never referred to it as Swing Street or Jazz Street, just 52nd Street, that said it all. Some people have referred to 52nd Street as Swing Street but there is quite a difference from that type of music to jazz, which is deeply soulful, passionate, low-down and sometimes rough. Swing is a kind of music played by bands headed up by Benny Goodman, Tommy Dorsey, and Glenn Miller. I think the name "Swing" may have been derived from people dancing—and swinging—together. It was fine but it was definitely white man's music.

The whole length of 52nd Street between Fifth and Sixth Avenues was largely made up of brownstones on either side of the street with the 21 Club on the north side close to Fifth Avenue. The small nightclubs were in the basements of these brownstones.

All the clubs were pretty much alike. As you took the steps down there was a window looking out—required by the Police Department so they could look *in* at the goings on. On the right-hand side there was a stand up bar and at the far end there were bare tables and chairs and a small bandstand. Generally there were four to five musicians that played piano, drums, sax, double bass, trumpet, or jazz violin (i.e., Stuff Smith). The musicians referred to the work as "six sets-four" or "six sets-three"—the second of which was obviously the preferred one. The translation: you play six sets of music within three or four hours. Drinks were served and smoke billowed throughout the room.

The state liquor authority required that a nightclub had to serve food and all the clubs up and down the block had ham and cheese on rye in their kitchens waiting for an order. Some of these sandwiches outlived the clubs.

The three "rooms" my dad had an interest in were The Onyx, The Famous Door, and The Open Door. Great musicians played at all of them: Jack Teagarden, trombone; Slam Stewart, bass; Wild Bill Davidson, trumpet; Lester Young, sax; Oscar Pettiford, sax; Joe Jones, drums; Bobby Hackett, trumpet; Cozy Cole, drums; Milt Hinton, bass; Charlie Parker, sax; Teddy Wilson, piano, Joe Bushkin, piano; and Quincy Jones, trumpet.

At the time, all of the jazz musicians were earning their keep by playing dance music in big bands in cities around the country which allowed black musicians "to play" in white clubs and when they came to New York they were hungry for real music — jazz — and would drop in for jam sessions that would go on for hours after the closing time of 4 A.M.

I was in love with jazz. Throughout my high school years my buddy, Eddie Rose, whose older brother, Mel, was a jazz aficionado (so much so that he spoke in the style and lingo of a black jazzman), and I would spend hours listening to Commodore Record jazz recordings. My dad's clubs were heaven to me. I'd sit around with him and listen to the exciting soulful music. He also had a fantastic collection of jazz records.

The first time I ever went to a jazz club was with Eddie, when I was 12 or 13. This was before my father had gotten involved in jazz clubs himself. Eddie and I were meeting his brother Mel at Nicks in Greenwich Village. At least that was our goal. It was New Year's Eve and appropriately it was snowing. There was a long line of people waiting to get in to Nicks. The bouncer refused to let us in, saying, "You're too small and too young." I protested, "But we were invited by Mel Rose." This made no impression on the bouncer, but a man smoking beside the door suddenly took an interest in Eddie and me. He put his arms around us and, to our surprise, pushed us into the club, saying, "Have a good time, boys." Our benefactor was Sidney Bechet, the famed tenor sax man. Mel had attended Sidney's jazz sessions in and out of clubs for many years and the two had become friends. Just as we walked into the club, midnight struck. For the first time in my life I saw groups of adults kissing, hugging, rubbing, smooching. It turned out to be a very exciting and happy New Year's for both Eddie and me. I have loved jazz clubs ever since. I became more deeply immersed in jazz and to this day the station I turn to while driving my car is a jazz station.

As the 52nd Street era began to fade, my dad and his partner, Ralph Watkins, took over a club on Broadway and 52nd called the Rio Bamba—a few blocks north of Lou Walters' Latin Quarter (Lou, by the way, was Barbara Walters' father). I was out of the army by this time but was soon enlisted by my father to be a male host to dance with the single women who came in. The only problem was I didn't know a flamenco from a tango. So I was taught by one of the Spanish waiters. We only got as far as my dancing Spanish on my right foot. My left foot refused to fall in line. This meant I could dance only in circles (a prophecy of my theatrical future perhaps?). The older women would grudgingly accept the one-way routine to be close to a young body.

As luck would have it, just as my dad and Ralph took the club over, the Spanish sun was setting over Broadway so they decided to return to the jazz beat. Ralph was very knowledgeable about this music. They hired Charlie "Bird" Parker as their first attraction and in short order renamed the club "Birdland." George Shearing appeared there regularly and wrote the song "Lullaby of Birdland" that became as wildly popular as the club. Gerry Mulligan, Dave Brubeck, Oscar Peterson, Dizzy Gillespie, John Coltrane, Charlie Mingus, Thelonius Monk, and many other great jazz artists played Birdland. Musicians loved the ambience (which my father helped create) and they enjoyed playing there—at least in part because they were earning more money than they had on 52nd Street.

One of the greatest artists ever to play Birdland or any other spot in the universe was Billie Holiday. She'd just been released from prison in Lexington, Kentucky, for drug offenses and had not been on the New York scene for some time. Her felony conviction did not make her a favorite with the Police Department who doled out the cabaret licenses that you needed in order to perform in a New York City nightclub. So Billie Holiday was barred. I thought what a great idea it would be if Birdland could rescue her and intervene with the authorities. My dad and Ralph agreed. Birdland was so respected in City Hall for running a clean operation that when Ralph asked for a card on her behalf she went downtown to the police department and the card was issued to her.

Lady Day became an enormous hit and her career quickly reignited. She even began recording again, with a big non-jazz string orchestra. Although this new background music was like something arranged for Doris Day, Billie's genius was such that she overcame even that musical arrangement obstacle. Every night when she performed at Birdland, her last song would always be "Strange Fruit." The house lights were taken out, everybody became silent; as the band played the introduction, a single spot shone on Billie. At the end of the song, she'd just walk off; there were no encores after the haunting melody and lyrics about lynching. The song was written by Abel Meeropol, a Jewish New York City schoolteacher.

One day my dad took my four-year-old nephew, Arthur, backstage to meet her and when he came in, she picked him up and put their noses together, asking, "What song would you like me to sing for you, sugaah?" Arthur chirped, "play one of your records!" Lady Day answered "You'll have to pay for that, sugaah." As she wrapped him in her arms she sang to him "God Bless the Child."

Birdland had started in 1951. The life cycle of nightclubs was fairly short. Later Birdland was fading too and closed in the early sixties.

My father and Ralph weren't quitters, however. I definitely inherited major doses of perseverance from my dad. They decided to move over to the East Side, taking a big space on 48th Street and Lexington that became Basin Street East. One of the first things dad did with this new club was move the bandstand to the center of the room. Obviously, he'd been taken by Circle's three-quarter configuration. And there you have the first clear evidence that I influenced my father a little in return.

Artists who played there were Dave Brubeck, Earl "Fatha" Hines, Charlie Mingus, Peggy Lee, Errol Garner, Roy Eldridge, Oscar Peterson, George Shearing, Herb Alpert, Dakota Staton, Thelonius Monk (who came along at the same time as Dizzy Gillespie and played the same kind of music), Cab Calloway, Jimmy Rushing, Charlie Barnett, Dizzy, Billy Eckstein, Della Reese, Sarah Vaughan, and Ella Fitzgerald.

Some years before a young, bedraggled hippie girl with unkempt hair had come to audition for me at the Circle for a role in a play which she didn't get. But something about her rang a chord inside me. Not much later, I read that the same actress was singing at the Bon Soir and I went to see her. Afterwards, I called my dad to say how wonderful she was and that Basin Street should book her. Dad hired her as the opening act for Benny Goodman's quartet, the star attraction. This young waif who would be the hit of the nightclub circuit wore a red checkered dress she'd designed herself. Her name was Barbra Streisand.

My father was out in San Francisco in 1963 at a shopping center and heard the then unknown Trini Lopez performing solo. My father signed him on the spot as an opening act for Mort Sahl. The engagement with Mort was a couple of months away and in the interim when Trini recorded "Live at PJ's" it became a big hit. So big that they had to expand Trini's quartet into an eleven-piece orchestra and he became the star attraction at Basin Street.

Count Basie and Louis Armstrong and his band and Duke Ellington and his orchestra also appeared at Basin Street East. The Duke's fading career, in fact, was strongly revived by his engagements at the club. At the time of his engagement, I believe he hadn't appeared in New York in ten years. No club would take a chance with him, not even The Apollo.

Stan Kenton's band was another attraction with a lot of brass—very, very loud, so that the trombones and trumpets had to be muted. My father brought his knowledge of jazz musicians to this new club and actively helped book it. He'd audition artists for opening acts. For trumpeters he had them play "One O'Clock Jump." For pianists, he had them play "C Jam Blues," also known as "Duke's Place," written by the Duke.

Comics besides Mort Sahl who also appeared were Buddy Hackett, Allen and Rossi, Don Rickles, Jack E. Leonard, and Bob Newhart. When my father was hospitalized for a couple of weeks I came in and worked at the club. I vividly remember one night, after closing, as the staff of 65-plus-year-olds was sitting around talking. Naturally the conversation got around to women. One commented, "Boy, would I like to have a young, firm 55-year-old."

Basin Street was very successful but finally its cycle also ended in 1965. In retrospect, none of these clubs survived more than seven years.

In 1948, before Birdland, my father and Ralph had opened a restaurant nightclub, The Embers, on 54th Street and Third Avenue, which had excellent food and music. My father was painfully aware of the cyclically short life of nightclubs contrasted to the long life of restaurants, so he combined the two so that food was the main attraction and music the side show. The sagacity of this decision was proved by the Embers' sixteen-year run.

In 1951, when they began renovating and redecorating the Embers, which coincidentally was the same year that the Circle was starting at Sheridan Square, I scavenged for stage curtains, chairs, and nightclub tables for possible future use. One of those Embers hand-me-down chairs was the very same one Marilyn Monroe would leave a lasting impression upon, but more on that tale anon.

My dad hired a five-star chef and an experienced butcher whose sole job was the selection and preparation of meat for the club. The food was of the highest quality specializing in large portions of aged steaks and roast beef. The meat was so good that at closing time some of the waiters were discovered with uncooked steaks strapped to their bellies under their shirts. Generally in restaurants, when the staff steals it's from the cash register or the liquor cabinet. At ours, it was from the freezer.

The interior of the club was luxurious with fine tablecloths, napkins, and silverware and a top selection of wines and liquors. My dad supervised the entire operation as well as the maitre d' and the waiters so that they would be courteous and patient with the customers. What my dad was never able to accomplish, nor do I believe any other restaurateur in history has done, is restrain the physical impediment of the maitre d's extended hand awaiting a gratuity.

As I said, fine dining took top billing. Ham and cheese was not on the menu. After people had their sumptuous meal, they'd sit back and luxuriate with a glass of wine or hard liquor and listen to the music played by the Jonah Jones Quartet (sixteen weeks every year) famous for soft jazz, Buck Clayton, Al Hirt, George Shearing, Milt Hilton, Henry Red Allen (trumpet), Sonny Greer (drums), and pianists Oscar Peterson, Dorothy Donagan, Marian McPartland, Barbara Carroll, and Don Shirley. Musicians that also performed there were Meade Lux Lewis, Dizzy Gillespie (who experimented with an innovative new musical approach to jazz with sharp changes in notes), Earl "Fatha" Hines, and the great Joe Bushkin who I convinced to come out of retirement. At the Embers, music truly became —or at least greatly complemented—the food of love.

After many years of top business, the club began to slow down. My dad and Ralph tried valiantly to save it by introducing vocalists, even though this added 20 percent to the customer's bill. But even this innovation didn't help and the Embers closed shop in 1964. The only good thing about the closing was the maitre d's could no longer get tips dropped into their outstretched right hands. Though I'll bet they stayed by the door with palms held out to the demolition crews as the building was torn down. Once a gladhander, always a gladhander.

CHAPTER 8

A DOCTOR MAKES A HOUSE CALL

Now back to finding that play for Gerry. One night Emily, Jason, and I were standing in front of the theatre discussing the plays we had read. José was coming towards us from Seventh Avenue with the street lamps shining behind him which gave him the glow of a halo. As he came closer he shouted, "I found it! I found it!" And we all said, "What? What? What?" He was waving a script in the air. "The play for Gerry!" It was Tennessee William's *Summer and Smoke*. We immediately took the script upstairs—and we sat around reading it and realized it was perfect for her. I went over to Gerry's apartment at 1 Christopher Street and I told her about our decision to produce *Summer and Smoke* and asked her, "Would you play the leading role?" She shyly questioned, "I'm going to play Alma?" and I said, "If you want to." Then with a mischievous grin and twinkle in her eyes she said, "I'll show them what I can do."

Lee Richardson was cast as Dr. John, Lola D'Annunzio as Rosa (probably the predecessor of Rosa from the *Rose Tattoo*), Kathleen Murray as Nellie, Bernie Bogin as the Salesman, Jason Wingreen as Dr. John's father, Sydney Stevens as Rose's father, Walter Beakel as Alma's father Reverend Winemiller, and her "dotty" mother was Estelle Omens. Emily Stevens was in charge of technical staff and was also a member of the cast, playing Rosemary. The last seven listed here were all that remained of our original twenty-member company.

When I had time, I sat in on the rehearsals. They were extraordinary.

The creative forces with José, Gerry, Lee and the rest of the cast, were as though they had waited for this play all their young lives. Everything they'd done previously had brought them together in this moment in time. Their ideas bounced like ping-pong balls. The atmosphere in rehearsal was stimulating, electrifying and happy. Fortunately we were rehearsing on the set of *Yerma*, which was an empty stage, so the actors were able to "think" the *Summer and Smoke* environment. Keith Cuerden designed a simple set that allowed for the Winemiller home downstage. The pole was covered with wallpaper. Upstage was Dr. John's father's office and in the center, the park, on which the statue of the angel lived. (This kind of statue is very common in Southern cemeteries. I saw many of them in Thomas Wolfe's hometown of Ashville, North Carolina, when I was there researching a possible stage production of his novel *Look Homeward Angel*.)

José was in full throttle. It was glorious to watch him and to be part of his enthusiasm with his deep love for the characters and material. It was during this rehearsal period that I decided I'd do anything to help serve José's aspirations. From the beginning, in Woodstock, that day when José, with tenderness and compassion for my lost love June, reached out to help me was a defining moment in our relationship. The second was the inspiration I felt from his work with *Summer and Smoke*. I wanted to be his "Diagalev" his "impresario" to help make his dance of art come true.

On the night of the opening May 24, 1952, I dutifully went to the New York Times building on 43rd Street and got a copy expecting another review of dismissal from Mr. Atkinson, as he'd done with *Bonds of Interest*. Instead it was good—it was great! It was supergreat! I was so excited I flew back from 43rd Street all the way to the theatre. As I entered the front doors our opening night party was in session. I caught my breath and walked slowly into the theatre. Everybody was drinking, talking and laughing—the noise was deafening. I jumped up on the bar of the old nightclub and stood there observing the bacchanalian scene with the newspaper dangling from my hand. Slowly the group became silent and I began to read the review. My heart started pounding like it would bounce out of my chest. Each positive comment was cheered. When I completed the review I held the newspaper above my head and threw it

Lee Richardson and Geraldine Page in Tennessee Williams' *Summer and Smoke* (1952), directed by José Quintero

up in the air and war-whooped. The actors were kissing, hugging, and crying tears of joy. I jumped off the bar. José and I hugged and then Gerry came up to me with tears in her eyes, wrapped her graceful arms around me and whispered in my ear, "Bless you." I breathed in her sweet scent which was like spring flowers. We had achieved a miracle—finally a great review.

I've always remembered the first paragraph of Mr. Atkinson's review.

It's funny how sometimes when something is happening to you, you know it's important, and you store it in your memory, marked, "important; never forget." That night I memorized that first paragraph of Mr. Atkinson's review and I've never forgotten it. "Nothing has happened for quite a long time in the theatre as admirable as this production at The Circle in the Square…."

Mr. Atkinson went on to praise Geraldine, José, and Lee and to re-evaluate the play, which had failed on Broadway several seasons earlier.

We didn't choose this play or any of the earlier revivals because they'd failed on Broadway. Plays such as *Antigone, The Enchanted,* and *Burning Bright. Summer and Smoke* had been done four-and-a-half years prior to our production but we hadn't seen it nor any of our other revivals. We did what we loved. There was no pre-thought of "Let's show them how to do them the right way," we were just trying to make good theatre.

The day after the opening, we were not prepared for the impact that a good review in *The New York Times* by Mr. Atkinson would have. As I rounded the corner to come to the theatre, there was a line stretching a half block to Seventh Avenue. I opened the door, twenty people followed on my heels, and the phone on my little desk was ringing off the hook! As soon as I answered it and hung up, it rang again, again, and again. All day long it was like firecrackers going off and ticket buyers kept pouring in. It was an explosion.

Writing here about Gerry reminds me of an incident that happened during the run of *Summer and Smoke.* She was onstage waiting for the telephone to ring so that she could answer it. The ring didn't come and it didn't come and it didn't come. So Gerry picked up a feather duster and dusted, and dusted and dusted—until there was nothing left to dust except maybe members of the audience. So she stormed over to the sound booth and told the technician Alvin Aronson to, "Ring the god-dammed bell!" The bell rang and she returned to the stage and Tennessee's dialogue. Geraldine Page went on to a screen career after the Circle's *Summer and Smoke.* She did a film version of it with Lawrence Harvey. A strange choice for Dr. John, but I understand he was the boyfriend of the widow of a studio executive who had total control. Geraldine also played in films with Paul Newman, Clint Eastwood, and

John Wayne. She was a great actress in whatever medium she was in. Who can ever forget her in the Horton Foote film *A Trip to Bountiful?*

There we were with a hit off-Broadway and within days all the other major critics finally came to our theatre and confirmed what Brooks Atkinson had written. We didn't realize at the time what we had accomplished but it has later been acknowledged that our production of *Summer and Smoke* was the birth of off-Broadway. And one might also say that Mr. Atkinson's review was the doctor in the delivery. This thunderbolt of critics and audience revealed there was a public for quality plays off-Broadway and theatres started popping up all over the place, like stalks of corn in Kansas. Even the Provincetown and Cherry Lane came back in operation.

Summer and Smoke ran for a year. José was rightfully lionized for his sensitive work and Gerry became a star—she was offered many other roles.

During this time a young, aspiring playwright Alvin Aronson worked for us doing multiple theatre jobs and became a lifelong fan of Geraldine. He had the small role of Vernon in the poetry scene in *Summer and Smoke* and thereafter when Gerry spoke or wrote to him she called him Vernon. Over the years he and I have talked on occasion and almost every time he brings up Gerry and the wonder of her performance. We reminisce about how in the play she called out like a song, "Johnny, oh, Johnny." And how beautiful the music was by Ravel and Saint-Saens.

The elite, well-known movie stars, society people, and artists of all disciplines came to be part of this phenomenon and the excitement kept growing. I think the success of this production also helped generate the regional theatre movement around the country because it became clear that there were audiences out there hungry for good theatre. There had been lots of newspaper and magazine stories around the country (including features in *Life* and *The New York Times*) telling about this little off-Broadway theatre that had achieved such great success.

One night, Lee Strasberg, head of the famed Actor's Studio, came with a group of friends, among them Marilyn Monroe. At intermission, Marilyn, Lee, and friends were standing in the bar area. Onlookers were on the steps surrounding her in a wide circle. All eyes were slightly tilted down, savoring her glorious derriere. She was clothed in a dress as tight as a mermaid's skin. Everyone's eyes were riveted to that painfully slow undulating posterior. She appeared totally oblivious to the erotic sensation that she was causing.

After the show I went up to see Gerry. She was excited about Lee and Marilyn having seen the show. Gerry had in fact attended classes at the Actor's Studio with Marilyn. When we came back downstairs into the empty theatre, Gerry asked where Marilyn had sat. We walked over to the nightclub chair of Embers' heritage and its padded leather seat. She'd apparently sat on her program and the heat of her body had warmed the seat and the program. The wonder is it didn't catch fire. As she rose and lifted the program, she'd inadvertently left a print of her famous derriere. I kept that chair for many years, but, ultimately, it disappeared. I hope it resides in a Marilyn Monroe museum someplace because I still get nightmares about somebody re-upholstering it.

There was another amusing incident that happened when Tennessee Williams came to see his play. Afterwards, he went backstage with his long-term companion Frank, to see Gerry. José and I accompanied him. We were both nervous of what he might say—suppose he hated the production or didn't like Gerry's performance? It'd been raining and Tennessee, wearing a raincoat and carrying an umbrella with a sharp point on the end, started to talk with Gerry and congratulate us. He leaned back on his umbrella. The point had landed on José's shoe but rather than stop Tennessee's affirmative comments, José endured the pain for the pleasure of hearing Tennessee's uninterrupted praise. It was manna to our souls. Tennessee became a good friend of José's and of the theatre and a lifelong friend of Gerry's.

After about six months Gerry left for her Broadway debut as Lily in Vina Delmar's *Mid-Summer*. Betty Miller took over the role and we continued to sell out. So there we were with little to do because we had a successful production running. Each play up until *Summer and Smoke* had run five weeks or less. I felt we should, and could, expand. I'd even envisioned that we might, someday, have Circle in the Square Theatres all over the country.

CHAPTER 9

You Win Some, You Lose Some

About this time I met Sam Schwartz, a general manager and producer who was running Philadelphia's Academy of Music where opera, symphonies, and ballets were regularly presented. I don't know which came first, my vision or Sam's idea of having a theatre in the ballroom of the academy, but the two interests found each other. He invited me to come down and look at their Foyer (a large ballroom with beautiful crystal chandeliers). I realized from the dimensions of the space that it was not possible to create a three-sided theatre for seating as we had on Sheridan Square. But we could have a space in which the audience sat on two sides of the stage. This would be similar, but larger than the one David Ross had down on Fourth Street where he'd very successfully presented Chekhov. (David had been one of the fortunate friends that accompanied Marilyn the night she saw *Summer & Smoke*.) Sam said we could have the Foyer rent free and no charge for electricity and porter service. This was starting to sound like a dream set up. Little did we know what was in store for us. The board, now consisting of Jason, Emily, José and myself came down to see the potential theatre. They were pleased with the facility and the possibilities for us.

So the plan was hatched to open a Circle in the Square at the illustrious Academy of Music right on Broad Street with its own separate entrance and box office. There were lots of old dollars down there and I thought because of the publicity we'd recently received it would be easy to elicit their support. I didn't count on our out-of-towner status, however, and quickly learned that the "Main Line" people do not welcome "foreigners." We got some small amounts, but ultimately the money for the creation of the theatre and production came from our *Summer and Smoke* surplus in New York.

We decided we were going to open with *Summer and Smoke* then do Jean Anouilh's *Legend of Lovers* with Felice Orlandi and Kathleen Murray, José directing both. But there was a lot of work to do before that could happen. We had to create and build the space. We brought down our lighting designer, Noah Kalkut, as well as Keith Cuerden to design the theatre. Later, Karl, our near-sighted carpenter, arrived and he and Noah built it. The beautiful chandeliers remained in place. Noah was at least ten years older than the rest of us with deep creases in his face and moved like a tired ballet dancer. He also spoke like a record playing at a slower speed.

Jason agreed to be our representative on site and he rented an apartment during the time of construction and the two productions. I think he received $150 a week to pay for his room and board.

I commuted back and forth almost daily, sometimes staying overnight at one of the nearby cheapest hotels. There was a wonderful restaurant across the street that we liked to frequent, and many a happy or anguished meal was had there.

Our Philadelphia *Summer and Smoke*, with Betty Miller, who'd taken over for Gerry in New York, was a superb production. Betty was vulnerable and touching giving a sensitive performance. The rest of the company was about as good as the actors who'd performed it in New York, except for Lee Richardson—nobody could top him. I was confident we'd get great reviews again and that our first flagship theatre was about to take flight. In fact, the reviews were just as I'd hoped they would be.

The next morning after the opening, I stood across the street from the theatre certain that I'd see swelling lines of people responding to those reviews, as you would see in New York. There was a light drizzle and then it came down a little heavier. As time went by, pacing between the pay phone and the restaurant, I realized the Philadelphia audience wasn't coming out. I thought maybe it was because of the rain. But as time went on and the rain stopped, I realized they weren't coming at all. It hit me hard—like a shot to the gut—that Philadelphia is not New York. The reviews for *Legend of Lovers* were okay but also failed to generate much business. This predominantly Presbyterian and Catholic city just doesn't respond the way they do in New York. Here we have a large number of people who love theatre and when a good review comes out they race to the box office. I think Philadelphians think about it, digest it, and by the time they decide to go you've already closed. We limped on hoping that the Philadelphians would wake up and show up, but to no avail. So we had to throw in the towel on my vision of Circle in the Square around the country. It was a tremendous defeat for all of us, but I felt personally responsible. I had campaigned for this, extolling the virtues of expansion, convincing everyone to go along. And the worst was that I had used up the *Summer and Smoke* surplus funds to do it.

CHAPTER 10

Born Again

While running around in circles and squares in Philadelphia we still had to mount our next production in New York. After a year's run, *Summer and Smoke* was about to close. We chose Truman Capote's *The Grass Harp* as our next production. José was directing with Ray Stricklyn, Clarice Blackburn, Ruth Attaway and my then girlfriend Patricia Brooks.

I have to pause for a moment or more to explain how I met the love of my life.

I first saw Patricia when José and I went to audition some people who had advertised a children's version of Stravinsky's *Peter and the Wolf* in the weekly theatre publication *Show Business*. I always wanted to do shows for kids on Saturday and Sunday mornings. As we walked into the apartment there were three performers, a short blond girl, a thin dark fellow, and a girl with long hair clasping a guitar to her chest. She looked like Picasso's "Woman in Blue." Introductions were made followed by chit chat, then José and I headed towards the couch to hear the audition. As we crossed the room I turned to José and said, "I'm going to marry that girl." He said, "Which one?" I responded, "The pretty one, of course."

After the audition, we said we were interested in their work and wanted them to perform it at the Circle. I also invited the girl with the long hair and the guitar to dinner.

Patricia was about 17 and had just finished Performing Arts High School. I was 26. We began dating. Patricia told her mother she was going out with an older man. Within a month we began living together in my room behind my office on the second floor of the theatre. The windows looked out on the alleys and fire escapes and rooftops of nearby tenement houses. I always thought that this is the way Paris must look. The bathroom down the hall had no shower or tub.

Patricia's parents were unique. They were supporters of many liberal causes. Her mother, Eda, was from Butte, Montana where her father had been the sheriff. She'd been a singer, had performed on the road on the Keith Circuit all over the country, and had appeared in a couple of plays on Broadway with Bert Lahr. She could also play a mean ragtime piano. Eda's mother (Patricia's grandmother) went to any show that came to Butte and when she came home afterwards she'd sit down and play the whole score even though she couldn't read music. This says a lot about Patricia's musical inheritance. Eda herself gave vocal lessons. While other professionals were charging $50 or more, Eda maintained the same fee, $10, until she had to stop in her early 90s. Patricia's father, Jerome (Brooky) was a writer, researcher, a wit, and raconteur. Public-school educated only, he nonetheless knew all of Greek mythology, Shakespeare, and regaled Patricia and her sister Joan with those tales. He'd written several books about the history of tobacco for Phillip Morris and produced two volumes for their private archives—he never believed in the harmfulness of tobacco and smoked all his life, which came to a close at age 92. He also contributed to *The New York Times Book Review* and wrote a well respected book titled *America's Cup* (about the annual races in Newport, Rhode Island). He was an avid sailor and kept his boat in Northport on Long Island Sound.

When we first met, dance was Patricia's love, and she was working very hard with the New Dance Group, and particularly the choreographer, Donald McHale. I of course was heavily involved with my theatre. Some evenings after the show our big adventure was to go to 42nd Street and see two films and stagger back out about 4 A.M. At the theatre in our room above the stage there were no facilities for cooking so all of our meals were courtesy of the local restaurants. Sometimes at Marie Crisis Café, across Seventh Avenue, we were welcome guests because of favors my father had done for Marie in the past. Some evenings we ate at my parents' apartment. They loved Patricia. She became their daughter.

After Patricia and I lived together for a year, I felt we either had to split up or get hitched. We decided to wed and when we did we found a small, one-room apartment on Minetta Lane. It was a tiny room, which served as a bedroom, living room, dining room, and kitchen. We moved in with my black Lab Geno and promptly invited both sets of parents to dinner. Patricia had little experience cooking (successfully bringing water to a boil was a major achievement) but she decided to cook a roast beef in the Dutch oven—on the one burner of our electric stove. Four hours later, it was still percolating. The parents were getting fidgety sitting on the bed, which at that hour was known as the couch. ("Where do you sleep?" my mother inquired upon first glancing around the room. "Oh," I casually replied, "we have a bedroom.") When one of us went to the bathroom those sitting in the main room had to talk loudly to drown out the toilet flush. During the whole evening, Geno investigated the visitors, dog fashion! My mother was shocked but Eda thought it was the funniest thing in the world. Finally, in the fifth hour, the roast beef was "ready." Ravenously, we all plopped on the bed-couch, plates in lap—it was now 1 A.M.—and gnawed through our Roast Beef á *la Patricia*.

Patricia was my perfect soul mate. As a young boy in Brooklyn, I observed gaggles of mothers sitting and conversing on benches amid their baby carriages. They looked so bored. At that early age somehow I realized I didn't want to be married to somebody whose main activity was child care. All my adult life, I have only been attracted to women in the arts, and Patricia was a complete artist in all ways, a true original. She didn't follow the rules; she invented new ones.

She even became an imaginative cook, concocting unique recipes. She also liked to change traditional eating habits, such as serving chicken for breakfast with Jello as a first course. When I questioned the sagacity of this unusual morning repast, she indignantly replied, "Well, you eat eggs and drink juice for breakfast, don't you? Don't be so Victorian."

Patricia was not judgmental and discovered affirmative qualities in almost everyone she met. She'd find justification for their shortcomings and would refute my criticisms by saying, "She was born out of wedlock," or "His mother was gay," or, "She's from a mixed marriage," or, "She never knew her father."

Patricia and I were married in 1953. The reception took place at the original Circle in the Square at Sheridan Square on the set of *The Grass Harp*. Patricia was performing in the play and we couldn't go on a honeymoon. The actual vows were made at The Drake on Park Avenue so that night after the reception Patricia and I had a New York City honeymoon. The next morning we had breakfast after which I said let's go out and take a walk. Patricia said, "I can't. I only have my wedding dress." What had happened was Patricia and her mother had been so frantically preoccupied sewing her into her wedding dress for the marriage ceremony that they didn't bring anything for the next day.

I said, "Let's go over to Saks Fifth Avenue and I will buy you a dress." Patricia said, "I can't go out the front door on Park Avenue in the morning in my wedding dress." I suggested, "I'll put my tuxedo on and let's go down the freight elevator and exit out the hotel back door. People will think we just finished shooting a commercial." Patricia liked that idea and agreed. I helped her pull the wedding dress back on as she sucked in her breath. After we selected a new dress we went down to the Circle to collect our wedding gifts—me still dressed in my tuxedo. Most of the gifts had disappeared. Patricia said don't worry, whoever took them needed them more than us. That was how Patricia was. Material possessions meant very little to her. Music and dance possessed her.

For years I could not remember the name of the hotel in which we were married, the one where we actually spent our honeymoon night. I remembered the dress and the back elevator, but not the name. Quite recently, I was rummaging through the bottom of a closet at home and came across a box containing old bottles of aspirin and vitamins. A metallic gleam in one corner of the box caught my eye. It was an old hotel key, for a room at the Ambassador Hotel. I had saved it as a memento of our wedding.

Patricia had been brought up as a Unitarian but even there she created her own set of beliefs and was more spiritual in every moment of her life than most. She was one of the few people I know who lived her life in the moment, and by that, she was able to relish each day anew. She was an enthusiast for other people's creative work without jealousy in the otherwise tough, competitive world of opera.

In time, she would reach the heights of the opera world through her acclaimed performance as Violetta in *La Traviata*, as Manon in *Manon*, as Gilda in *Rigoletto* and as Lucia in *Lucia Di Lammermoor*, among others. One story from this period, in fact, illustrates my wife's beautiful nature. Despite her fame, she agreed to help me by performing in two Circle productions for a couple of weeks without pay. The first was Henry Livings' *Eh?* with Dustin Hoffman, Dana Elcar, and Elizabeth Wilson. Elizabeth had to leave for a couple of weeks to do a film. Patricia, coming from the opera world, was shocked by the profanity she encountered in a theatre dressing room. Moreover, during and after the performances, the actors in the play would come to her and give her notes: "In comedy you can't move this way or that when I deliver my line, because you're killing *my* laugh." Or, "You have to enter a beat later because you're stepping on my laugh." Or, "When I enter and say my line, don't move." She patiently, as a good producer's wife, listened to all the comments of the other performers. Now it was her last night, the performance was over and Dana Elcar grabbed her by the arm before she could get into the dressing room and urgently said, "I have some notes for you." Patricia, surprised, replied, "But, Dana, I'm not performing anymore." And he pleaded, "*Please* let me give you my notes!" Patricia bobbed her head yes and patiently heard them. Dana smiled with pleasure.

Now back to our production of *The Grass Harp*. Patricia at the time had been studying acting with Uta Hagen, while continuing her folk singing with Pete Seeger's Weavers and dancing with the New Dance Group.

Harp is a charming play about a boy and his elderly cousin who defy the conventions of a materialistic society by retreating into a tree house, only to discover that to live together, compromise is necessary. It was a lovely production that failed to get strong reviews. The critics found the play limited. Maybe it was a mistake to do a second Southern play that was compared unfavorably in the critics' minds to the great *Summer and Smoke*.

Next, we moved on and did a new play by Victor Wolfson, *American Gothic*. *Gothic* explores lonely God-fearing patriarchs, wayward sons and wandering drunks in turn-of-the-century New England. The play featured Jean Stapleton (Edith Bunker from TV's *All in the Family*),

Clarice Blackburn (Addie), and most notably a young unknown actor Jason Robards, Jr., as Addie's husband.

This was more than fifty years ago, but in my remembrances some long gone events are as vivid as the present—like meeting Jason. When we were casting the male lead in *Gothic*, we had read a lot of actors and then Jason appeared and easily got the part. He had black wavy hair, a square lantern jaw and looked like a character in a Norman Rockwell painting—but something about him was definitely off-center. Jason as the character had a rakish way about him cut from the same cloth as the New Englander, Clarice, but he was different— like he didn't belong. He was an outsider. Like a blue bird in a leafless tree.

Jason and I became friends and we used to retreat, joking all the way, across the street to "Doc's" drugstore with its soda fountain and rows of paperback books. Jason was very engaging and charming. He had been an unemployed actor just hanging around New York hoping for a good role and here it was. He'd been bored and was so happy to get the lead role in a meaty part. We were excited too—a new play, telling an American story. It's funny to think about it now but he and I would go across Sheridan Square and schmooze with "Doc" at the counter. Booze was still a couple of years away—chocolate and vanilla sodas were our poison.

Jason was living way out West, just off 14th Street, in an apartment above a meat packing plant with his wife, Eleanor. Like Patricia and I, their children had not yet arrived. Jason was articulate, with a great devilish sense of humor. Even then he had that deep rumbling laugh.

We had photographs taken of *Gothic*, of all the individual cast members posed in front of a stone wall to add a sense of grave auster-ity befitting the play's setting, rural New England. The wall was in Isabelle Halliburton's tiny courtyard on 33rd and Park—she was José's personal secretary, a tall elegant lady with a wonderful dry sense of humor. When we had a photo session on the set, Jason was absent. I asked him why and he said, "Eleanor was sick." So we had no pho-tographs of Jason on the set of the play! But there is one photograph taken in a second floor room above the theatre, Jason, foot on stool, leaning in talking to Clarice. I think that before he achieved stardom, Jason might have been camera shy because there are lots of later photographs of Jason as Hickey in *The Iceman Cometh*, his breakthrough role.

Unfortunately, both *The Grass Harp* and *American Gothic* failed to produce sufficient monies at the box office. Combined with what we'd just spent to create the Philadelphia Circle in the Square we were once again broke. A condition we seemed to slide into very easily.

CHAPTER 11

MY LOVE

After those two failures, I'd like to discuss something funny. In 1968 Patricia did another acting turn for me. The Circle had rented the Henry Miller Theatre on Broadway to perform three one act plays: *Morning, Noon, and Night* by Israel Horowitz, Terrence McNally, and Leonard Melfi. Patricia stepped in for Charlotte Rae who had to fulfill television commitments. Patricia wouldn't take any pay, but insisted that her name not be used, which was of course by then well known in opera. She used the name of Virginia Kuntsler, an inside joke of ours. When I'd call home long distance or from overseas, I'd make the call person-to-person and ask for Virginia Kuntsler, who, of course, would not be at home. This way, Patricia would know I'd arrived safely without the expense of a call. (William Kuntsler, the well-known civil rights attorney, had been my counselor at Camp Mahopac when I was 13.) I wonder how many other families had similar codes to help out their household finances?

Patricia had made her debut with the City Opera in Hugo Weisgall's *The Inspector General*. Julius Rudel, the company's artistic director and conductor, had heard her in the annual "John Golden Award for New Talent" presentations that were sponsored by the League of New York Theatres. She performed "Glitter and Be Gay" from Leonard Bernstein's *Candide*. She won the award for her wonderfully funny and stylish performance as the most outstanding new talent. Her interpretation was delicious and very different. Opera is tradition-bound and a fresh look is always a healthy way to go.

Her next New York City opera performance was in Robert Ward's *The Crucible*, based on Arthur Miller's Pulitzer Prize–winning play. She got very good notices for her interpretation of Abigail, for both her voice and her acting, and the opera was later recorded.

So back to *Morning, Noon, and Night*. This great diva, my wife, agreed to perform for her husband once again. Patricia's bio in the *Playbill* read, "Virginia Kuntsler was born into a theatrical family. She started to perform at age four as the hunchback Richard III, and as a teenager she played Lear in *King Lear*." All of this is Pat's rich mischievous sense of humor. Quite a few opera fans of Patricia's found out she was performing and at the end of the play we heard the familiar opera acclaim, "Brava, Brava!"

The last public performance Patricia did, in fact, was at the Circle in the Square Theatre when we did a special evening dedicated to Eugene O'Neill and August Strindberg. Various artists performed to a sold out crowd. In the audience were Oona O'Neill, the King and Queen of Sweden and Paul Newman and Joanne Woodward. At the party afterwards one of the guests asked me if he could introduce his daughter to Paul Newman — if she got to meet him this gent would contribute $5000 to the Circle. I relayed this request to Paul and he smiled and said, "Show me the way. I'll kiss her." After observing the rapturous embrace, the grateful father gave us $10,000.

Sadly, by this time my wife was quite sick with multiple sclerosis. The disease had been progressing over a ten-year period to the point where she was forced to rely on crutches. For that evening, she bravely pulled herself up on stage without them, however, balancing herself on a handrail from the set and sang two songs that O'Neill loved. Her voice was as beautiful and vulnerable as ever. Whenever I heard her sing and she hit the tender part of a song, it always brought tears to my eyes. There was such a depth of feeling in her, like an echo of longing. Patricia had soul.

Of all the opera performances I heard her sing, there were only two or three with which she felt satisfied. Those other times, I'd go back stage to congratulate her, with her fans, cameras and flowers in hand, stopping me along the way to gush, "Oh, Mr. Brooks, congratulations! What a wonderful performance!" But when I reached my wife's dressing room, she'd be sitting at her table, in costume, dejected. I would take her in my arms and tell her she sang beautifully. She'd shake her head slowly, weeping, "The First Act aria was this, or the Second Act aria was that." I'd try to calm her down, but Patricia usually felt she hadn't accomplished what she knew had to be done. We'd go to a party and, after half an hour, I wouldn't be able to find her anywhere. I'd look around and discover her in a bedroom or closet studying a score. In her mind, she was already beginning to study for her next role. Later, however, when we got back home, she'd immediately become chipper—happy to see our boys. She'd march into the kitchen to prepare their breakfast for the next day.

Every morning, seven days a week, was dedicated to vocal warmups. I would imitate her as if I were an inmate in *Marat/Sade*. I'm a teaser. Some people love it, and some abhor it. Thank God Patricia was among the ones who loved it. My son Andrew has continued my cynical but funny view of life, as does his young son Samuel.

Patricia had given birth to our first son, Andrew David José, in September of 1959. In the early days of our marriage Patricia and I talked about having children and decided that we would like to wait until we were really ready and we thought that would be about five years. Our first son Andrew was almost on target having been born six years later. Our understanding was that when we did have children we would hire an in-house person to take care of them twenty-four hours a day. There were two reasons for this, one was so that Patricia could pursue her career and the other was selfish—I wanted to have time with my wife, I didn't want the romance to end. How naïve I was to believe that the little darlings would not also win my heart.

We had met George and Betty Marshall through Brett Weston, who was visiting us—eating his meals with us but sleeping in his photography van parked on the street. While Patricia was pregnant, George and Betty invited us to stay at their guest cottage, which was in the middle of a field of apple trees in Sands Point, Long Island, about twenty-five miles off Broadway.

One morning Patricia woke up saying it was time to go to the hospital which was way back in New York City. We jumped into the car and I attempted to fly over the traffic of the Long Island Expressway. Patricia writhed in the seat beside me, deep breathing and singing an aria to try and distract herself from the pain. After several near crashes we arrived at the hospital. And I waited and waited in the nondescript hallway which had hard wooden benches, the torture seats for would-be fathers.

At about 1 A.M. I heard a loud wail reverberating down the long dark marble corridor. Andrew José had been born. Patricia and I had spent many days walking on the Sands Point beach to find the correct first name that would rhythmically compliment Mann.

At this time we lived in an old tenement house on Barrow Street right around the corner from the Circle. Living above us was John Wallowich—an accompanist and a voice coach. Some of the voices we heard through the cracks were okay, but a few were more painful than little Andrew's wailing down the hall. Maybe he was training to be an opera singer too. Opera can always use a good tenor. The noise above hastened Patricia's desire to return to singing. She longed to hear correct vocalizing.

Our first maid/friend/cook/housecleaner/spiritual advisor was the beautiful, honey-skinned Hannah Mattis from Jamaica. She remained our friend these many years and was the beginning of a long long string of twenty-four-hour help, most of whom were from Latin America. Elsa was from Germany and had aspirations of being a tap dancer in America. Kinichi was from Japan and was chosen by Patricia when the boys were in their young teens so that he could be their basketball teammate and nurse. It was a great idea except the kids found out that he couldn't play basketball; so they taught him. We hear regularly from him; he's now a married father back in Japan.

When Jonathan was born, Evie Johnson, from rural Georgia, came into our lives. She was an elderly black lady who disliked all white people except us. Jonathan was born at Mt. Sinai Hospital. The night before he was born we were staying at our apartment on Seventh Avenue. Late that night Patricia slid out of bed. I said what are you doing? She said, you sleep I'm going to the hospital. I said just stop, sit on the chair. I got dressed and ran to get a taxi and she waddled down the steps like a tugboat about to go into battle. Patricia glowed in pregnancy and this night she had a big broad smile on her face. Contractions were nothing new to Patricia. She learned all about them working with Martha Graham.

When we went to the hospital I was once again, as all husbands are, shunted aside. I waited about four hours and in the wee hours of the morning I decided I couldn't wait anymore. I wanted to see my wife but the nurse explained that she was in the delivery room. I knew that was the last place Patricia wanted me to be. She never wanted to be seen, even by me, in a distraught state. So I asked if I could wait in her room and the nurse said, "Yes, if you are very, very quiet." It was now about six o'clock in the morning.

I was exhausted and I flopped down on her hospital bed and promptly fell asleep. I was awakened by the sound of clicking heels approaching the room. The door opened and a nurse screamed upon discovering a male on the maternity floor.

It was now 9:30 A.M., I had an appointment at ten. I called my office to have them postpone it to the next day. My secretary said, "Mr. Mann, where are you? They are looking all over for you." I said who? She said the hospital. I said I'm in the hospital in her room and she said didn't they tell you? Tell me what? I wondered. "Congratulations!" she continued. "Pat gave birth to a baby boy!"

The next helper was a single English woman in her early 20s whose name has long since escaped my memory. On days off she wandered down to where the ships and sailors docked on the West Side. One night when I came home the boys were eating dinner with a visiting sailor. The next day a different sailor was in her bedroom. I let her know, as discretely as possible, that this was not a good idea. Later that night when Patricia came home from rehearsal at the City Opera, I said we can't have sailors sleeping in her bedroom; they have bunks aboard the ship. Patricia said you are such a prude. I said no, I'm not. She could have sex with them right outside our doorstep and I'd step over them quietly and not interfere—but not in our house. Pat's response was, "You're so Victorian."

Our next housekeeper was Elsa, the tap dancer, who took care of making our beds, cooking, sweeping, serving, taking care of the children and all the while practicing her tap routines. Elsa and her boyfriend Hans, who also aspired to be a tap dancer, went back to Germany after they failed many musical comedy auditions. He was shorter than Elsa and they must have made quite a pair when these German-speaking tap dancers came in and auditioned for a Broadway show.

After Andrew was born in 1959, within two weeks Patricia began rehearsing as a chorus member for the opening of Rodgers and Hammerstein's *Sound of Music* with Theodore Bikel and Patricia Neway. At this time she was not yet a diva. My wife Patricia had started out as a high school award-winning classical pianist, and earlier had won a roller-skating championship in Central Park, then she became a dancer with the New Dance Group and performed in Donald McKayle's modern dance piece *Games*, after which she began to study with Martha Graham and Martha asked her to become a member of the company. After several months of rehearsing for performances, Martha took Patricia aside and said in her soft hushed voice, "I hear you singing all the time and I think that's where your heart is." Patricia protested, "No I love dance and want to stay with the company." Martha only gently patted her knee and prophesied, "I know your future is in opera." Patricia continued to protest, however, and Martha allowed her to stay.

Patricia, since I first met her, was always singing, humming a tune and even when she slept—both of her fingers would rest above the folded sheets at about chest level and in her sleep she would "play" the piano and hum the melody. Patricia sang all the time in the bathtub or while she was cooking or cleaning.

As Martha Graham was preparing for their fall season fate stepped in and Patricia badly sprained her knee. No more dancing.

She took Martha's advice to heart and she began studying voice with her mother, Eda, who had been an actress and was now a voice teacher. At the same time Patricia was also studying acting with Uta Hagen, which helped Patricia enormously when she later performed in operas. Patricia was highly regarded for her musicianship—I think that came from her genes and early training in classical piano. The combination of all these elements: dance, theatre, musicianship, and a vulnerable heart helped catapult Patricia into the front rank of opera singers in a very short time.

Patricia had a glorious career at New York City Opera. Her first major success came in 1967 as Violetta in *La Traviata* with Placido Domingo directed by Frank Corsaro. Her reviews were spectacular. The critics compared her to Maria Callas, whom Patricia never met but adored, in particular for her dramatic insight. *The New Yorker* said, "Patricia Brooks is one of the great Violettas of our time."

She had now become a diva. Fans would flock backstage to see her after every performance, but she never played the diva. She was always kind, warm, friendly, and patient to her admirers. Several fans became close friends and would visit at the apartment. One of her earliest admirers was Matthew Epstein, who'd loudly lead the "Bravas" for Patricia at the curtain calls. He became her dear friend and mentor, and helped her with interpreting many performances both in concerts and opera. Matthew, formerly the Artistic Director with the Wales Opera and the Chicago Lyric, is now an artist representative of some of the most important opera singers back at his old job at Columbia Artists.

At home, Patricia was still our sons' "little mommy"—cooking, telling stories, playing games, and taking the boys on adventures. Before the maid arrived for her day's work, Patricia had to clean the house furiously so the maid wouldn't think she was a messy housewife and mother. Patricia had some wonderful, memorable idiosyncrasies. One involved hot, summer days, when she'd pre-cool her brassiere in the freezer. During winter, she relied on the oven.

Patricia also had great successes in Puccini's *Manon Lescaut* and Debussy's *Pelléas et Mélisande* and as Gilda in *Rigoletto* both with Louis Quilico. At that time, Beverly Sills was the leading diva at New York City Opera and Patricia followed her in *Baby Doe* and *Lucia*. In all of her opera performances, Patricia was appreciated and heralded for her acting, singing, and graceful movement. Her final act in *La Traviata* broke your heart. Violetta, who was near death, suddenly burst back to life upon hearing Alfredo was coming to see her. As he entered, she got out of her sick bed, ran into his arms and miraculously she was well and happy, then suddenly her body sagged, her arms still draped around his shoulders. Violetta had died. No one who ever experienced Patricia in that opera will ever forget her.

Patricia performed *La Traviata* in Chile with their National Opera Company. At a dinner afterward in her honor, she was so tired that her face fell, fast asleep, into her dessert of baked Alaska during the official speechmaking. Around this same time Patricia began studying with Daniel Farrow. She loved working with him, which she did at least twice a week. When she was in rehearsal for an opera their sessions were even more frequent. Daniel is one of the best vocal teachers in New York City.

In 1969, Patricia performed at Covent Garden in Rimsky-Korsakov's *The Golden Cockerel*. Her dressing room was the same one recently used by Beverly Sills, and in a top drawer of the dressing table Patricia found a single ballet shoe with a note, "Break a leg, Bev." What a heartwarming surprise it was for her to find this thoughtful gift of camaraderie on such an important night in a foreign country.

Unfortunately, Patricia did only three opera recordings: Robert Ward's *The Crucible*, Haydn's *La Canterina*, and Dittersdorf's *Arcifanfano* with Eleanor Steeber and Anna Russell. There are also many performances of her on tape, including a concert version of *Norma* with Beverly Sills, conducted by Richard Bonynge, husband of Joan Sutherland, and Bellini's *I Capuletti ed I Montecchi* with Marilyn Horn. Patricia also performed in operas with each of the three tenors: Luciano Pavarotti, Placido Domingo, and José Carerras, as well as Dominic Cossa and Richard Fredricks. Since Patricia's death on January 22nd 1993, Dominic calls me every Christmas to talk about her and how much he misses her. She affected everyone that way. Patricia had an exuberance for life whose heart embraced everyone that she met with compassion and understanding. She was also a great mother, making quality time for her two sons, who have both grown to possess her wonder and warmth. On a recent fall day, Jonathan who is now a father was out playing with his children, Jackson and Dakota—they were trying to win the game by catching a falling leaf before it touched the ground. Pure Patricia.

In March 2001, there was an article in *Opera News* about sopranos who have performed *Manon*. In it, Steven Blier wrote: "Given that *Manon* has proved such a chameleon, could anyone ever capture her essence for all times? I think one artist did: Patricia Brooks."

Throughout Patricia's long illness—at least fifteen years—we tried to stem the disease in every way that came to our attention.

As her illness progressed, Patricia had to use first crutches and later a wheelchair. I got a mechanized one which she drove around the house and also the shopping malls. She loved it and referred to it as her legs. Patricia was so alive and alert and positive even in her illness that friends would never think of her as wheelchair-bound but rather in glorious motion. She truly levitated.

Heat is a terrible debilitator for an MS patient. When Patricia was in the early stages we stayed one summer at Brett Weston's house in Carmel Valley. Patricia benefitted greatly from the dry climate, so in 1980 we began renting a house in the Valley each summer. We did that for two years until I realized our rent was almost as much as mortgage payments. So I began to look for a house in the valley that would be comfortable for Pat. I must have seen forty houses before Harper Brown, a lovely delicate man and wonderful poet, took us to a house a friend had built for a handicapped son. It was perfect, on top of a hill with large picture windows so we had a spectacular, nearly 360-degree view unobstructed of the valley. We bought it in 1983 and for the rest of Pat's life she would go out to the Valley from May to October. Patricia was so happy there. She had a full-time companion, Iara Godin, a very lively Brazilian woman. We invited Pat's mother Eda to come and she was a great companion for Pat. Eda played the piano daily and on some days Patricia would sing for a few minutes. Amazingly, the voice was still there—it was as though a treasure box had suddenly opened. The sound was so beautiful and moving but Patricia didn't want to sing unless she had the breath and technical control. She couldn't stand hearing herself if it wasn't perfect.

CHAPTER 12

SPRINKLERS

Our next play after *American Gothic* was *The Girl on the Via Flaminia*, by Alfred Hayes, in 1954. As I am writing this I am trying to remember the name of the man who brought me the script. Last night I got a call from Felice Orlandi, who I hadn't heard from in forty years, just to say hello. He was in *Flaminia*, and of course, we talked about the play and he gave me the name I was searching for, Alfred Sachs. Mr. Sachs, a total stranger, came into the theatre one afternoon to announce he had a very good new play and asked if I'd read it—which I did. The other board members agreed it was indeed a very good play. I called Mr. Sachs and told him we'd like to produce it. He said, "There is one condition." I thought, "Oh god, there's a girl involved in this." He continued "I have the rights from Alfred Hayes and he wants me to direct it."

I knew not a thing about this guy or his work. I thought if Mr. Hayes had given him the rights to direct he must be good. José was exhausted after directing the last five plays in a row anyway. He'd always encouraged the idea of bringing in other directors but every time I would suggest someone he'd wince. Here was the opportunity to bring a new director on board. José relented and proceeded to cast the play with Betty Miller, Leo Penn (Sean Penn's father), Lola D'Annunzio, and Emilie Stevens, and of course Felice. After about two weeks of rehearsal, it became clear to me this production was not going to work with this director. I asked José to step in, but he was reluctant. After much pleading and cajol-

Circle board of directors (1954): *left to right,* José Quintero, Theodore Mann, Emilie Stevens, Jason Wingreen

ing and desperate requests he agreed to take it over. He wouldn't use his own name, however, because he was coming in with such a short rehearsal period. He provided the pseudonym of Joseph Benjamin (his first and middle names anglicized).

Like an expert marksman, José targeted the play scene by scene, moment by moment and found its heartbeat. The actors flourished. He attacked the weak section first and then proceeded at lightning speed to fix the whole play. All of this was done in a matter of several days. I remember how Felice, Betty, Leo, and Lola's faces—which had been sullen for weeks—began to beam. The critics gave it great reviews. Suddenly from the edge of extinction, after one box-office failure after another, we had a major hit! And I was back in the good graces of my sulking mistress. The audiences were flooding in. It was like *Summer and Smoke* all over again, two years later. We were dancing and jumping with joy—Sweet Fate had saved us again.

Of course it was much too good to last. *The New York Times* announced that the newly appointed (by Mayor Robert F. Wagner) Fire Commissioner, Edward J. Kavanaugh, in his first week in office was closing us down because we were in violation of the Fire Department Code requiring sprinklers. But we *did* have sprinklers in the dressing rooms. I had the sneaking suspicion that Kavanaugh might be trying to make a name for himself by finding us in violation. Smash hit play. New commish. A combustible combination indeed. But the public had to be "protected." The irony is that back when we were starting out I would have done anything for any kind of coverage in the *Times*.

Nevertheless, our cabaret license was revoked forthwith and we were prohibited from having any performances in the theatre. We had a huge hit but no theatre! In fact, the Fire Department was mistaken but more on that later. What could we do? The further irony was that because of our success with *Summer and Smoke* all the other off-Broadway theatres were occupied and we had no place to move *Flaminia* to. Jason Wingreen said, why don't you move to Broadway? Wow what a challenge! So I said, "Yeah let's try to put it together."

Within days, and with the help of our Press Agent David Lipsky, I made an arrangement with the owners of the 48th Street Theatre (the very place where I saw *Tobacco Road* as a boy) to move *Flaminia* to Broadway. This was our first venture into the big time and amazing things lay in our future. I was able to work out a low rental deal for the theatre and by April 1, prophetically April Fool's day, we reopened uptown. I'd gotten the funding in bits and pieces from lots of people. I think it cost $75,000 to make the move to Broadway. We had a little left over for advertising.

I didn't know anything about Broadway. I thought that on the strength of our reviews in the papers, particularly the *Times*, we'd succeed uptown and that there'd be an instantaneous audience. I hadn't counted on uptown's uppity attitude about off-Broadway. We were in a *serious* play with exactly *zero* stars. Even Atkinson's re-review of the play failed to sway this audience. Broadway theatregoers at that time were conservative and snooty and just not interested in anything that had originated below 42nd Street. The unions were cooperative but still our costs were five times more per week than they had been off-Broadway. I was unprepared and just completely out of my league. I made the fatal mistake of moving an off-Broadway show to Broadway without sufficient funds for advertising. We limped along hoping that each week our fortunes would change. We kept expecting a big article in *The New York Times*. This didn't happen. We didn't get the Sunday *New York Times* piece that any dramatic show needed then and still does today. By Memorial Day we had to close.

So, there we were in the summer of 1954: no show, no theatre, and no money. I rented a small walk-down office on Christopher Street next door to Frances' Typewriter Repair Service. We couldn't pay ourselves anything. We crowded our records into that tiny shop. We had nothing to do. Suddenly, after five years and eleven plays of furious theatre activity, could the Circle really be slipping away? Was there no hope? We'd plummeted from the peak of a wave of great reviews for *Flaminia* to the bottom of the sea. Jason, Emilie, José and I would meet every day in this tiny office, which barely had room for us to sit. It was in the middle of summer and it was hot-hot without air conditioning. One of Frances's sideline activities was fixing air conditioners. I would salivate as I watched the repaired air conditioners depart the premises next door to chill someone's plush office somewhere. All we could afford to cool were our heels.

We were trying to make plans for the future. It was during the time of these fruitless meetings and the frustration of our depressing, uncertain future that Jason Wingreen and Emilie reluctantly decided, with regret, to leave. Jason had accepted an offer for a Broadway play and Emilie headed for California to pursue her career. Then it was just José and I. I think José hung on out of loyalty to the dream of our own theatre; also he had confidence in me, that I would find a way to get us reopened.

Now back to the fire department and those sprinklers. Once again, I looked in the New York City code and found "in a space of public assembly, sprinklers are required where the seating exceeds 299." Since our seating was under 200 we were well below the code requirement! The fire department was "all wet!" An assistant to the commissioner had obviously misinterpreted the code. I then tried desperately, through my old municipal friends, to get the Circle back open. But to no avail. It was a dead issue. The Commissioner had spoken.

In October, I volunteered to work for Franklin Delano Roosevelt, Jr., who was running in the Democratic primary for Governor of New York. I had not forsaken the theatre for politics, however. My intention in taking the volunteer job was to find a politico to "help" clear up the mistake the fire department had made in closing us. I needed to find a magician who knew how to make red tape vanish.

In F.D.R. Jr.'s campaign I was the front man arranging "spontaneous" demonstrations of support for the candidate. I hired a black, six-man band that proceeded F.D.R. Jr.'s walks playing "Franklin D. Roosevelt Jones." People knew the song and the sight of this tall, good-looking son of FDR striding behind the band excited them. At one of the demonstrations on Eastern Parkway in Brooklyn, with people lined up on both sides of the street, somebody ran up to me and bellowed, "What a wonderful turnout, what a response! People love him, he looks just like his father!" Of course I had staged it all, including some cheerleaders inserted into the crowd. I got them saying, "Yeah, F.D.R. Jr.! Yeah, F.D.R. Jr.!" encouraging others to join them in the chant. Theatre is theatre, whether on a stage or a city street. Come to think of it, this was my first directing job.

The Democratic Convention for Governor took place at the Armory on Lexington and 26th Street. There was much opposition to F.D.R. Jr. within Democratic circles, particularly in the Catholic community. He was said to have endorsed something or other that had raised their ire. At the convention, he was denied permission to stage a demonstration, or hang posters or banners in the armory. "They" were afraid a demonstration would erupt and sway the delegates to support him. But we weren't going to be denied that possibility. They hadn't counted on the cleverness and the resourcefulness of his public relations manager, Richard Harrity. Harrity went about enlisting the support of the Longshoremen's union to help us overcome the convention leaders' lack of vision and manners.

The band, the longshoremen and I gained surreptitious access to the Armory in the dead of night. We secreted banners, large posters of F.D.R. Jr., confetti, balloons and ribbons in the steel rafters. With the union's help I positioned the band in the basement. All of this was done while Harrity and his cohorts diverted the armory security personnel. The longshoremen nimbly climbed the dangerous scaffolding. From the balcony they hung banners and large photographs—all to be unfurled at the right time. Yours truly was nervously guiding this whole operation, standing in the middle of the armory, looking over my shoulder fearful at any moment that the security guards would rush in swinging their billy clubs; fortunately, Harrity knew how to "lift a drink" for himself and anyone in his close proximity. Thanks to him, the guards failed to notice us, or much else, that night.

Later that day, the convention began and when Frank's name was put into nomination the band popped up from their hiding place in the freight elevator, belting out "FDR Jones," then proceeded to march around the armory. Conventioneers fell over themselves to join the parade. A huge demonstration burst out and more and more delegates were marching behind the band. Banners, posters, confetti, and God knows what else was released by the longshoremen and floated down over the whole hall. It was spectacular!

I ducked into a small storage room to catch my breath. The room had a single lamp hanging from the ceiling; chairs were piled up helter skelter on top of each other. Sitting in front of the TV monitor was a tall slender woman all by herself; it was Eleanor Roosevelt. I introduced myself and said I was working for her son. A bit surprised, Eleanor asked, "What are you doing for the campaign?" I responded by pointing to all the hullabaloo in the main hall still filling the TV screen. Her beautiful long hands were resting folded on her lap and she turned to me and said, "Young man, that is the finest demonstration I've ever seen at a Democratic convention." Boy, was I thrilled. I had long been a New Dealer from head to toe thanks to my father. This praise coming from one of America's great women was exhilarating, to say the least. I still get chills as I'm writing this.

Of course the powers that be prevailed and F.D.R. Jr. was defeated in his bid for Governor. He was a wonderful man with liberal ideals. His defeat was a loss to both State and Country; this man had brains and charisma. As I said, the Catholic Church was against him. I think the Democratic bosses also didn't want him because he was not their chosen candidate. (Averill Harriman was and he became governor.) F.D.R. Jr. was too independent-minded and, as famous and beloved as he was, not quite powerful enough to buck both church and party.

The campaign was over and weeks went by before I got up the courage to call F.D.R. Jr.'s campaign manager to ask for his advice on how to get my theatre reopened. I told him of the fire commissioner Edward Kavanaugh's snafu and he responded, "That sounds totally wrong. I know Ed, he's a good friend of mine. I'll make a call." I hurried to add that we had under 200 seats so the city code didn't require us to have sprinklers anyway. He said, "That's good; this will be a breeze."

Within two weeks the fire department issued a press release and in the *New York Times* it read something like, "The Circle in the Square violation has been corrected" and the fire department's prohibition against the Circle in the Square had been withdrawn. In the entire release there was not one mention of sprinklers. The damned thing is that we hadn't made *any* physical changes to the theatre. Ah, that beautiful New York municipal red tape! Now you see it, now you don't. I'd like to have seen Houdini try to free himself from *that* kind of entrapment.

But hold on—we still had to hurdle having all of the city departments inspect us again, a laborious, delicate dance during which I'd meekly follow each inspector as he investigated his area of expertise. Finally, came the building inspector, who took a long tour of the whole place, roaming around downstairs to the kitchen, then the furnace then up to the second floor offices and studios, the dressing rooms and finally the theatre itself—the main event. He'd move around the theatre with me standing in the center of the stage trying to keep the conversation light. It was like a ballet without music. I would try to bring up subjects that would distract him, such as, "Say, what's your bowling score?" or "The Giants look good this season," or "Do you like spaghetti and meatballs?" (a gentle hint that I would take him to lunch if his inspection were successful). Of course, if the fellow had been Irish I'd have praised the St. Patrick's Day Parade and sworn by corned beef and cabbage. Or by knishes, or by whatever ethnic dish applied. But he approved us, and, as any honest bureaucrat would, he refused the free lunch. He said "Everything looks fine. You're O.K. but I've already eaten." During the entire time of his inspection I was holding my breath. When he walked out the door I finally exhaled in great relief. Getting through the quagmire of the city inspections made the parting of the Red Sea a cake walk by comparison. After all the city departments at long last okayed us, the Police Department issued a new cabaret license.

While all these inspections were going on, I also had to negotiate a new lease with the landlord, Loomis J. Grossman, under the same terms as the previous lease. He agreed with one proviso—the lease had to be on a month to month tenancy so that he could terminate by giving us one month's notice for the purpose of demolishing the building. Loomis was a good, stiff negotiator. I had never met anyone with that first name before and somehow the sound of it was chilling. Like a villain out of a Dickens novel. The termination clause made me very nervous. It was like having an ax hanging over our heads. But there was nothing I could do. He was as unmovable as the Sphinx. Where we got the money to reopen the Circle in 1955, I don't remember, but in those days, we could still put on an off-Broadway show for a couple of thousand dollars.

This entire Herculean effort of reopening the Circle had taken a lot of phone calls and meetings with a multitude of city departments, and of course input by my friend in F.D.R. Jr.'s campaign manager's office and advice and spirited assistance from Richard Harrity. In retrospect, I raise a tall toast to him and them. New York State may have lost a great governor, but it regained a vibrant theatre.

CHAPTER 13

WELCOME HOME AND GOODBYE

José and I were so grateful to get back into the theatre, which had remained empty throughout our City Hall travails. It had been a tremendously painful period of time to be without it. All sorts of fears and trepidations had crept into my dreams, but we were saved! We'd just gone through a tumultuous struggle for nine months and had given rebirth to my mistress. We had hung on. Our faith, and belief, had been sustained.

During this long hiatus and after F.D.R. Jr.'s campaign, Roger Stevens, the producer/real estate developer and financier, had befriended me and given me a job as an assistant stage manager/understudy in *Goat Mountain* by Baruch Lumet (Sidney's father). It opened in Detroit which we traveled to by train, after which the play was scheduled for Broadway. The renowned Boris Aronson designed the scenery. The play represented country life in Europe with a series of mountains of differing levels that the leading actor had to climb up and down. We had to cancel the run in Detroit because the actor began suffering palpitations! The play never opened on Broadway, probably the only one in theatre history done in by acrophobia.

Roger was the head of the Playwright's Company, a group of prominent playwrights who had joined with him to present their plays. They took their careers in their own hands—that's a lesson for playwrights today who carp about the paucity of serious plays on Broadway, namely their own! Those who banded with Roger were the leading playwrights of the time: Robert Sherwood, Maxwell Anderson, Robert Anderson, and Elmer Rice. Robert Whitehead participated in the company as a producer. Whoever came up with that idea was smart. Roger did the funding or fund-raising and Bob did the hands on producing. He did it as he did everything in life—with great style and finesse. The playwrights company encouraged and produced other writers outside of the group, as well. In today's world, the only playwrights I know of who have actively helped other playwrights work are Edward Albee and David Mamet, founder of the Atlantic Theatre Company.

Roger hired me again as an assistant stage manager/understudy and to play the small one-line role of the Western Union Messenger, "Telegram for Mrs. Daigle," in Maxwell Anderson's *The Bad Seed* with Nancy Kelly, Evelyn Varden, Thomas Chalmers, Eileen Heckart, and 13-year-old Patty McCormack. Reginald Denham, a debonair English gentleman in both his manner and attire, was the director. He always wore a gray double-breasted suit or a jacket and tie. He never loosened his tie or unbuttoned his jacket no matter how stressful the rehearsals were or during the heat of the day. He was an unflappable guy. We'd often go to lunch where he humorously regaled me with the trials and tribulations of his life in the theatre while elegantly puffing on a cigarette in his long cigarette holder. His wife Mary Orr, the well known playwright and screenwriter of *All About Eve*, accompanied us on occasion. During the run we had understudy rehearsals twice a week. Roy Pool was the overall male understudy. When the female understudy was out, I'd play the Patty McCormack role in rehearsal. Over the years, Roy performed in many plays at the Circle, including the Chief of Police in *The Balcony*. We had lots of laughs whenever Roy would mimic me reciting Patty McCormack's lines.

Seed played out-of-town in Detroit for two weeks and then to New York. There was a theatre shortage at that time so Roger and The Playwright's Producing Company took a musical house, the 46th Street Theatre. During the out-of-town tryouts, a bit of friction developed between Nancy and Evelyn. I became the focus of their competition. When I rang the bell to the house as the Western Union messenger, they were both standing downstage of the couch on either side. Upon hearing the bell, they both made a dash for the door. Evelyn wanted me to open the door wide enough for the audience to see me and hear my line, "Telegram," etc. Evelyn wanted this young kid to be seen and heard. Nancy would open the door slightly, grab the telegram and slam the door.

The race for the door was pretty even—Evelyn winning most of the time even though she was older! The show was a big success, ran for over a year, and made a star of Patty McCormack.

I left *The Bad Seed* early to reopen the Circle and get ready for our first play. For our reopening in June of 1955, I recommended Francis Ferguson's much admired but rarely produced *The King and the Duke*. Richard Watts Jr. of the New York *Post* had written lovingly about this play. It was an adaptation of Mark Twain's *Huckleberry Finn* with the king and the duke as the principle players.

The lead role, Tom, was played by Ralph Williams. The music was by G. Wood, who wrote several memorable songs that Patricia and I relished for years.

I had long thought this score and another G. Wood wrote for us, *F. Jasmine Adams* (based on Carson McCullers' *Member of the Wedding*), were lost. Quite recently, however, I got a phone call from Betty James, who had been with our company in the early days. It turns out she's still in contact with G. Woods' sister, "Woody," whom I called and who told me, in her mellifluous Macon, Georgia drawl, "Oh, yes, we still have all his scores in his old apartment." She'll be sending us copies so that they can be included in our archives at Lincoln Center.

The King and the Duke was a beautiful and touching play, well directed by José but, for some reason, the critics didn't like it. We were taking in enough money to pay the absolute necessities: actors, Con Ed, rent, telephone, coal, payroll, and payroll taxes. We were back on a familiar one-rail track called financial trouble.

We had to get another play on quickly so we chose Arthur Schnitzler's *La Ronde* which consists of six interconnecting love scenes. It's about the duplicity of love. The cast included Betty Miller, Phillip Manor, Grayson Hall, Katherine Ross, Felice Orlandi, Ralph Williams, and Susan Oliver, directed by José. We had it up and running within three weeks. I conceived of an idea for a print ad with sexual undertones. I told the photographer Roy Schatt my idea. He photographed Felice, dressed in his Prussian uniform and hat, a suggestive smile on his face, partially obstructed by his fellow actress, Katherine Ross. She, in a turn of the century off-the-shoulder dress and hat, was tightly held in an embrace by the Prussian Officer with a slight smile on his face. I thought the photograph was mysterious and provocative and that the ad would lure audiences. It was a striking photo but I guess it didn't project what I'd hoped. Oddly enough, my present-day assistant, Holly Ricciuti, has fallen in love with the photograph. She contacted Roy's widow to get a copy of it that now hangs in her living room. Perhaps a photograph, like a play, can be ahead of its time. The reviews for the play were mixed, and so, again, a quick closing after five weeks.

For our next production José chose *Cradle Song*, by Gregorio and Maria Martinez Sierra. It tells the story of a mother who leaves her baby at the door of a convent of Dominican nuns. José and I had a big argument about doing it—I didn't think it would draw. We were standing in my office that had an unusable fireplace and we were both leaning on the mantelpiece looking directly at each other, hotly arguing about doing the play, and I said, "The Jewish audience won't come to see a play about a convent." José said, "The trouble with you is that you are anti-Christian." I responded "No, I am neither for nor against Christ," and continued sardonically, "I just want a little business of my own." But José insisted that it would succeed so we went ahead. The financial noose got tighter. And of course, *The New York Times* dutifully informed the public that the play takes place in a convent. Why couldn't they keep that a secret? I think this was one of the few disagreements about play selection that José and I had ever had during our eleven-year partnership. In the end we were both right. Once again, José directed it beautifully, the critics praised the play *but* the audience didn't come.

We had had too many shows in a row that didn't produce sufficient audiences. After José finished work on *Cradle Song*, he was hired to direct a new Broadway play, Theodore Apstein's *The Innkeepers*, at the Golden Theatre. This was the first time José had worked in a theatre outside of the Circle. Things were pretty grim financially. It looked like we might expire at any moment. We had no idea what we would produce next. My mistress's wardrobe was getting more and more frayed.

We kept *Cradle Song* running even though it was losing money.

Sometimes I found that we lost less money that way than if there were no show in the theatre at all. I was also marking time until José was available for our next project. I was very scared and I decided to reach out and try to find a play for us to do. I began scouring the theatre section of the libraries and the drama bookstores.

Shortly before this, in 1955, out of fear of losing my theatre and my shirt on any given month to my landlord's dreams of lucrative apartment units, I leased at my own expense a nightclub around the corner on Seventh Avenue South. I had to take it in my own name in part because the Circle had zero financial credibility. I paid the bills and the rent. I wanted my darling Circle to have some place to go if Loomis the landlord struck. For eight months it was successful. I called it *Seventh Ave So* and presented music and performance artists. It was a hot spot. Lots of people came. The entertainment was very improvisational. It helped give birth to "Happenings." People would get up spontaneously and do a reading, a monologue, sing a song, or break into dance.

At a recent birthday celebration for the composer David Amran, he and I reminisced about his recurring performances at *Seventh Ave So* with some of his friends—who included Jack Kerouac, Leroy Jones, Terry Southern, and even James Dean. They would read poetry with David playing accompaniment. I had previously done midnight concerts with his friends at the Circle on our dark nights, which were the first jazz/poetry concerts ever done.

Seventh Ave So was dynamic and exciting but the bartenders were getting hungry. I hoped that I was breaking even. Because I didn't charge admission and the main source of income was liquor, it was hard to control the dollars coming in and the expenses going out. I complained several times to the bartender's union representative about the insufficient bar receipts. There's a line in *Iceman* when Harry Hope's talking to Rocky the Bartender about the small receipts from his saloon, "Sure you share with me, and everything that sticks to the ceiling belongs to me." I couldn't keep up with the bartender's sleight of hand with dollars—they are the greatest magicians in the art of "disappearing money." The club became a losing proposition, so when an opportunity came along to rent it out for a play, I grabbed it.

I rented the space for *Career* by James Henry Lee, starring James

Patterson. The play was a success. Once again, I was saved at the brink of disaster by Fate's good nightclub sister. But after a month of sold-out houses, the owner of the building objected to the space being used as a theatre. He said that we couldn't do a play in there because it was zoned as a cabaret. So he terminated the lease. Sound familiar? Another irony, this time where "cabaret" was tweaked *against* me. If only there were a city code for condemning building owners!

CHAPTER 14

RESURRECTIONS IN SPADES

It was now March 1956. For years I'd wanted to do an O'Neill play. Eugene O'Neill was America's forgotten playwright, denigrated by the leading literary lights of the day (Eric Bentley and Mary McCarthy to mention two). They considered him long-winded, repetitious, and ponderous. O'Neill had just died three years earlier with limited media coverage of that fact. I had seen in my late teens the John Ford film of two O'Neill one-acts titled *Long Voyage Home* (*Bound East for Cardiff* and *Long Voyage Home*) with an extraordinary cast—Thomas Mitchell, Barry Fitzgerald, Ward Bond, Mildred Natwick, Arthur Shields, and John Wayne (before he became America's cowboy hero). Many of these became members of Ford's film repertory company. A few years later, while in the army, I saw the film of *The Hairy Ape* with William Bendix and Susan Hayward at an art-movie house in Carmel. In 1947 I also saw the film of *Mourning Becomes Electra* with Michael Redgrave, Katina Paxinou, the famed Greek actress, and a miscast Rosalind Russell playing Lavinia. All these films had a tremendous impact on me—I had never seen anything so truthful, powerful, and emotional. They whetted my appetite to read O'Neill's *Desire Under the Elms*, *Emperor Jones*, and *Ah, Wilderness!* All of which made me realize there was majesty in his plays. I thought what a sweet victory it would be to bring him back and give him the respect his work deserved, to have another victory like Tennessee's *Summer and Smoke*. It was the kind of challenge that excited me. The danger and thrill of going against the grain has always energized me. As I think about this, fifty years later, my heart beats with the same excitement.

In the thirties, O'Neill had been our most important playwright. He is to this day the only American playwright ever awarded the Nobel Prize for literature. He was honored with the Pulitzer Prize four times, one posthumously, when we produced *Long Day's Journey Into Night* on Broadway in 1956.

O'Neill was first presented on Broadway in the twenties with afternoon performances at the Morosco Theatre of *Beyond the Horizon*. It was performed on the set of a play that was being done in the evenings. I think some of the actors from that play also performed in *Horizon*. Critics—in particular, George Jean Nathan, leading drama critic of the era—came to see it and lauded the play and then it went into a regular run. In the seventies, Circle in the Square put a plaque outside the Morosco commemorating it as the site of O'Neill's first success. Unfortunately, the theatre was demolished when Broadway was being rebuilt in the eighties. The plaque disappeared along with the theatre.

In 1956, O'Neill's plays were being produced all over the world and especially in Sweden at the Royal Dramatic Theatre, but very few were being produced in America. He was revered everywhere except in his own country.

So here we were looking for a new play to do. I suggested O'Neill, but José had never seemed interested whenever I previously brought up O'Neill's name. We continued to read and search for the next play. Primarily, it was Leigh Connell—a new board member and a close friend of José's since 1955—and I reading because José was busy with the *Innkeeper*. After all the ups and downs—and mainly downs recently—I think José was ready to throw in the towel with the Circle. But Fate's wand was once again waiting in the wings to touch us.

So this year as I did every year, I called Jane Rubin, O'Neill's literary agent, asking for permission to do one of his plays. I'd always been rejected, but this time she stunned me by saying, "Which one?" I thought Mrs. O'Neill would only let us do one of the more obscure plays so I submitted a list of three rarely produced ones, *Lazarus Laughed, Great God Brown* or *Dynamo*. Jane called me back and told me that Mrs.

O'Neill had said, "If you can choose any O'Neill play which would you like to do?" So José, Leigh and I began reading O'Neill's better known plays.

Leigh proved his invaluable worth when he told us he'd just read *The Iceman Cometh* and thought it was a great play. It had been modestly received on Broadway in 1946. José and I didn't even know of its existence. But after reading it, we agreed with Leigh's assessment. I called Jane Rubin and told her that *The Iceman Cometh* was the one.

In late 1955, Leigh Connell had joined the Circle in the Square. Leigh was a 5'7" man with chiseled features and short blond hair who hailed from Nashville. Good-looking with a soft Southern accent, he was a very intelligent man who loved literature and classical music. He had been afflicted with polio as a young boy. As a result he always had to use a cane and could never bend his knee. He began coming around the theatre as a companion to José. At the time, José and I were the sole producers. And after several months José asked me to have Leigh join us as a producer. There was no particular job or specific role for Leigh, but José was very persuasive and demanded that Leigh become our co-producer. Leigh certainly was an invaluable advisor to José, but he hardly ever came to the theatre and when we did have meetings he listened and rarely participated verbally. The comments he did make were very brief. He wore dark glasses, which made it difficult to read his thoughts—"the eyes are the mirror of the soul." With his championing of *The Iceman Cometh* he turned our world around and spoke volumes, justifying Leigh's earlier silences. Later, after we presented *Long Day's Journey Into Night*, Leigh returned to Nashville.

The Iceman Cometh is over four and a half hours long with a cast of nineteen. I thought if the Circle was gonna go down let's go down big. The image I had in my head was of the *Normandie* slowly listing on its side and sinking into the mud of New York Harbor. But how was I ever going to find the money to get it on even if we got the rights?

Mrs. O'Neill summoned us to her hotel. We bathed and attired ourselves properly. Shirt, tie and jacket; even shined our shoes. We had lunch with her and she ordered her favorite drink—a Monterey Cocktail. As the meal progressed she told us that she was going to give us the rights to *Iceman*. Fate's magic wand had reached down and tapped us on the shoulder. I could barely breathe. We humbly thanked her. She told us the reason she was granting us the rights is "because you are a young Greenwich Village theatre group just like Gene. And the failure of *Iceman* was a torture to him." As she bid us goodbye, she hoped our production would bring the proper recognition to the play that had not been successful on Broadway. "Oh, how Gene had suffered; that production broke his heart." He'd labored hard, writing at the Tao House in California during WWII, and considered it one of his best plays.

Because of Mrs. O'Neill's gift, I felt that I had a tremendous responsibility to help get this production right. José was transformed and rejuvenated. As rehearsals began he embraced the play as though it were the Holy Grail.

The *Iceman* has a large theme. The cast of multiculturally mixed bottom-of-the-barrel inhabitants of a Manhattan saloon in 1912 was exciting to me. These people have one last hope, a treasured pipe dream, until Hickey comes in and destroys even that by forcing them to face their own reality.

But was mounting the monumental *Iceman* the Circle's last pipe dream? Was Hickey going to step on stage and dash our hopes too?

José was always very good in his casting selections which were usually through readings followed by personal meetings with any actors he was interested in. Now with *Iceman*, he was even more passionate and focused than ever. We had a commitment from Howard DaSilva to play Hickey, but about a week before rehearsal was to start, he notified us that he couldn't do it. A film job had come up. We couldn't blame him—our salary was $25 per week and he would be making thousands during the same period of time. We were crushed. We sent out a call for actors for the role. Many came in but were rejected—including Jason Robards Jr. In fact, José had already cast him in the smaller role of Willy Oban. After *American Gothic* three years earlier, Jason had come to our casting calls for succeeding productions when he was in town.

It looked like our pipe dream was going to burst even before Hickey showed! We had an emergency meeting between Leigh, José and myself in my second floor office to discuss our Hickey dilemma. I said, "Without the right Hickey we can't do this play!" Someone came into the meeting and told me Jason was downstairs and had to see me. When

I came down, he said he wanted to read again. Before I could say no, he launched into Hickey's fourth act monologue. I could tell he'd had a couple of drinks, but as I heard him read, I felt a shiver go through me—no one had ever come close to what Jason was doing. He pleaded for another chance to audition. I ran upstairs and told José, "Jason wants to read again. There is something special coming from him." José rolled his eyes as if to say "Oh, no, not again," but dutifully went downstairs to the theatre. A half hour later, he came back exhilarated with that wonderful José smile of sparkling eyes and shiny teeth. He said to me, "Ted, you were so right. Wait until Jason gets home to telephone him and when he gets on the phone say, 'Hello, is Hickey there?'" We had found our man and we began rehearsals the next day.

A couple of years ago I was at a benefit at a college in Connecticut. Jason read some O'Neill—his voice still had the same timbre and warmth in it and vulnerability. In O'Neill roles he had a heartbreaking desire to be needed, with his arms down or outstretched cupped palms—offering the essence of himself and his character. His heart was bare and exposed and this created a magnetic pull that made an audience feel they had to help him. This was the time Jason showed me the script he had under his arm covered with his notes on most of the pages with heavy underlining for his role. In the recent revivals of O'Neill plays that I had seen performed, I always hear Jason's unmistakable cadence and that wonderful growl. It's a voice that has haunted every successive production and haunts me still. I long to hear it again.

Now back to the rehearsals, which were going well but we still didn't have any money! It was just too big an undertaking to follow my old play-financing methods of delaying payment to creditors so I could pay the actors and build the set. The total salary for the nineteen actors was $475 per week. I didn't know where that was going to come from on Fridays. What to do? Where to turn? Who to turn to? The *Iceman* ship was out of the harbor and unless I got some money immediately the ship was going to hit a reef and go down. We'd been in existence off-Broadway since 1951 and had had several successes, but they didn't make up for the money we'd lost with plays that had failed. I was frugal and watched for every penny. Leigh, José, and I were salary-suffering along with the actors.

Jason Robards, Jr., and Farrell Pelly in Eugene O'Neill's *The Iceman Cometh* (1956), directed by José Quintero

Then I thought of Roger Stevens' kindness in hiring me for *Goat Mountain* and then *The Bad Seed*. Roger was also a very successful real estate man. He'd bought and sold the Empire State Building and was in a lot of deals all over the country with his company City Investing. Roger had a passion for the arts, particularly theatre. He initiated the plans for Lincoln Center. It never materialized for him but he started the ball rolling.

However, he was singularly responsible for building the Kennedy Center in Washington. He was all over the theatre world helping playwrights, directors, and actors and never looking for a payback. He had a heart bigger than any of the buildings that he erected.

I went to Roger's fifth-floor office at 1545 Broadway, nervous as hell because this was my last chance. I had exhausted all other avenues for money. I had told Roger over the phone that I wanted to see him. In his usual casual style he didn't inquire, "Why?" As the elevator landed on the fifth floor, Roger was going out, throwing on his hat and coat to fly to D.C. He waved to me, "Come on," as we got in the elevator he said, "What do you need?" And I said, "We need your help to put on *The Iceman Cometh.*" He laughed and asked, "Why do you want to do that play? It's so depressing." As the doors closed, I said, "Oh no, it's a great play and it's got a lot of laughs." Roger turned to me as he buttoned his overcoat and asked, "How much do you need?" I explained that we didn't have any money and needed $2,500 to mount the show. As the elevator landed at the street level, Roger stepped out without responding, just heading toward his waiting taxi to Washington, D.C. My heart fell through the elevator car floor and I felt like I was sinking in the mud like the *Normandie.*

Suddenly he spun around and called out: "Go back upstairs and tell my secretary Jean to give you a check for $2,500." And he got into the cab and sped away. I never got out of the elevator. I pounded the button for the fifth floor. I told Jean what Roger had said. In a few minutes I had the check in hand and rushed downtown to tell Leigh and José the good news and, of course, to get the money in the bank. The $2,500 was enough to pay salaries and get by all the other expenses to put the play on. I was wrenching, squeezing, and stretching every dollar.

In rehearsal, the relevance of the characters to José's own family and Catholic upbringing became apparent. He'd tell stories about the church and his family and he wove them into the life of the characters in the play.

When you hear laughter in rehearsals you know things are going well. There was also a lot of soul bearing, with each actor telling of incidents in their own lives. José had put together a wonderful cast that included many young professionals, one old timer, and even some people new to the theatre, like Al Lewis (Grandpa in *The Munsters*) and his *Iceman* drinking partner Phil Pheffer. They were big heavy-set fellows, without theatre experience, but they fit their roles perfectly. Farrell Pelly, a gem of a man and a divine curmudgeon of an actor, played Harry Hope—the owner of the saloon. Years before, Farrell had come over with the Abbey Theatre and stayed in the U.S. He'd been working in New York many years but by this time he'd stopped performing. An actor friend, knowing we were looking for an older Irishman, told Jason Wingreen about Farrell. He met with José who instantly liked him and offered him the role. Farrell was very reluctant to start performing again. He told me he was too tired and was afraid he couldn't remember the lines. I urged him to read the play, and when he did, all his self doubts disappeared and his energy reemerged. His Irish lilt was magic for the play. Joe Marr played the day bartender, Chuck Morello, the same role he'd played in the original Broadway production in 1946. The night bartender, Rocky Pioggi, was played by a young kid from Hartford with a small amount of experience. He had played in O'Casey's *Shadow of a Gunman* at the Cherry Lane and had one good eye and the swagger of a peacock. His name was Peter Falk and he endowed Rocky with a tough exterior and a soft inside.

Some years later, Peter told me about meeting movie mogul Louis B. Mayer for a film job and his future career. Mayer said, "We got to fix your eye. We can't use a guy with one eye in the movies." Peter stood up and walked out without uttering a word; the rest as they say, is history. I guess it was Mr. Mayer who didn't have very good vision.

The "girls" were Gloria Scott Backé, a buxom blond, warm and gregarious from a classy Connecticut family. Dolly Jonah with a heavy New York accent played the tough dame who wants to marry Joe, the day bartender; and my wife, Patricia was the "third girl," a curvaceous, sexy, rough-talking, pushy Italian. She dyed her hair black and played Pearl, the fast talking Italian, perfectly. She and Scotty played a wonderful scene in which they've come from a night of trying to find "Johns." They frisked a drunken sailor in an alley—holding him up against a wall and making him laugh from the tickling as they fleeced his pockets. José blended them and the entire cast into a mesmerizing ensemble. It was a flawless production. José surpassed all his earlier work. He understood

In rehearsal for *The Iceman Cometh*: *top*, Al Lewis, Farrell Pelly, and Phil Pheffer; *bottom*, Dolly Jonah, Gloria Scott Backé, Patricia Brooks, and Peter Falk

O'Neill completely—the fear as well as the zest for life of his bottom-of-the-barrel characters. O'Neill is saying that every man, however low, has to have a dream.

Iceman, in addition to being a great neglected play also had special resonance for me. Our theatre had itself been a lower Manhattan night-club—the successor of saloons like Harry Hope's. Furthermore, the Bowery bums in Lower Manhattan were very much still with us forty-four years later. In 1956, when we did *Iceman*, the Bowery had not much changed. It remained a flourishing beaten-up district from Houston down to Canal Street. The conditions were identical to those in O'Neill's play. At the street level, there were stores for electrical fixtures, plumbing supplies and used restaurant equipment. Sprawled out on the sidewalks were stoves, refrigerators, sinks, anything you needed to outfit a restaurant, along with chairs and tables. Above them on the second

Patricia Brooks in *The Iceman Cometh*

and third floors were flophouses populated mostly by men who rented a bed for fifty cents during the day or a dollar for the night. These guys spread out wandering around the city panhandling for food or a drink. In contrast to today, there was minimal sleeping on the streets. Where they got the money for their nightly rooms, no one knew and rarely cared. On the streets, people ignored them—they were invisible.

One effect *Iceman* had was to awaken theatregoers to the realization that the bums they saw on the street were human beings. They had a life—they had a story. The play made some people generous and curious about these poor blighted souls who'd lost their families, their jobs and themselves. This was probably one of the main reasons O'Neill wrote the play—to encourage empathy for even the lowest of the low. He had lived among them in his 20s, and wanted to show the bliss they achieved by escaping from the world through a combination of hope and booze. When people saw these bums at the beginning of the play, awakening from a drinking bout, and begging for their next shot, the viewers only tolerated them for the laughs that they provided. But by play's end, each character was clearly etched into their minds and they showed by their applause how much they loved them. Who knows how this might have affected them to give to a charity or to a beggar on the street? My father's own opinion had been changed; he now had much sympathy for those lost souls. After *Iceman* he never walked past a derelict seeking a handout without dropping money into his hat.

At that time, curtain time in New York was at 8:30 P.M. and whether the play was over or not, the first-string critics had to leave the theatre by 9:30 P.M. to make their deadline for the next day's edition. Well, we had a four-and-a-half hour play! If we started at 8:30 P.M., they'd barely see the first act! After conferring with our press agent, Louis Sheaffer, I set the opening at 3 P.M. and he persuaded the critics to agree to come at that unusual hour. Lou had been a drama critic at the *Brooklyn Eagle*. After the *Eagle* decided not to review plays anymore we were Lou's first press agent job. Lou's work with the play obviously stimulated his mind to the extent he wrote a biography of O'Neill, for which he won the Pulitzer Prize. It's funny how life stitches things together.

So there we were on a sunny weekday in May of 1956. May seems to be a significant month in my life. My father, my son John and grandson Dakota and myself were all born in May; *Summer and Smoke* and *The Girl On the Via Flaminia* on Broadway were both in May—and here we were with *Iceman*. As the rhyme goes, April showers bring May flowers.

On the opening matinee our "cabaret theatre," seating 199, was mostly filled with critics. The old nightclub, formerly The 19th Hole, was a perfect environment for the play. People felt they were really in Harry Hope's saloon. David Hays, who later founded the Deaf Theatre Company, designed a brilliant turn-of-the-century New York City bar. Remember those nightclub tables we'd stored when we first took over the cabaret? The ones that, for some unknown reason, I'd been saving all these years? Those became the tables in Harry Hope's saloon. The three poles dissecting the stage, the audience surrounding the actors, and David's beautiful period bar all worked in concert for the play. The entire space had become Harry Hope's saloon.

Jason's entrance in the first act comes about forty-five minutes into the play. All the characters are waiting for Hickey whom they can count on to buy them a round of drinks. Jason would sit out on the stoop facing Sheridan Square chatting to passersby with one ear cocked to the half-open

Theodore Mann and José Quintero in the Sheridan Square Arena Theatre

stage door. About five minutes before his entrance he'd stand up, stretch and wait in the foyer, peeking at the audience and calculating how they might behave that night. Then he'd burst in with joy to see his buddies in Harry Hope's saloon. Boy, were they depressed when Hickey told them he was on the wagon. Later in the play, after Hickey's confessional speech, Harry refers to him as the *Iceman Cometh*—the messenger of death.

The real-life windows in our theatre behind the bar had been painted black years before, but the paint had chipped, allowing streaks of daylight to enter the theatre. After the intermission at the opening performance, as the house lights went out and the actors came back to take their places for the second act, these little beams of light picked up the stooped forlorn figures of Harry Hope's saloon—like ghosts returning home. The audience, en masse, stood up and applauded. I'd never seen that before. I hope that other producers have had that same thrill—a standing ovation after intermission! As I write this, a chill runs through my body as it did that day in 1956. The critics lavished us with praise. *The Iceman Cometh* was a great success! It was probably the biggest hit that off-Broadway ever had, with both audiences and critics.

Iceman ran a year and launched us into a whole new dimension of importance in the theatre. We didn't realize the sensation we had set in motion. To this day, more than fifty years later, it is recognized as the seminal event in the O'Neill canon, as it unleashed a rejuvenated interest in his work. People still talk in aching memory of the production. In particular, the resonance of Jason's performance as Hickey and his total command of the role; the tough leprechaun quality of Farrell Pelly as Harry; the swagger and the Italian cocker spaniel style of Peter Falk as Rocky; and the laconic strength of Conrad Bain as Larry and, of course, Patricia's delicious tempestuous spaghetti-like energy as Pearl—none of which has ever been matched.

At that time, Actors' Equity Association rules allowed an actor to leave a production, "for more remunerative employment with five days written notice." With a cast of nineteen, replacements had to be made in almost all the roles on a regular basis, including Leo Penn as Hickey and Eileen Ryan as Cora. Leo and Eileen fell in love and were married shortly thereafter. Their marriage gave forth another great actor, Sean Penn. But of course, with that parentage what would you expect—a standup comic? Leo was a different Hickey. He employed a more gentle approach to convince the denizens of Harry's saloon to follow his right path. But he was still unrelenting in his obsession to convert the boys "to give up booze and their pipe dreams."

The ex-policeman, played by Al Lewis, and Phil Pheffer's circus grifter stayed the longest—they were living the play and actually grew afraid of leaving Harry Hope's saloon. It was amazing that with all of the replacements we had to make, the *Iceman* ship kept going. Strangely, Carlotta never saw our production of *Iceman*.

Two years after the Fire Department had knocked us on our heels, *Iceman* had a fantastic ride of success with all kinds of rewards and terrific audience response. Each night as the *Iceman* boat left port for its four-and-a-half-hour journey, it couldn't be stopped! Even though the original cast was gone, the production remained solid. It was a great tribute to both O'Neill and José.

It's amazing the fireworks which exploded from that production: O'Neill and *Iceman* were instantly elevated. Productions of O'Neill's plays began to pop up all around the country and an editorial tribute to our production appeared in *The New York Times*. Shortly thereafter Barbara and Arthur Gelb began the work on their great biography of O'Neill and more was to come in his honor.

CHAPTER 15

CARLOTTA AND THE CHILDREN

After the opening of *Iceman*, I went and had lunch with Mrs. O'Neill in the restaurant at the Carlton House on Madison where she lived. She had her usual Monterey Cocktail. Afterwards I drove her down to the Village to meet the actors in my old station wagon. The front seat was propped up with a wooden stick and as we hit a bump the stick gave way and we both sprawled backwards! Mrs. O'Neill's legs went up in the air, her skirt flying backwards. She laughed uproariously and thought it was the greatest fun! I pulled her upright and reset the supporting stick. We continued on our journey.

She insisted that we go down MacDougal Street. Carlotta said, "Please stop at my Gene's Provincetown. *The Hairy Ape* played there."

She repeated how the failure of the 1946 production of *Iceman* had, "broken his heart since the play was so much about his own tumultuous young life in the Village he loved." She recalled the disaster of opening night: "Gene and I were not present. We never attend openings." She went on, "I was told by a friend that James Barton (Hickey) was paid a visit before curtain by his close friend and drinking buddy Babe Ruth. They must have had quite a few because when Barton came out in the fourth act for his long speech he couldn't remember his lines. The stage manager called them out to him but he was drunk and stumbled through the rest of the play." As Mrs. O'Neill spoke she became very agitated and muttered some unintelligible words about Barton.

Carlotta Monterey O'Neill *(Compliments of The Hammerman Collection and eOneill.com)*

Mrs. O'Neill and I arrived at the theatre while rehearsals were in progress. We sat and watched for about ten minutes. At a break, José introduced her to the company and she chatted with them amiably. Of course, the actors were nervous as hell. As rehearsals started up again and we retook our seats, she was very absorbed. To my surprise, after about twenty more minutes, she stood up, thanked the actors, particularly Jason and Farrell Pelly, and embraced José and referred to him, as she did very often, as "my darling." All the cast was in silent awe of this great man's wife, dressed in her customary black dress, string of pearls, dark stockings, black heeled shoes and a black box hat. She wore her dark glasses as she almost always did for her weakened eyes and complained, "I ruined my eyesight copying from his insufferable small script." She took the glasses off to wipe the tears from her eyes. I then drove her back to her apartment and she barely said a word. It was a memorable afternoon with this ultra-gorgeous and dignified 70-year-old, bumping along in my car on a journey back through her past in Greenwich Village.

Mrs. O'Neill and I enjoyed many other lunches together, sometimes with my boys Jonathan or Andrew. On one occasion, when she and I were alone and she could speak as frankly as she always did, she proclaimed in her grand theatrical voice, "I had appeared in *The Hairy Ape* on Broadway but Mr. O'Neill didn't pay any attention to me. I thought he didn't know who I was and then, one day, I met him again at a friend's house in the country. I was with someone else at the time. Gene was a black Irishman with intense eyes who kept staring at me. One afternoon he showed up at my apartment and just sat on the couch in silence and I thought, 'Good grief, what is he doing here?' and finally he said to me, 'I want you to be my wife, nurse, secretary and mistress.' I laughed, what did he expect me to do? Give up everything? But he sat there on the couch, so sad and forlorn that my heart just went out to him. I fell in love with Gene. I took care of him. I took him to my tailor and had suits and shirts made for him, he was dressed so poorly, like a beggar. Gene loved the attention and shyly smiled at the tailor who was measuring him."

She'd stop and take a deep drink of her Monterey Cocktail. It was her own special concoction. She never revealed its recipe but I suspect it was gin from the smell. She loved that drink and it was brought to her whenever we sat down for lunch in her hotel restaurant.

Then she'd begin again (often referring to her husband as Gene, That Black Irishman, or Mr. O'Neill), "After Gene and Jamie's mother died in California, Jamie returned to New York by train. Gene didn't meet him at the station. So Jamie went searching for him and found him in Washington Square Park. Jamie told him about the blonde he had met on the train while his mother's body rested in the mail car." As far as we know Gene never attended his mother's funeral. This story about the blonde was immortalized in A Moon for the Misbegotten where she was identified as a floozy. And that the word "met" that Mrs. O'Neill used regarding the train trip in fact meant that, "he had her." Then Mrs. O'Neill said, indignantly, that "Jamie had introduced Gene to his first 'woman.' They used to get so drunk together that they would fall to their knees and then would pull themselves up by the towels [that hung] from the bar rails. They were terrible drunks."

By now she'd be immersed in the past, telling stories as though they were happening right then and there. When she spoke about O'Neill it was as though she were talking to him. She shared many of their private incidents while we visited in her apartment such as the argument when "Gene stormed out of the house into the freezing cold weather. He fell, hurt his leg, and crawled back to the house, banging on the door pleading with me to let him back in." On another occasion she told me, "Gene would go into his study first thing in the early morning and close the door. He would write standing up at his desk. I would hear these awful noises and shouting and torturous cries, as he acted out the scenes playing all the roles. Then after several hours he'd come out totally spent, looking just awful. He wouldn't let anyone but me type his manuscripts and that's how I ruined my eyesight—trying to read his impossibly small writing."

As she continued in her remembrances sometimes she got angry and it frightened me. She was confronting Mr. O'Neill right then and there in her living room. She went on, "Late in his life when he was very ill he was lying in bed and he'd try to get up but he fell. He called to me to help. I came in from the next room and was aghast to see him lying on the floor. 'Help me,' he said. I tried to pick him up but he was a big man. [O'Neill was 6' and Carlotta about 5'3".] To pick him up, I had to slide my body underneath him and on all fours start to lift him. As I did, he put his hands around my neck and tried to choke me." She paused.

Often I felt like an observer at some great theatrical event. I wanted to remember so much of her memories but, alas, the mind can only take in so much.

"We lived in Tao House [California] for several years," she continued. "His friends complained that I wouldn't let them see him. But I was only doing what Gene wanted so that he could write. After the war we moved back to a hotel in New York. Gene had become ill and was losing his ability to write. He didn't want to be in New York City so I arranged for us to move to this lovely hotel in Boston where I nursed him and had all kinds of doctors come to see him and try to help. I decorated the hotel rooms with the things he loved. I'd always taken care of choosing the houses we lived in and furnishing them at great expense. We had lived in France in a beautiful Château . . . "

"The chateau," Carlotta explained, "was inland and Gene wanted to be near the sea. So, I bought a house for him in Sea Island, Georgia, right on the water where he could swim every day. Oh, how he loved the sea! He was like a seal in the water and he'd stay out for hours. I would select the food that he would eat and had fresh cut flowers every day. He was like a child; he loved the attention."

In the summer of 2004 my wonderful partner Paul Libin was honored in Tours, France for his work with the O'Neill Society. One day we visited the Chateau Le Plessis where the O'Neills had lived in 1929. It's a three-turret building sitting on many acres surrounded by a forest. On the exterior of the house are full-length windows with wooden shutters.

The current owners invited Paul, his wife Florence, his daughter Andrea and her friend John High to come into the chateau. The rooms were beautifully laid out, and spacious with a real sense of comfort. They told us that it rained a great deal of the time and how depressing this was. It got me to thinking that the O'Neills had lived there while Eugene was writing *Mourning Becomes Electra*—we all know the importance of shutters in that play and how easily one could become melancholy living there.

Carlotta then began talking about the children, "When Oona married 'that little Jew,' she was 18 and Charlie Chaplin was in his 50s. Gene never wanted to see her again. He felt that she had married her father."

His son, Eugene Jr., was a Greek scholar and professor at Yale University and was close to his father. Carlotta explained, "They corresponded regularly until he got involved in politics—Gene thought he was wasting his life." In 1948, I met Gene Jr. at the Woodstock Art Gallery after he'd finished delivering a speech supporting Henry Wallace for President. Gene Jr. was a big burly man with a barrel chest and sandy hair, soft eyes and a Van Dyke beard. From the photographs that I have seen of his grandfather James, he seems to have inherited his barrel chest.

After his speech, we had lunch and drinks with my friends Jack and Sophie Fenton, both artists. Jack, who was a very curious intellectual, asked Eugene Jr. about Greek theatre. Eugene expounded a bit, then he went on to comment on the beauty of Woodstock. He also talked about his disgust with the Republicans and the Democrats and with conditions in the country, which explained his support for the Liberal Party candidate Wallace.

Aileen Cramer, one of the co-founders of Circle in the Square, and a longtime Woodstock resident, was a close friend of Eugene Jr.'s, but "not a girlfriend." They had met in Greenwich Village and had partied in various Village haunts along with his longtime woman friend and his brother Shane. One of the haunts was the Minetta Tavern. Aileen described Eugene Jr. as, "warm, humorous and funny. He was tall like his father, over six feet. He rented a small house on top of Ohai Mountain in Woodstock. Amazingly, he didn't know how to drive a car and I taught him on the back roads." In our first summer at the Maverick Theatre in Woodstock, Eugene Jr. was one of our supporters and attended the final party we had at the theatre. At the time, I had no idea of the importance Eugene Sr. would eventually play in my life, and for our theatre company.

The O'Neills' journey from Georgia to California was a convoluted one. The O'Neills initially left their Georgia home to seek a house in Seattle. The fog and rain deterred them and they soon left Seattle in search of a better climate. Carlotta's daughter Cynthia drove them down the coast to San Francisco with O'Neill singing out intermittently, "Fog, fog, fog!"

The O'Neills' house search was interrupted by Mr. O'Neill's appendectomy in 1936. Carlotta took a room next to him in the hospital, as she told me, "to keep the chorus girls away." The operation was successful. But while still in the hospital he became infected and, as O'Neill wrote about it, "an interior abscess burst and flooded my frame with poison." Still in the hospital he received his Nobel Prize in February of 1937 for "his creative drama, for characters marked by virility, honesty and strong emotions, as well as depth of interpretation." Recipients usually must go to Sweden to accept the honor but an exception was made in this case due to O'Neill's frailness. Carl E. Wallerstedt of the Nobel Prize committee presented O'Neill with the award. Wallerstedt reported, "As he tried to stand, O'Neill's feet wobbled and his hands shook." Wallerstedt helped O'Neill to sit down. The ceremony, such as it was, took less than five minutes. Carlotta was not present because she was selling their Sea Island house and its furnishings in Georgia.

O'Neill was released from the hospital. But the doctor told him he should rest and not work for a year. While Carlotta was still in Georgia, O'Neill had his nurse Kathryne drive him to meet for the first time Carlotta's mother, Nellie Tharsing (Carlotta's maiden name). This was rather late to be meeting one's mother-in-law. Perhaps Carlotta was embarrassed by her mother's colorful past with the mayor of San Francisco. Kathryne served as O'Neill's nurse for the entire time he lived at Tao House.

After he got out of the hospital, they rented a house in Lafayette, California, and then later purchased land which would become Tao House, in Danville, California, 160 acres far away from any other humans and with the quiet O'Neill needed to work.

In 1937 the road from Danville to their property was almost totally uninhabited. Today it is crowded with suburban homes, one acre or less. When the site was designated by the Government as a National Historic site the National Park Service was assigned responsibility of the property. Then tourists began arriving to visit the site. They drove on the now populated road and a court battle ensued when one of the neighbors, an attorney, objected to the tourist traffic. The battle went on for many years until the parties came to a settlement by which the park service must provide a bus and driver to transport visitors to Tao House on a limited visitation schedule. So today if you want to visit the home of America's greatest playwright you must call the tour service for Tao House first to make a reservation Monday through Wednesday for either 10 A.M. or 12:30 P.M., then you wait in a parking lot in Danville for the bus to take you to the house. A maximum number of fourteen people is allowed in the two buses that travel to the house. Furthermore when I was in the city of Danville recently I didn't see any street signs that indicated the direction to Tao House. According to the National Parks Service roughly 2,500 people visit Tao House annually. The best time of the year is the spring. But other times of the year they may have one or two people or none on any given day. So O'Neill and Carlotta have the kind of privacy that they have always wanted through the help of the National Park Service. And the final irony of this tale, that O'Neill would love, is that the bothersome lawyer was later found guilty of fraud and disbarred.

At Tao House, O'Neill began working and thinking about his eleven play cycle A *Tale of Possessors Self-Dispossessed* that was to cover 150 years of an Irish immigrant family in America, from 1775–1925. This cycle included A *Touch of the Poet* and *More Stately Mansions*. The Theatre Guild, his longtime producers were anxious to present one or more of the plays but he wanted to complete all of them before they went into production, saying, "Productions are only nerve wracking interruptions. The play as written is the thing and not the way actors garble it with their almost-always-alien personalities (even when the acting is fine work itself)."

Two plays survived. *More Stately Mansions* was never completed; but was produced in 1967 on Broadway directed by José with Ingrid Berg-

Tao House exterior *(National Park Service, Tao House)*

man, Colleen Dewhurst, and Arthur Hill. Sections of the play were admired as were the actors, although it was highly criticized because they had presented an unfinished O'Neill play. *Touch of the Poet* was the only play of the cycle which he was to finalize in 1942.

Half way through 1937 Carlotta began overseeing the building of Tao House. She had total creative control of its construction. The house was finally completed in the spring. Carlotta confessed, "It was like living through one of Gene's long plays."

The house is surrounded by a six-foot wall with a wooden door bearing the Chinese letters for "Tao House," which means "the right way of life." As you entered the courtyard garden, one path went off sharply to the left and the other to the right, both paths ending at solid walls. The center path went briefly straight ahead then veered to the right and then came back to the center. By oriental tradition these paths that went off left and right were intended to mislead potential intruders. The front door entrance is at the far left of the house which is built of cinderblock painted white.

When you walk into the house to the left is the dining room, pantry, kitchen, and then servants' quarters fit for six people. When you go right at the front door you come to Rosie's room, which contained O'Neill's player piano, which he had named Rosie. Bookshelves lined two walls of the room which held innumerable classical, jazz and blues records as well as books of all description. The bookshelves were filled with hundreds of books and plays and research material including works of Chekhov, Strindberg, Shaw, O'Casey, Wilde, etc. On the walls opposite the piano were photos of his father and actors of that period. The living room in the days when the O'Neill's lived there contained oriental furniture as well as bookcases. The floors were Spanish tile. The ceiling was dark blue. Beyond the living room was a guest room. On the second floor at the top of the stairs was Carlotta's bedroom, bath, and dressing room all with wood floors and a dark blue ceiling. Continuing to the right is O'Neill's bedroom. O'Neill's bed, in the oriental tradition, faced East and West. It had been at one time in a fancy opium den; the ceiling is white. The floors of his rooms are also wood. Next came his bath and dressing room. In his study, the beamed ceiling is painted Chinese red. There is also a closed sun porch. His desk and chair in the study look out at the distant Mount Diablo. Behind the house, on a long arduous sloping path, is the pool O'Neill swam in every day, which had never been heated.

In 1938 O'Neill suffered from neuritis and had to suspend writing altogether. Carlotta said, "it broke her heart." O'Neill's spirits were down because of his illness and the Great Depression, which he blamed on, "The Spanish Civil War, the rise of Hitler and corrupt U.S. politicians."

That same year, his son Shane, who was in school in Colorado, was reunited with his father for the first time in two years. Shane had gained a reputation as an editor at his prior school's newspaper and was also admired by schoolmates for his drinking capacity.

Eugene O'Neill turned 50 on October 16, 1938 and spent the day laid up with rheumatism. In June of 1939 he had completed a revision of *A Touch of the Poet* but had permanently set aside his eleven-play cycle.

By 1939 it had been eight years since Oona had visited O'Neill. In July of that year, in a letter to Oona, he wrote that he was anxious to see her and get to know her again. He continued, that he was, "looking forward to the great happiness of seeing you." He wrote in a letter to a close friend that he was "very apprehensive," but didn't know, "what she might be like." During her ten-day visit to Tao House, Carlotta took her to the Golden Gate Exposition and to go shopping. Carlotta also gave her silk blouses she had purchased in China. Every day O'Neill would stop writing about 1:30 P.M. and afterwards he and Oona would have lunch together and then go to the pool. The bathhouse of the pool had photographs and posters of James O'Neill in *Monte Cristo* and other plays in which he had appeared. She loved to swim and he was very proud of her ability. On the last day of her visit, September 1, 1939, Germany invaded Poland and World War II began.

Eugene and Oona O'Neill. You know they're father and daughter—note the similarity of the smiles, the eyebrows, the right ears, and the twinkle in their eyes *(Left photo: National Park Service, Tao House; right photo: Corbis)*

The O'Neills kept a map of Europe on the wall at Tao House and tracked the battles of the War. O'Neill was deeply affected by this turn of events, shouting, "Jesus! The incredible, suicidal capacity of men for stupid greed."

I've attended many O'Neill conferences, including the gathering in June of 2005 in Provincetown, at which many papers were submitted on wide-ranging subjects regarding O'Neill, but never one about his children. I was very curious to know more particularly about Oona because as a young man I saw her photograph constantly in newspapers and magazines, and I as well as many others fell in love with her. As a matter of fact the first love of my life, Kraig Short, looked very much like Oona—black hair, brown eyes. So while writing this section about O'Neill and his plays and my relationship with Carlotta, Oona was on my mind. I was thinking about the father–daughter relationships in his plays. For example, in *Anna Christie* her father, Chris, abandons Anna, but in the end he tries to make up for the pain he has caused her and wants her to marry the sailor, Mat Burke. In *A Moon for the Misbe-*

gotten, Josie has been living with her father, Phil, all her life and they have a very playful, warm relationship, though he is anxious for her to get married and hopefully to Jamie. In *Mourning Becomes Electra*, Lavinia's father Ezra is a very cold man, and upon his return from the war does not show any affection to her. She strongly identifies with him, and when he dies, she is determined to destroy her mother's relationship with Adam Brant, a sea captain. In *A Touch of the Poet*, Cornelius Melody's relationship with Sara is remote and denigrating and he only becomes interested in her when she has a potential marriage with a wealthy neighbor that he believes would benefit him. So I was curious about O'Neill and his children—particularly Oona.

Within a very short time after Oona left Tao House in 1939, things between Oona, Carlotta and her father changed drastically or shall we say dramatically, when Oona was named debutante of the year in 1942–43. When Oona was asked in an interview if she was lace curtain or shanty Irish, she responded, "I am shanty Irish and proud of it." There were many stories and photographs about her in newspapers and magazines, which always noted that Nobel- and Pulitzer Prize-winning playwright Eugene O'Neill was her father. This upset him because he disliked the idea of his daughter "riding on his coat tails." Oona began to frequent the Stork Club in New York, a hangout for wealthy people and debutantes. She was photographed being escorted to the Club by older men in their 40s and up.

Through his attorney, O'Neill learned that Oona wanted to study acting at the Neighborhood Playhouse. O'Neill was angry and wrote to Weinberger, "I will not provide tuition for an insolent daughter that mocked her heritage. She had little talent [for acting]." Oona had appeared in a summer stock production of *Pal Joey*, and O'Neill had heard unfavorable reports about her performance. The letter to Weinberger continues, "If she had really serious ambition, she would get a job in the theatre. The way to act is to get a job in the theatre [something he had done as a young man, though, in his case, his father hired him], not to go to acting school." He felt that she wanted to go on stage because it was easy and his name was the key. He said that, "Having the name of O'Neill as an actor would make it more difficult." He further wrote he was sure "she'd fail because it takes genius to pull something like this off, and she was no genius." He referred to her as a "spoiled, vain, lazy little brat." In comparing Oona's plans with Jamie, his letter said that "Jamie had drawn on his father's name, went on the stage and turned into an embittered third-rate actor. That his easy start had murdered the life he might have had."

O'Neill overlooked the fact that alcohol was Jamie's undoing. O'Neill said, "Oona should wake up and realize the U.S was at war and it was no time for young Americans to aspire to be on stage. If she wanted training that meant something, she should train to be a Red Cross nurse, or to do any war work that might make a real woman out of her. Her yearnings were apt to make her a tart. Drama school was more laziness, more sly evasion. Pure Boultonism." (Referring to his former wife and Oona's mother.)

Oona, Carol Marcus, and Gloria Vanderbilt became friends and were the most beautiful, radiant girls you ever saw. They all had luminous pale skin that they powdered white. They all had one thing in common: Gloria's father died when she was 17 months old, and Carol was born to an unnamed father. Though Oona's father was neither unknown nor deceased, Carol said that Oona knew her father but that she was fatherless.

There was a fourth friend whose name I don't remember but who wanted to be a ballet dancer. In planning their marital future these four young ladies made a pact that they'd all marry famous older men. The dancer did become a seasoned ballerina and married John Huston— which, if that ballerina were her mother, would account for Anjelica Huston's great legs. Carol married William Saroyan, Gloria married Leopold Stokowski and Oona married Chaplin. They fulfilled their pact.

Carol Marcus invited Oona to Sacramento. On her way, Oona wrote a letter to her father at Tao House and gave him her telephone number at a hotel in Sacramento. She never heard from him so she called him and Carlotta answered. Carlotta put the phone down and returned saying that O'Neill would prefer not to see her. Determined to see her father, Oona drove to Tao House and was met at the door by Carlotta who refused to let her in. O'Neill later wrote her a letter saying she had not sought his advice about her life choices and he, "was disappointed with the woman she was becoming." He had wanted her to seek his advice on her life choices and help her avoid her mistakes. "You don't want to see me. Your conduct proves that. Let's cut out the kidding. I don't want to see the kind of daughter you have become in the last year. I had hoped that there was the making of a fine intelligent woman in you, and would remain fine in whatever you did. If I am wrong, goodbye. If I am right, you'll see the point in this letter and be grateful." This was the last time Oona received a correspondence from her father. After leaving Tao House in 1939 she never saw him again. Over the years she continued to try to contact him but was rebuked.

After Sacramento, Oona went to Los Angeles to try to pursue a film career. She met Chaplin at a dinner party and later turned up at his studio. Her agent advised Chaplin that Fox studio wanted to sign Oona. So Chaplin quickly signed her to a contract with his film company. He then began giving her acting lessons at his home.

According to Carlotta, when Oona married Chaplin, O'Neill referred to him as a little Jew. Strange comment since his producer at the theatre guild, Lawrence Langner, and his attorney Harry Weinberger were also Jews. In his divorce from Agnes, Weinberger also represented him. And in his 1952 divorce action from Carlotta, Winfield Aronberg, another Jew, represented him. Oona was a voracious reader and loved to give her opinion, as a teen and later in a discussion with Carol Marcus she advised Carol not to read T.S. Eliot because he was an anti-Semite.

Chaplin at the time was having a lot of well-publicized difficulties. First was a paternity suit filed by Joan Barry claiming that he was the father of her child. Although blood tests proved otherwise, the suit still continued. Then he was to be called by HUAC (House Unamerican Activities Committee) in 1951 because of "Communist leanings." Chaplin stated that he had never been a member of the Communist party. He and Oona were outspoken liberals. At parties at their home they had people of all denominations and ethnicities. The blacklist stain was on him. In those days, if you were blacklisted you couldn't work in Hollywood. And thirdly it was revealed that for all the years that he lived, worked and prospered in the United States, he had never become a citizen. And the fourth problem was that the government was claiming back taxes from him.

Because Chaplin feared that the government would seize all of his assets, he determined that they should leave the country. Oona, at Chaplin's instruction, went to all the vaults and banks and withdrew their assets. When they sailed for England on the Queen Mary she wore a fur coat. Sewn into the lining were as many $1,000 bills as she could fit. In 1952 they decided to establish residence in Lausanne, Switzerland, on Lake Geneva. He bought a chateau. Oona gave birth to her fifth child, named Eugene on August 23, 1953. She sent her father an announcement of the birth, but he was very ill and he did not respond. Eugene, Oona's father, died three months and four days later.

On Christmas Day in 1977 Charlie Chaplin, the greatest comic of all time, died. Oona began drinking heavily and continued for the rest of her life. She maintained residences in Switzerland as well as New York and traveled between both. In 1988, The Circle in the Square honored Strindberg and O'Neill with performances by the Royal Dramaten of Sweden and Circle O'Neillians: Colleen Dewhurst, Jason Robards, etc. The king and queen of Sweden were in attendance as were many American celebrities, amongst them Paul Newman and Joanne Woodward. This was the hundredth anniversary of O'Neill's birth. I met Oona that night and we had a chat in which she thanked me profusely for the work we had done for her father and expressed her gratitude and told me that she had secretly seen several of our O'Neill productions, and felt that her father would have been honored.

She had had a long correspondence with Louis Sheaffer, the Pulitzer Prize winner of the O'Neill biographies: *Son and Artist; Son and Playwright*. Through that correspondence she was able to understand and forgive her father and said, to Sheaffer, "The misery about me and my father should be forgotten and forgiven in his heroic battle to become an artist."

Because of the fine literary quality evidenced in her letters Sheaffer and many of her friends tried to encourage her to write a book, but she refused. Oona died September 27, 1991. By this time her brother Shane, Eugene Jr., her mother Agnes, Carlotta and her father all had passed away. All that furor and heartbreak was just a memory.

In 1942, O'Neill completed A *Touch of the Poet*, in which the father finally reconciles with his daughter, whom he has berated throughout the play, when he gives up his false posture as an Irish war hero. Was this O'Neill trying to come to terms with his own daughter? With his own behavior toward her?

Back in Tao House in 1939, despite his fragility, O'Neill started work on *The Iceman Cometh* and completed the first draft in two weeks. At the time he said that it was as if he had "locked myself in with my memories." The setting of *Iceman* was inspired by one of O'Neill's old hangouts, The Golden Swan. The play is "based on people I once knew or knew of, although none . . . is exactly a portrait of anyone." For example the character James Cameron, "Jimmy Tomorrow," in *Iceman* was based on a man who was a habitué of one of these saloons who interestingly had been James O'Neill's press agent. The character Don Parritt in *The Iceman* who commits suicide mirrors O'Neill's own failed attempt at suicide in 1912. (*Iceman* and *Journey* are both set in 1912. Obviously O'Neill viewed that year as pivotal in his life.) It may be that the press agent was one of the men responsible for saving O'Neill from his attempted suicide. Larry Slade is based on Terry Carlin, an anarchist whom O'Neill respected and was very fond of. After the draft of the *Iceman* he then began work on *Long Day's Journey Into Night*. This was to be the beginning of a seminal period in O'Neill's playwriting life. Over the next four years he would write four of the most important plays in his career and in the history of the American theatre. This is especially true if one considers the influence these plays have had on such eminent playwrights as Arthur Miller, Tennessee Williams, Tony Kushner, Edward Albee, David Mamet, and August Wilson.

In 1942 he wrote *Hughie* and in 1943 *A Moon for the Misbegotten*. I am proud to say that these four masterpieces were all produced by Circle in the Square and I have had the privilege of directing three of them. I am particularly honored that I was the producer of *Long Day's Journey*, acknowledged as the greatest American play ever written. Arthur Gelb, the O'Neill biographer, recommended to me, "That should be the first line of your Who's Who in *Playbill*." I agree with him completely.

O'Neill's abandoning of his eleven-play cycle to begin work on these four plays begs the question of what was happening in his life that made him change direction. As noted, he had recently written to Oona to try and reestablish their relationship. And later in a letter he wrote to Oona he said he was, "exceedingly proud" of her. He was on a track totally different from his earlier plays, many of which contained oblique references to his own family. Now he was writing plays about experiences of his life and the ghosts that had always haunted him. Because of his physical condition which put in question his longevity he must have felt he had to face these ghosts which had tormented him his whole life and finally deal with them before he would lose his capacity to write. This struggle gave birth to these great plays at immeasurable cost to him. After completing the fourth play, *Moon*, he was never to write another play again. The last plays that were produced during his lifetime were *The Iceman* in 1946 and *A Moon for the Misbegotten* which went on tour first to Columbus, Ohio in 1947; it was then banned in Pittsburgh. In Detroit *Moon* was closed on the second night of performance by the police censor for "an obscene slander of American motherhood." Armina Marshall producer of the Theatre Guild objected and wrote to the police censor that O'Neill had won the Nobel Prize and the censor responded, "Lady, I don't care what kind of prize he's won, he can't put on a dirty show in my town." It then played St. Louis where it finally closed. Despite entreaties from the Guild to recast and reopen the play, O'Neill refused, exhausted from the troubles of the tour. That production never opened on Broadway. The play was done with Wendy Hiller and Franchot Tone at the Bijou Theatre on Broadway in 1957 but it didn't succeed. In 1968, I directed and the Circle produced *A Moon for the Misbegotten* with Salome Jens and Mitch Ryan. It was recognized as a minor masterpiece.

O'Neill did not live to see the publication of *Journey*. It is about his family and set in their Monte Cristo Cottage in New London. Now he was not inventing new characters. This was his own father, mother, and brother and the problems that they were living through all compressed into a single day. The four new works are all naturalistic. As lengthy as some of them are (*Iceman, Journey*), they are naked, stripped to the bone and deal forthrightly with the issues of the lives of the characters.

Based on the visit with Shane and his welcoming letter to Oona and her later visit, I believe O'Neill wanted to leave for them the truth of himself and his family. Perhaps having turned fifty was another aspect. I know for myself, at that turning point, I realized that time was short—life is not infinite—so I decided to concentrate solely on that which was important to me, my wife Patricia, my two sons Andrew and Jonathan and my seductive, dangerous mistress, Circle in the Square.

The play *Hughie* is about a drifter con man Erie Smith, a character that O'Neill definitely would have met in his low life living in cheap hotels. Erie desperately seeks the companionship of the night clerk as though he were the last man on earth. The night clerk is as silent as a gravestone and Erie needs to wake him up. The setting is a "flea bag" hotel in Times Square east of Broadway. It is also a play that sums up O'Neill's basic belief that a man no matter how low must have companionship and at least one hope or pipe dream to survive.

A Moon for the Misbegotten is about his brother Jamie and takes place on a farm close to the O'Neill family's New London cottage. Jamie seeks his mother in the person of the character Josie—a 28-year-old unmarried farm daughter. By the end of the play Jamie finally finds peace in her arms.

The fifth play completed during this period, in 1942, was *A Touch of the Poet* which deals with a tempestuous father–daughter relationship. Perhaps *Poet* was O'Neill's attempt to examine and to further understand his own relationship with his daughter.

On September 28, 2005, I attended a commemoration ceremony in a park in Danville, California, celebrating Eugene O'Neill. At the luncheon that followed, I met Kathryne Radovan Albertoni, who was Eugene and Carlotta's nurse from 1937–1944, while the couple lived at Tao House. She was now 95 years old, a tall woman with pure white hair, agile, and sprightly. She loved talking about O'Neill. Kathryne would arrive at ten in the morning and leave at six. In 1937, when the O'Neills moved in, Eugene had an appendicitis operation. During his recovery period, nurse Albertoni chauffeured him to what he always referred to as "Frisco," a forty-five minute drive from Tao House (O'Neill never learned to drive). She also took him to see college football, to movies and to the Cliff House Restaurant. Kathryne called him papa. Perhaps this is a name O'Neill relished to supplement the absence of his children.

Kathryne also told me that: "One day when Oona was visiting, Carlotta and Mr. O'Neill went shopping in San Francisco and bought Oona a mink coat." This was the same coat that Oona sewed Chaplin's $1,000 bills into when they escaped from the IRS to Europe. So, unbeknownst to him, O'Neill blessed the marriage he had opposed in a way he never imagined.

I met at that same luncheon Janet Washburn, a beautiful woman, slender, dark-haired, about 5'5" with a wonderful glow of joy emanating from her face with sparkling dark eyes. She spoke very clearly and was very chipper—a happy lady. She had been O'Neill's typist since she was 22. "My mother, Carlotta's convent school friend, had recommended me to work with O'Neill. So I became his typist." I immediately understood why O'Neill would want to have her around. I could imagine how beautiful she must have been when she was 22. Kathryne the nurse was like Carlotta in that she was rather grand, but Janet was just the opposite, fun-loving and approachable. Even now, in 2005, she was devilishly charming.

Carlotta told me that she had, "lost my eyesight typing his plays." Maybe several people, Janet, Carlotta, her daughter Cynthia all helped to transcribe O'Neill's plays which were written in long hand. As he got older, his handwriting diminished making the words very difficult to read. Carlotta told me that at Tao House, "his hand writing was so damn small; I had to use a magnifying glass."

Janet told me that she would "arrive at Tao House at ten o'clock in the morning and be greeted at the front door by Mr. O'Neill who was wearing trousers and suspenders without a shirt or shoes." She smiled and giggled. It's no wonder O'Neill liked having this youthful charmer close by. "After greeting me," she continued, "he would walk with me to his study talking all the time as he stopped at his dressing room to put on a shirt and shoes. I sat at a desk directly behind Mr. O'Neill's. As we sat down to work, he would begin writing the plays in what looked like a ship's log book. As he finished each page, he would hand it to me and I would type it. We worked like that for several hours, then would stop for lunch joined by Carlotta. O'Neill loved jokes and was a very handsome, charming man.

"Mr. O'Neill would turn on a blues or a jazz record and ask me to dance. I liked to dance and so did he. Carlotta did not mind and joined in the fun. While we were dancing, he would whisper in my ear, I love you. And another time while he was writing *Moon*, he turned to me and said, "I want you to play Josie." In his flirtations, O'Neill forgot his own

O'Neill in his study, Tao House *(National Park Service, Tao House)*

description of the character (Josie): "She is so oversize for a woman that she is almost a freak—5'11" in her stockings and weighs around 180. Her sloping shoulders are broad, her chest deep with large, firm breasts, her waist wide but slender by contrast with her hips and thighs." This is the complete opposite of the slight 5'5" Janet Washburn. The only similarity to Josie was that they both had dark hair.

There has been much written about the fact that Carlotta kept visitors away from Tao House, and I've always been curious about that because O'Neill was a strong independent man. So I asked Janet, who had been on the scene, "Who was responsible for keeping people away from Mr. O'Neill? Was it Carlotta?" She shook her head with a smile on her face and said, "No it was him. No one told Mr. O'Neill what to do." She emphasized "him." Of course, this is coming from an impressionable employee. Is there a wife who never suggests what a husband should do (my own wife's loving style)?

Janet said that the O'Neills were, "very fine people and fun."

When I visited Tao House, at the time of the commemorative service for O'Neill, I was fortunate to gain special access after hours through the good offices of Diane Schinnerer, former president of the O'Neill

Foundation, which has done so much to preserve Tao House. My visit was able to take place when there were no tourists around. With a National Parks Service Guide at my side, I was allowed to wander around the house and ask innumerable questions. When I walked into O'Neill's study and saw what Janet had described, two desks back to back, with a log book sitting on his desk—a chill went through me. I was in his place of work. The guide volunteered that they had a Dictaphone recording, and a CD of O'Neill reading from Edmund's speech in *Journey*, Act 4. (It had been converted to a compact disc and she played it for me.) O'Neill spoke wonderfully with a theatrical enunciation and a definite New York accent. She said they also had a CD converted from the Dictaphone recording of him singing a song, but that "Mr. O'Neill was drunk when he did this." I asked to listen to it, and O'Neill was not drunk at all. In fact what he was doing was acting the role of an old sailor singing a sea chanty. I heard Carlotta's laugh in the background and that excerpt brought him right into the room. I put my hands on his chair where his back rested and I could feel the vibrations of O'Neill still emanating. He has never left Tao House, he is still there.

In 1952, their nurse Kathryne received a letter from Carlotta in Boston asking her to come help them. "When I arrived, I found them in two separate hospitals. O'Neill was very frail—he weighed 120 pounds—and Carlotta had had a nervous breakdown. He was suing her for divorce and Carlotta was suing him. My job was to get them back together again. I did get them out of the hospitals and into their hotel in Boston."

So Carlotta and Eugene were united again during his final days in Boston. She was definitely with him in the last moments of his life. All of the play inscriptions by Mr. O'Neill to Carlotta are filled with love.

Mrs. O'Neill told me that in the months before O'Neill died, the playwright burned the unfinished plays from the eleven-play cycle in his fireplace to prevent future productions of them. I can imagine that heartfelt scene. However, a completed *A Touch of the Poet* and the unfinished *More Stately Mansions* survived.

O'Neill died the next year in 1953. His dying words, according to Mrs. O'Neill were, "God damn it! Born in a hotel and died in a hotel!" He was buried in the secluded Forest Hills Cemetery in Jamaica Plain, Massachusetts and only four people were in attendance: his physician,

Carlotta, his nurse and his butler. O'Neill had told Carlotta that he didn't want to have a priest or a minister. He said, "If there is a God we'll meet and talk things over." His gravestone reads:

EUGENE O'NEILL

BORN NEW YORK CITY OCT. 16, 1888

DIED BOSTON MASS – NOV. 27, 1953

REST IN PEACE

When Carlotta died in 1970, she was buried alongside O'Neill and her name was added to his gravestone.

CHAPTER 16

A MYSTICAL GIFT

At the time the Circle was doing *Iceman*, Brooks Atkinson of *The New York Times* befriended me, which was and is an unusual thing for a drama critic to do. They generally are remote—what seems to emanate from them is "don't try to influence me." But Mr. Atkinson was a man of a different cut; his theatrical reviews expressed how much he loved the theatre and its people. Mr. Atkinson placed the American theatre on the same level as ballet, symphony or opera. His criticisms were constructive rather than destructive. Even when he wrote a negative review he'd find something positive to say about a production. I loved him for that and also for his wit.

One afternoon he took me on a walking tour of the Village to show me the O'Neill haunts where the site of the Washington Square Players (now a bowling alley), the Provincetown Playhouse, and the Golden Swan (the inspiration for Harry Hope's saloon in *Iceman*) were. He also pointed out to me an apartment house on the corner of MacDougal and Fourth Street, which faced Washington Square Park. O'Neill had told him he was going to set up a machine gun on the second floor to "mow down the capitalists when the revolution came."

That day Mr. Atkinson also talked about the stage size of the Moscow Art Theatre. I asked him what he thought was the ideal theatre. And he responded, one whose stage is the same size as the audience area. That thought remained in my memory. Years later, when Paul Libin and I came to build our new theatre on Broadway the stage was built to be just as large as the audience.

While *Iceman* was running and reviving interest in O'Neill, there was a production in Sweden at the Royal Dramatic Theatre of his then unproduced play, *Long Day's Journey Into Night*. It had been published by the Yale University Press in the United States, but the production rights were withheld. The Dramaten as it's known in Sweden had done many O'Neill plays during his lifetime, even while he was out of favor in America.

In his will there was a clause prohibiting *Journey's* not being produced until, "25 years after my death." Mrs. O'Neill explained the clause was intended to protect the privacy of living family members.

By 1956, when we did *Iceman*, O'Neill had been dead for three years. Eugene Jr. had committed suicide in 1950—following the classic style, slitting his wrists while lying in a bathtub in Woodstock. His other son, Shane, was still alive but was an alcoholic barely in contact with the world. He had come around several times while we were rehearsing *Iceman*. He was in bad shape, dressed in dirty clothes, tie-less, his hair long, barely able to speak. As for Oona, O'Neill refused to see her again after she married Chaplin in 1943. According to Carlotta, "He considered her dead."

Mrs. O'Neill told me that she felt she was not bound by the prohibition in the will because the two surviving children were dead to O'Neill. Therefore she granted permission to the Dramaten to produce *Journey* in recognition of the previous body of O'Neill's work they had presented. (Interestingly, the great Swedish stage and film director, Ingmar Bergman, had never directed an O'Neill play for them, until he directed *Journey* in 2002 at the Brooklyn Academy of Music.) The original Swedish production in 1956 was hailed by the international press as a masterpiece and a furor broke out among New York producers to obtain the rights. It seemed every other week Sam Zolotow, theatre columnist for *The New York Times*, would print a rumor about yet another Broadway producer securing the rights. Robert Whitehead, Billy Rose, Herman Shumlin, Kermit Bloomgarden, were all rumored at one time to have secured them, as were all the other top-flight producers. I read all the stories in the paper and it never crossed my mind, "Why not us?"

These top guys seemed the only ones with enough reach to grab the brass ring.

Mrs. O'Neill was criticized for her release of the play, most notably by Bennett Cerf, O'Neill's friend and editor at Random House, and by many others, including the Theatre Guild attorneys. But she stood firm, and God bless her that she did! She was determined that O'Neill be acknowledged as our greatest playwright, and with her sense of the dramatic and her timing, she accomplished nothing less.

Mrs. O'Neill was a mystic and believed that powers beyond man's control forced actions to be taken, that to deny that power was to stand in the way of what was inevitable. By the time she'd given us *Iceman* she'd already contracted with Sweden's Royal Dramatic Theatre to present the world premiere of *Journey*. After our astounding success with *Iceman* and the enthusiastic international reception for *Journey*, Mrs. O'Neill decided that rather than going with an established producer, she'd make the most startling decision and give the United States rights to us, a small off-Broadway company much like the Provincetown Players O'Neill had come out of in the twenties. People have said that Mrs. O'Neill released the rights to *Journey* because she needed the money. But the reality is that if she had gone with one of the big Broadway producers, she would have gotten an advance of $25,000 to $50,000. Instead, she gave the rights to us without any advance at all. Mrs. O'Neill's mystical belief had guided her to this action and wasn't she right! With these three master strokes: allowing us to revive *Iceman*; the world premiere of *Journey* in Sweden; and granting us the U.S. rights to *Journey*, she single-handedly resurrected her husband's reputation.

When *Journey* opened on Broadway, audiences flocked to see our production. Carlotta had put O'Neill back on top where he belonged. This had all happened in the space of one year. One has to wonder what level would our theatre be at today if Mrs. O'Neill had not followed her mystical forces.

The slights by the public and the press hurt her deeply. She had suffered these indignities with her husband and was fiercely determined to return him to his appropriate status. In the course of making that decision, literary standards for the American theatre were raised. (The same standards O'Neill had fought for his whole career.) Mrs. O'Neill dedicated the rest of her life to this responsibility and, God bless her, before she died, she saw the fruits of her labor, with productions of O'Neill's plays all over the country. For years no Broadway producer had wanted to do any of O'Neill's plays.

So how *did* it all happen for us with *Long Day's Journey?*

One day I received a call from O'Neill's literary agent Jane Rubin that Mrs. O'Neill wanted to see José and me the next morning at 10 A.M. As José and I put on our ties and jackets (José borrowed one of mine), we wondered if we'd done something wrong. I had observed Mrs. O'Neill's tempestuous turns of dissatisfaction towards other people. There were some she liked and some she didn't, and when she didn't like you there was no uncertainty.

We arrived, shaking with fear. Jane opened the door and as we walked in, Mrs. O'Neill at the far end of the room stood straight up from her wing-backed chair and in a demanding tone said, "Do you want to do *Long Day's Journey* this season—on Broadway?" We babbled "uh uh uhhh," and weakly replied, "yes." She ordered us, "Then sit down!" As we obeyed her, she sat back in her chair and said, "now there is only one condition you must agree to, do not cut the play." On the spot we agreed. We, of course, had read the play and realized what a great work it was. She said, "Good, now of course you'd like Peter Finch to play the father?" Before we could answer she shot in, "I think he would be perfect for the role." The way she said it I thought, "Mrs. O'Neill is in love with him." José and I looked questioningly at each other about her choice and then he volunteered, "I think it would be better for us to have an American play the role." She let the idea of Peter Finch float away. We asked for time to think about it but we all agreed right then and there that Jason should play Jamie.

This brief conversation was managed in a very businesslike fashion by Mrs. O'Neill. She wanted to stick to the agenda of getting the play on and quickly. It was very important to her that we get the show on that year. It was already late August, so we had only four months left to finance, cast, rehearse, and bring it to Broadway. As it turned out, we went into rehearsals in October and presented the play in November.

We spent a little more time with her. She relaxed as she lovingly showed us around the apartment, including the furniture that had been with them since Tao House. She pointed out photographs of Gene and took one of them off the wall and handed it to José and said, "Your hands remind me of Gene—I want you to have this." The photograph was of O'Neill dressed formally, resting his cheek on his hand; his eyes were very contemplative. She repeated what she had told me about his process of writing plays and how he was even more exhausted writing this one. Gene would "shout and holler loud enough to raise the dead." She reiterated that she was giving us the play because of our work and the success of *Iceman*. And then we were summarily dismissed.

José and I rode down the elevator in silence. It felt like the breath had been kicked out of us. We were stunned. This meeting with Mrs. O'Neill had lasted only a half hour. We stumbled into the bar of the hotel. I'd never had a drink in the morning, and I don't think José had either but we ordered scotch; we drank and then looked at each other. We were somber and sober. I said, "José, everything will change now." He shook his head yes and we remained silent for several minutes contemplating the enormity of what had just transpired. She had entrusted us—*us*—with her most valued possession! We felt empowered and stronger than we were before, but at the same time terrified of our responsibility. We got drunk, we got giddy. We laughed and laughed at the absurd unpredictability of life. Here we were, a little off-Broadway theatre only five years old, and we'd been given the gift of this great play—one we'd be producing not off-Broadway but *on* Broadway.

We stood up weaving and wobbling into the bright sunlight of Madison Avenue and went down to the Circle. As we traveled our feelings intensified as the profound event sank in.

By the next day, we already had Fredric March in mind for James Tyrone. Mrs. O'Neill agreed with the choice, and repeated her sense of trust in what we would do. I met with Freddie's agent who told me that Mr. March agreed to do the play, with the proviso that his wife, Florence Eldridge, be cast as Mary Tyrone. They would commit for a year. We knew Freddie was perfect for James Tyrone and that Florence was a gamble but it paid off because Freddie was so fantastic as the father. Florence and Freddie had done other plays together, Lillian Hellman's *The Autumn Garden*, in 1951, among others, and she was a star in her own right through her stage and film appearances. I later learned that Freddie had

already been studying the role of James Tyrone for several months prior
to this—even before the Swedish production—in anticipation of snagging
the part from whichever producer got the rights to the play!

We were hoping to start performances in New Haven in October, and
then on to the Wilbur Theatre in Boston but we didn't have any money
and we didn't have a Broadway theatre. Once again, I was furiously trying to raise money. People were interested but no checks had come in
yet. In order to plunge into rehearsal of our five-cast-member play, I
needed to post a bond with Actor's Equity Association for two week's
salary for the actors and put down a deposit for a Broadway theatre.
Despite the success of *The Iceman Cometh*, we lacked the thousands of
dollars required for those bonds and the deposit. *Iceman* admission was
only $1.50 and we had 199 seats and nineteen actors, so the surplus each
week was only a few hundred dollars, and that was being used to pay off
old, patient creditors.

Once again I approached Roger L. Stevens. We needed a total of
$50,000. Roger agreed, adding, "I'll put up the money and I'll let you
use one of my theatres to do the play and I'll wave the deposit." Roger
made it even easier for us by allowing us to use the theatre for rehearsals,
rent free. All of this was done while Roger was handling three telephone
calls and dealing with his assistants who were coming in and out of his
office. He didn't insist on billing or extra points for putting up this *risk
money*, referred to as *front money* in theatrical parlance. Front money
means literally what it says—monies put up which can be spent before
the production is totally financed. If, for some reason, the production
doesn't happen, this money is lost to the investor.

I thanked Roger and told him, "We are going to give you billing above
the title." He replied, "That really isn't necessary. I'm doing this because
I know you will be able to get the rest of the money and get the play on."
My chest swelled. After the play opened and we were in a position to
start paying the investors back, I made sure Roger got his money first.
Roger also made the distinguished Helen Hayes theatre on 46th Street
available to us. It was the best dramatic house on Broadway, though later
demolished—over the protestations of Joe Papp and Colleen Dewhurst,
among others—to make way for the Marriott Marquis.

I still had to raise the entire production cost of $95,000. One day I was in the dentist chair getting a tooth drilled. I caught a breath and told my dentist about the play we were producing by Eugene O'Neill. He said, "Who's that?" I jokingly said, "He's a dentist!" He responded, "I never heard of him. Where does he practice?" Then I got serious and told him about O'Neill and asked if he'd like to invest in our production. He put his drill down and said, "Yes—how much do I have to invest?" I said, "Well, a minimum share is $500." He said, "Yes, I'll do it—I play poker with other dentists every Thursday. I'll ask them if they want to join in the fun." Most of his friends became gamblers and invested in the show. The rest of the money came from family, friends, a few actors and some theatre investors. The money came in very fast; I even had to say "no" to some that wanted in. It would be an act of noblesse oblige—or perhaps hari kiri—today for a producer to deny potential investors.

Just a note as to how the world has changed, *Long Day's Journey Into Night* was later produced in 2003 with Vanessa Redgrave, Brian Dennehy, Philip Seymour Hoffman, Robert Sean Leonard, and Fiana Toibin. It cost just under $2 million to produce. I invited Vanessa to use my apartment while she was rehearsing *Journey*. She came every day, studying her lines and practicing a Schubert sonata that she was to perform in the play. She laboriously worked on the piece every day. Vanessa, who is not a pianist, insisted on performing live in the play, though in most productions, including ours, Mary Tyrone's piano sonata is recorded. When I questioned Vanessa about this, she explained, "My playing is not good so it will sound like Mary's crippled fingers playing."

Vanessa was very curious to hear my thoughts about the play, so many mornings we sat and discussed different aspects of her character—Mary's recurring recall of the convent school she'd gone to as a child, her relationship with her husband and with her two boys, and also her familiarity with their maid. Vanessa asked to see a copy of the *Playbill* and photographs from our original 1956 production.

Of all the thousands of *Playbills* we had printed there was only one left. I made a copy for Vanessa so she could study the changing styles evident in the *Playbill*'s advertisements. She also yearned to see photographs from our production. She was particularly taken with one of Florence standing behind Freddie, gently embracing him. Vanessa turned to me, let out a deep breath and said, "What love there is between them."

I said, "That is the basis of the whole play. Without that the play can become an angry shouting match."

She asked me to come and see her in the preview performances. Afterwards I gave her my thoughts about what I felt she needed to work on. At the opening night party she thanked me profusely and told me how important our talks had been. Robert Falls, the director thanked me for my input. Vanessa won the Tony Award for Best Actress. Accepting the award, she acknowledged the 1956 production and said, "Thank god for those dentists!" I wonder how many people in the television audience understood that reference.

Wow! How the economy has changed — $95,000 in 1956 and just under $2 million in 2003! I suppose it's not surprising considering how much dining out costs these days. I remember the first time this hit home with me. I went to lunch with Patricia and her mentor and friend Matthew Epstein in Bedford, New York, and the bill came to $100 for the three of us. We were gleefully astonished at spending so much money, which could have financed an entire production when we were starting out in Woodstock.

This O'Neill play was four-and-a-half hours long. We set an early curtain time so the audience could get out by 11:00.

The brilliant David Hays was entrusted with the scenic design to create the set for *Journey*. Later when the company went to visit the O'Neill house in New London we were amazed at how much of its ambience was captured by David.

I stopped by the theatre many times to see the play and to stand at the back to soak in the audience's response. One night after the curtain calls, two women were walking up the aisle and I heard one say to her friend, "I could've been in Miami in the same amount of time." The other one said, "but it was good." They both bobbed their heads affirmatively. Almost unanimously, audiences loved the show and were on their feet applauding after every performance shouting, "Bravo! Bravo!" Obviously the play resonated with their own lives—the frustrations in a life of marriage; the sibling rivalries between Jamie and his younger brother Edmund, and the guilt Edmund felt for being the cause of his mother's morphine addiction. At the very core of the play was that deep love that James and Mary Tyrone feel for each other. And of course the love of the father for his sons, despite the slights and indignities "the old miser, the cheapskate" has to endure from them. James feels the future of the family lies within Edmund when he tells him, "Yes, there's the makings of a poet in you all right."

James O'Neill, the playwright's real-life actor father, did try to help his sons, and Eugene worked briefly as a stage manager for him. He arranged for Jamie (O'Neill's wastrel older brother) to get acting jobs. Jamie failed him by often appearing on stage drunk. Jamie was a brilliant student up through high school. He had a beautiful speaking voice and made excellent grades. At some point, however, he lost his joy for life and became a self-destructive drinker. His female companions were always prostitutes. He humiliated his father by his grandiose drunkenness and "female companions." Ironically, the father's own drinking was, according to him, always controlled. For all the years he was performing on the road, he was never inebriated during a performance. He says to Mary in *Journey*, "I was never drunk onstage." But he drank heavily with his friends after the show.

Journey embraces a dysfunctional family and their aching inability to live a normal life. Jamie adored his mother and was always in competition with his father for her affection.

Some critics complained about O'Neill's repetitions in the play. But this is in fact a source of strong identification for audiences, reminding them how all families talk. We repeat and repeat our burning complaints about other family members. I think that O'Neill's repetition is really the musicality of his writing. Just as in a symphony, the theme is repeated and embellished and repeated again.

The first day of rehearsals the actors and José sat around a table on the stage of the Helen Hayes and read the first and second acts. When we came back after lunch to rehearse, the first thing Freddie wanted to work on was the solitaire card game the father plays in the fourth act. Freddie had to get every particular and sequence of the game right in order for him to incorporate James's lines. Freddie referred to the scene as "prop dialogue." He had to get the props/cards right in order to make James' words truthful.

José was patient and each rehearsal day he allowed Freddie his time to work on "the game." José worked very slowly, and carefully, which made the actors feel perfectly safe. The actor after all is the one who has to create the character, to make him a living being on the stage. The actor can best do that when he feels confident the elements underneath his feet are solid—the blocking, interior motives, scenery, costumes, and lighting. José didn't push, he just let the flower evolve and slowly open up. Rehearsing in the theatre where we later performed made a tremendous difference in the working process, as well as in the comfort the company felt.

This should be a routine procedure for every play (assuming the theatre is unoccupied) but, because of the union rules today, it is financially prohibitive to rehearse in the theatre. If you choose to rehearse in the theatre before opening, you must have on salary a prop man, a carpenter, and a head electrician, even though there is no work for them to perform.

I went before the stagehands' union and pleaded my case that stagehands not be assigned to us during our rehearsals in the theatre explaining that we had an unusually long play—four and a half hours—and we had not provided in our budget for stagehand salaries during rehearsal. The head of the union at this time was Sol Pernick, whom I knew from off-Broadway union dealings. He was tough—tough as nails—but somehow my pitch about the length of the play, the intimate nature of it and a few of my jokes at the meeting, got him to ease off and the union made a big exception in our case. Mr. Pernick concluded, "You can do it but you have to have one prop man for all rehearsals and I'll tell you who he is." And he named the very same prop man that I had worked with when I was the Assistant Stage Manager for *The Bad Seed* in 1954. This prop guy was the best in the business. He was short, bespectacled and in his early 60s. He was an easygoing hard-working man but also very quiet. Usually stagehands love conversation and sometimes their unscripted dialogue unfortunately seeps out from the wings to the audience.

Allow me to digress here, back to the early days of off-off-Broadway when Mr. Pernick first came into my life, or shall I say when he exploded into it! Sometime after *Summer and Smoke* opened, I was summoned to a meeting of all the theatre unions concerning how their representation was going to operate for the future at Circle and off-Broadway. At the meeting, I was told that they were going to put three stagehands in the Circle in the Square Theatre and later in all the other off-Broadway houses. I haltingly but bravely responded, "That's impossible. One stagehand's salary would be five times what we're paying any of the actors and we can't afford it. We won't be able to continue. And if you try to do it in any of the other houses they will also collapse." I showed them a list of the salaries at Circle which at this time had risen to the mighty sum of $50 per week. One union stagehand's salary would be $275. This argument went on for sometime with all off-Broadway theatres fiercely resisting the attempt to have stagehand union representation. We of course had stagehands but they were nonunion and were paid salaries equivalent to or less than the actors'. We were all small operations just squeaking by and couldn't take what the union proposed.

If you don't accept our terms, Mr. Pernick threatened, "We'll put a picket line around the theatre and them actors won't cross it." I left the meeting very dejected, not knowing what to do. When the actors arrived at the theatre, I decided to tell them what was going on. Consequently, they appealed to their union, Actor's Equity Association, but to no avail. I had a meeting with Fred O'Neal, the Actor's Equity President, and laid out to him what the situation was and he said he would take it up with the board of Actor's Equity. We were trapped in a negotiation with all of the unions. The future of the off-Broadway movement was at stake. I kept squirming and delaying the stagehands and finally Mr. O'Neal interceded on our behalf and notified Sol Pernick that they would not honor the picket line. That broke the deadlock.

This threat of union representation was the reason that Paul Libin, Noel Behn, Robert Kamlot and myself founded the League of Off-Broadway Theatres, to fight the union so that off-Broadway would be able to survive and have a unified voice in future negotiations. I'm happy to say that the League still exists today. Paul Libin was the president for many many years and with his skill, imagination, forcefulness and acting ability, fought off all of their succeeding attempts.

Now back to *Journey*. As we moved toward performance, Solly Pernick was out for blood again, even though he'd kindly allowed us to have only one stagehand for rehearsals. Solly didn't forget—his skin was as leathery as an elephant, with a slightly bent nose and looking very much like what one would imagine Marlon Brando's father would look like—*after* he'd been punched in the face. With rehearsal period over, Solly wanted to increase the union personnel for *Journey*'s performances. We got into a big fight but finally Solly backed down and we were able to go ahead with the crew of three that had been agreed to. Then Local 802 got on the bandwagon wanting musicians because there was some incidental music in the show. Arnold Black, violinist/composer, had written the music for *Journey*, which was used throughout the play. I told the musicians' union that there was "some" music, but mainly foghorn sounds and that the music was only three minutes in length. And they bought it—so no musicians on payroll.

Jason had immersed himself in O'Neill and made numerous notes in his script about the family, the plays that Jamie performed in, and everything he could find about the character. Jason was a good influence on the company; his past success with *The Iceman Cometh* made him like an assistant director, and maybe even a guardian angel.

The actors also loved José, who was a great storyteller to the point of hypnosis. His own family seems to have had the same combustible mixture of antagonism and intense love that was tearing apart the Tyrones. With his charming Panamanian accent, he used his family stories and painful personal experiences to elucidate the play for his cast.

O'Neill's home in New London, where he and his family spent their summers, is the setting for the play. It was the only permanent residence the family ever had because James O'Neill toured every year, performing a wide variety of plays but mostly *The Count of Monte Cristo*, which became his greatest financial nest egg. When his family did follow him on his travels, they stayed in Manhattan hotels, including The Barrett House on Broadway and 43rd Street, where Eugene O'Neill was born. In 2001, Paul Libin and I placed a commemorative plaque at that site which is now an office building, 1500 Broadway.

In the fourth act of *Journey*, the father, James, talks to Edmund about "that play" (*The Count of Monte Cristo*) while playing cards late at night. He explains how he's been trapped and how he, as a young man, had performed with Edwin Booth, and says: "I played Cassius to his Brutus one night, Brutus to his Cassius the next, Othello to his Iago and so on. The first night I played Othello, he said to our manager, 'That young man is playing Othello better than I ever did!' That from Booth? The greatest actor of his day or any other!"

He continued, "Then I took on The *Count of Monte Cristo*, thirty-five to forty thousand dollars net profit a season like snapping your fingers. . . . A fortune in those days—or even in these. What the hell was it

I wanted to buy, I wonder, what was worth all of that—Well, no matter. It's a late day for regrets."

Freddie (James Tyrone) would stand up on his chair during this speech, wearing his worn-out flannel bathrobe with the sash untied, and unscrew all the light bulbs except one to save electricity. He was reliving that moment with Booth and in his face and body you could see the despair and anguish he felt for having squandered his talent. That moment is etched forever in my mind, with Edmund listening to his father with deep warmth and understanding. Edmund goes on to say that now you told me your dreams, I'll tell you mine. And he starts reciting poetry. At the conclusion of which the father tells him, "You have the makings of a poet." The subtext of James' speech, of course, is that he sacrificed his own poetry for his family's security.

Freddie told me of the excitement of his early acting days and how that helped him relate to James Tyrone. Freddie and James had similarities in their careers, particularly in that they both achieved great fame. James just explained to us what caused his fall. Freddie's movie roles had thinned out, because of his alleged left-wing friends, which got him in hot water during the Hollywood blacklist days—a terrible time in our history and a terrible thing to have happened to one of our great actors. I've seen many productions of *Journey* since, and no one has ever come close to Freddie's art. In his portrayal of James Tyrone he embodied the low peasant and the great classical actor. When Freddie spoke Shakespeare's lines you imagined him in a costume of that period. A directional note that José had given Freddie was to hold himself like a prime minister—shoulders back, chin up.

Throughout the play James is under attack for being cheap—by hiring "the quack doctors" that attended Mary during her pregnancy; the cheap doctor in the play that he has just taken Edmund to for his cough; the pittance of money he begrudgingly gives Jamie who's going into town that night; Mary's accusations about hiring uneducated immigrant Irish peasants to be their maids; Jamie's attack on his father's choice of sanitarium for Edmund; Mary's sarcastic comment about his real estate "get rich quick" schemes and also Mary's complaints about the second-hand car that he bought for her and the cheap hotels he made her live in. Poor James, your heart goes out to him. He is a victim of his impoverished upbringing and his fear of ending up in "the poor house." But despite the family's attacks he rises in the audience's eyes and hearts to a father trying to shepherd his family through a minefield of problems: his drinking, Mary's addiction, Edmund's consumption, and Jamie's alcoholism. Nothing is hidden from the audience and yet at the end of the play, what comes through is the love the family feels for each other. This is a real tribute to the superb work that José and the actors did on the play.

Our premiere took place in New Haven at the Shubert Theatre with a split week of four performances. Opening night did not go well. The press was mixed, some of them commenting on the play's length, which didn't help sales. Our confidence had been shaken by the indifferent reception. Each day we continued to rehearse even more intensely. We were determined to achieve O'Neill's intentions.

I inquired if it would be possible to visit the O'Neill house in New London and found a real estate agent who could let us in. So after leaving New Haven, on our way to Boston, we went to the O'Neill home in New London on Pequot Avenue—a street name that always calls to my mind the *Pequod*, the ship in Melville's *Moby Dick*. We all went together—the whole cast, José and Leigh. As we drove along Pequot Avenue I was dismayed to see the commercial development: souvenir shops, fast-food joints, and cheap five-and-dime markets. They were all one- or two-story buildings, garishly painted, sprawling out onto the avenue and taking away from the beauty of this waterfront town.

It was a clear and freezing cold day. As we approached the house, I saw the bedraggled bushes that are lovingly referred to when Jamie and his father go down to "trim the hedges" in *Journey*. It's an early section of the play intended to display the humor and camaraderie of the family. Alongside the hedges were three steps. We walked on the path alongside the lawn, stopped midway and looked up to absorb the house. It is a two-story Victorian wooden structure with a beautiful gabled porch—on which stood the real estate agent.

He greeted us enthusiastically—and was so happy to show us the house; it had been empty for several years. At the top of the porch steps, he pointed out that when James O'Neill lived here there had been a shingle which read, "The Count of Monte Cristo." He went on to say that mail was still being delivered addressed to The Count of Monte

Cast of *Long Day's Journey Into Night* at Monte Cristo Cottage, O'Neill's New London, Conn., summer home

Cristo. Imagine—it had been forty years since he stopped touring! It shows what a powerful impact he had on the theatre-going public.

The agent said he had something special to show us and took us around the back of the house. As we were walking, he told us, laughingly, "young people dressed funny [remember these were the beatnik days], they come here at night, build a fire and have a powwow with Eugene O'Neill. They think they are talking to him and then they read one of his plays." I looked down at the ground and sure enough I could clearly see the burn marks of old fires. It was exciting to me that young people were interested in O'Neill despite the fact that theatre in New York and around the country had ignored him. Those young kids and others like them became the catalyst for the future interest in O'Neill. I felt that we were part of the continuum of O'Neill diehards.

Next we went inside the house. I took a deep breath in anticipation of being in the house of our play. As we stepped in it smelled musty. There was dust all over the place. It had a very somber feeling—a great atmosphere for ghosts. There wasn't a single stitch of furniture. It was totally empty. This was 1956. O'Neill had died just three years earlier.

We stood in the dining room described by O'Neill. It was thrilling to be in the original setting of the play. Then I walked up the stairs, holding the wooden railing and felt the distant vibrations of the family. The real estate agent showed us where Jamie had carved his initials into the staircase post. One can imagine how upset the father must have been to discover it. The railing is so significant in the play because it is used by Mary to steady herself as she ascends for her morphine injections. The bedrooms were small, with paper-thin walls, and very close together. A sound made in any of the rooms could be easily heard in the others. Imagine the noises at night from this tempestuous verbal family: The father snoring, the mother wandering around from bedroom to spare room, and the boys pretending to be asleep while they listened to the mother's movements. Downstairs we examined the kitchen, the cupboard, and the rear of the living room where the piano had sat.

That visit had a profound effect on us—to be in the place where O'Neill grew up, to breathe in the air that he breathed. We were at the very origins of *Journey*. It was like finding a rare treasure at an archeological dig—it sent reverberations through all of us and has remained embedded in my mind and many times has entered my dreams. Being in that environment made me realize how important our mission was—to be completely truthful to the O'Neill family. I also felt an obligation to the spirit and reverence of the young people communing in the backyard. We were all links to O'Neill. Imagine being in that living room and being able to see and smell the Long Island Sound and hear the bell buoy—the water in which Eugene swam and the beach on which he walked and immortalized in Act Four.

Edmund also recites his poems to his father about the sea, the fog, and the beach in Act Four: "I was set free! I dissolved in the sea, became white sails and flying spray, became beauty and rhythm, became moonlight and the ship and the high dim-starred sky!" And: "The fog was where I wanted to be. Halfway down the path you can't see this house. You'd never know it was here. Or any of the other places down the avenue. I couldn't see but a few feet ahead. I didn't meet a soul. Everything looked and sounded unreal. Nothing was what it is. That's what I wanted—to be alone with myself in another world where truth is untrue and life can hide from itself. Out beyond the harbor, where the road runs along the beach, I even lost the feeling of being on land. The fog and the sea seemed part of each other. It was like walking on the bottom of the sea. As if I had drowned long ago. As if I was a ghost belonging to the fog, and the fog was the ghost of the sea. It felt damned peaceful to be nothing more than a ghost within a ghost. Don't look at me as if I'd gone nutty. I'm talking sense. Who wants to see life as it is, if they can help it? It's the three Gorgons in one. You look in their faces and turn to stone. Or it's Pan. You see him and you die—that is, inside you—and have to go on living as a ghost." How could anyone read those and so many other passages and not acclaim O'Neill as a poet?

Recently I was in a theatre in Romania for an O'Neill conference and played a CD for them of O'Neill reading Edmund's speech. His deep voice reverberated throughout the balconies and orchestra of the vast Stalin-built theatre. When the recording ended the Romanian audience sat in reverential silence for several minutes. An elderly leading actor of the company who had played Ephraim in *Desire Under the Elms* broke the silence by standing up and declaiming, "Now I understand O'Neill. He was an actor!"

Jason Robards and I would later reminisce about Freddie and the play, the fog and the foghorn and the difficulties we had making the fog machine behave and work on cue. To create this fog on stage is a difficult problem because it's sprayed backstage and the slightest draft blows it out into the audience making them cough and choke. You have to have fog that doesn't make your audience bolt out of the theatre.

After New Haven, *Journey* continued to Boston and we began loading the set into the venerable Wilbur Theatre. One of the old stagehands told me that James O'Neill played the *The Count of Monte Cristo* on this stage. Wow! We're going to do his son's play in the very theatre that he performed in! The stagehand took me under the stage and pointed out the boulders on which the theatre had been built. In the several cave-like recesses, he demonstrated with a sheet of flexible tin how shaking the sheets made the sound reverberate through the caves up to the stage and in to the audience. This 5'4" octogenarian stagehand shed decades as he deftly hoisted up the tin sheet, which was about six feet high and two feet wide. He was revisiting the sounds he had created for *The Count of Monte Cristo*. I ran up into the audience and could hear very clearly his thunderstorms. Before I parted, I asked him what James O'Neill was like, and he responded in a lilting Irish accent, "He was a *fine* gentleman."

The load-in for the show took three days and on Thursday night we were to perform our first preview, but without Florence—she'd lost her voice that Monday. Florence was laid out in her hotel room in the Ritz Carlton, her sore throat impairing her ability to speak. Tuesday, Florence was worse but she was hopeful she would regain her voice. On Wednesday there was the snowstorm of the year, all planes were grounded at New York and Boston airports. Freddie called his doctor in Connecticut but he couldn't get there. The local theatre doctor was a general practitioner and he couldn't help and wouldn't come out in the storm anyway. I was desperate and frantic. I kept seeing Mrs. O'Neill in my mind the day she entrusted us with the rights to the play, and after our mild reception in New Haven, here we were in Boston with a disaster about to happen.

I knew Dr. Max Jacobson, from New York City, who had treated my father very successfully as well as other friends who all reported superlative results from stomach viruses to throat and chest problems. Among his patients were such illustrious people as John F. Kennedy, Leonard Bernstein, Maria Callas, Alan Jay Lerner, and Judy Garland. Dr. Max had helped many people with voice problems and relieved their tension and stress with an injection. At the time no one knew, or even worried about, what the ingredients of the injections were. He was fondly known as "Miracle Max." When I asked him once what the ingredients were, he waved his hand in a cavalier fashion and said with his Viennese accent, "Don't vorry. It is all goot things."

I needed somebody to see Florence quickly so she could perform the next night. I called Dr. Max and asked if there was someone he knew in the area. He didn't, but he volunteered, "I vill come." I said, "Thanks but all flights out of New York are grounded. There is a big storm up here." He said, "Don't vorry; I'll fly up in my own plane." And I replied, "In this storm! It's impossible, no planes can land." He repeated again, "Don't vorry, I will land in Boston." That was in the morning, and by two o'clock he was at the Ritz-Carlton Hotel. I never found out whether he himself had piloted his plane or how he made it to the hotel—since no traffic was moving. He was indeed Miracle Max—of course Max loved stars and would do anything for them.

The snow was coming down like pillow cases. I took Max into Freddie and Florence's bedroom which had twin beds. He opened up his medical bag, turned it upside down on the adjoining bed and out dropped what looked like fifty vials, bottles of medicine, a stethoscope and syringes. I saw Florence hunch her shoulders with fear when she saw the supplies. Florence began to explain to him how she felt, but Dr. Max cut her short and commanded her in his Viennese accent, "Don't whisper and don't say another word. Don't talk on the telephone, whispering and telephone talking put a strain on the voice."

Dr. Max was a well-dressed, handsome man with black wavy hair and dark intense eyes with a perpetual suntan, as though he just came back from Bermuda. His manner was kind but like all doctors acted superior and definite—a benevolent god walking among us. In this day of health insurance they only let their benevolent light shine on you for fifteen minutes per ailment. And as he ordered, Florence stopped talking. I guess the sight of all those vials tumbling on the bed and the needle scared her plenty, as they did me. He pointed to the door and commanded Freddie and I to "Go!" We put our coats on and trudged over to the theatre.

I had notified Ruth Nelson, Florence's understudy, to get ready. The poor woman had not had one day's rehearsal, but she worked with Freddie and the company that day and performed the first preview the next night—script in hand. She did very well, the company helping and encouraging her all the way. Ruth was an original member of the Group Theatre and was married to John Cromwell who directed that wonderful film, *The Goddess*, about Marilyn Monroe, with Kim Stanley. John was blacklisted during those terrible McCarthy days. Freddie and Florence remained their steadfast, close friends through all their hardships.

Florence slept all that day of Dr. Max's visit and most of Thursday. She returned to perform in the show Friday night. Her voice was com-

Cast of Eugene O'Neill's *Long Day's Journey Into Night* (1956): *top left, seated*, Florence Eldridge and Fredric March; *standing*, Bradford Dillman and Jason Robards, Jr.; *top right and bottom*, Fredric March and Florence Eldridge

pletely recovered and she was anxious to have her role back. Max had lived up to his moniker once again.

The preview audiences were thin and a little perplexed by this three-and-a-half-hour drama but those perceptions changed overnight when Kevin Kelly, drama critic of the *Boston Globe* and one of the most important critics in the country, gave us a glorious review! We sold out the rest of the two-week run. His review and our sold-out houses had a tremendous impact on the New York theatre crowd and it created a buzz and excitement and brought us in on a wave of high expectations.

We were bringing to Broadway O'Neill's first new play in ten years, since the debacle of the original *Iceman* in 1946. Heading the company were Freddie and Florence, both Hollywood film stars, the expectations of what Jason would do with his new O'Neill role and, of course, José, who had directed our tremendously successful revival of *Iceman*.

We settled back into the Helen Hayes Theatre where we had rehearsed. From the first preview performance we were sold out. In another way the opening night was also an astonishing event. As the actors came out for their curtain call there was total silence in the audience. The actors were in shock and looked at each other as though they were asking, "What the hell is going on?"

I was standing in the back of the theatre just as perplexed. As I ran back stage, only a minute or two had gone by, I heard this sudden thunderous noise. I peeked out through the curtain at the audience. They were on their feet, applauding wildly. And then they started approaching the stage, en masse, applauding and vociferously shouting "Bravo!" Audiences did not stand up in theatres in the fifties. I think this might have been the start of the standing ovation on Broadway.

The reviews were unanimous raves! There were long lines at the box office out into the street. I had coffee served to the anxious customers. With the astonishing success of *Iceman*, then followed by the praise of *Journey*, we landed a one-two punch in audience and theatre circles. When O'Neill received, posthumously, the Pulitzer Prize for *Journey* this was the final seal of approval—acknowledging his significant contribution to the world of theatre, which has never again been doubted. What a thrill for us to have helped achieve this for our greatest playwright. We won all the awards that season—Antoinette Perry (better known as the Tony Awards), Outer Circle Awards, etc., etc.

I have seen many productions of *Long Day's Journey Into Night* since then, including scenes from the Royal Dramatic Theatre's production, and none even vaguely compared in emotional truth, sadness and audience euphoria to our 1956 production.

Freddie left his mark on the role of James Tyrone forever—just as Jason had with Jamie and as Hickey in *Iceman,* and just as Brando had as Stanley Kowalski in Tennessee Williams' *A Streetcar Named Desire.* All other performances are always compared, in the audience's mind, to them. It pains me that in succeeding productions of *Journey,* no critical mention is made of Freddie's majestic performance. Whenever Jason and I got together, the conversation would always swing around to Freddie as we rhapsodized about him—Freddie's Irish peasant lilt in contrast to his fine delivery of Shakespeare. Believe me whenever Freddie would say in *Journey,* "that young man is doing Othello better that I ever had," I swear I saw Edwin Booth in the wings, smiling and nodding his head in approval.

I'd go back to the dressing rooms to chat with the actors and comment or compliment them on their performances. (Actors want to know what you think.) Freddie was not interested in my praise of him as much as, "How do you think Florence did tonight?" And I would respond, "very good, wonderful," etc. Or whatever was appropriate. And Freddie would put his arm around my shoulder and say, "go tell her," and then added, "isn't she the greatest thing since sliced bread!" Every night before the performance, Freddie would stand behind the curtain and look out through a tiny peephole at the audience. We sold out regularly but sometimes on stormy nights there were a few empty seats. Freddie would turn to me with a mischievous smile on his face and say, "There must be a big dance in Newark tonight." (A humorous theatrical observation popular in the twenties.)

I had invited Mrs. O'Neill to the opening on November 7, 1956. She said she would not be there, that "Gene and I never go to openings, Gene hated them." When Brooks Atkinson's review in *The New York Times* came out, I called her at her hotel, The Carlton House, and read her part of it. She began to cry and said, "I'm so grateful for what you've done." It had been a long battle back for her and Gene, from the disappointment of *The Iceman Cometh* on Broadway in 1946 and the out-of-town closing and disaster of *A Moon for the Misbegotten* in 1947.

On the telephone, Mrs. O'Neill repeated the story of James Barton drinking at the opening night performance of *Iceman.* It was not unusual for Mrs. O'Neill to repeat her stories, but they were always consistent with earlier versions.

Jason Robards, Jr., and Bradford Dillman in *Long Day's Journey Into Night*

One day late in the afternoon while we were performing *Long Day's Journey Into Night*, Jason called me from his apartment on Ninth Street. He said his wife, Eleanor, was not well and could I please come over and help with the kids. I dropped everything and rushed over and when I arrived in the apartment, the children were in chaos running all around. Jason was very distraught and didn't explain what was wrong or what had happened or where Eleanor was. He pleaded with me to stay and take care of the kids, adding that help was on the way. He then left to do the show. The children were frightened and crying. I tried in vain to calm them. It was one of the most painful scenes I have ever had to deal with. The turmoil continued for another hour until a friend/relative arrived to take care of the kids. I was shaking and the first thing I thought was to go to the theatre to tell Jason the children were okay and see if he was all right.

I got up to the theatre just as Jason's big fourth act with Edmund begins. Jamie comes home drunk and almost immediately tells Edmund to beware of him, "Make up your mind you've got to tie a can to me—get me out of your life—think of me as dead—tell people, 'I had a brother, but he's dead.' And when you come back [from the sanitarium] look out for me. I'll be waiting to welcome you with that 'my old pal' stuff, and give you the glad hand, and at the first good chance I get stab you in the back."

Jason had always been great in the role and particularly in this scene where he opens his heart to save his brother. His need to defend Edmund against himself is so strong that Jamie becomes the devil telling his brother to run from him. I stood in the back of the house and watched the scene with tears streaming down my face because Jason had done what only great actors are capable of: he had internalized his personal pain (his wife and children at home) into the character he was performing. I think without that outlet of emotion which he experienced in that scene, Jason might have done physical damage to himself. I had just witnessed one of the greatest performances I'd ever seen.

When I went backstage after the show, Jason didn't ask me anything about what had happened at home. I volunteered that Eleanor was okay and that "so-and-so" was with the kids. For all the years Jason was with us after that he never mentioned this incident. I always had a funny feeling that Jason bore some resentment because I had accidentally stepped into his personal life.

While we were running *Long Day's Journey* to sold out performances and big returns for the dentist investors, *The Iceman Cometh* still continued at the original Circle on Sheridan Square. *Journey* ran until 1958 having only been interrupted to be part of the international festival in Paris. Freddie, Florence, and Jason stayed on to the last performance in New York.

We began to plan a nationwide tour with a new cast. Many film companies wanted the rights to *Journey*, and we were offered $750,000 but on the advice of our attorney, who insisted, "I will get a million dollars," we held out. He wanted to have the honor of achieving the highest figure ever paid for a dramatic play—but no film company was ready to pay that amount. As time went on the offers got lower and lower and then our right to participate in the film sale revenue expired. Eventually Mrs. O'Neill practically gave away the film rights to Eli Landau for, I was told, the astonishingly low figure of $50,000. He presented it on Channel 13, starring Ralph Richardson, Katharine Hepburn and Jason as Jamie. It was a good lesson for me to take the best offer you can get—don't be greedy and I forgot to remember what my father had told me, "You the client are the best lawyer."

When *Journey* closed we felt that we had fulfilled our responsibility to Eugene O'Neill and particularly to Mrs. O'Neill who entrusted us with this invaluable treasure. Having helped to reestablish O'Neill's prominence as America's greatest playwright we also at the same time, by virtue of our work, had placed Circle in the Square at the forefront of American theatre. Since those grand years of 1956–1958 we have done seventeen productions of O'Neill plays, more than any other theatre in the world.

The circumstances of casting Bradford Dillman in the role of Edmund in *Long Day's Journey* make an amusing side note. He was a young actor out of Yale who after college worked as a clerk in a New York bordello run by the mob. His job was to verify the identity of the prostitutes on arrival. One night he inadvertently let a non-member prostitute enter and pursue her craft, which got him fired. He was submitted to us by his agent who had three clients: Brad, Peter Falk, and another whose name I don't remember.

Brad reminded me about the day he went to visit Mrs. O'Neill and told me that José had said to him, "As far as we're concerned you have the part but you have to be approved by Mrs. O'Neill." (This wasn't really necessary because Carlotta actually gave us full approval for the casting and I think José was just trying to flatter her.) Recalling the visit with a moan, Brad said to me, "I got very drunk the night before and when I came into her apartment [at the Carlton House], I was smashed, really smashed and I found the nearest chair to steady myself and sunk into it—hiding. I was afraid to speak. I felt such self-loathing for myself that I would do such a stupid thing and get drunk for this most important meeting. I answered a few questions that Mrs. O'Neill asked me as best I could. José asked Carlotta what she thought of me and Carlotta reflected a moment and said, 'Well, I like him.' and José asked 'Why?' She responded, 'He's just like my Gene; he doesn't say much and when he does you can't understand him.'"

Brad's parents were very much against him becoming an actor but after they saw him in *Long Day's Journey* his father would proudly say to all, "My son is in the theatre." Jason and Brad became very good friends and backstage would joke and imitate Fredric March's vocalizing—"High me, low me, high me, low me." Freddie's vocal coach would often be in the audience and advise him after the show of his vocal enunciation and projection.

In Act Four in the scene between Jamie and Edmund the audience was always very quiet. One night, the actors on stage and the audience heard a moan that filled the entire theatre. The actors were startled, not knowing where the sound emanated from. It was coming from a deaf and blind woman in attendance that night, responding to the emotions emanating from the stage. After the performance she was brought backstage to Brad's dressing room and she went up to him and felt the bones and all the features of his face and then she kissed him. The woman's name was Helen Keller.

I hadn't seen Brad since he left the cast of *Long Day's Journey* fifty years earlier to pursue a career in film and television. Recently, I had a reunion with him at his book-filled home in Santa Barbara. He met his future wife—the most famous model Suzy Parker—when they made a film together in London and it is she, in fact, who is the big book collector and reader. One night she came to see *Long Day's Journey* pretending that she came to see Jason but afterwards she came back to Brad's dressing room and confessed that she had really come to see him. Brad has written four novels and has been an unpaid scout for professional football teams including the San Francisco 49ers for years.

It has been half a century since that momentous New York opening night of *Long Day's Journey Into Night*. I cannot let that milestone pass without calling attention to the great contributions made by José and Jason. Carlotta, it's true, was the driving force, compelling audiences to pay attention to her late husband's genius. But it was, to my mind, the genius displayed by both José and Jason that not only made *Journey* a triumph, but which was instrumental in reclaiming O'Neill's lost reputation. I honestly wonder if, without those two great interpretive artists along with the incomparable Freddie, Florence, and Brad, O'Neill would today be as highly regarded as he is. As we have seen in other productions, the play can descend into a harangue of anger without the underlying love in the family.

CHAPTER 17

Discovering Two Mountain Ranges in New York City

While *Journey* was running on Broadway we produced, downtown, Edwin Justus Mayer's *Children of Darkness*—which takes place at Newgate Prison in London in 1725. Originally produced on Broadway in 1930, Richard Watts Jr. of the New York *Post* would often lovingly and longingly refer to it in his review of other plays. Right away a young lady who'd been getting good off-Broadway reviews came to audition and José offered her the role without a reading. What director wouldn't with that great smile and warmth exuding from the tip of her toes to the top of her head? She was a sunburst! It was Colleen Dewhurst and she recommended her good friend J. D. Cannon for the role of Count La Ruse. Once we hired an actor to play the part of Lord Wainwright, we were off and into rehearsals.

After a week, we became dissatisfied with the actor playing Lord Wainwright and gave him notice. We put out a call for actors to come and audition for the role. There was only one scene that Lord Wainwright appeared in so we were able to continue rehearsals while we searched, but no one seemed right. It was getting dicey; everything was going well except—no Wainwright. Auditions continued and one morning around eleven as I passed the dressing room on the way to my office on the second floor, I caught sight of a tall man lying on the cot—not an unusual occurrence in a dressing room. But I felt something like a gust of wind hit me. I said,

"Whoa." I tiptoed backwards to get a glimpse of this sleeping giant. His eyes were closed, a threadbare overcoat on, collar pulled up, unshaven, hands clasped on his chest, lying on his back. A beautiful strong nose was his most distinctive feature. Even though he was immobile, I felt a force about him, something like coming upon an ancient wooden shipwreck lying on the beach. I stood stock still gazing at him, then made an about face and ran downstairs two steps at a time to José who was auditioning and breathlessly said, "You gotta stop auditioning. I'm bringing down Lord Wainwright." José said, "I'd like to meet him." This was unusual for me because I rarely got involved in casting although I did supervise the choice of replacements in all the shows including *Iceman*—José, once the show was up rarely came back and so instead of leaving the responsibility solely to the stage manager I oversaw those decisions. I went upstairs and whispered to the sleeping figure tentatively, "Excuse me." He opened his eyes, "We would like you to come downstairs and audition." He slowly rose majestically to his full height, which was a foot taller than me. Then he proceeded to the staircase taking his time—clearing his head and walking down like an emperor. When he got downstairs, José and I looked at each other and Jose shook his head affirmatively and I turned and said, "We'd like you to play the role of Lord Wainwright." George said, "What would you like me to read?" and I answered, "that's not necessary you already have the part here's a script. Rehearsal is tomorrow at 10 A.M." The next day at the first rehearsal I said, "I'd like you to meet Lord Wainwright. George Scott," and he whispered to me "George C. Scott." I repeated, "I'd like you to meet Lord Wainwright, George C. Scott." I once asked George why he insisted on the initial "C" in his name and he responded "it takes up more room on the marquee." The letter C also stands for Campbell which is his extremely talented actor/director second son's name. This also was the first time that Colleen had ever seen him up close, and as they say it was "love at first sight." More on this later. As we went into rehearsal, George was letter-perfect in all his lines. When George looked at the lines for a role he instantaneously retained them.

We now had one more week before previews. The rest of the play was ready but the scene with George, which was with Colleen, needed to be worked on. With José guiding them, the scene was ready in a few days. George had this idea to use a four-foot-long walking stick like you would see in a movie about the French royalty (before the revolution). George, at about 6'2" inches, almost floated with his movements and he rested the stick at arm's length, so that his body was always in an elegant posture. He wore a long braided wig of the period that folded down his back and framed his strong profile.

Once George and Colleen got through the rehearsal and the play opened to excellent reviews the fireworks between them that had been lying dormant exploded! Within days they were in love and couldn't bear to be separated. Remember the feeling? They asked me if they could be alone in the same dressing room. So I gave them the only unused space we had — a tiny room that in the nightclub days had been the storage closet for mops, brooms, and pails. It was barely big enough for the two of them. When I would visit them, the room was so small I could only stand in the door frame to have a conversation. But these two giants loved the tiny space, in which they cooed to each other like birds. They also began living together and they referred to each other in terms that only lovers know. I don't know if they had other attachments at the time, but if they had, those just evaporated.

They were just so happy. My wife, Patricia, George, Colleen and myself all became lifelong friends. Early in our friendship they asked me to manage their finances. Their salaries from the Circle were $75 a week. They agreed that I would give them half for pocket expenses and the balance I would save for them for a rainy day. This was 1958, $35 was probably the equivalent of $350 today. Imagine, doling out an allowance to these bigger-than-life people. Their out-of-pocket didn't last very long. George went to the race track. He loved horses and betting on his favorites. Unfortunately, he lost most of the time. Colleen always needed more, what she spent it on I don't know — dresses, shoes, and some jewelry. She was more judicious, but as the week neared its end they both needed more money, so of course I always relented. I was trying to get them in the habit of not spending everything they earned so that when and if they made big money (which we all expected) they would be more responsible. Many times their "allowance" money was all used up and I advanced them some from my pocket so they could make it through the rest of the week. How could I refuse these glorious human beings anything? In 1958, they were really America's first rockets.

Recently, I had a dream that I was on the street looking up at a big plated glass second floor window. George had fancy cowboy clothes with sparkles on. He was looking at himself in the mirror and brushed his hair back so it set smoothly—admiring himself like he did in Noël Coward's *Present Laughter* playing the role of Garry Essendine. In the dream I walked into the building and as I came out I was carrying Colleen in my arms to get across a heavily trafficked area. End of dream.

Patricia and I became more intertwined with them as our friendship continued to grow, visiting each other almost every weekend. Around the same time we both began our families. Pretty soon George left *Children of Darkness* to do a small role in the movie *The Hanging Tree*, with Gary Cooper. In that small role George walked off with the reviews! Then he was cast on Broadway opposite the grand diva Judith Anderson in *Comes a Day*, and once again, he got the reviews!

Now money was starting to roll in and George and Colleen moved from their tiny apartment to a penthouse on top of a commercial building on West 56th Street. The money coming in was so substantial—I felt I didn't know enough about investing so I stepped aside. What they needed was beyond my knowledge, and they moved on to an influential attorney and financial manager.

As time went on, our friendship deepened. Colleen stayed on in *Children* to play opposite George's replacement Richard Dysart. It ran for a couple of more months but business had fallen off so we were on to the next play.

CHAPTER 18

A New Home

Brendan Behan's *The Quare Fellow* starring Liam and Tom Clancy and Lester Rawlins was our next production. I remember Liam's happy apple-red cheeks and innocent eyes and Tom's sturdy, definite unrelenting manner.

Lester Rawlins, that wonderful actor who must have done a hundred roles off-Broadway, played the prison guard. The play takes place in an Irish prison. Most of the experience of the play, in fact, comes from Brendan's own incarceration. Brendan was a rebel and a big drinker. We wanted cuts in the text, which was repetitive in places, but our requests for changes in the script went unanswered. Brendan just couldn't do it, poor dear.

The Quare Fellow had been done in London to excellent reviews. The British-Irish conflicts that the inmates were going through correlates with the troubles in Ireland—which we know is still not resolved to this day. Our production fared well—the Clancy boys were adored by one and all, and later went on to become the singing group the Clancy Brothers with other members of their family.

Next we chose Thornton Wilder's *Our Town* with John Beal as the stage manager, Jane McArthur (Emily), Clint Kimbrough (George), Dana Elcar, and Daniel Kiese as the fathers. *Our Town* is one of the most beautiful American plays and it was perfect for us because it was written to be performed on stage without scenery. When Emily has died and comes back to invisible life to celebrate her birthday is one of the most achingly heartfelt passages in American literature.

The production received good reviews but the nighttime audiences were small so I decided to reach out to grade schools and high schools in the area to see if I could spark interest for daytime performances. Teachers knew the play and immediately started organizing groups to come, so much so that we stopped doing midweek evening performances and did matinees for

Thornton Wilder

the young people. Sometimes we did the play twice in one day, once at ten in the morning and again at three in the afternoon. The word of mouth spread as to how good the play was and pretty soon buses were rolling in from as far away as Massachusetts and as close as Brooklyn. The play thrived with that wonderful young audience for six months.

After losing *Seventh Ave So* as a potential Circle replacement in case Loomis exercised his option to terminate our lease, I hunted around the Village to see if I could find another space to move to. In the course of the search I had called Charles Abrams, the Commissioner of Buildings at the time, and asked for his advice. He was a lover of art and a frequent visitor to our theatre. He called me back a couple of days later to tell me that his brother Ralph would help me look at buildings. Ralph was in real estate in the Village and owned a couple of movie theatres. So Ralph and I met and I told him what I was looking for. We began doing biweekly tours of the Village from Third Avenue and 14th Street west to the Hudson River looking for a space.

Ralph was a wonderful, patient man and I think he thought of me as a lost son. Of all the different spaces we looked at I didn't like any.

Jane McArthur and Clint Kimbrough in Thornton Wilder's *Our Town* (1959), directed by José Quintero

One day we were walking past the Amato Opera house on Bleecker Street and Ralph said, "What about this place?" I responded, "I don't think they will want to rent it." He said, "Well, call and ask." I knew the space, having seen several operas there, and I immediately visualized our three-sided theatre fitting in. So I got Sally Amato on the phone and she said they weren't interested. I kept calling back because I wanted to speak to her husband Anthony. One day, I got him and he repeated what his wife had said but volunteered that he'd be interested in selling it. I asked, "How much?" He told me and I went to Ralph and told him what the price was. I thought it was beyond our reach. Ralph was elated, though, and explained that if you paid it out over thirty years your mortgage payment would be exactly the same as we were currently paying in rent. Ralph arranged for a loan with the bank and for an attorney, Morris Hellman, to handle the transaction. I told Anthony that we were interested and showed José the space. We agreed that we would take it. The Circle didn't have any money to put up the security with the bank so I borrowed $30,000 from my father. The bank approved the situation and the deal went through. We now had a new theatre to move into when and if Loomis gave us notice.

So I went about having our future home renovated. The Amato was a proscenium theatre with 299 seats—100 more than we had at Sheridan Square. David Hays did the design, a three-sided theatre, that improved the conditions for the production as well as for the theatre audience.

A friend of mine, George Kogol, who is in real estate, arranged for the renovation and rebuilding at no charge to us. We now had a sparkling new theatre which had originally been built as a Nickelodeon at the turn of the century. It had a previous theatre history as being the home of Jean Paul Sartre's *The Respectful Prostitute* with Meg Mundy. So rather than wait for Loomis to give us notice we gave him notice and moved our production of *Our Town* to our new theatre which of course didn't have any scenery, only props. George and Colleen and other actors helped us carry the ladders and chairs over to the new Circle in the Square at 159 Bleecker Street between Sullivan and Thompson Streets.

That same night we performed *Our Town*. Remember the columns on Sheridan Square? Well, believe it or not, we installed three columns into the new space because we had become so comfortable with them. After *Our Town* though, we came to our senses and had the columns removed for future productions.

CHAPTER 19

A Momentous Exit

In 1960, while Jean Genet's *The Balcony* was running at the Circle, we also produced Tennessee Williams' *Camino Real*, with José directing and starring Clint Kimbrough, at an upstairs theatre on 8th Street and Second Avenue called St. Mark's Playhouse.

During *The Balcony*'s one-year run, there was a continuous turnover of actors. The Actors' Equity five-day notice rule was still in effect. Every week we were replacing one actor or more because of the Equity clause.

As usual, José wasn't interested in either selecting or guiding the newcomers, so it was left to the stage manager. The results were not good—the choices had to be better so that the production remained at the level of José's superb direction. At that point, I had learned a great deal from José, sitting in and observing rehearsals of all the plays he'd done. I had also helped actor friends prepare scenes for auditions for other plays other than our own, several applying for admission to the Actors' Studio, and I seemed to get the language and communication with these actors. George Segal was one of the beneficiaries of my burgeoning knowledge.

Grayson Hall was about to replace Nancy Marchand (who was leaving to do a movie) in the role of Madame Irma, owner of the brothel. Since I felt very uncomfortable with the situation of *The Balcony* replacements, I took over the rehearsals. I found it went very smoothly.

Grayson and I worked well together. Even after she began to perform the role we continued to work trying to achieve the depth of the character and the play. I loved the process and I realized that I was working on one of the great plays of the 20th century. From then on, I did all the *Balcony* replacements. The play continued to flourish.

The costumes by Patricia Zipprodt were extraordinary—each an extension of and a further insight into the character. Salome Jens played "The Pony Girl."

Salome Jens in Jean Genet's *The Balcony* (1960), directed by José Quintero

Patricia costumed her in a tight low-cut top with leather puffing, curving around the upper part of her thighs—and what a pair of legs and what a performance! She was the human embodiment of an independent self-willed horse. José gave Sally the key to this characterization and led her through the role like a groom gently taking her by her reins showing her the way.

I remember José in rehearsal with Salome throwing his head back and whinnying like a horse and gesticulating with his arms, hands, legs making neighing sounds, imitating a horse prancing. And he used her striking physical ability to help her become the horse, far smarter than her bedraggled client The General (Jack Dodson), who fantasized that he was a General leading his troops into battle riding gloriously on his steed. One of the memorable lines, of which there are many, was when The General, speaking of his courage in battle, says, "I was so calm I began to snow, to snow on my men."

Patricia's costumes for The Pony Girl and The Slave all had ele-

Nancy Marchand and Roy Poole in *The Balcony*

ments of leather in the design. Within the next few years and to this day, leather as clothing has become the fashion rage and I think Patricia started it.

During this period I was making all the replacements for the show. Our gorgeous production lived on for a full year. It had received all kinds of awards and press. It was the event of the year and had a tremendous effect on the increasing importance of the off-Broadway movement.

The play was owned by Lucille Lortel who had sent it to me to co-produce with us. After reading the first four scenes I was knocked out and was ready to produce *The Balcony*—I didn't care what the rest of the play was like but on completing the reading I realized this was a major new work. José concurred. Lucille's husband, Louis Schweitzer, gave us some of the money for the production and I quickly found the rest.

We cast the play and went into rehearsal. This was the first play that we had ever co-produced and so we didn't know how to react to a third party on our turf. Fortunately, Lucille never came to the rehearsals and never interfered.

The cast included Nancy Marchand as Irma, Roy Poole (my *Bad Seed* understudy partner) as The Chief of Police, Betty Miller as Carmen, Fred Kimball as The Bishop, Arthur Mallet as The Judge, Sylvia Miles as The Thief, Salome as The Pony Girl, Jack Dodson as The General, and John Perkins as The Executioner.

After the second week of rehearsal José did a run through. We found there was a lot of extraneous material that stopped the flow of the play. I showed José my recommended edit, he agreed, and we announced the cuts to the cast. Of course, there was a lot of pain—no actor likes to lose his lines. But when we ran it through with those changes they all realized the correctness of the editing. The play had come together, like polished steel.

José Quintero

The Balcony takes place in a brothel during a revolution in an unknown ravaged country (for today's audiences it would be Iraq, with explosions and people being shot in the streets). Madame Irma provides costumes and a female companion to help the male "guests" act out their fantasies. All of the men have taken their lives in their hands to get to Madame Irma's. In one scene, a plumber wants to be a bishop and in another a carpenter wants to be a judge. When the man is fully clothed as a general and mounts his horse to lead his troops into battle—that is his ecstasy. When the magistrate humbles himself by kissing the foot of the thief who had been on trial in his court—that is his "moment." And so this goes on in different scenes—as each character acts out his or her fantasies all of which is overseen by Madame Irma. Suddenly, a man announces himself as the representative of the Queen, who he says is dead, missing or hiding. To keep the populous in check, he needs Madame Irma to assume the role of the queen. She reluctantly agrees in order to save her brothel from destruction and leads the other impersonators (the magistrate, the judge, and the bishop) out of her brothel to be adored by the populous.

In the *Balcony* there is no overt sexuality; it is inferred sensuality but no actual sexuality. Any production that goes against that is a disgrace to the play because the audience has to fantasize just as the characters do.

As luck would have it, opening night it snowed. It snowed and snowed—thick white stuff. Most of the critics got there. Later that night, it was still snowing, I nervously got the early edition of the *Times*. I quickly read it. I was so excited I rushed back downtown to the Circle's opening night party to read this wonderful review. I was so surprised. I thought that the review would be like a frozen igloo of denunciation, because the *Times* was conservative and the play has to do with a brothel and its orgiastic subtext. We were a hit and even bigger as the rest of the reviews rolled in. This new play was the first new production in our theatre on Bleecker Street.

In 1961, José began expressing a desire to leave the Circle. He had directed the last seventeen plays and he said he wanted new challenges and was pursuing motion picture possibilities as well as plays with other producers. He had a commitment to do a film of Tennessee Williams' novel *The Roman Spring of Mrs. Stone* with Vivien Leigh, which he was preparing for, to be filmed in London. When filming began I visited José on the set and the shooting was going well. Vivien Leigh was very slender, quite short and very beautiful. She was flirtatious. She, José and I had dinner together several times and once I had dinner with her alone. We of course talked about Larry (Sir Laurence Olivier) and her experiences of filming *Gone With the Wind*. She was very curious about the Circle and what we were doing.

I had hoped *The Balcony* would replenish José's energy and make him want to continue with the Circle. Either way, we still needed a new production. I invited William Ball to direct Dylan Thomas' *Under Milkwood*. I had seen it in Minneapolis with Bill directing. I also saw a few years earlier a short-lived Broadway production of the play at the Henry Miller Theatre with a cast of over forty and starring Richard Burton. Watching that production, I was confused and overwhelmed by the attempt to follow each character. The production unsettled me, but I loved the text. When I heard about Bill's production, I went to see it.

It had a cast of ten, the women dressed in wool skirts, sweaters, cardigans, and an occasional shawl and the men in dark trousers and turtleneck sweaters. These costumes coincided with the imaginary Welsh sea village and they helped to enhance the environment of the play.

Years later when my son Jonathan was studying acting in London we drove to Wales and then drove on to a village near Dylan's home. When we were there the ocean was very agitated with strong winds and fierce rain. I saw Welsh women pushing baby carriages in that stormy atmosphere. The carriages were covered with plastic to protect the babies, the women strolling along like it was an ordinary summer day. When we went to the local golf course gift shop to buy some mementos, we saw two golfers striding in towards the building. The shopkeeper told me they had just played eighteen holes. The golfers were dressed in rain slickers head-to-toe with golf bags over their shoulders. As they entered the shop, they were jubilant and immediately began talking to each other about the splendid golf game they'd just completed. Throughout our whole visit it was a pleasure to hear the Welsh dialect and experience the friendliness of the people and the dwellings they lived in and to visit the ancient Roman ruins—including the remains of a small coliseum. Wales may be attached to England geographically but is worlds apart in its culture.

Bill's concept for *Milkwood* was to have two narrators upstage left and right standing on platforms minus podiums. The entire action of the play takes place downstage in front of them—with them observing and commenting on what they see. The direction was very fluid. There was no set; the words are the scenery, the smells, and the sounds. The audiences quickly grasped who everyone was and where they were in Dylan's Town. *Milkwood* is very similar to Thornton Wilder's *Our Town* in that both plays are performed with imaginary props, a narrator, and no scenery. Both are about a small town—one in Wales and the other in New England. For the audience, they are both memory plays of an earlier era showing both the good and the meanness that existed in those societies.

Milkwood was very well received and attended. This was the first time I had sole responsibility for the choice of a play for the Circle. Its success gave me a great deal of confidence. I felt like a young chick who with great trepidation, fearlessly crosses the heavily trafficked highway all by himself to get to the other side.

Bill and I had a very happy director–producer relationship. I admired Bill and I worked with him again in 1963 when I produced Pirandello's

Six Characters in Search of an Author at Paul Libin's Martinique Theatre. If José did decide to leave, I thought Bill might be my next "José," —another director that I could help blaze the way for, but Bill got an offer to start a theatre in Minneapolis, which ultimately led to his founding the American Conservatory Theatre in San Francisco.

Then one of the most extraordinary events of my life started to unfold. I received a letter from Thornton Wilder. He told me that he was writing a cycle of one-act plays based on the seven ages of man and the seven deadly sins. I thought, "Oh, boy! That's fourteen plays!" A major theatrical event had just landed in my lap, a series that might keep us occupied for years to come. He asked, "Would you be interested in reading three that have just come out of my oven?" Thornton had come to see several of our plays in the Sheridan Square theatre and would always sit in the same seat on a third row riser. Remember those little tables I wrote about earlier? Well Thornton would put his chin in the cup of his hands and would lean forward with his elbows resting on the table, intensely absorbing the play. Thornton had a high forehead and wore metal-rimmed glasses—in that position he looked like an ancient owl perched on a limb.

His telephone number was in the letter so I called and said, "Of course we would be interested." He sent them and after José and I read them we agreed to produce the three plays he had completed: *Infancy*, *Childhood*, and *Someone from Assisi*. (*Assisi* was from the "Sins" cycle and the other two from "Ages.") Thornton decided to title the evening *Plays for Bleecker Street*—which honored and thrilled us that being our location. This great playwright was giving us his new one-act plays.

Each play was cast individually: Betty Miller and Lee Richardson in *Someone from Assisi*, Dana Elcar and Betty Miller in *Childhood*, and Richard Libertini and Fred McIntyre Dickson in *Infancy*—two actors from our earlier production of *Stewed Prunes*. As Mr. Wilder had done with *Our Town*, there was no scenery for any of the plays. The most fascinating of these three was *Infancy* which tells of two nurses in Central Park attending to their infants in their carriages as they chat. The babies are fully grown men but have always been talked to in baby talk—so they're physically mature but not in their minds. Thornton was sending a pretty powerful message to parents. (I have always talked to my own children and five grandchildren as though they were adults.) The

MacIntyre Dixon, Mary Doyle, Charlotte Jones, and Richard Libertini in *Infancy*, from Thornton Wilder's *Plays for Bleecker Street* (1962), directed by José Quintero

baby carriages had to be specially constructed to hold those full-grown babies.

Prior to *Plays for Bleecker Street*, Thornton had totally disappeared from the Broadway scene and had not written a play for the New York stage in probably ten years. Our announcement that we were going to produce these plays was big news. Arthur Gelb of *The New York Times* did a front page story about this coming event. In the interview, Mr. Gelb asked Thornton where he had been and he replied, "I was in the desert"—I think he meant this metaphorically. Gelb also asked him, "Why are you writing plays without scenery?" and Thornton shot back, "the eyes are the enemy of the ears." I have found this to be one of the most profound truisms of the theatre. For example, our productions of George Bernard Shaw plays were all written for the proscenium stage but in our three-sided theatre they were done almost scenery-less thereby allowing the words and the intricacies of his wit to freely and successfully float and resonate without any visual encumbrance. It was as though his delicious words, like butterflies, had been set free. All of the Shaw plays that we did were enthusiastically received by audiences. The success of those productions reinforced Thornton's truism: that the eye *is* the enemy of the ear. How many plays have you seen where the only thing you remember is the scenery?

Thornton came one time to a rehearsal of *Bleecker Street* and after sitting and watching for twenty minutes he stood up and bolted out the door without saying goodbye to anybody. I was astonished and ran after him. Thornton was a very fast walker with a warm ebullient personality. I caught up to him after two blocks and asked him if everything was okay and he said, speaking with a serious tone in his voice, "My work is done. I'll come back at the opening." With a twinkle he added, "I want to hear the director sing." And away he went.

I had to come up with a piece of art for newspapers, flyers, etc., that would convey to the reader that these plays are dealing with universal truths and eternal questions that Western Civilization has always pondered. After doing research for some time, mainly looking through art books, I decided that the artist most likely to have an appropriate work would be Ben Shahn. I scouted around to find out where Mr. Shahn lived. A fellow artist, Chaim Gross, told me that Ben lived in Roosevelt, New Jersey. Franklin Delano Roosevelt wanted to provide low-cost homes for artists—actors, painters, sculptors, etc.—and so the Federal government provided funds and Roosevelt, New Jersey was created. This socially conscious concept came out of the WPA era.

When I arrived in Roosevelt, I saw dozens of homes simply constructed of wood with one or two floors and a large plot of land around each house. I told Mr. Shahn about the plays that Thornton had written for us and that I was hoping to find a work of his that I could use for advertising. I asked, "Would you object to my using your art in that fashion?" He quickly responded, "No, not at all. I like Mr. Wilder's work and I admire what you're doing." He took me into his studio to browse his entire collection. He was a very gracious stocky man, about 5'7", wearing baggy corduroy trousers and an old vest with drawing pencils and brushes sticking out of the pockets. He had wire rim glasses similar to Thornton's and I thought, wow, this was meant to be. He said he didn't have the time to create something for us and that I could chose one of his works. I looked through over a hundred pieces of his—until I saw the one that I thought was perfect. The work I selected conveyed to me the ages of man because there are three heads all coming out of one body. Each face had an individual expression. The work made me feel that we are all one. I also knew it would tell our audiences that there are three different stories without explicitly stating we

Ben Shahn's poster for *Plays for Bleecker Street*

were presenting three one-act plays—which generally are anathema for audiences.

The production was fairly well received by the critics but the business was modest. So I decided to bring back *Milkwood* and perform it on the same evenings with a new production of an old play of Thornton's, *Pullman Car Hiawatha*, which José was eager to direct (even though he continued to say he was going to leave the Circle). I think this was the first production of *Hiawatha* in New York, and I was hoping against hope that doing it might change José's mind. But all of my cajoling and coaxing—couldn't convince José to stay. I pleaded with him and offered to reduce his directorial responsibility but he was determined to leave. He said with his heavy Spanish accent, "I want to be free!" In earlier times, when he said how tired he was from directing, I had offered to bring in other directors. That offer would always make his tiredness disappear and suddenly the energy was there again. The reality was, he didn't like anyone else to "sing" on his turf. But finally it happened.

José officially left the Circle after *Pullman Car Hiawatha*. We had lots of handshakes and hugs. I was always unclear why he really left. I never believed it was just to be "free." He had said his leaving had nothing to do with our working relationship but what was the reason?

Many people thought we had a falling out. A couple of years ago, a very close friend of José's told me that the real reason José left the Circle was that he needed money to help his sister at a critical juncture in her life. We had previously agreed that if he left he would receive $10,000, and I wanted to give it to him, but I didn't have it. Fortunately, I was able to borrow it. I gave him the $10,000. It took me five years to pay the bank back. So José went off and worked on other projects. Despite the gossip we remained friends. In later years, when José visited New York, we would meet and he would see the plays that we were presenting.

After *Hiawatha*, George and Colleen talked to me about their interest in doing O'Neill's *Desire Under the Elms*. I asked José if he would come back one more time as a "guest" director for *Desire*. He agreed. We started rehearsal in December and opened in January 1963. By this time, George, Colleen, and I had already formed the Theatre Company of Michigan (more on this later).

Now I had to take leadership of Circle in the Square on my own, without anyone to confer with except my darling wife, Patricia. She was a great support and advisor. In my first year alone I had a very active time, at several different theatres, producing or co-producing: *Desire Under the Elms, Six Characters in Search of an Author, Strange Interlude, Trumpets of the Lord* and *The Trojan Women*. Where I found the time and the money to do all this, and to squeeze in breakfast and basketball (every Tuesday and Thursday at 4 P.M.), I have no idea. I guess the old adage "action begets action" was at work.

CHAPTER 20

GETTING AWAY FROM THE BIG CITY

One day in 1961 George C. Scott and I were having lunch and he expressed dissatisfaction with Broadway, "I'm fed up with Broadway—as though everything in theatre only happens here. There is a whole country out there wanting to have good theatre." We talked a great deal about this and came to the conclusion that we wanted to do something about decentralizing the Theatre. So we decided to establish a theatre company that would rehearse and produce its plays outside of New York.

Los Angeles, Chicago, Denver and San Francisco—none seemed right to us. They were too far away for me, I would not be able to take care of Circle's activities. Philadelphia was a no-no based on our experience of non-interest and non-support from the Academy of Music days. George and I both hated L.A. and the movie/TV pressure that exists there. Then George brought up Detroit. He'd been born in Michigan, and he'd also just made the highly acclaimed film *Anatomy of a Murder* in the upper peninsula. He felt harmonious with that city because he was a rabid Detroit Tigers fan—to the extent that he wore a Detroit baseball cap and jacket. And so we said, "Let's go take a look."

When George was performing at the Circle and the baseball season was on, he always had his radio tuned to the Tiger game in his dressing room and would listen up until the last second before he made his entrance. The transformation from baseball freak to Willy Loman or Astrov was near instantaneous. One night during our run of *Uncle Vanya*

George was hunched over the radio listening to the game and then his cue came in over the loudspeaker—he straightened up, brushed his hair and strode out onto the stage as Astrov. As soon as he came off he asked me, "Teddy, is the game still on?" "Yes." "Are the Tigers ahead?" "Yes." With no further questions he ran to his dressing room and donned his Detroit Tigers cap and sat hunched over the radio listening to the game. One reason George chose Detroit for our theatre experiment was so he could see them play, but he was so busy he never got the chance.

George was the star pitcher and batter on our softball team in the Broadway Show League. One day, however, he was getting hit pretty good. As the manager, playing second base, I ambled up to the mound and asked him if he wanted to go on. He said, "No, I better stop. I can't seem to get anybody out." George strode off the mound to sit in the stands and cheer the team for the rest of the game. Our infield included Bob Loggia, Tony LoBianco, Charlie Deerkup, and myself at second. Our outfield consisted of Bruce Dern, Louis Gossett Jr., and John Perkins. Another of our starting pitchers was Jason Robards. The opposing teams would hit him like they were family.

Our plan for the theatre company in Michigan was to hire New York actors, directors, and designers, rehearse in Detroit and present exciting new plays and while we were at it do TV and film. But we didn't have a theatre so I went to see David Nederlander who owned several theatres in town. There wasn't much road activity for dramatic houses at that time and The Shubert Theatre was empty. He was sitting in a small office in the back of the theatre at his desk with two wooden chairs, nothing on the walls with a bare bulb hanging from the ceiling. He was dressed immaculately—tie, jacket, and shined shoes. David was in his 80s but still vigorous and the head of the company. During our meeting, he picked up an old-fashioned phone with a receiver on the side that hung from the main stem and called his sons Jimmy and Joey and told them, "Come over and meet George C. Scott and Ted Mann. They want to rent the theatre." There was a pause and David shook his head and said, "Yes, that's right George C. Scott and Ted Mann from New York." While we waited he regaled us with stories of victories and defeats of his theatre-owner career in Detroit, and the stars that had appeared for him since the turn of the century. George, an avid student of the theatre, guffawed as only he could with full appreciation.

When Jimmy and Joey arrived we walked into the theatre proper and Jimmy asked in his charming Michigan accent, "Where's the money coming from?" George turned and slammed the palm of his hand down on the railing separating the orchestra pit from the audience and said with a growl, "We'll get the money!" The slam was so ferocious and so intimidating that the Nederlanders didn't ask any further questions. (Remember George's slam of the rock in John Huston's film *Moses*?) George continued with the smile of a shark, "Ted and I will bring in the money!"

Years later, whenever I'd see the Nederlander brothers they would mention George's slam of the hand with awe.

Detroit at the time was in pretty bad shape—there had been race riots, the streets were dangerous, department stores and restaurants closed early and by 9 P.M. the town was asleep. But the section where The Shubert was located was active with the wonderful London Chop House practically next door. We took the plunge and rented the theatre for two new plays, *Great Day in the Morning*, about an Irish Catholic family, by Alice Cannon (J.D. Cannon's wife), starring Colleen, Tom Carlin (Frances Sternhagen's husband), and Cliff James; followed by *General Seeger* with William Bendix and Ann Harding, written by Ira Levin (author of the novel and then the screenplay of *Rosemary's Baby* starring Mia Farrow and John Cassavetes).

George and I walked away from our meeting with the Nederlanders with the same question Jimmy asked us, echoing in our wake. "Where is the money coming from?" We didn't have any idea. George was now a star, having done Robert Rossen's *The Hustler* with Paul Newman and Jackie Gleason. Somehow the money would come. The Nederlanders must have felt the same way—they gave us the house without the usual required deposit.

By this time G.C. and I had been in Detroit for some time trying to hustle up money, with Colleen coming in for special company needs, such as a fundraiser at the home of a fatcat. George, Colleen and I would drive to a home of someone who had gathered their friends for a fundraising evening. After some hors d'oeuvres and cocktails I would get up and make some introductory remarks about our company, why we were in Detroit and that I had brought along blank checks with me for those who wanted to contribute. I then introduced George and Colleen who would proceed to read scenes from the two plays. Then I'd pass checks out to the guests trying to pick up some money. Mainly these events failed. On our way home we would roar with laughter at the cultural apathy of these Midwesterners. We laughed so hard we had to stop the car.

In fact, the only successful fundraising parties we ever had were set up by Max and Lois Pincus in Bloomfield Hills. We did get some investments and later some attendance from that Jewish population. We were presenting the exact same home events with George and Colleen. The difference, I think, is that in the non-Jewish homes we were just a show, whereas in the Jewish homes we were seen as "culture."

To try to raise more money I set up a fundraiser and publicity event in the main ballroom of The Woodward Hotel. The Mayor and other dignitaries were expected to attend. The ballroom was lined with mirrors that ended at about waist height. The Mayor showed, but very few others, maybe fifteen altogether. There we were; a huge ballroom, loaded banquet tables with food and drink, and white-jacketed waiters hovering around and with only a few people in attendance. I was heartbroken.

G.C. was seethingly furious at this inhospitable slight from the Detroit movers and shakers. While we waited for people to come, he began to drink and pretty soon he got out of control and began to curse Michigan, Detroit, and the hotel! The Mayor quietly slipped away and so did everyone else. Then G.C. started to smash the mirrors with his fists. George continued to smash, but finally Colleen and I, mainly Colleen, calmed him down. The next morning when I went up to their hotel room Colleen was frying eggs, buttering toast, and serving coffee. She and George were cooing to each other in lovers' baby-talk fashion. They were all smiles. No mention was made of the tumultuous night before.

This failed fundraiser and the earlier disappointments at fatcats' homes began to have its effects on G.C. and myself. Colleen had asked me to contact José to direct *Great Day*, which he agreed to do. He did cast in New York but we still didn't have the money to go into rehearsals. We were in a crunch, although "vise" would be a more appropriate word.

We were still practically broke. George brooded for days on this dilemma, and then one day while walking to the theatre George said,
"I got an idea of how we can raise money for our company; let's sell
stock." I said, "You mean shares of stock?" He said, "Yes." I said, "For
how much?" He said, "Two dollars a share." I said, "Whoa that is not
much money." He said, "Yeah, but if it's inexpensive a lot of people will
buy it and then come to see our shows." I said, "Maybe this will get some
of those fatcats to finally crack their wallets."

The usual way Broadway shows are financed, then and now, is by
forming limited partnerships, where the investors become limited partners and the producers the general partners. The latter have full liability
and control whereas the limited partners have, as the term indicates,
limited liability. They are liable only to the amount of their investment.
These limited partnerships were always readily approved by The Securities and Exchange Commission. Broadway producers were forever talking about forming corporations and selling shares of stock as a way to
produce a play and get the funds. But they were dissuaded because of
the intricacies of that route with the Securities and Exchange Commission. In financial matters, all producers feel safe by following tradition.
We would now go against the grain, trying to do what other producers
had been talking about for years—so I said to George, "Let's do it. Let's
form a corporation."

I went and talked to the attorney son of the Nederlander family, Robert. He agreed to draw up the necessary papers for The Theatre Company
of Michigan, Inc., to incorporate. The Nederlanders have always had an
optimistic point of view about life. So Robert was following in the family
tradition of embracing new ideas in the theatre. He liked our plan.

We took a large ad in the Detroit newspapers in the financial section,
offering shares in the company. George and I had rented a small office
so we could have a Detroit business address. We didn't have enough
money to put the name of the company on the door of room 309 which
was ten feet by ten feet with a high ceiling and two desks. The day after
the ads appeared, we went to see if there was any response. We were
hoping to find a couple of envelopes. As we approached the door, we
saw what appeared to be a large shadow. I asked "What is that?" and
George replied, "I don't know. Maybe someone is inside." We had dif-

ficulty opening the door, but when we did we discovered a dozen big fat mailbags stacked to the ceiling. When we opened them hundreds of envelopes cascaded towards us. It was the gentlest rain I had ever experienced. I wanted to kiss each one. George and I were ecstatic and we danced around the small open space and he cackled that large parrot laugh of his. I stopped dancing and started to open envelopes. They were stuffed with $2, $4, $8 and $10 checks! I immediately opened an account in the bank downstairs. Suddenly, we had money to pay the expenses and start the shows. And those envelopes kept coming in every day for weeks!

George was about to do a series for CBS, *East Side West Side*, in which he was to be the director/star and have full approval of the script, with David Suskind as the producer. One day there was an announcement in *The New York Times*, in the TV section. At the top of the page the headline read, "CBS to invest in Scott Theatre Co." The story went on to say that in effect Mr. Scott had formed the Theatre of Michigan Company to produce plays in Detroit, with his partner, Theodore Mann. After which the plays would move on to Broadway. It went on to say that CBS would invest $175,000 in the company.

I was delighted—with a huge injection of dollars and this publicity! George had never mentioned this to me. I only found out about this by reading the article.

I think George took less money for himself from the TV series to encourage CBS to invest in our theatre company. George always put his money where his mouth was. It was typical of George to deny himself to help fulfill others' dreams. George was one of the most unselfish people I have ever known. People who have only seen him in films probably find this hard to understand—but working with him so much, I fully appreciated the breadth of his generosity.

George was a big man physically and morally. The first day of rehearsal for Bernard Sabath's *The Boys in Autumn* at Circle in the Square Theatre in 1986, George looked around the theatre and observed with a growl that, "Your carpet looks pretty shabby, Teddy." I agreed and explained, "We can't do anything about it because we don't have the money." He asked, "How much would it cost?" I answered, "About $10,000." He said, "I'll give it to you."

Some weeks after the *Times* story about CBS and George—with the envelopes still filling up our tiny Detroit office—I was summoned to a meeting at the Securities and Exchange Commission office in Chicago. The S.E.C. made it clear that we had to cease selling shares of stock because we were a Michigan corporation that only had authority to sell stock in that state. We had exceeded that authority because of the investment from CBS, a New York corporation. I was stunned. I had thought that CBS had made the investment through a Michigan affiliate. But, there was nothing to do. I asked the SEC representative if we could keep selling shares if I returned the CBS money. No deal. We had to stop selling shares to Michigan residents or anybody else immediately. I tried to explain that we had not solicited CBS, that they had given the money of their own volition. This explanation did not fly with them—we had to stop selling shares of stock!

Well, this stopped us dead in our tracks. Fortunately, the SEC didn't require us to give back the money to the individual $2 shareholders that we had already collected. That allowed us to go ahead, plus George putting in $50,000 of his own money. I've often thought what the fate of the company would have been if the CBS mistake hadn't happened—if CBS had invested the money through a Michigan affiliate— telling this story I'm getting nervous all over again! So, George and I went on to produce *Great Day in the Morning* and *General Seeger* both at the Shubert in Michigan and later on Broadway.

After that Chicago meeting I was very depressed but before returning to New York City I stopped off in Minneapolis to see that terrific production of *Under Milkwood* I described earlier. Fate has its own ironic methods. It knocks you down and picks you back up.

Great Day got good reviews in Detroit but didn't do much business. The big surprise to us was that the shareholders didn't come to see the plays. I could never figure that out. If they invested in the company, I would assume that they would want to see our plays. But they were investors—not theatregoers. Well, so be it, another lesson on the path of theatre.

George and Colleen took it like the warriors they were—undefeatable! *Great Day* came in to Broadway to the wonderful old Lyceum Theatre filled with the history and the ambience of past productions.

Colleen made the role her own—she was magnificent! José's direction was insightful. Hope for success stirred in our hearts.

The New York Times review was bad but I had some innocent hope because the *Daily News* critic, John Chapman, was glowing and we tried to ride on that. I thought maybe Chapman's review would bring in audiences. We hoped the Irish Catholic audience would respond to the play and since the *Daily News* readership is primarily of that persuasion we prayed for box office redemption. But we probably weren't helped by Colleen being a Christian Scientist, George being a Presbyterian non-believer, and me a very non-Irish Jew.

Shoulders bowed but unbeaten we immediately went on to *General Seeger*. George directed.

In Detroit, Colleen, George, and I had adjoining rooms in the hotel. I would fly in, take care of business, spend a few days and then go back to New York to take care of my mistress the Circle. When we began the theatre company in Michigan, I was almost always exhausted from the traveling back and forth.

George and Colleen were as happy as two sweet larks—they both always loved theatre and here we were putting on plays on our own terms. In the evening, after rehearsal they would be playing cards with members of the cast. They'd greet me upon arrival after my flight and I'd lie down on the couch and chat with them and pretty soon I'd fall asleep. It soothingly reminded me of my childhood when my dad and uncles, Ben, Tom, and Sam, would be playing pinochle and the kids would fall asleep. Hearing George and Colleen and the cast's banter, laughter, and the cards clicking, I got sleepy as I did in my childhood. Many nights they just let me sleep there on the couch and the next morning Colleen would be up, all chirpy, making coffee and eggs. It was a happy time—we were a big family.

As *Seeger* rehearsals progressed George began to be dissatisfied with William Bendix's portrayal and his dissatisfaction kept escalating, with George getting hotter and hotter. Then one afternoon, George was drinking, and insisted on firing Bendix then and there. That night was to be our first preview. I thought if we could get through this night maybe things would get better, which I told George. He agreed, adding, "You better be right, Teddy."

A couple of hours later, the show was on, I was in the theatre and I hear this terrific pounding on the exit doors—it was George! I ran to the front of the house to tell the house manager, "Don't let Mr. Scott in. He's upset." The performance still had another hour and a half to go. He kept pounding, now at another door and after a terrifying half hour he suddenly stopped. When I went outside, I cautiously walked around to all of the exit doors. I thought I would find George resting against one of them. But he was gone.

The show went on but George was right, Bendix was not up to the role. After the curtain I found George at our nearby favorite hang out, the London Chop House. I sat down with him, he amazingly had sobered up. We had a rational discussion that Bendix was not cutting the mustard—but then what do we do? Who could we get? And what do we do until that person is ready? George had the answer—he said he would do the role! He would step in the next night!

George had a photographic memory so the lines were already learned. He had a film commitment eight weeks later, still leaving us enough time to get into New York and if the reviews were good we could replace him. But first Bendix had to be told and I told George I would do it. But George said, "No Teddy, I'll do it." He undertook to do that thankless task himself. In most cases, the producer performs this unpleasant business, but George was an upfront man. When he was directing, he always took full responsibility—to gently explain his decision to the actor.

George, as General Seeger, is having an authority conflict with his officer son. George was powerful in the role. At one point he is standing up and to emphasize a point, he slams the palm of his hand down on the desk. The papers jumped and so did the audience. Somewhere in Detroit the Nederlander brothers also probably jumped.

We had bright hopes when we opened at the Hudson Theatre that we could keep our dream of the Theatre Company of Michigan alive. But those hopes were dashed when *The New York Times* and others including the *Daily News* gave negative reviews to the play.

Now, with George's film commitment and our having spent all the money raised, we decided to throw in the towel and swallow the bitter pill of defeat. We closed the Theatre Company of Michigan operation down with no regrets. We had tried to do something unusual, we had started and produced two plays whose home base was not Broadway, but Detroit, where we stirred the theatre lethargy of the city. And it's interesting that there were, throughout this time, other companies being thought about in San Francisco, Pittsburgh, Denver, Minneapolis, and Los Angeles.

We could be proud that we were among the first, that we kids helped to start the regional theatre movement. Maybe our example showed it *was* possible to have professional theatre outside of New York City.

CHAPTER 21

Dancing With a New Partner

In 1963 Paul Libin and I teamed up. At the insistence of our mutual
attorney Sy Litvinoff, Paul and I met in Sy's office to discuss the possibility of our joining together. We had known each other since the late
'50s when we founded the League of Off-Broadway Theatres and when
I produced *Six Characters in Search of an Author* at his Martinique
Theatre, an off-Broadway house at 32nd and Broadway. I instantly felt
comfortable with him. After the meeting in the lawyer's office we went
out and had a bite to eat. We talked of our hopes for our theatres and
particularly about Circle in the Square. I had always liked working with
a partner, to bounce ideas off one another. We decided to join together
at Circle in the Square. We shook hands and that has been our contract
ever since. Paul maintained his own interest in the Martinique for some
time and we never wrote down terms of our understanding; we just let
the partnership evolve. Paul took full control of all the business affairs of
the theatre and I the selection and mounting of the plays. Of course we
overlapped into both categories. I've always respected Paul's opinions,
suggestions, and guidance. Since that time we've done over 150 plays
together and have rarely disagreed on anything.

Paul's interest in the theatre all began in 1949 when he went to see
Thomas Mitchell in *Death of a Salesman* in Chicago with his young
woman friend and another couple. After the show, the friends went to
get the car while Paul and his girlfriend waited near the stage door.

Coming out of the theatre was Mr. Mitchell. To Paul's amazement, he saw that Willie Loman was alive! That moment ignited his unquenchable thirst for theatre.

That summer he went to work for a stock theatre company in Malden Bridge, New York, as a juvenile actor, and with his unending curiosity he also became involved in the technical side of theatre. That fall he transferred from the University of Illinois to Columbia University. While at Columbia he studied acting with Gertrude Lawrence and received the Gertrude Lawrence Award as best actor and $500 prize money. That year in New York he was also seeing as many plays as he could on and off-Broadway. In 1951 he saw *Yerma* with Geraldine Page at Circle in the Square. Unbeknownst to either of us our paths were beginning to converge. The Korean War was going on while he was at Columbia and he was drafted into the army to Fort Hood, Texas, armored division. He was assigned to the mail department. He was yearning for theatre and started a company at the fort and produced and directed Sidney Kingsley's *Detective Story*.

After his discharge, he returned to Columbia to complete his studies and while there he taught stagecraft at Queens College. Jo Mielziner, the designer/producer, then hired him, as his production assistant on the musical *Happy Hunting* and later Paul became a stage manager on the production. While working at Mielziner Studios, he joined forces with others to create the Martinique Theatre in the Martinique Hotel.

In 1957, the theatre came to life in a formal ballroom, which was the first of many theatres that he was to conceive over the years. For his first production he presented Arthur Miller's *The Crucible*, which became a major off-Broadway hit alongside our *Summer and Smoke*, and *The Iceman Cometh*, and Carmen Capalbo's *Threepenny Opera*.

Paul has an ebullient personality and he makes people immediately feel at ease in his presence. At 6' tall he is a handsome man with an imposing presence. Paul is a careful person and extremely orderly. Any project or subject submitted to him he studies thoroughly. In our forty-three years of partnership Paul has never thrown his hands up and walked away from a problem. He is a person who completes things and is highly adaptable, coming up with ways to solve unfathomable mysteries. Paul has never lost his actor instinct and has a great sense of humor that can be attested to by any union negotiator he has dealt with. In the writing of this book he has always been the last word for me on obscure incidents that I have tried to remember. He brings clarity and his memory is dependable in a world of "undependables." The first production he and I worked on was *The Trojan Women* at the end of 1963. He is a deeply loyal friend. A quote about Sir Thomas Moore pithily describes Paul better than any words of mine, "He is a man of singular learning and angel's wit. I know not his equal."

In 1963, before Paul joined me, I produced *Six Characters* with Claude Giroux at Paul's Martinique and *Strange Interlude* at the Hudson Theatre. *Strange Interlude*—what a cast! Geraldine Page, Jane Fonda, Richard Thomas, Franchot Tone, William Prince, Ben Gazzarra, Pat Hingle, and Betty Field! Earlier in the summer of '62 Gerry Page had invited me to a staged reading of the play at the New School with her and Franchot Tone. I liked what I heard so much I acquired the rights. When Lee Strasberg head of the Actor's Studio expressed an interest in doing the play with Gerry, I agreed to co-produce with José directing.

There were a lot of problems in our *Interlude*. José wasn't focused, he was drinking. He had fights with Lee Strasberg and a shouting match with Rip Torn in front of Gerry and me in the lobby of the Hudson Theatre while the play was still rehearsing. Rip Torn was furious and screaming at the top of his voice. My heart broke for José to be criticized in such a public manner. Rip chastised him for his slowness and unresponsiveness to the cast. I defended José then took Rip aside and calmed him down so that José wasn't in danger of being fired. The production opened to good, not great, reviews. When *Interlude* was originally produced, it had been presented on two successive evenings. We decided to do it on the same evening with an early curtain at 7 P.M. with a dinner break. The public didn't take to the play and it closed after four months.

Desire Under the Elms was still running at the Circle. Every day George arrived three hours before curtain to apply makeup and glue to his neck, hands, forehead, ears and face to give him Ephraim's age. And he whitened his hair. When he walked out on stage he was an old man by virtue of his body movement and makeup, but a very vigorous one. George at that point was 36—the reason he put all this stuff on was to fulfill O'Neill's description of an 80-year-old farmer. There was a lot

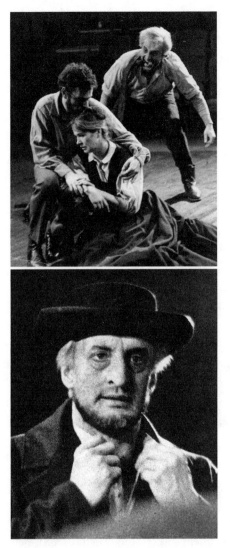

of tension in the rehearsal. George was suspicious that Rip Torn was flirting with Colleen and threatened, "I'll wrap this pole [a metal scenic piece] around your neck if you continue to bother with her." Of course, flirting could not be farther from the truth. Rip was happily married to Geraldine Page, and Colleen was in love with George. When I relayed the pole threat to Colleen, she let her head fall back and she roared with the kind of laughter only Colleen could erupt with. And when she recovered and caught her breath she said, referring to G.C.'s jealousy, "Oh, the poor baby."

Desire is about the love affair that evolves between Ephraim's young son, Eben, played by Rip, and Abbie, his young wife (Colleen), so of course they were flirting and being romantic, but not in real life. It was actors doing good work. They were so good that it obviously convinced George! Aside from that, rehearsals were wonderful. José was sharp as ever. He executed a beautiful production.

Top, Rip Torn, Colleen Dewhurst, and George C. Scott in Eugene O'Neill's *Desire Under the Elms* (1963), directed by José Quintero; *bottom*, George C. Scott in *Desire Under the Elms*

Early on in the play we hear the sound of a horse and carriage arriving. George and Colleen enter standing at the front edge of the vomitorium. Ephraim, looking at the farm, says to her, "Har we be t' hum, Abbie." And Abbie says, "Mighty purty farm." These are two simple lines with profound implications for the rest of the play.

Desire got great reviews but George had to leave to make a movie. Colleen stayed and Carl Low took over George's role. Alan Nixon replaced Rip and later Salome Jens replaced Colleen. Then, Betty Miller replaced Salome. *Desire* ran for ten months.

However, José and I knew this would be the last play he directed for the Circle. José did come back to conduct special seminars for Circle in the Square Theatre School acting students. These were incredible events. José by this time was suffering from throat cancer and he needed special amplification via a microphone to his vocal cords. He spoke haltingly. He started off the seminars telling of a little boy he met on the street who saw him using the microphone. Hearing José's voice, the boy pointed to him and said, "Are you an alien?" and then José with a broad smile replied, "Yes, I'm from Mars." The audience laughed. With that anecdote, José denied the tragedy of his condition. Instead we heard his passion and listened intently to his stories and interpretations of *Summer and Smoke, Long Day's Journey Into Night, A Moon for the Misbegotten,* and *The Iceman Cometh.* These seminars were thrilling and inspiring. His charm, wit, deep love, and insight into the material won his audience.

The week that he took very ill in New York City, I spent several days with him. The last day before he went into the hospital, his companion, Nick Tsacrios, asked if I could come and stay with him while he went to see a doctor at Sloan-Kettering about José's condition. Nick was going to plead with the physician to admit José for special treatment. Nick and José were staying at Liv Ullman's apartment—a good friend of José's from their work in the theatre together. After Nick left, José and I sat at a table opposite each other and played a game of cards. I would say something and José would nod. Then I would add something more and he would smile. And then I would make another comment and José would write a note of response on his notepad. So the conversation went on. We did not want for subject matter. I think José declined to use his microphone because speaking must have caused him excruciating pain. José's smile was on his lips and in his eyes. As always, it warmed my soul.

He got very tired and asked if I could help him to the bed, which I did and made him comfortable. He took a nap. When he awoke we continued to talk in the manner that I described for the rest of the afternoon. We restated our love for each other. I felt very fortunate to be with him. My heart went out to what this beautiful man was suffering. When Nick had left he hadn't told José whom he went to see, but when he came back you could tell from his manner that his plea had been rejected. The next day, José was in another hospital.

I was with José during his last day, along with Nick and José's sister Carmen—one of the beautiful souls of this world. She and I cried and hugged and talked about her brother. As I left the room I hugged and said goodbye to José knowing full well what that meant, and walked down the hallway. I had to catch my breath, I was dizzy and leaned against the wall and took deep breaths. The sobs pounded up through my being. This man, whom I grew up with culturally, was such a significant person in my life. A deep and meaningful friend was leaving us. I couldn't grasp the reality of this loss. For days afterwards José was continually in my heart and my mind.

CHAPTER 22

THE TRUMPET BLOWS

The same year, 1963, I produced (with Will B. Sandler) *Trumpets of the Lord* based on James Weldon Johnson's poems *God's Trombone*. It was Johnson's interpretation of black rural Southern ministers' sermons. We selected the poems and added gospel music under the superb musical direction of Howard Roberts. It was an uplifting, joyous, foot-stomping evening that started at the Astor Place Theatre, where it had been directed and choreographed by Vinnette Carroll until Donald McKayle took over. The Astor Place was tiny and dirty and across the street was an abandoned library which was to become Joe Papp's Public Theatre — but at this time Lafayette Street was a wide, rarely foot-trafficked street. It looked like Hoboken on a dark night. I decided because of the dirt and the loneliness of the theatre to move *Trumpets* to the former Cafe Society Downtown at 1 Sheridan Square, right across the street from our original location.

The gospel show fared well. Cicely Tyson was discovered in the production. It also featured Theresa Merritt and Lex Monson in the cast.

Jean-Louis Barrault, famed for his role in *Les Enfants du Paradis*, one of the most illustrious men of theatre in the world, and also the husband of Madeleine Renaud, came to see the show and after the performance introduced himself. I was very moved to be in the presence of this great actor. He was presenting an international festival at his theatre, the Odéon, one of the oldest theatres on the left bank in Paris and he invited

Trumpets to participate. The festival would include companies such as Olivier's National Theatre, as well as companies from Czechoslovakia, South Africa, China and many others. We would be the sole American representative.

But where was the money going to come from? As we would be there on behalf of the United States I asked The State Department for assistance, but they declined to support us. Sam Zolotow, theatre columnist of *The New York Times* ran an article about our dilemma, in which I was quoted as saying that, "We didn't have the money to go," or words to that effect.

Two days later I got a call from one Irving Rossi who invited me to his office on Wall Street overlooking the Hudson River. Mr. Rossi, in his early 80s was a sturdy man with steel-gray hair, a ruddy complexion, a gentle smile and a twinkle in his eye. I've always trusted a man with a twinkle in his eye—they see the humor in life. People have often said that I have a smile like the Mona Lisa, which I'm told is mysterious but inviting.

Mr. Rossi's back was as straight as a marine sergeant's. He attributed his longevity and robust physical fitness to daily horseback riding at his home in New Jersey. His other health secret was an annual visit to a Swiss spa. I've been looking for that spa ever since! I'll let you know if I find it. Was Ponce de León Swiss?

Mr. Rossi wanted to help me to bring *Trumpets* to Paris and give us part of the money to make the journey possible. Mr. Rossi became a good friend of the Circle and contributed to several other productions. He was a personable and witty man who never wanted any recognition for his contribution. He told me that he had made his fortune in the steel business, by a special process that preserved the spill when steel is subjected to intense heat.

Howard Schwartz helped us with the rest of the money. He was anxious to videotape *Trumpets* after we came back from Paris. So Will B. Sandler, who was also an attorney, took care of getting the television rights. After returning to the U.S we went to Canada and televised the production under my direction. James Earl Jones and Jane White joined the company.

I also directed the show in Paris with American actors living in Europe. We rehearsed in a studio in the Odéon surrounded by old theatrical trunks and the kind of large, curved windows you might see in films about the French Revolution. The trunks were filled with costumes some 100 years old. As we breathed deeply we smelled antiquity and the ghosts still inhabited the skirts, jackets, and pockets. In other words it was pretty musty up there but a thrill to be working in the middle of all this theatrical history. It reminded me of a song my son Jonathan wrote, "Haunted Clothes," about a dude who's just outfitted himself at a used clothing store and as he's strutting down the street he hears strange voices—out of his pants pocket, out of his shirt pocket—the ghosts of the previous owners.

The night we opened, the audience was in a riot of enthusiasm and stopped the show many times shouting bravos. The next day the critics were "plus, plus," and Parisians were lined up outside the box office onto the street, which made me very happy. But I realized that the line was not moving. The French box office manner is very different from the United States and particularly New York's. Each ticket buyer was asked by the treasurer to identify where he wanted to sit by looking at the seating chart on the little counter at the box office. Then there would be a prolonged discussion between the treasurer and the prospective patron about the pros and cons of the desired locations.

As we got closer to curtain time, I was desperate for the line to move quickly because we still had empty seats. There were plenty of people to fill them if only they could get past the box office confer-ence. Part of the receipts went to us and we needed the money to meet our expenses. I tried cajoling the treasurer with the little French I knew from high school, "Vite, vite!" And then resorted to Italian, "Pronto, pronto!" Then finally English, "Faster, faster." As much as I pleaded with them, the box office staff went their sublime, dignified, plodding French way.

Have you ever observed how slowly French diners cut their salad with a knife and fork? As contrasted to the American style of fork crashing down on lettuce and jamming the whole leaf into mouth. How fastidi-ous the French are about this process. Now place that picture in your mind and merge it with a mustachioed treasurer proceeding at the French lettuce-cutting pace. They were too grand to rush. Even though people were abandoning the line because the curtain had gone up! It

Cicely Tyson, Theresa Merritt, and Lex Monson in
James Weldon Johnson's *Trumpets of the Lord* (1963),
directed by Donald McKayle

was the first time in my career I questioned the adage "The show must go on!" Yes, but not yet!

But still we were a hit. *Le Figaro*, France's most important newspaper, compared us to Britain's National Theatre, which had just performed a Shakespeare play at the Festival, and declared the American actors in *Trumpets* were "superior" to them. We were such a raving hit that Lars Schmidt (former husband of Ingrid Bergman) invited us to his theatre—it was now August. In the summertime all French citizens flee Paris. I gained that knowledge through my son, Andrew, who has lived happily in France for the last fifteen years. We limped along for several weeks but, by September we had expired, evaporated with the famous Parisian heat.

It was a wonderful time for all of us. On opening night, the United States ambassador to France, William Bullit, held a reception for us at the embassy. Where we were wined and dined.

I visited Versailles with my literary advisor Gillian Walker, a brilliant, charming woman who is now head of the Ackerman Family Institute. The King's Palace was closed but we had a most pleasurable experience walking around the gardens. We saw trees that extended as far as the eye can see in three different directions. (Unfortunately, the storm that swept through Europe several years ago destroyed most of these trees.) It was late in the afternoon and there were only a few visitors there and I was able to imagine myself in that time, strolling among the people in their royal costumes and long curled wigs. Still in my mind I was using a four-foot walking stick as G.C. did in *Children of Darkness*. There wasn't a single scrap of paper or cigarette butt to be seen. And the grass was pristine. Gillian and I accepted this unspoken invitation and rested in it. In my many visits to France to see my son Andrew and his children we always go to the national parks or forests and they are immaculate. The French respect their treasures. The famous French fastidiousness has its benefits.

During the run of *Trumpets*, I was invited to reside at the American Embassy in Paris. What a beautiful chateau—surrounded by a thin iron fence and two armed marines always on duty at the gate. Those were the days. Pre–cement security blocks.

I slept in the same room and bed that Charles Lindbergh had in 1929 after his historic flight from Long Island to Paris. Each night, before I went to sleep, I was expected to leave a note for the butler with my breakfast, newspaper, and arousal-time orders. My shoes were to be left outside the door to be polished.

In the morning at the designated hour a butler entered, drew the bath, pulled back the heavy drapes and brought in my breakfast to the bed on a tray. Then he brought back my now clean and highly polished shoes. What luxury! I felt like I was Lindbergh and the crowds were outside cheering for my beautiful production.

One Sunday morning I woke up and there was no butler. I was shocked and indignant. How could I possibly pull the drapes back and draw the bath all by myself! I felt faint. My shoes were not shined and there was no newspaper! I rang for service and no one answered. I got dressed and went in the hallway, called out, but there was no response. I went walking down the corridors to try and find someone but incredibly there wasn't a single person in the embassy! I thought there'd been a military attack of some kind! I made my way to the front door and found the two marine guards who informed me that as it was Sunday everyone had gone to an official event and the embassy was closed for the rest of the day. I had to go out all by myself and find a croissant and coffee!

The performance of *Trumpets* in Paris was inspired, the actors were enthused by the passion the audience had for the poetry, music, and acting. It was a stunning engagement, and a great honor to be America's cultural representatives.

A couple of months later Paul and I brought the production to New York thinking that the international hoorahs would spill over to Broadway but as Maurice Chevalier has said, "Paris is not Broadway." Oddly enough, Baltimore was. The black audience came out in huge numbers when we opened there in the enormous Mechanic Theatre (operated by James Nederlander) and filled the seats for two solid weeks. We had also had a sold out stay at Ford's Theatre in Washington, D.C., and next we took it to Los Angeles.

Because of time considerations we had to fly the set from Baltimore to Los Angeles. Paul hired the Flying Tigers Airlines—independent pilots who flew cargo from India to China for General Chenault for the U.S. Army and were lovingly designated as the Flying Tigers. The set was a replica of a small southern rural church. So it was really just wooden slats with a small stained-glass window in the center to give the impression of us being in the church. From the airport to the theatre the set was transported in a long cargo truck. We had hired the Flying Tigers because they assured us that they would protect the set. When it arrived at the theatre the driver opened up the back of the truck, I looked into the darkened interior. I asked, "Where is the set?" and the driver said, "up front" and up front I saw a pile of wooden slats neatly tied together. They had preserved it all right but had disassembled it!

We were supposed to start a technical rehearsal that morning. The stagehands were already in the theatre to put up the set. Instead, all of us had to get down on our hands and knees and reconfigure it. Fortunately nothing was lost and we were able to get the set up in about nine hours. Finally at five o'clock we had the set ready for our technical rehearsal.

In Baltimore and Washington, the word of mouth in the churches brought out our audiences, but in L.A. the churches, like everything else, are so spread out, we never could generate the same contagious word of mouth.

CHAPTER 23

A Quiet Dinner in Rome

Desire was winding down and I needed a new production. Once more the wand of fate tapped me on the shoulder.

In the summer of 1962, I was interested in making a film of Elmer Rice's *The Adding Machine.* I was going to produce it with Jerry Epstein, Charlie Chaplin's good friend and assistant. Rod Steiger had expressed interest in doing the film. So I flew to Rome to meet with Rod and went on the set where he was making a film with Shelley Winters. When they finished shooting for the day, Rod invited me to his home for dinner and to meet his wife, Claire Bloom. There's a big difference between seeing an actor on screen and across a dinner table—Claire's exquisite beauty close up had a glowing porcelain fineness to go along with her extreme gracefullness. Their maid served dinner and the conversation was convivial. I asked Claire what she had been doing and she told me she had recently finished performing a production of Euripides' *The Trojan Women* at the Spoletto Festival in Italy. A bell rang in my head. When she told me that Mildred Dunnock had played Hecuba in that production—the bells rang even louder and my heart started to race. When I heard Milly's name, one of our most esteemed actresses (Linda in *Death of a Salesmen*), my mind instantly called up her "Attention must be paid." The bells were ringing even louder and I most definitely was paying attention.

I cautiously asked Claire, "Would you like to come to New York to the Circle and repeat your role as Andromache?" Her eyes shone and with a big smile she vigorously shook her head and said, "Yes!" and she added, "I know Millie would like to do it again." Rod then volunteered that he would allow us to use his recorded voice reading the lines of Poseidon.

I asked her who the director was. Claire answered a wonderful Greek, Michael Cacoyannis. I thought this will throw the whole project off: a Greek director who can't speak English, and whose name I couldn't even pronounce. I hopefully asked her, "Does he speak any English?" And she said, "Oh yes."

After this happy and exciting exchange during dinner, tension between Rod and Claire started to surface. They began to speak very icily and briefly to each other, which made me sitting in between them very uncomfortable. I was embarrassed to my soul by how they were treating each other.

Claire went off to bed to terminate the acrimony. Rod continued to speak enthusiastically about the *Trojan Women*. He urged me to do it. He was not interested in *The Adding Machine*, which was the purpose of my visit, but lo and behold here was another potential project with the wonderful dew-like beauty Claire Bloom on the horizon and so out of a missed opportunity came something very good.

The next day Shelley Winters saw me in the lobby of the Hilton and invited me to sight-see Rome and have lunch together. She had a studio limo at her disposal. We had a great two days together seeing the sights and enjoying the Italian food—her big limo honking its way through the narrow, crowded streets of Rome.

The next day I was leaving to go back to New York, but the hotel desk clerk wouldn't take my check. I called Shelley on the house phone and asked her, "Would you please tell the clerk that I am trustworthy?" She got angry and said, "What kind of a producer are you? Don't you carry a credit card?" This was 1962, credit cards had just barely hit and they had not reached me. She refused to help and slammed the phone down. There I was in the lobby and I offered to do dishes or whatever they wanted. I assured them the check was good. They looked me over and decided that my doing their dishes was more risky than taking my check.

I dashed out of the hotel and leapt into a taxi—piloted by a cabdriver right out of John Huston's *Beat the Devil*, a little fat roly-poly man with a mustache wearing an ill-fitting suit and chauffeur's cap. He was driving his own cab and proceeded at an escargot's pace. I kept bellowing,

"Pronto! Airplane! Pronto!" But he stopped—he had to get his coffee as well as gasoline. He stirred the coffee slowly with a small spoon to cool it off. Meantime, I'm going silently crazy since the plane was about to leave. My delay at the checkout counter at the Hilton had made my arrival for the flight quite precarious.

As we arrived at the terminal twenty minutes before departure, I saw my Alitalia plane taxiing out on the runway. I shouted through the thick glass, waving frantically to try and stop them. The plane kept moving. I ran to the ticket counter and began shouting at the Italian clerk who said in broken English, "Yes, we leave early because plane filled." Gathered around the desk were other irate passengers, Chinese, German, English, Japanese, American all shouting in their native tongues, at the top of their lungs. I saw their jugular veins popping. I stopped and thought what am I doing? Nothing can change the plane leaving. Shouting will not bring it back. I took a deep breath and waited four hours for the next flight.

Claire had given me Cacoyannis's number in Athens and I called him when I got back to New York. We agreed he would come and direct *The Trojan Women* for the Circle. I was so pleased to hear him speak such perfect English; he'd been educated in London. Later, after his visit to the United States, Michael felt the Spoletto production of the play would fit perfectly into the Circle. Michael and I talked about the scenery and he wanted to have a cyclorama in front of which were platforms, Greek columns and steps leading down to the stage where most of the action took place. The costumes would be in the period of the play with the music of Jean Prodromides.

CHAPTER 24

AN ESCAPE ROUTE

When I took the leadership of the Circle in 1962, I met with Mrs. O'Neill to ask permission to produce O'Neill's *Hughie*. She granted me that. And also gave me the rights in perpetuity for film and television.

Sometime before Paul and I produced *Hughie* in 1964, I had taken Mrs. O'Neill to see *Laterna Magika* a Checkloslovakian Company at Carnegie Hall. They used voiceovers for actors' inner thoughts. After the performance, as we strolled back towards her hotel, Mrs. O'Neill brought up the voiceovers and said if that method had been invented, Gene would have used it for *Hughie*. I stuck that idea in the back of my head. Those inner thoughts of the night clerk in *Hughie* were written so beautifully but are inaccessible to audiences because they're in the stage directions and not normally spoken. Audiences didn't know what the clerk was thinking, so I thought maybe we could use the Laterna Magika method to relay his inner dialogue. I knew that it had to be delicate so as not to interfere with the play.

Later, when we were ready to produce *Hughie*, Paul and I went to see movie mogul Joseph E. Levine about partnering with us. As we entered the long hallway towards his office, the walls were covered with posters of films he had produced. When we were ushered into his office, sitting behind the desk was a suntanned, short, heavyset man. The wall behind him was all glass with a magnificent view of New York City. He was on the top floor of this building on Sixth Avenue. I commented,

"Mr. Levine, what a view from the top of this building." And he said, "Yeah, I'm so high up, I can kiss God's ass." At the meeting he agreed to participate with us. Joe put up all the money for the production—I think it was $75,000.

In our production, Jason Robards played Erie Smith and Jack Dodson was the night clerk, directed by José at the Royale Theatre on Broadway. I loved the idea of all of us working together again. We were reunited, with David Hays once again creating magic with his scenic design. We'd been through the wars together and understood each other very well. We hadn't all worked together since *Long Day's Journey Into Night* in 1956.

Jack Dodson and Jason Robards, Jr., in Eugene O'Neill's *Hughie* (1964), directed by José Quintero

Erie is another version of *Iceman*'s Hickey so Jason was raring to go. Jack as the night clerk, had a long face with a dour cast and expressionless eyes. He is the confessional priest that Erie desperately needs to get him through his mourning for the loss of Hughie, the night clerk who had just died. Erie loved Hughie because, "He gave me confidence."

As I am writing this, Al Pacino's reading of the word "confidence" jumps back into my head (we produced *Hughie* with Al at the Circle in 1996; more on this production later)—Al said "CON-fi-dence." He broke it up into three syllables, pausing slightly on FI and then pushing home on DENCE. The way he pronounced the word was like the excitement of a horse race.

Hughie is fifty-five minutes long so I tried to find another one-act to match it with. But I never did find the right mix. With a new O'Neill play starring Jason Robards (the star of *Iceman* and *Journey* and a burgeoning movie career) I thought we could succeed even though the evening would just be a long one-act play. So Paul and I decided we'd produce it by itself, knowing full well some people might complain about its brevity—I felt it was a masterpiece and the audiences would be more than satisfied.

The reviews were excellent—in fact many did indeed acknowledge it to be a minor masterpiece. The audiences were excellent too, and after a decent run on Broadway we took it to San Francisco. This was the third play of O'Neill's (with *Long Day's* and *Moon*) that I premiered in the U.S. as a producer.

In San Francisco, Paul and I met for lunch with the owner of the Curran Theatre, Louis Lorie, and he told us interesting tales about theatre in San Francisco that went back fifty years. He was an elegant elderly man, dressed as sharp as a gambler, and his stories complemented his attire. He had an associate with him who helped him sit down at the table, but as he told the stories his strength and vigor rebounded. In fact, he subsequently rose and walked out of the restaurant without assistance! After San Francisco, where good reviews brought good business, we went on to Los Angeles to Jimmy Doolittle's Huntington Hartford Theatre to great acclaim!

Years later in 1996, as I said, the Circle produced *Hughie* with Al Pacino. Al had Erie's street smarts down to his fingertips. In this production, The Night Clerk, who is as stone-faced as a Mayan statue, was played by Paul Benedict. He looked like death until towards the end of the play when he comes to life through Erie's prodding. I remembered what Mrs. O'Neill had said about the voiceovers in *Laterna Magika* so when I directed Al in a workshop the year before at the Circle on Bleecker Street, we began to experiment with the idea in rehearsal. We realized it fit perfectly and gave Erie "silence time." While the night clerk spoke his inner thoughts, Erie/Al invested his own thoughts and was just as alive in his silence. When Al later directed and starred in it for us at the Uptown Circle, he used the voiceover technique we had worked on.

A few years later, Circle co-produced *Hughie* with Gordon Davidson at The Mark Taper Forum in Los Angeles with Al and Paul repeating their roles. Once again it was a total sellout. Al's presence obviously helped its success, but I also believe that the amplification of the night clerk's inner thoughts was an important added element for the audience to understand the play more deeply.

Back in 1964, when we produced *Hughie* in L.A., John Carradine came by to take Jason to lunch at the Brown Derby. Several hours later they staggered back to the theatre. I can still see them stumbling their way arm in arm down the sun-blinded L.A. streets, holding each other up. They were both sloshed, I mean to the ground, and as they entered the theatre Carradine announced to Jason in magisterial Shakespearean tones, "I have better projection than you." And to prove it he crawled up on the stage on his hands and knees. He managed to get to his feet and staggeringly delivered Hamlet's "To be or not to be" soliloquy, while Jason, at the back of the theatre, weaving, held onto a theatre seat to steady himself. To Carradine's credit, while his body was unsteady, his voice was unwavering, thundering throughout the house. Jason called out, in his best Shakespearean tone, "I say, old chap, what did you say?" Carradine responded with, "You come up here and I will go to the rear of the theatre and I will see if I can hear you!" Then they reversed—Jason onto the stage, where he did Macbeth's speech "that we but teach Bloody instructions, which being taught return to plague the inventor." Of course, neither thought much of the other's abilities. As drunk as they were they were letter-perfect in their soliloquies—God bless actors! Paul and I cajoled them, assuring each that his projection was better than the other's. So Carradine wandered off in the direction of the Brown Derby and Jason went to his dressing room and promptly fell asleep, each comforted by his projection victory.

The L.A. run was successful and all of Hollywood came to see Jason. He was partying and enjoying the lionization of the Hollywood community.

One night in New York I was having dinner with Jason's agent Peter Witt at Dinty Moore's restaurant right next door to the Helen Hayes Theatre where we had performed *Long Day's Journey Into Night*. Peter was a Viennese man and one of the most important actor agents in New York. He was friendly and very chatty with a delicious sly sense of gossip and humor and he enjoyed a good laugh. This particular night we were seated at a table in the back near the kitchen doors. I wondered why Peter had chosen this particular table when the restaurant was practically empty. I was later to find out the answer.

While he was laughing and telling me a funny story he saw Jason out of the corner of his eye entering the restaurant. Jason was obviously tipsy. Peter's smile dropped as fast as a guillotine and without saying a word, clutching his napkin he darted out and disappeared through the kitchen doors, which had a separate exit to the street. Jason found some friends in the front corner and sat down with them. I quickly paid the bill but did not employ Peter's same escape method—I walked out the front door. As wonderful a person and actor as Jason was, sometimes when he'd had a few drinks, it wasn't pleasant. In fact, this eventually would strain our friendship for a number of years.

In 1997, a memorial service for Travis Bogard, the great O'Neill scholar, was held at the Monte Cristo cottage in New London, Connecticut. We were all standing in a semicircle in the living room of the O'Neill house and various speakers got up to express their feeling about Travis. Amongst them were Arthur Gelb and Jason. After Jason finished he crossed to where I was standing and stood alongside of me listening to the speakers. After a while he gently put his arm around my shoulder. And after a couple of beats, I did the same. We turned and faced each other smiling broadly remembering the good times we had together, standing in the place where all of our dedication to O'Neill had started.

From that time on Jason and I remained good friends and on October 16, 2000, Paul Libin and I, for Circle in the Square, placed a plaque on what had been the Barrett House Hotel at Broadway and 43rd where O'Neill was born on October 16, 1888. At the luncheon afterwards, Jason got up to speak at the end of which he said, "My career was made possible by three people, Eugene O'Neill, José Quintero, and Ted Mann." I was deeply gratified by Jason's gracious acknowledgement.

CHAPTER 25

A RETURN TO THE CLASSICS

Back once more to 1963. I went with the serendipity that had placed me at Claire Bloom's dinner table in a not so tranquil little villa outside of Rome. I quickly got a copy of *The Trojan Women* and fell in love with it. I had read it in college and thought it was a great play but now with us involved in the Vietnam War I felt it would have great significance for the audience. The play deals with very human emotions in times of war. Some of my associates reminded me of the time when Greek classics badly done had been the death knell of the off-Broadway movement of the 1940s. I've always believed if you fall in love with a play, do it, and besides I'm a Taurus. So I took a gulp and went against the opposition. Thank God Patricia stood firm with me.

Michael Cacoyannis arrived in New York and the casting began. He is very musical, having studied and aspired to be an opera singer. He needed a chorus that could speak clearly. He tested them all for their singing ability and then the way they moved.

He came with his close friend, Yael Dayan (daughter of Israel's General Moshe Dayan) and she was very helpful to Michael. She is also diplomatically skilled and helped to smooth over rough patches because Michael is very precise; he knows exactly what he wants and he can, and does, demonstrate the rhythm of speech. Michael did not allow any variation of tone, volume, or enunciation. The actor had to speak it exactly the way Michael had just done. And he would repeat it

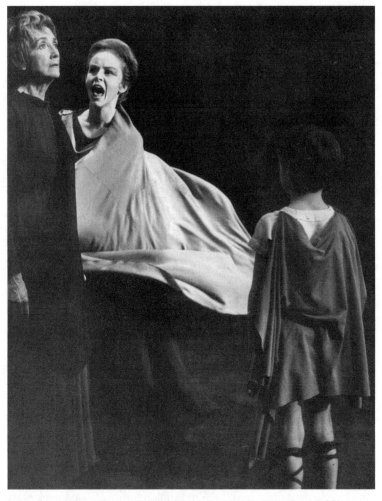

Mildred Dunnock, Joyce Ebert, and Michael Walker in Euripides' *The Trojan Women* (1963),
directed by Michael Cacoyannis

fifty times if necessary to make sure it was spoken the way he wanted.
These demonstrations are known as "line readings" and there is nothing
American actors hate more. There were some ruffled feathers and Yael
was constantly gently patting them back down.

Mildred Dunnock agreed to repeat her role as Hecuba, Joyce Ebert
was Andromache (as matters turned out, Claire Bloom couldn't repeat
her Spoletto role because of a film commitment), Carrie Nye played
Cassandra, Jane White took on Helen of Troy and Robert Mandan got

the role of Menelaus. Mildred (Millie) was the only one in the cast who had performed the play in Spoletto. Jane White is the daughter of William White, a famous black activist. She is a beautiful woman and I was determined to stray away from the traditional dewy blue-eyed blonde in that role.

While we were rehearsing, we got the news that President Kennedy was assassinated. We were stunned and people wept. Michael and I asked the actors if they wanted to continue and they said yes. So after several hours we resumed, but the rehearsal became a very solemn, important event and there was still more weeping and crying. We realized the only way we could get through that day was to go on with our work because this great antiwar play symbolized everything the President had stood for. The production became our dedication to John F. Kennedy. Some of his family must have felt the same, as Robert Kennedy and other family members later came to see the production.

Michael's precision and the insistence on his line readings paid off. The production was tight and powerful, running just one hour and ten minutes. The play's message was felt very deeply by the audience. Our production became one of the earliest anti–Vietnam War statements.

During the run of *The Trojan Women* I met Irene Papas, the superb Greek actress, an impressive beautiful woman with ravishing black hair, fine chiseled bones, and the nose of a Greek sculpture. Irene loves to laugh and we have had many great times together. She was anxious to do a Greek play with us. One of the funniest moments we shared was when she got members of the New York Greek community together at a Greek restaurant to interest them in funding future classic Greek plays that we would do. They were all friendly and cordial but did not donate a single drachma. They reminded me of the fatcats in Detroit. Smiles and charms evaporated as soon as I mentioned money and their hurried frantic departure followed soon after. Irene and I were left alone in the restaurant and we laughed convulsively about the money ship that sunk before it reached port.

In 1964, *Othello*, directed by Gladys Vaughan with James Earl Jones and Mitch Ryan, was performed in the Central Park Shakespeare Theatre. I asked Joe Papp if I could bring it to off-Broadway and he agreed. So I leased the Martinique, which Paul was still operating, and we de-

James Earl Jones in Shakespeare's *Othello* (1964),
directed by Gladys Vaughn

cided to do two plays in repertory—maybe this could be the beginning of a repertory company. The second play was *Baal*, one of Bertolt Brecht's earlier works.

Mitch and Jimmy were terrific together as Iago and Othello. I've never seen a more passionate "Moor." Jimmy literally did fall in love with his Desdemona, played by Julienne Marie, and in real life married her. (They are since divorced, with Jimmy now happily married to his darling Ceci.) Mitch played Iago and Bette Henritze his wife Emilia. Mitch's Iago was a conniving, brilliant, cowering peasant with tremendous charm. It is interesting that in both plays, *Othello* and *Baal*, the leads were in the throes of love—in *Othello* his love for Desdemona was the source of Iago's jealousy and the inspiration for his revenge; in *Baal* the two men for each other. At one point in *Baal* Mitch and Jimmy kiss passionately on the lips. Audiences were shocked—another first for Circle.

Jimmy was majestic as Othello and handled the language beautifully and portrayed the conflict he suffers with genuine human feeling. At the same time we put *Othello* on, Laurence Olivier was performing it in London and several critics commented that Jimmy's *Othello* was far superior. However, my dream of a repertory company evaporated as Jimmy and others were lured away by more remunerative projects.

In 1966, Paul and I saw a series of one-act plays at La Mama which we decided to move to The Martinique. We entitled the evening *Six from La Mama*. For these six writers this would be their first time off-Broadway. The playwrights were Sam Shepard, Lanford Wilson, Leonard Melfi, Jean-Claude Van Itallie, Paul Foster, and William Hoffman.

Paul and I felt that these young writers were extremely talented and deserved to reach a larger audience. Their later success has certainly justified our belief in them.

In the preceeding month Andy Warhol told me that he wanted to create a theatre film experience and asked me to find him a place to do it. He said, "I need a wall I can project my film on." I thought, what about the theatre part of it? I was elated to experience his masterful idea.

I found The Polish Hall known as the Dom on East Eighth Street with a large audience space and unobstructed back wall. But we could only have it for the month of April since it was rented thereafter. We presented what Andy called *The Exploding Plastic Inevitable* with his Velvet Underground band who became world famous. I set a low price of admission of $6. It became an instantaneous hit and was filled to the brim every night. All the proceeds went directly to Andy's place of work, the Factory.

I now saw what he meant by "film theatre." Andy had created something completely innovative with performers on stage either speaking, singing, or reciting poems while behind them on the back wall was film footage that Andy had shot earlier of the actors. I thought Frank Sinatra's people should see this. This would be fantastic for him. I don't know if they ever did but sometime later it must have come to the attention of the MTV people and they copied the idea. Andy had launched a new concept that was to become part of our culture as evidenced by the rock music concerts we see today with films behind the performers and smoke floating in from all directions.

Andy was a fan of Patricia's and we became very friendly. One night he came over with a little book in his hand and said, in his whisper-like voice, "I want to give this to you." It was twelve pages of handdrawn cats. Patricia was pregnant with Jonathan at the time. She loved them. Two of the cats have survived in a mural on the wall in Andrew's bedroom that Patricia painted in her always creative efforts. It depicts a country scene with the oncoming baby Jonathan, Andrew, Patricia as Alice in Wonderland, and our Jamaican housekeeper.

I'd been speaking to Michael Cacoyannis about doing a Greek classic for Irene Papas. I wanted very much to do a Euripides play because I felt his work, more than any other Greek classical writer, speaks to contemporary audiences in emotional terms that are more accessible—especially when translated by Edith Hamilton. I began to read his plays to see what was best for Irene.

In 1967 Michael, Irene and I finally settled on *Iphigenia in Aulis*, the heartbreaking story of a mother having to sacrifice her daughter to satisfy the Gods.

The role of Agamemnon was played by Mitch Ryan. I admired Mitch as an actor and as a person and I knew he was a heavy drinker, which disrupted the production on several occasions. One night, he was late, and I jumped in my car, trying to find him in one of the bars in the Village. While I was wildly hunting for him, he came in and he'd had a few drinks. He assured me that he would be okay and that he could do the performance. But his first line when he came onstage was "Clytemnestra, baby." Irene, whose back was to him, turned slowly in a profound lengthy silence and fixed her two eyes on him like a death ray. It instantly sobered him and he finished the performance without a single mistake. There is no stronger wind than a female Grecian fury—but the next day she was as calm as the Aegean Sea.

Frank Langella played Achilles and irony of ironies just before the first preview he sprained his ankle! I took him to the hospital and when I came back to the theatre the show was on and Michael was reading Frank Langella's part, book in hand, in his Italian silk suit and pointy shoes. It was quite a sight against the backdrop of the Greek temple and the costumes and the flowing female robes. It was brave and honorable for Michael to do that. Frank couldn't return and was replaced by Christopher Walken, always a dynamite actor. The music by Marvin David Levy was very modern and exciting. We got through the rest of the run fine and the play received wonderful reviews. It was successful but not to the degree that *Trojan Women* had been. Irene's performance confirmed that she is one of the greatest actresses I have worked with.

CHAPTER 26

HUNTING FOR GOLD

In 1964, Peter Shaffer's *Royal Hunt of the Sun* opened at the National Theatre in London to sensational reviews—the kind that playwrights dream about—directed by John Dexter. It was optioned for New York by Joseph E. Levine, David Suskind, and Daniel Melnick. One day Joe called and asked us did we want to co-produce *Hunt*? It was a show any producer would jump at. We asked how much money we would have to raise. He said, "I'll take care of that." Then we said we'd like to read it. Joe said, "Why read it when you can go see it. Go to London and see if you like it. Tell me if it's good—I haven't seen it myself."

This was to be Joe's second venture on Broadway having previously done *Hughie* with us. He was a veteran film producer who entered the business when he got involved with the United States rights to *Godzilla*. He'd come from a poor immigrant family in Boston, with no high school education. He was of the streets and now he was on top of the world. He loved to tell stories about his upbringing, in particular about his dominant father, who would come home from work and knock Joe and his siblings around to remind them who the boss was. They were fiercely funny stories in which he went into detail about his family's behavior at the dining room table—forks, knives, spoons, and dishes flew in the air.

Shortly after our meeting with Joe, Paul and I hopped the plane for London. We saw the play and loved it. So Paul promptly went to work and negotiated all the contracts including Peter Shaffer's agent, the National Theatre, Michael Annals as scenic and costume designer, Madame Claude Chagrin the mime choreographer, and director John Dexter. Paul made arrangements with the National once the show closed in London to ship the scenery, costumes and props in the hold of a ship bound for New York. In effect, we were piggybacking *Royal Hunt* to New York, saving us the great expense of building it here.

I went to the prop man's house and he showed me around. I admired an antique brass bed that was taken apart and leaning against a wall. He said it was junk. He was throwing it away. I asked if I could buy it and he said no, I'll give it to you. "We're buying a good modern bed," he explained. So the "junk" traveled in the ship's hold as one of the Inca artifacts and has been my bed ever since.

After these accomplishments, we came back to New York and went to Joe Levine's office. He stunned us with the announcement that he didn't want to do the production and was stepping out of the project. So there Paul and I were with this fantastic play and contracts in hand but no money to produce what was to be one of the most expensive dramatic productions ever done on Broadway—about $350,000. Remember, this was 1965! And this was with a cast of twenty-four! Today a Broadway production with a cast of just four people can cost up to $2 million.

Joe's backing out didn't deter us, in fact it inspired us. And Paul and I were like two producer firecrackers burning up the telephones trying to raise money. Philip Langner of the Theatre Guild agreed to come on board and help.

For several years before this event was taking place, Paul and I had sent bus and truck tours of Circle in the Square Productions to theatres and college campuses around the country. One of the most esteemed settings was the Greek Theatre at the University of California at San Francisco run by Travis Bogard. The Ravinia Festival outside of Chicago, run by Hope Abelson, had invited us to participate and present *The Trojan Women*. We got very good reviews and the next season she invited me to bring another play. I chose William Alfred's *Hogan's Goat*, which I directed with Mitch Ryan and Joan Potter.

Both Mitch and Joan were excellent. He's a troubled priest, which Mitch, being an Irish Catholic, understood down to his fingertips. She's a prim and proper lady struggling with the conflict between spirituality and lust. We presented it in a Seminary auditorium so our Gregorian choral music fit the surroundings perfectly. The music even echoed through the hallways, filled with priests walking around, adding to the whole atmosphere of the play. The show got very good reviews and we were nominated for several Chicago theatre awards.

When the whole financial quagmire with *Royal Hunt* arose I called Hope Abelson to ask her if she would participate. She agreed to help. The last to come on board was Gerard Oestreicher.

As the money came in for *Royal Hunt*, Paul and I began to see sunlight in the dark cave that a producer inhabits before funds are in place. We invited John Dexter to come to New York to begin casting. After looking around at several Broadway theatres to house the production we chose the ANTA Theatre, now the August Wilson, which was owned by my good friend Roger L. Stevens.

Christopher Plummer agreed to play Francisco Pizzaro; the commander of the Expedition and David Carradine was cast as Atahuallpa, the Sun God of his Inca Empire (Peru, where the Spaniards came to find gold).

Once casting was complete rehearsals began. John Dexter was friendly to begin with, but as he got through the second week he got very tense and ordered that rehearsals be closed to any viewers. He particularly didn't want the producers to watch. This was a stupid idea and we fought him about it. Ultimately he relented. During rehearsals he would pick out an actress playing a small role and berate her brutally in front of the other actors. Needless to say he became very unpopular with the company.

John Dexter had been lionized for *Royal Hunt* in London as well as for other plays he had done, so he was feeling his importance and wanted everyone to bow down to him. During rehearsals Dexter complained defiantly about the color of the walls in the audience section of the theatre. He said that they conflicted with the set and insisted that they be painted. Obviously this became a great problem. We only had four days of technical rehearsal. To paint the theatre would take at least a week, not to mention the tremendous cost of doing it. Paul dealt with Dexter on this problem and each day he would show him samples of colors for the painting. And each day Dexter in his usual noncoopera-

David Carradine and Christopher Plummer in Peter Shaffer's *The Royal Hunt of the Sun* (1965), directed by John Dexter

tive way would reject them. By the fourth day, he had totally forgotten about the color of the walls.

Despite the scenic pieces and props that were coming from London there were still sections that had to be built here in New York. The set piece that we had the most difficulty with was the sun, which hung on the back wall. All eight petals had to open and close simultaneously for the Sun God's entrance and exit. If one petal was out of line, the entire mechanism didn't work. The building of all these pieces and the operation of the sun were under Paul's genius technical supervision. The working of the sun was particularly difficult and kept getting stuck during rehearsals. Everybody was perplexed, throwing up their hands in disgust. But Paul solved the problem by meticulously coordinating the machinery for each petal.

Christopher Plummer was fabulous in the role and his performance led the production to a wonderful success. Chris is one of the finest actors of our time. During the run of *Royal Hunt*, he, Jason and George became drinking buddies and would all hang out after their respective shows for a relaxing interlude. Recently I was at a private screening of *Eugene O'Neill: a Documentary Film* created for PBS by Ric Burns. Chris and I embraced with all the good feelings in our memories of the *Hunt*. Chris looks as handsome as he did forty-one years ago. He is still a striking man and as robust and quick-witted as ever.

I've seen many productions of *Long Day's Journey Into Night* and the greatest James Tyrone has always been for me Fredric March from our

'56 production until I saw Chris in the documentary. His performance in the fourth act scene was astonishing and every bit as touching, warm and vulnerable as Freddie. When Chris spoke a line from Shakespeare he did it with the command of a great Shakespearean actor. At the same screening Jason was once again up there on the screen as Hickey and to hear his deep rumbly yearning voice again brought tears to my eyes.

Later we had a panel discussion of the film with Barbara and Arthur Gelb, Zoe Caldwell, Lloyd Richards, and Chris. Chris told a very funny story about how one night in a narrow bar just off Broadway where he and Jason were drinking a mounted policeman was outside. Jason invited him in and later the horse. They all had a round of drinks including the horse. The policeman had to return to duty and they had a very difficult time turning the horse around. It was finally accomplished and the policeman and the horse weaved out of the bar back to duty.

George, Jason and Chris's drinking was a kind of twenties thing. They were reliving the days of John Barrymore, when heavy drinking was a mark of social distinction. It was glamorous. Jason and Chris eventually gave it up but George couldn't and wouldn't. Most of the time the booze had little effect on him. During all the shows I did with him, he only missed a couple of performances because of it. I think he worried that he wasn't completely fulfilling the character and drank to overcome this. I have to say though, when he did return whatever fear or panic I felt was more than washed away by the glory of what he was doing on stage.

Jason had a serious auto accident in California and Lois, his wife, helped him recover. Christopher had his new wife for support. George was married to Colleen twice then was married to Trish for over twenty years, but even their love couldn't stop his drinking—nothing could.

After the run of *Royal Hunt* we sent it out on tour with a new cast and it did very well. Its last stop was Los Angeles where it played outdoors at the huge Greek Theatre in Hollywood. To watch this play under the stars was the perfect setting (which I doubt any color of paint could reproduce). When the Incas first saw Pizzaro and his men bestride their horses, they thought they were Gods because they had never seen a horse before. As a result, the Sun God and his people all willingly cooperated with the Conquistadors who impoverished the people, pillaged all of their gold, and ultimately destroyed what had been a glorious harmonious civilization. They also killed Atahualpa and demolished his city. I was sure that someday *Hunt* would be made into a wonderful film. It did happen but, unfortunately, it wasn't successful. By the way, the horses that Pizzaro's Conquistadors brought to Peru eventually spread throughout North America and later became the horses of the American Indian.

CHAPTER 27

A Blackout and a White Devil

Our next production, *The Zulu and the Zayda*, which Doré Schary adapted and directed, starred Louis Gossett Jr., Menasha Skulnik, and Ossie Davis.

The play is about the relationship of Zayda (a grandfather) and a smart young black native man in South Africa. It was a sweet play in which the characters try to bridge the differences of the two cultures by showing their similarities. It had only a couple of months' run at the Cort Theatre on 48th Street because the critics thought it unimportant and dismissed it. Before the critics came to render their Olympian opinion, it had sold out all preview performances with wild appreciation from the audience. AHHH! The glorious power of the pen. And UG-GHH! The destructive power of the critical pen!

Before we opened, at one of our early previews, the great New York City blackout occurred. I was playing full court basketball at the YMCA on 47th Street. My fellow basketeers were Burt Bacharach, composer; Phil Berger, novelist; Ira Berkow, sports columnist for the *Times*; and others. All ten players stopped and touched their hearts to verify that they were still alive. It was now about 5:30 P.M. and I got in my car and drove across town to the theatre. Self-appointed traffic cops made the traffic even worse. I finally got to the theatre around seven. There were a bunch of customers standing outside wondering if there was going to be a show. I said, "I don't know." Televisions and radios were not working. These were the days before cell phones. I went into the dark theatre and at stage left I saw a dim orange light shining from backstage. I proceeded to stumble over seats and finally reached the source of the light. It was Menasha's dressing room. He was fully dressed in his costume with a candle on his table. Menasha was 86 and lived way uptown and I said, "How did you get here with no trains, cabs, or buses?" He said, "I walked," and added pointing his finger at me, "I'm here! You must pay me! It's Actor's Equity rule!" He was the oldest of any of the actors, by I think, fifty years, but he was the one who got there. Talk about the show must go on. Of course all performances on Broadway were canceled that night.

When I got home my little boys Andrew and Jonathan, six and four, respectively, were huddled and frightened around their tiny eating table with one candle. The Jamaican maid was trying to comfort them but they wanted mommy and daddy. Patricia was rehearsing at the State Theatre. When she got home we all went to the Russian Tea Room, which had no more electricity than anyplace else in the city. Candles adorned all the tables and it was magical with all their permanent Christmas decorations glittering in the candlelight. The oven was working. We gratefully accepted what was put on the table. This was one night in which the customer had to take what was served to him. It was a night we have all remembered.

With the negative reviews for the *Zulu and the Zayda*, audiences stopped coming—even after the electricity came back on. Paul and I had borrowed $50,000 from a friend to put the play on, which we were unable to pay back until Paul put together a summer stock tour of *Zulu* throughout the Northeast. We were confident that the Jewish audience would come out to see Menasha. In fact they did and almost all the performances were sold out. It was a very hot summer but we were cooled by the dollars blowing in and we were able to pay the friend back.

After a year's run, our production of *The Trojan Women* at the downtown Circle wound down and I was back to searching for a new show. A number of years before I had heard a reading of John Webster's *The White Devil* at the Phoenix Theatre. With its astonishing plot of love, sex and murder, I knew it was a play that someday we must do. I inquired and found that the director of that reading, Jack Landau, was available.

Off we went to put on this delicious Elizabethan play. It has glorious language and a delectable tale of upper-class vice. Webster was a contemporary of Shakespeare and I thought it important for us to present a voice from that time.

We cast Carrie Nye and Frank Langella in the leads, both seasoned off-Broadway actors very well equipped to handle the language. We got stellar reviews. The great British actress Glenda Jackson told me that our production was the best she'd ever seen of an Elizabethan play, a thrill for me coming from her. But unfortunately we were not attracting audiences. This was very unusual for off-Broadway. In all our previous productions good reviews meant good audiences, especially if *The New York Times* review was as positive as it was here. It was early 1966. This was the first indication Paul and I had that the boom of off-Broadway was waning.

CHAPTER 28

Dusty

I went to see a production of a new play at St. Clement's Church with a young actor who knocked me out. He portrayed a paranoid person who was extremely precise in his behavior so as to protect himself. After he shut the door he made sure that all ten locks were neatly closed. And, having completed that, he did it again, then again—three times in all. I was sure this was not in the script but came out of the actor's improvisation. He was the guy for me, the kind of actor I love. After the show, I met and liked him right off the bat and told him I wanted to find a play for him. He responded in his now-famous sweet nasal adenoidal tone, "Sure that would be swell." He probably thought that this was the usual after-show blather and he'd never see that guy again. His name was Dustin Hoffman.

I was determined to find a play for him. I began looking at the classics and anything new I could get my hands on. I came across Henry Livings' *Eh?* I don't remember how it came to my attention. I think Melvin Bernhardt, who'd directed it at the Cleveland Playhouse, sent it to me. I thought it had a perfect role for Dustin as Valentine, a Chaplin-like boiler repairman's assistant who does the wrong things but everything always turns out right anyway.

Bernhardt's Cleveland production had gotten good reviews, so I chose him to direct. We cast, beside Dustin, Elizabeth Wilson, Joe Maher, Linda Lavin, and Dana Elcar. All were top-flight off-Broadway actors that I'd seen perform comedy material. After about two weeks of rehearsal it was clear that the work was not going well. Elizabeth Wilson, one of the few people that ever used my full name, called me aside: "Theodore, the production is not going right." Dana said the same.

I sat in on rehearsals and did not find this comedy funny at all. The next morning I got a call from Mel asking me what I thought of the rehearsal. Before I could answer and say I was unhappy, he said, "What's wrong with this production is Dustin." I quickly responded, "The reason I'm doing this play is because of Dustin!" There was not much more conversation. I advised him that we were going ahead and sticking with Dustin. Mel was out and now I had to find another director.

I had seen Alan Arkin in *Enter Laughing* on Broadway and liked his work very much. For some reason the humor I saw in his performance seemed just what we needed from our new director. So I called my good friend and attorney, Sy Litvinoff, who represented Alan and he told me Alan was indeed anxious to direct.

I explained the situation to Alan and invited him to come and watch a rehearsal. He had never directed a play but if you saw him on stage as I had, you knew he was a thinking actor besides being a brilliant comic. He had been trained by and performed with Second City in Chicago. After the rehearsal he said that he would like to direct the play but he didn't want to use his name because he was a new director and was afraid that a bad review would ruin his directorial future. He invented a name or borrowed it from a former Brooklyn Dodger baseball player—Roger Short. Dustin claims that the name was a derivation of a jazz musician's. It turns out that Alan and I grew up across the street from each other in Brooklyn on Eastern Parkway.

From the moment he began rehearsals he had the actors laughing. When I came back a couple of hours later the actors were standing on their heads—and loving it. I knew he was the right director. We opened to wonderful reviews for the play and all the actors, especially Dustin, who Walter Kerr of the *New York Times* compared to Charlie Chaplin. The play was a big hit—and everybody who was anybody flocked to the theatre.

After a few months into the run, Elizabeth got a film job that would take her away for two weeks. This was when my wife Patricia coura-

Dustin Hoffman and Elizabeth Wilson in Henry Livings' *Eh?* (1966), directed by Alan Arkin

geously agreed to step into Elizabeth's role. The actors were so into the play and their roles, and each one knew how the other roles had to be played in order for the comedy to work. They all had their opinions and had to give their notes to Patricia and to each other or die. God bless the actors.

When Elizabeth got back, Dustin went to Hollywood to screen test. When he came back he was as bubbly as ever. I asked him how it went and Dustin said, smiling, "Not well, they thought my nose was too big, I'm too short, and I'm Jewish." How wrong he was, the screen test was for *The Graduate* to be directed by Mike Nichols. Mike or his assistant had seen Dustin in our production. After Dustin's screen test, Mike asked him to call him in Hollywood. When Dustin was eating breakfast in New York he made the call. Dustin woke Mike up and was afraid the director would be annoyed with him. In response to Mike's sleepy hello, Dustin sheepishly whispered, "This is Dustin Hoffman." Mike said in his inimitable fashion "Well, you got it"—the kind of underdog success story Hollywood loves. Fortunately, Dustin never changed his lovely nose. The *Graduate*, of course, made Dustin a superstar.

Dustin's great gift for farce has rarely been used in films but he's had success in every kind of role—a single father in *Kramer vs. Kramer*, a savant in *Rainman*, a cross-dresser in *Tootsie*, the degenerate "Ratso" in *Midnight Cowboy*, a reporter in *All the President's Men*, the obsessive runner in *The Marathon Man*, even a press agent in *Wag the Dog*, but the only farcical role he did on film was *Tootsie*.

McIntyre Dixon replaced Dustin. *Eh?* went on for several more months quite successfully, during which time I launched a workshop of an early Bertolt Brecht play, *Drums in the Night.*

The workshop was not going well and after I saw a couple of run-throughs I decided to cancel it. I notified the director Gladys Vaughan who had directed *Othello* and *Baal.* I gathered the actors together to tell them of my decision. They asked, "Why, what was wrong?" I began to explain what I felt was not working. To illustrate my concern, I asked some of the actors to play a scene and then I began critiquing, using the director-actor language I had learned helping actors prepare for auditions.

Suddenly, I was directing and some of the actors got excited and said let's continue and others, not so excited, left. I felt comfortable working on the scene and wanted to continue. So we went ahead with the workshop. I recast it and suddenly I was directing my first play.

I felt very at ease. Directing a play is really a very complicated job, blending the emotions of the actors with the requirements of the play, but I guess I had been absorbing more than I realized by observing rehearsals of all our earlier productions and I stepped right into this new role. The workshop also presented me with my perfect first play to direct—it was like finding a diamond ring under the carpet of your own home. But I do have one little secret to reveal here. Though *Drums* was my first New York directing job, I had earlier directed a summer stock tour of *The Fantasticks* with Ed Ames in the role of El Gallo. He sang "Try to Remember" in his glorious baritone voice better than anyone I'd ever heard, including Sinatra. This was the year before *Drums* and my son Andrew, who was five, came with me and helped the stagehands build the sets with his little hammer. Since he grew up to become a carpenter and now a project manager, I wonder if this was the inspiration for his career. He has always loved working with his hands —his grandfather, Brooky, was a Mr. Fix-It.

Since my workshop of *Drums* was going so well, Paul and I decided to roll the dice and fully mount the play at the Circle. This would be the first time *Drums*—a play by one of the world's great writers, Bertolt Brecht—would be seen in New York. We had a new set designed; costumes built and opened the play.

Drums takes place just after World War I and depicts the deprivation the German people were suffering. The play got good reviews and an excellent one in the *Times*, and had a decent run.

At the same time we put on Shakespeare's A *Midsummer Night's Dream* directed by John Hancock with Gloria Foster at the Theatre De Lys (now the Lortel). The sets by Jim Dine were beautiful. I still have props from the show displayed on the walls of my home. John Hancock had the idea of having the roles of Titania and Helena played by one actor—which emphasized the dream aspect of the play—and it worked very well.

CHAPTER 29

How a Failed Play Becomes a Minor Masterpiece

I thought the next play at the Circle could be Eugene O'Neill's *A Moon for the Misbegotten*. I had seen the production on Broadway with Wendy Hiller and Franchot Tone in 1957, the year after we did *Journey*. The production was not well received but I thought this is a play I'd like to do someday.

I read many actresses for the role and read Salome Jens six times before I cast her as Josie. Then I cast Mitch Ryan for James Tyrone. Mitch, Salome, and I got together and read *Moon* to make sure that we could achieve what was required in the text. In this way, we became very familiar with the play so that by the time we got into rehearsal we were feeling very comfortable with the work that had to be done. James in the play is a thinly disguised Jamie, O'Neill's big brother.

Mrs. O'Neill commented to me on a relationship that had developed between Gene and Mary Welch while *Moon* was touring: "I think Gene was attracted to Ms. Welch and that is why she was cast in the role. I can't imagine why, she was such a big horse of a woman." The green-eyed devil called jealously was still bubbling in Mrs. O'Neill years after that production.

In our production I cast, W. B. Brydon as Phil Hogan, Josie's father, and Jack Davidson played T. Stedman Harder, the next door Sunoco millionaire. The set was by Marsha Eck, the costumes were by Domingo A. Rodriguez.

There was an abandoned farmhouse up the hill near where I live in Bedford. I brought Marsha up to view the site and I took photos for us to study. There were so many elements about it that fit the description of O'Neill's house, including an old iron bed, broken chairs, a wobbly kitchen table and old curtains barely hanging onto the windows. Marsha was inspired by the farmhouse and did wonderful work in recapturing the entire environment. The scrim of the set was a painting of the woods with a little bit of light coming through. This enabled me to depict different times of day. I also tramped through woods near my home in Bedford with a tape machine recording the sounds of nature . . . birds, crickets, etc. There is no sound in the world louder than crickets at night. I used these sounds throughout the play to underline the time of day.

I also brought the actors to the farmhouse to spend some time soaking up the atmosphere of the imagined Hogan house of O'Neill's play. This was a real house with a roof and four walls so in our minds it was the backdrop to where the action of the play takes place, downstage of the house. Salome, Mitch, and I rehearsed there for the better part of a day and the impressions that they received that day stayed with them throughout the run.

My driveway is a quarter of a mile long and I would walk up this hilly path and imagine myself as Jamie and how difficult it must have been for him to manage the incline in the heat of summer after he had hoisted several drinks.

We had a very creative rehearsal period—the actors melding together perfectly—especially Mitch and Salome. Mitch completely understood the spiritual and religious significance of the role. Salome is from Wisconsin, and grew up and worked on a farm; she is an extremely vulnerable soul. She didn't have any trouble conveying Josie's physical size required by O'Neill. Salome has a healthy statuesque figure at 5'9". She didn't have to act out her character's physical qualities. They were already part of her.

Josie Hogan is a symbolic Virgin Mary figure and James Tyrone is the child being embraced and protected in her arms. Josie has a lusty laugh and good sense of humor. Which helps her cover up her heartbreak for Jamie and craftily deal with her conniving cantankerous father, Phil. W.B. Brydon has a stentorian voice and is a passionate husky man and played the role very well.

Salome Jens and Mitch Ryan in Eugene O'Neill's *A Moon for the Misbegotten* (1968), directed by Theodore Mann

Later, after the play had opened Brydon had to leave for another job and was replaced by Stefan Gierasch who played Phil as dumb but wily. Stefan was very much in the Barry Fitzgerald tradition—a bit of a leprechaun with the devil in him. The character of Phil is similar to Joxer in O'Casey's *Juno and the Paycock*.

Clive Barnes writing in *The New York Times* called *Moon* a "Major minor masterpiece." And Walter Kerr in the Sunday *Times* was equally enthusiastic. After these reviews a producer contacted me about moving the play to Broadway.

Our past history off-Broadway had been that when a play got great reviews *in The New York Times*, as we had, it would run for a year or more. This could be more profitable than a Broadway run, given the cost of the transfer and advertising. So Paul and I decided to sit tight and as the run went on, we realized that the conditions had changed off-Broadway and the flame was flickering but we continued to run. Business was good but not the kind we had experienced in the past with positive reviews. We did run for seven months and received Obie Awards (the off-Broadway equivalent of the Tony Awards) and a lot of followup press.

We first took *Moon* on the road to Ford's Theatre in Washington, D.C., where it was very well received. To continue the tour, Jimmy Nederlander helped us, and we took it to his Mechanic Theatre in Baltimore. Our next stop was the Studebaker Theatre in Chicago, where we got great reviews and won several Drama Critics Awards.

Next we took the production to the Lindy Opera House in Los Angeles. I referred to it as the White Elephant. It had been a movie theatre in the late '20s, seating over 5,000 people. The enormity of the space put fear into all of us. It was a huge adjustment the actors had to make to accommodate the size of this theatre.

We took a full-page ad in *Variety* citing all the critical acclaim and awards we'd won, along with a photograph of the cast and myself showing us proud and defiant, staring right into the camera. We were riding high with a very successful show—but Fate was about to withhold her wand.

Presale was good at the box office and we were happily rehearsing. Mitch was late this one particular day. When he arrived he had his coat over his shoulder like a cape and his cigarette in a holder. He shocked us with the news that he had just been cast in a new movie with Lee Marvin and that he had to be on the set the next day and then he said "Goodbye." We were speechless, but then got his understudy, Jack Davidson up on the role for the production. The reviews were good but we missed the magic of Mitch. We did well in L.A. despite his absence. The next time we saw him he came to the theatre driving a Bentley convertible with the top down, looking every bit the Hollywood glamour boy.

Our last stop was Boston, always a receptive town to an O'Neill play. We were booked into the only available house, the Colonial, one of the largest dramatic houses in America. In effect, we were going from one barn to another. I remember standing on the stage and trying to see the last row of the audience, but it was so far away, I couldn't. We did well but we missed Mitch every inch of the way. Or, as an actor would say, moment by moment.

Working on the play with Salome and Mitch was one of the great experiences of my directing career. It was so happy that we have continued to talk ever since about another project still to be found. Recently Paul and I, to celebrate the fiftieth anniversary of my production of *Long Days Journey Into Night* arranged with a booking company to send out a tour to colleges and universities starring Mitch and Salome. Brochures and flyers were printed, and mailings were sent out. After a year the booking office asked me if I would cut the play. The scene of myself and José in Carlotta's apartment fifty years earlier came back into my mind—Mrs. O'Neill saying, "I'm going to give you the rights to do the play on Broadway but you must not cut one word of it." I honored that condition then and I will honor it to the rest of my days. The booking office was unable to book the tour blaming the colleges and universities in that they would not accept the play in its full length. It's a sad day when U.S. colleges will not present the greatest American play ever written in its entirety. Paul and I were shocked and disgusted by the booking company's failure. We canceled the project.

Salome and I have remained very good friends and have participated in O'Neill conferences in Romania, Bermuda, and the Tao House in California. In all of these conferences, Salome has always performed Josie's monologue in the last act of *Moon*. It still brings tears to my eyes. I feel very proud that Salome, Mitch and I were able to resurrect this forgotten play of O'Neill's and bring it to the position that it deserves as a "major minor" masterpiece.

CHAPTER 30

THE F WORD

Terrence McNally called to tell me of a play project that he, Israel Horowitz, and Leonard Melfi were working on. It was to be an evening of theatre, three one-act plays, not related in theme, but connected by the time of day. The first one takes place in the morning, the second at noon and the third at night. That, in fact, was the title: *Morning, Noon and Night*. It was an exciting idea, an evening of work by new, young writers, with me directing.

Paul and I had worked with Terrence and Leonard in their one-act plays with *Six from La Mama* in 1966, and Terrence's Broadway debut with the full length *And Things That Go Bump in the Night*. We had admired Israel's off-Broadway *An Indian Wants the Bronx* with a young actor named Al Pacino. So it was a happy collaboration. Terrence's play was ready and Israel's as well, Leonard was still writing his.

The Circle was busy with *Moon*, so we decided to bring these exciting new talents to Broadway and we rented the Henry Miller Theatre on 43rd Street from James Nederlander. Before *Moon* at the Henry Miller was Jack Gelber's new play, *The Cuban Thing*.

For *Morning, Noon and Night* we cast Sorrell Booke and Robert Klein (I had met him in Williamstown in 1962 when I directed *A Taste of Honey*). and the deliciously kissable Charlotte Rae. We played two weeks of previews and were selling out to a young audience which had followed us from off-Broadway. They loved it, especially the obscenities which made it very revolutionary. Hearing the expletive "fuck" on a Broadway stage tititlated them.

Terrence's play was set, but Israel was unhappy about his ending. We experimented with several different versions during previews. Finally he agreed on one and we performed it that way several times and were getting a very good audience reaction. Then after one of the shows he kept insisting that we go back to his earlier ending. I felt the audience was responding well to the ending as performed. I didn't want to change it; it would have been very difficult for the actors since we were just about to open. The rule I've always worked with is that you make whatever changes you want during rehearsals and previews, but none in the last week before the opening. The actors have to feel confident and do the same words and blocking for the last week before the opening.

One night still during previews, the audience was gone and Israel continued to argue for the restoration of his ending as we walked onto the stage. I kept saying, "We can't make any more changes." As I walked downstage from him, he got angrier and angrier. He suddenly strode across the stage and with a roundhouse punch swung at my jaw. Instinctively, I ducked as I had learned to do when my brother practiced boxing on me when we were kids. As Israel took aim again, Paul, who was much taller than Israel, picked him up—off the ground—by the shoulders and put Israel behind himself. Israel tried again to get at me, but Paul blocked him. We all finally went home and the ending we'd been performing was what we opened with.

Israel's play *Morning* is about a black family who have taken a pill the night before and when they wake up, they're all white but still speak lower-class black. The mother, Charlotte Rae enters and sees her husband lying in bed and the first line that she speaks is, "Git yo matha fuckin' black ass out of that matha fucking white bed!" Before the father (played by Robert Klein) could respond, the older people in the audience, shocked, stood up mumbling and wagging their heads as they escaped up the aisles. This response was in contrast to the young people's enjoyment. I believe this was a historic moment in the American theatre, because it was the first time that that four-letter word was uttered on a Broadway stage—to the best of my knowledge.

Noon, Terrence's play, was about a young man (Robert Klein) who had taken an ad in the personal column for a young lady to have an afternoon of fun. When he opened the door, expecting a beautiful young thing, instead a short, squat, rounded couple entered dressed in middle-class clothes, he wearing a black hat and carrying a black suitcase — Sorrell Booke and Charlotte Rae. They perfunctorily acknowledge Bobby then proceed to disrobe and get into their S&M costumes, taking out their whips and chains from the suitcase. Bobby's character tries to stops them, saying this has all been a mistake. Sorrell's character, disappointed in this reception for what he thought would be a delicious afternoon, laments, in a heavy German accent, "Mine hart is heavy!" as they pack up to leave.

Leonard Melfi's play, *Night*, was about a man who dies — his body's onstage in a coffin — and comes back to life. The meaning of the play was unclear to all of us including Leonard. I kept asking him, "Leonard, what are you trying to say?" After much discussion, Leonard decided that the man in the coffin had to be the assassinated Robert Kennedy. We all went along with that and Bobby played it with that in mind.

The New York Times review found the whole evening unsatisfactory, but the New York *Post* loved it. We knew the kids were out there who would like to see the show, so Paul said to me, "Let's reduce all prices to a couple of dollars again, like we did for Terrence's *And Things That Go Bump in the Night*." This time it worked. People were lined up down the street and the theatre filled. But we weren't covering our costs. Then Paul and I thought, since the audience is so enthusiastic, let's raise the ticket price and thereby cover our expenses. I guess we were being greedy because as soon as we announced the higher ticket prices the audiences dwindled. We did manage to run for seven weeks after the opening. Terrence acknowledged our valiant efforts in his introduction to the publication of the plays.

Two months before *Morning, Noon and Night* at the Henry Miller. we did Jack Gelber's *The Cuban Thing*. As luck would have it, across the street from the theatre sat the offices of a "Free Cuba" organization. They decided that the play must be pro-Castro, even though they'd never read it. On opening night, an anonymous caller notified the police there was a bomb in the theatre. The police department emptied out the audience and after a couple of hours of dog sniffing and police searching, they realized it was a false alarm—no bomb, however, except for the play. It closed and Paul and I said goodbye to the Henry Miller. By this time we both wanted to start a permanent theatre on Broadway where we could produce for a broader audience. The excitement downtown was dimming and we felt that the work that we were doing would be appreciated on Broadway.

Girl on the Via Flaminia, Long Days Journey Into Night, Hughie, And Things That Go Bump in the Night, The Royal Hunt of the Sun, Trumpets of The Lord and *Morning, Noon and Night* were Circle's seven valiant forays onto Broadway but we still did not have a home there. In Early 1968, I had gotten a call from an official in Mayor Lindsay's office asking if we would be interested in having an off-Broadway theatre *on* Broadway. I responded, "Yes, of course." How did I know where such an answer might lead? I immediately forgot the call, thinking it was someone with a macabre sense of humor, since we'd just flopped on Broadway.

The production of *Morning, Noon and Night* at The Henry Miller was made possible by the brilliant contracts Paul worked out for the rent and the stagehands. A couple of years later when Circle in the Square uptown came into being, those contracts became the format that the unions used for our nonprofit theatre.

After *Moon* we produced Jules Feiffer's *Little Murders* at the Circle on Bleecker Street. It had failed on Broadway, but I felt it was a fine up-to-date comedy. We asked Alan Arkin to direct again and he put together a sublime cast of actors with the comic touch—Elizabeth Wilson, Linda Lavin (both in *Eh?*), Vince Gardenia and Fred Willard, who played the young son, with divine performances by all. *Little Murders* is about a city family besieged in their apartment by the random violence that exists on the streets. They have one mission: Survival. The Father (Vince) says, "We'll put a fence around the apartment and we'll beat the shit out of anyone who tries to get in." Eventually they take rifles in hand to shoot the potential perpetrators. Needless to say the play had resonance for New York City audiences and it was very successful.

Several years later, I was invited to select and direct a play at the Dallas Theatre Center. Dallas was now the city famous for the assassination of JFK. I thought that *Little Murders* could be a sobering play for the people there. On opening night when the actors pointed their rifles toward the imaginary street below there was some panic in the audience—for obvious reasons. But they stayed and we had meaningful discussions afterwards with the cast, and me. I cast Ed Herrmann , then a young unknown, as the son. After the run, I invited Ed to come to New York and told him that I would help him find work. It was obvious from the first time I saw him that he was an extremely talented actor.

CHAPTER 31

LBJ AND ABE

In 1964, Lyndon B. Johnson was running for office. I was asked by the Democratic Party to help rally support for him. So I reopened the El Morocco nightclub and renamed it the "LBJ Disco Tay." Large signs were made with that name for outside the building so that anybody walking or driving on the avenue would see it. I had the walls covered with posters and pictures of LBJ, mounted a disco ball, and hired a disc jockey. People came in, drank, and danced on election night to celebrate his victory. I thought that Johnson was a terrific president, having pushed along civil rights and other legislation for poor people that had lain dormant for generations. Johnson enacted the Civil Rights Act of 1968, the Head Start program, as well as sponsoring a series of bills and acts creating programs such as food stamps, work study, Medicare and Medicaid, which reduced the rates of poverty and improved living standards for the poor.

Ford's Theatre in Washington, D.C., is the infamous site of Lincoln's assassination and had remained closed as a performance space. On January 30, 1968, over a century later, it reopened. Patricia was invited to be one of the artists along with Henry Fonda, Harry Belafonte, Odetta, and many others. As Patricia and I entered backstage with me carrying her performance gown there were at least twenty-five federal agents with walkie-talkies checking out all the artists. The area was crowded and in minor chaos. Harry Belafonte, a tall elegant man, was in front of us and he was stopped and questioned by an agent who growled in the manner of a rural cop, "Why are you here?" I thought to myself, didn't we win the Civil War? I tapped the agent on the shoulder to tell him Harry Belafonte is a very important singer who came tonight to celebrate the reopening of this theatre. Finally they whisked him inside.

Patricia sang two arias (from the operas *La Sonombula* and *Lucia di L'ammermoor*) which I have on videotape. The evening was very well received by an audience of dignitaries, politicos and big-time corporate executives. LBJ's key administration personnel were there, along with members of the Supreme Court and Hubert Humphrey.

That night there was very tight security everywhere, not just backstage. President Johnson didn't attend, but Lady Bird did, as did their daughter Linda. Afterwards there was a dinner reception at the White House and Johnson greeted the entire company of performers. During dinner I saw an aide walk up to the President and hand him a note. With no expression he put the note into his pocket and continued the conversation with those at his table. When Patricia and I walked back to the Mayflower Hotel and turned on the TV we found out what the note was about—the Tet Offensive had begun, which overran the South Vietnamese and American troops. We didn't know it at the time, but America lost the war that night.

In June of the same year Patricia and I were invited to the White House for a black-tie cultural evening honoring Pablo Casals. Patricia had performed with him at the Marlboro Music Festival in Vermont. My dear friend Alexander (Sacha) Schneider, violinist/conductor, Budapest String Quartet, gathered the rest of the classical performers for the evening's entertainment. Afterwards at dinner, I saw an aide hand another note to the president. He read it. The expression on his face was anguish. He then crumpled it in his fist and let it fall to the floor and sat silently. Robert Kennedy had been assassinated in Los Angeles at the height of his bid to secure the Democratic nomination for President.

During the intervening years between Lincoln's assassination (by the brother of James O'Neill's colleague Edwin Booth, by the way) and its reopening, Ford's theatre had been used as a warehouse, I've been told. In 1969 Paul and I were invited by the Department of the Interior to take charge of the theatre. We decided for our opening production we would put on a play by America's greatest playwright so we did Eugene O'Neill's A *Moon for the Misbegotten* with Salome Jens, Mitch Ryan, and Stefan Gierasch.

In effect what we were doing was moving the same production from the three-sided Circle in the Square to the proscenium stage of Ford's Theatre. We found that the set fit perfectly into the space and only minor blocking adjustments had to be made. Mitch as Jamie, on his first entrance, entered through the vomitorium at the Circle, and at Ford's he entered through an aisle of the theatre, and up onto the stage. *Moon* was quite successful and as a result we decided to tour it, as I discussed earlier. The fact that the proscenium was so harmonious to our production allowed us to travel the play to the proscenium stages of other cities.

I became fascinated with the circumstances of Lincoln's assassination. John Wilkes Booth had acted many times in that theatre. As he walked toward the Lincoln box no suspicions were raised and the guard assigned to the president was missing. Lincoln and his wife, accompanied by a naval lieutenant and his wife, were watching *Our American Cousin*. One day, I entered the Lincoln box which is always off limits and a chill went through me thinking of the shock of that night. I stood in the Lincoln box and put my foot on the ledge and imagined I was John Wilkes Booth. It didn't look like much of a jump but Booth broke his leg doing it. He was wearing boots which probably caused him to slip. The audience watching *Our American Cousin* that night thought that the gunshot and then the jump were part of the play. In fact, Booth had cagily timed his shot to be drowned out by a laugh he knew was coming.

I then walked out the stage door through which he had fled and walked on the same cobblestones as he had, and in my mind got on his horse. Who helped him? With a broken leg he couldn't get on the horse himself. I then walked to the bridge where he had ridden out of Washington. I wandered around the city seeking out the sites of the conspirators and visited the house nearby alleged to be Mary Surratt's and any other sites that still existed, including the Seward House across the street from the theatre. There I saw the bed in which Lincoln had expired. I entertained doing a play based on this matter but decided that it would be inappropriate to recreate the event.

In 1968, Johnson had chosen not to run for reelection. The smartest of all politicians had allowed himself to be misled by his military advisors as to our victory in the Vietnam War. Richard Nixon defeated Hubert Humphrey and became the new President. The Vietnam War was still on and the country was in turmoil.

Nixon's White House took us under their wing and we were in direct contact with John Ehrlichman and Bob Haldeman, Nixon's aides-de-camp who visited us at Ford's Theatre and became our supporters. Paul pointed out to Haldeman that Ford's Theatre did not have exterior lights or a marquee and, as a result, people were having difficulty finding it. The very next day electricians appeared and began installing exterior lights that illuminated the theatre from the Seward House across the street. Several weeks later a flag pole with a large banner reading "Ford's Theatre" was fluttering in the wind. Now people could see us.

After the grand reopening in 1968, another group had run the theatre before us for a short time and then dissolved. It had been impeccably restored to its condition at the time of the assassination. The chairs were straight back cane chairs with wicker seats and were very uncomfortable to sit in. We wanted to have cushions but the purists were against the idea and besides that the Department of Interior would not spring for the money to have them made. So Paul and I did what we have always done, we stepped forward and found a way to do the impossible. To us, the addition of cushions was critical to the comfort of our customers and, therefore, to our success. So we started shopping to have special cushions made in the style of the period. Paul even found a photo of the original Ford's Theatre interior and, lo and behold, there *were* cushions! So the purist argument went out the window. And then Paul's research turned up a company in Arkansas that agreed not only to make the cushions but to donate them merely for a mention in the theatre's program. Now, over forty years later, those same cushions or a variety thereof are still being used at the theatre! Let's hear it for Arkansas!

Ironically, there was rarely a person of color who attended our shows, so we decided to really shake things up and remount a new production of *Trumpets of the Lord*. Word quickly got around to the black audience and the theatre filled up. At long last, the theatre was living up to Lincoln's legacy. It was such a success that we extended the run in D.C. and then moved the show to the Mechanic Theatre in Baltimore (run by James Nederlander) where it also sold out, then on to Los Angeles, which I wrote about earlier.

After Los Angeles, we brought it back to New York to the Brooks Atkinson Theatre where it had a short run. It had been quite a journey for *Trumpets*—one of the mainstays of all of those productions was the glorious Theresa Merritt. She had a fantastic voice and a smile and warmth like the sun. All the people who saw it loved her and the show.

In 1969 the Vietnam War was still raging. The division in our country we are experiencing now probably started at that point in our history. Or perhaps it started when President Nixon resigned to avoid impeachment on August 8, 1974. So the next production we chose to do at Ford's was one of an earlier time in our history that tells us of the virtues and positive values of an American family. The play was Eugene O'Neill's *Ah, Wilderness!*, his paean to America.

Symbolically this innocent comedy takes place on July Fourth, and shows the frictions within the family, with Geraldine Fitzgerald playing the mother. Mrs. O'Neill told me, "I dared Gene to write a comedy. All you write is serious and depressing plays." Before that he had written *Mourning Becomes Electra* in 1933, *Marco's Millions* in 1930, *Dynamo* and *Before Breakfast* in 1929, and the grand daddy of O'Neill's serious plays, *Strange Interlude*, in 1928. Gene took up the dare and three days later he had completed the play. The Theatre Guild, his longtime producer, put it on at the height of the Depression in 1933 with George M. Cohan and it became a great success. The play, with its nostalgic warmth and humor, was the perfect antidote for the tough times our country was going through in 1933 and 1969.

The family in *Ah, Wilderness!* represents a dream of what O'Neill's own childhood might have been. It was actually modeled after the family of the girl he had been in love with in New London. *Ah, Wilderness!* is one of the most popular and produced plays in the world. On opening night, Art Garfunkel, during intermission was heard loudly demeaning the play to one of the Washington critics, who later, repeated Garfunkle's pearls of wisdom, in his review that, "this was an old-fashioned, out-of-date play." As a result the run endured some "Troubled Waters."

Ford's Theatre is designated as a National Historic Landmark. The museum in the basement depicted events around the assassination. Every day hordes of tourists would visit the museum. Walter Hickel, Secretary of the Interior, asked us if we would allow the tourists to stand at the back of the balcony seats and watch rehearsals, and observe the box where President Lincoln was assassinated. We agreed. It is very unusual for anybody other than the company to view rehearsals. But we all felt that we were part of caring for and showing Ford's Theatre. Watching us rehearse the theatre came alive for the tourists.

The next play we did was *Iphigenia in Aulis*—the great Greek drama. The production was well received. Following that came a one-man evening of period songs by Max Morath.

The next play back home at Circle in the Square was a new one by Seymour Simckes, *Seven Days of Mourning*. It was a religious play about morality in the modern world in conflict with Jewish tradition. This brought in small audiences and I was soon off hunting for our next production.

Jules Feiffer had just completed a new play, *The White House Murder Case*, which he asked us to produce. I loved it and Alan Arkin agreed to direct, this time using his own name instead of Roger Short, which he had used when he directed *Little Murders*. The play was a strong criticism of presidential power and the falseness of the Vietnam War. It is just as pertinent today with the circumstances surrounding the Iraq War.

One day James Earl Jones called to tell me he had a new play he was interested in doing. It was by Athol Fugard, one of the English-speaking world's greatest writers. I asked Jimmy to send it to me. The play, *Boesman and Lena*, presents the circumstances of poor black people under the suppression of an extremely unfair national authority and how they deal with the actual destruction of their living quarters. Our production starred Ruby Dee, Jimmy, and an authentic South African, Zakes Mokae. It was very helpful having Zakes in the cast to amplify the cultural significances of the play and to help the other actors with the South African language and rhythms. Directed by John Berry, *Boesman and Lena* proved extremely successful for us.

Around the same time at Ford's Theatre, we put on another successful season, starting with *The Fantasticks* with Word Baker directing and we also did *Will Rogers USA* by Paul Shyre with James Whitmore playing the politically savvy cowboy.

Then at Ford's I directed William Gibson's *John and Abigail* with

Ruby Dee and James Earl Jones in Athol Fugard's *Boesman and Lena* (1970), directed by John Berry

Salome Jens and Michael Higgins. The play consists of the letters between John and Abigail Adams from the time of the first Continental Congress through the finalization of the Constitution. Bill placed the letters in juxtaposition so as to have dramatic context. In the play, John and Abigail rarely looked at or spoke to each other except where there were personal moments in the letter, but converse expressing their emotions and observations, through their letters. They were brilliant passionate and articulate people and it was a very provocative evening, which resonated with the audience.

Salome and I, as I've mentioned, like to do research for our stage work. We visited both John and Abigail's houses each of which are modest two-story wood frame farmhouses in Weymouth, Massachusetts, where they had lived as children. The houses were across a large pond from each other. I was told by some natives that folk lore had it that they had communicated to each other across the pond with hand signals. In John Adams' house the bed and the clothes were for people about five feet tall. It's surprising to think of how short these people were. The rooms and the windows were all very small with low ceilings. Considering that he was the second President of the United States I was surprised to see how modestly the house was being preserved!

A church that the Adamses probably attended, which Cotton Mather had preached in, was nearby. For Salome this was part of her preparation for the role and it helped deepen my knowledge about the play and added details rich in American History.

Actors are urged to research as many elements of their characters as they can think of. For example, where the characters lived, the clothes they wore, the food they ate and the roads they walked on. So we found a treasure trove and more when we went to the Quincy, Massachusetts— known as Braintree in their time—site of the Adams home when he was Ambassador to France. The house was a substantial structure—a graceful Tudor style home with a view of Boston Harbor. This was quite a contrast to the homes they had lived in in their youth. There was also a separate dome-top library containing all of his books from the floor to the ceiling. You can pick out any book at random and almost every page has margin notes scribbled by Mr. Adams. It was a thrill to hold one of his books in my hands and breathe in the atmosphere of their substantial quarters.

Abigail was the early liberated woman in America. She had strong opinions on the political events of the day; she was also a confidant of Thomas Jefferson. Both she and her husband wrote with the skill and style of a Jane Austen.

While we were rehearsing, Sal and I went up one weekend to visit John Jay's home on Route 22, outside of Katonah, New York. Jay, another founding father, also co-authored the Treaty of Paris and was the first Chief Justice of the Supreme Court. What was so interesting to us was to observe the kitchen quarters of his well-to-do Colonial era house—the fine silverware and plates, the giant hearth, the copper cooking utensils, all of which were imported from England.

By the time of our final play at Ford's, Paul and I were exhausted. The finale was *You're a Good Man, Charlie Brown*, directed by Joseph Hardy. And so our time at Ford's was over. We accomplished what we set out to do—re-open Ford's Theatre and present meaningful productions that would bring honor and audiences back to the hallowed place. It had been a mission—a theatrical, spiritual, and patriotic one—for both of us.

CHAPTER 32

THE MAYOR REQUESTS THE PLEASURE OF YOUR COMPANY

Remember that joke phone call about an off-Broadway theatre on Broadway which I had rejected? Well, he called us back.

He said, "The Mayor wants you to know that you have been selected from all the other off-Broadway companies to have a new theatre built for you on Broadway." I asked, "All the other theatres? Including Joe Papp's?" He answered, "Yes." I said, "Wow! That's a great compliment." I asked, "Can we see the plans?" The plans were delivered to us the next day.

Our theatre was to be where the old Capitol Movie Theatre stood. It would be built below ground in a large office building. This was being made possible by a bonus program initiated by the Mayor in the city zoning code, which normally limits the height of a building as defined by the building lot size. In this case, by building a new theatre the owner would be allowed to go much higher and thereby gain additional floors. As part of this development the landlord was to build a large musical house and also a 299-seat theatre built to our specifications.

A meeting was set up and Paul studied the plans. After about ten minutes he said, "Why do you want a two hundred ninety-nine seat theatre?" The representative replied, "That's what you have off-Broadway at the Circle." Paul said, "because of the location of the new theatre we will be subject to the union rules for a Broadway house. As I look at these plans you can fit in at least six hundred ninety-nine seats!" and Paul went on, "this is the minimum number of seats which we will need to satisfy the economics of the theatrical unions." That ended any further discussion of a 299-seat theatre.

We found out at this meeting that our landlord would be the Uris Brothers, one of the largest real estate developers in the world. Later on we had many meetings with the Uris people to discuss this

Paul Libin and Theodore Mann (1972)

new theatre. The basic conditions we worked out with them were that the number of seats was to be the maximum number possible but not less than six hundred; and further that the theatre be built to our specifications following the design of the downtown theatre, with added access for the actors' entrances and exits. As the plan for the theatre evolved, the design included passageway tunnels for the actors which were under the audience.

At the old Circle on Sheridan Square, those entrances and exits were outside and the actors were exposed to the weather—cold, rain, snow. Barry Primus also sat on the exterior exit steps of the theatre, the very same steps that Jason had nervously waited on for his entrance in *Iceman*. Barry was sitting there to fulfill his duty as understudy, and security guard, preventing people from wandering into the theatre without a ticket.

For the new theatre, there would be a large rehearsal area and offices beneath the stage. Paul and I also insisted that all the dressing rooms had to have their own sinks, toilets, and showers. At the original Circle on Sheridan Square there were no showers and on Bleecker Street there was one shower on the second floor which could only be used after the audience had departed because it made too much noise. This reminds me of the many rain and snow leaks we had from the Bleecker Street roof. Money was short at that time and the best I could do was to have the holes patched, which I did for twenty years to try to prevent rain from dripping on the stage or the audience. Finally, after one horrendous rain storm, Paul himself retarred a new roof with the help of volunteers.

At the new Circle on 50th and Broadway we also insisted on traps on the stage to allow openings to create access from beneath the stage for directors and designers to work with. The traps were used by director George C. Scott in the studio scene of Noël Coward's *Design for Living* and in Tennessee Williams' *Not About Nightingales*, by Corin Redgrave to enter from his below stage warden's office, and in *Holiday* for Laura Linney to enter into her play room as well as many other plays. We also needed a catwalk above the stage so the stagehands had easy access to the lights. Most Broadway theatres have a grid for lights above the stage only accessible by long A-frame ladders for focusing and adjusting stage lights. These ladders require two stagehands to hold it in place and another to climb it. Needless to say, this method is slow and expensive. So these stage necessities for the Circle were agreed upon by the Uris Brothers.

During the construction of the theatre, Harold Uris, the surviving brother of the company, would often come around to relish with us the process of creating this new theatre. He was joyous and proud of it like a little boy. He liked Paul and me so much that he allowed us to do a fundraising benefit honoring him. At that benefit we raised more money than we'd ever raised before.

There were many physical adjustments which had to be made as the theatre was being built. One of the most significant was the position of the two supporting columns in the theatre. As shown on the building plan, they would block the vision to the stage for a substantial number of audience members. Mr. Uris agreed to reconfigure the plan at a substantial cost to his company. Mr. Uris told his staff, "do what they want."

A lease had been submitted to us which we went over point by point with Floria Lasky, our splendid dedicated attorney who had been such a great help in many earlier issues that one faces in the course of running a theatre and producing plays. We always won with Floria by our side.

We were to become a Broadway Theatre! Wow! But there were many obstacles to get around or over—among them the lease required that Paul and I be the signatories, with the further important proviso that the space had to be used as a theatre. That was based on the city's requirement that the building include two theatres (the other was the large musical house next door to us, The Gershwin)—all part of Lindsay's drive to have new theatres constructed on Broadway. Because of this creative zoning the American Place Theatre also came into existence on 43rd Street, as did the Marriott Marquis on Broadway.

The lease required a security of $75,000! The Circle didn't have any money in reserve to meet this requirement. So Paul and I put up $37,500 each — a lot of money in 1968 — we mortgaged our homes and borrowed the balance, as required. Paul and I signed the lease. We were to start using the space in the summer of 1972.

While construction was going on Paul and I would excitedly visit the site and watch the excavation and the beginning of the foundation of what would become our theatre. It was thrilling to witness the slow evolution.

Paul would patiently explain to me where the actual theatre, seats, dressing rooms, offices and studios were to be located. Every time we went back he would have to explain to me these different locations. I felt a little bit like Lenny in *Of Mice and Men*. "Tell me again, George."

By this time we had formed a Board of Directors for the Broadway operation. We of course wanted reputable and well-to-do people. How one led to another I don't remember but I think Eugene Black Jr. was our first member which led to Lady Weidenfeld (Sandra Payson), Carolyn Lynch, and Joseph E. Levine. Then Carol Hausman became a board member. We had our first board meeting at her beautiful Central Park South apartment.

Paul and I began to plan what plays we were going to do. I had been in touch with Colleen Dewhurst, Irene Papas, Dustin Hoffman, Al Pacino, and George C. Scott to have them participate. I brought Al and Dustin on separate occasions to test the site lines and audibility. Dustin or Al would sit on the concrete ramps (where the seats would be installed), which looked like an ancient Roman amphitheatre. I would walk on the stage pretending to be an actor talking all the time and they happily affirmed that the sound was very good. I was so relieved because this was the first time the sound had been checked. Then they would go down and I would sit in the audience. And I remember Dustin saying, "This is a very democratic theatre; every seat is as good as any other." Al Pacino loved performing there and proved it by doing *Hughie, Chinese Coffee,* and *Salome* in addition to participating in several workshops at the theatre.

I began meeting with Colleen on a regular basis about what she wanted to do. At one point we had lunch with James Earl Jones. Jimmy

Set of *Mourning Becomes Electra* (1972) in the new Circle at 50th Street and Broadway

wanted to play Big Daddy in *Cat on a Hot Tin Roof* and Colleen would play Maggie. Color has never been an issue with Paul and me. So when Jimmy came up with the idea to play Big Daddy as a white man we readily agreed. This was an exciting project but it never came to fruition because Jimmy got a movie.

Because of our long connection with O'Neill, Paul and I decided to open our new theatre with one of his plays. We talked about *Anna Christie, Long Day's Journey Into Night, Strange Interlude*, and *Mourning Becomes Electra*. We selected *Mourning*, which had not been done since its original Broadway production in 1930. I felt it was one of his great forgotten plays. I had always loved the bigness of its theme. And, of course the role of the mother, Christine, is one of the signature roles of the American Theatre. It was originally performed on Broadway by the superb Alla Nazimova. Colleen was born to play Christine.

So that became the play to open our new theatre on Broadway. This would be the fifth theatre that Circle in the Square had opened: Sheridan Square and Bleecker Street downtown, The Academy of Music in Philadelphia; Ford's Theatre in Washington, D.C., and now, at long last, on Broadway!

CHAPTER 33

THE CIRCLE SALUTES A MASTER

For *Mourning*, O'Neill borrowed from *Oedipus*, combined it with *Antigone*, and created a portrait of an American family at the end of the Civil War. We are in the Mannon house of a New England wealthy family whose riches derive from slave traffic and ship building. The mother of the Mannon family, Christine, long estranged from her husband, has, during his wartime absence, fallen in love with the captain of a sailing vessel. Adam Brant is a free spirit who woos her with tales of his adventures in the South Seas. Their romance flourishes as they plan to live in that paradise. Her daughter, Lavinia, suspicious of her mother's new-found joy follows her to New York City and discovers the illicit love affair. Lavinia is dedicated to her father and threatens to reveal all to him unless Christine, the mother, ends the affair. Also, her brother, Orin, is returning from the war wounded in battle. Lavinia tells him of the affair, but Christine convinces Orin that Lavinia has imagined it all. Orin is so in love with his mother that he believes her.

Orin also hates his father who has always minimized his achievements. On the night of her husband's arrival home from the war, Christine and her husband retire to their bedroom. He suffers a heart attack, unable to reach his medicine and pleads with Christine to hand it to him. She coldly stands by and watches him die—with a knowing Colleen Cheshire smile on her face.

Ben Gazzara was cast as the father and Ben's wife, Janice Rule, as Lavinia. Before rehearsals started Ben dropped out for a film and I cast a

Canadian actor, Donald Davis, with lots of classical roles under his belt at the Stratford Company.

The theatre installation of seats, lighting, and sound equipment was completed.

What a challenge—breaking in a brand new theatre at the same time we were putting on this mammoth, three-and-a-half-hour epic play with multiple scenes and fifteen actors. The nuts and bolts of the new theatre were being tested and worked out as we were in rehearsal. Marsha Eck who had designed *Moon* on Bleecker Street did the set for this new production. The back wall was covered with framed portraits of Mannon ancestors looking down at the activities in the Mannon house in judgment. Then, as the scenes changed, they were turned around and became other elements of the set.

We went into rehearsal with an actor I had seen on television for the role of Orin. He had been strongly recommended by other actors who had worked with him. I auditioned him and thought he could do the role but after a week it became evident that he lacked the tools of a trained stage actor so I replaced him with Stephen McHattie whose stage work I had seen many times. Now in the second week of rehearsal, Janice Rule was unhappy and dissatisfied—she and I could not communicate at all. She left—We had no "Lavinia." I felt in my bones the right person was out there somewhere—someone whose work I'd seen.

Through all the problems Colleen was like a strong tree. She kept at her work on the role of Christine and was very positive and helped me to hold the whole production together.

The morning after Janice left I closeted myself in my office and thought and thought. Then I took out the Players Guide and began pouring over it very slowly, page by page. Most actors who have worked in New York have their photographs and credits in this book. After a couple of hours I came upon a photo and my heart jumped. I put my finger on her face and said, "That's her!" I had seen her, Pamela Payton-Wright, in *The Effect of Gamma Rays on Man-in-the-Moon Marigolds* off-Broadway and was struck by her tenderness and strength. I called but she wasn't in New York she was in California. I got a number for her and called at 8 A.M. California time and put the question right on the table. "We're doing *Mourning Becomes Electra* with Colleen at the Circle, we start performing in two

Pamela Payton-Wright and Colleen Dewhurst in Eugene O'Neill's *Mourning Becomes Electra* (1972), directed by Theodore Mann

weeks—would you be interested in playing Lavinia?" Without hesitation, she said, "Yes," took the red eye and was at rehearsal the next morning.

On the plane she'd memorized the first act—amazing! So we just went right at it. She and Colleen and Stephen all got along perfectly and the production began to take shape. We delayed the opening one week and had an extraordinary success.

Colleen received a Tony nomination for Best Actress and the production for Best Revival. The *New Yorker* magazine's esteemed critic Brendan Gill called it a, "Landmark production." We had launched a new theatre and re-established the importance of *Mourning Becomes Electra*!

Since it was a new theatre many kinks popped up. Such as: During one of the early performances of *Mourning*, the fire alarm system went off; people going to the theatre next door were heard walking on our ceiling which is the street arcade; and one night we heard horse hooves—which wasn't bad since this was a post–Civil War play. It turned out that the mounted police were using the arcade as a shortcut between 50th and 51st Streets. I pleaded with our precinct captain and he rerouted them.

When we announced our season—*Mourning, Medea* with Irene Papas, *Here Are Ladies* with Siobhan McKenna, and *Uncle Vanya* with George C. Scott, Julie Christie, Nicol Williamson, Cathleen Nesbitt, Lillian Gish, Barnard Hughes, and Elizabeth Wilson and directed by Mike Nichols, our subscription response was overwhelming—more than 17,000 in the first season!

By the time we hit March of our first season in 1973, we were doing *Ladies* but it was nerve-wrackingly unclear whether Mike Nichols
would finish his film *Day of the Dolphin* (and starring George C. Scott
to boot!) in time to start rehearsal for *Vanya* in June.

Joe Levine was the producer of the film and also involved with us.
He'd agreed to give us $250,000 and in exchange we would rename the
theatre Circle in the Square/Joseph E. Levine. Joe gave us $50,000 as
the first payment. The rest was to follow shortly thereafter. Joe was a very
friendly guy and Paul and I always had great times visiting with him at
his office. Patricia and I were regular guests at Joe's weekend parties at
his home on Long Island Sound in Greenwich, Connecticut. Joe had
the complete collection of paintings by James Wyeth and I expressed to
him how honored I was to see them. He took me aside and whispered,
"They're not the real thing. The originals are in the vault."

We were selling lots of subscriptions and using the money to mount
shows and meet expenses but the dollars were still short, and we were
very anxious about *Uncle Vanya*. Finally the film was finished and this
great cast was assembled.

On the day rehearsals began, Paul and I let out a big sigh of relief.
Mike worked beautifully with the actors and made them into one happy
family. This time we had the luxury of rehearsing on the stage we'd be
performing on. George and Nicol became drinking buddies and got into
scuffles with third parties and a couple of times the cops had to bring
them back to the theatre like two wet cats. But the next day they were
back functioning perfectly. Tony Walton did a lean, brilliant set. The
props and furniture appeared to the audience as though they were hand
hewn a hundred years ago. The actors were able to live and breathe the
play in the atmosphere Tony had created.

Everything was going along great—then one day I got a call from
George's agent, Jane Deacy, "George won't play matinees." I asked,
"Why?" She replied, "He saw a Wednesday matinee of *That Championship Season* and said he won't play matinees." I said, "Jane, we have
to play the matinees to give us eight performances per week." She answered, "Talk to G.C. but I don't think you'll change his mind. You
know how he is."

The next day at a rehearsal break I asked George if I could talk to him.

He nodded yes. I was very nervous, because I knew that when George made up his mind it was very difficult if not impossible to change his position.

We were standing in the narrow tunnel under the audience which is about three-and-a-half feet wide. George, who was taller than me, rested his elbow on the wall while I made my pitch—he was staring into my eyes and a stare from George was like hot iron.

I said, "GC, Jane told me you don't want to play matinee performances." He growled back, "That's right. I won't play to those fuckin' blue-haired ladies." I said, "Why?" He bellowed, "Because they sit there in their flowered hats whispering to each other, munching candy with their clacking false teeth." I didn't know what to say to this but I knew I had to say something and quick. I blurted out, "George, we don't have blue-haired ladies here. They're afraid to come down the escalator." He came right up to me, looked me square in the eye and said, "All right, Teddy, but if I see one fucking blue-haired lady I'm walking." He turned on his heel and started back into rehearsals and I called out, "Don't worry, George. They don't come here, they don't like drama." I raced upstairs to the box office and casually as possible asked, "By the way, have you sold any tickets to blue-haired ladies?" They laughed and said, "Yes, of course. For the matinees." I shouted back, "You can't. If they come to the box office tell them there's no performance. If they try to go down the escalator, tell them the show's been canceled." Mercifully, that was the last time George ever mentioned the infamous blue-haired ladies.

When we got into technical rehearsals, Mike Nichols made a big fuss about the noise the lighting instruments were making. In reality, the noise is infinitesimal and is absorbed when an audience is in the house, but Mike's hearing is acute and he refused to rehearse until this problem was solved. The actors were told to wait in their dressing rooms. This slight noise is only discernible when the house is empty. The problem went on for several days while technical rehearsals were suspended. Paul took charge of this whole problem and with his usual superior technical ability, solved it so that rehearsals could start up again. I'm biting my nails and my heart is beating quickly as I tell this story. We didn't want to delay the opening and lead the theatre community to think that the show was in trouble, especially with the rumors already floating around about the problems from *The Day of the Dolphin* movie shooting. We were under tremendous pressure to open at the announced date because the show was practically sold out for its entire run.

We began, on schedule, our two-week preview period. At this time, on any show that I had been involved in with George, he would always get very nervous which led to drink. So here we had to put his understudy on until he came back, which

George C. Scott and Elizabeth Wilson in Anton Chekhov's *Uncle Vanya* (1973), directed by Mike Nichols

would usually be twenty-four hours later. When he did return he was very contrite—he knew he'd done something wrong but couldn't remember what. Sometimes the play, his life, or his demons would get to him and he would go off on a bender. Paul and I would be frantically waiting, hoping he'd come back and then we'd get a call from Trish saying, "He's going to play tonight" and in he'd walk with never a mention of his absence and he would throw himself back into the role with his incomparable artistry.

George's wife, the actress Trish Van Devere, was always there for George and for us during this very trying but wonderful time of *Uncle Vanya*. Despite all the problems—Mike's with non-silent lights; the drinking; the blue-haired ladies—it was a happy time. We got a good reception from the press, but I felt Mike never got the praise he richly deserved. The dichotomy of a Chekhovian play is to find the humor, which provides a necessary contrast to the seriousness of the work. Chekhov had identified *Vanya* as a comedy and Mike was true to that description. It was a powerfully touching and funny theatrical event.

On the day of the opening, Mike gathered the actors in our rehearsal studio under the stage and there in complete isolation they did a speed-

George C. Scott and Conrad Bain in *Uncle Vanya*

through of their lines. This is an excellent thing to do because on this day, the actors are always nervous like race horses in the starting gate. This exercise brings them the warmth and comfort of their acting family. After the speed-through the actors went to their dressing rooms and rested on their cots.

During the run there was one more memorable incident. All the rooms have speakers so the actors can listen to the play and be ready for their entrance. George was in his dressing room. He loved playing comedy and getting his laughs. He believed that more is learned about the play and the character through laughter. But here he was in *Vanya* playing Astrov and he never got a single laugh. Astrov is an idealist, an early environmentalist, and serious in his one-minded focus of saving Nature from man's encroachment. In his dressing room over his speaker George could hear Nicol as *Uncle Vanya* getting howling laughter for his childish behavior regarding his passionate love for Julie Christie's Elena.

George was hearing this laughter performance after performance and this night it just boiled up inside of him—he couldn't take hearing it anymore, so he put his fist through the speaker. Now he could concentrate on

Astrov. George was sending a clear message in his own fashion that he didn't want a working speaker in his dressing room, and it was never replaced.

Julie Christie was mesmerizing in the role of Elena. Even after opening she continued to work on her role and would come in early each day and rehearse with our longtime stage manager, the excellent Randy Brooks. As a result her performance continued to grow. She is a hard worker. I admired Julie's tenacity and her focus. She wanted to be better and better. In performance Mike had her walking very slowly on the outer edges of the action, totally absorbed in her own thoughts, oblivious to the other character's attraction to her. She was mysterious and sensual in the role and captivating to the other characters and the audience.

By the end of the summer our first Broadway season was over. We didn't realize at the time but we had done something revolutionary—we had broken the Broadway mold—we presented three revivals and a new play; we had established twelve-week runs; we had attracted major stars; we revitalized subscriptions as a regular Broadway policy; we established Sunday matinees at 3 P.M., a time now being used by all Broadway shows. In addition, our success with the classics has encouraged similar presentations. The main ingredient here is a major star's commitment to a classic for a short period of time. I am proud that we initiated that on Broadway. And I think we also helped to remove the negative connotation of the word revival. Now on to our second Broadway season.

CHAPTER 34

The Iceman Returneth

We began with America's beloved acting couple, Anne Jackson and Eli Wallach in Jean Anouilh's *Waltz of the Toreadors*, a stylish comedy about a French General and his imagined affairs, or attempts, and his wife's reaction to them. Eli who had training as a dancer held himself with the erect posture of a military man and played the befuddled spouse beautifully, as did Anne as his betrayed ever-suffering wife who is always one step ahead of him.

I had been looking and talking to James Earl Jones about doing a play. He and I had worked together on *Othello* and *Baal* and done a recording of Eugene O'Neill's *Emperor Jones* for Caedmon Records. Jimmy had tremendous success in the Broadway production of *The Great White Hope*. He is one of the most charismatic and powerful actors that I know. I first met him when we were doing *Iceman* in 1956. He was a young kid from a rural part of the country and I remember in particular he was wearing leather shoes that laced up above his ankles. It looked like he wore them for support. His pants were too short and his gangly arms hung down below the cuffs of his jacket. He was gawky and very shy. He had come to see his father Robert Earl Jones, who was playing the role of Joe in our production.

Now it's 1973 and our second season—I wanted to do *The Iceman Cometh* again because I was hoping to establish a pattern of doing an O'Neill play each season to honor our great playwright.

Jason Robards in *Iceman* had left an enormous imprint on the role. I had spoken to several leading actors for the part of Hickey, but I hadn't found the right man so I had put it on the back burner. Jimmy and I talked about him doing it and I told him that I didn't have any problem about a black man playing Hickey because I felt that the main ingredient that Hickey has to have is emotional power and charisma—which I said, "you have in buckets." We both acknowledged the delicate relationship between Hickey and Joe, the black porter and felt that both of them being black would not affect their camaraderie, in fact, it probably would enhance it.

Hickey has to have a powerful personality so as to convince the inhabitants of Harry Hope's saloon to give up drinking and their pipe dreams. This is Hickey's most important characteristic—not the color of his skin. The inhabitants of Harry Hope's saloon have to buy his pitch. The audience must be as persuaded as the denizens are.

I was assembling the cast, but I couldn't find the right actor for Rocky the bartender. He had to be tough outside but a pussycat underneath. I was getting desperate, I couldn't find him. Now I'm about to make an admission of failure. David Margulies, an old friend from *Seven Days of Mourning* who I cast as Hugo in *Iceman*, recommended a friend for the role of Rocky. The actor he urged me to see was short, chunky, balding, and about the height of the bar counter. He was the then unknown Danny DeVito! He gave an okay reading but I didn't see his potential genius. He would've been great. It was one of the "big" mistakes of my career.

Outside of that I put together a wonderful cast including: Walter McGinn (Willy Oban), Stefan Gierasch (Harry Hope), Joe Ragno (Rocky Pioggi), and Lois Smith (Cora).

We were now of course in our Broadway house and the expenses of this production would be completely different from our 1956 off-Broadway run. We had a cast of nineteen, and it was necessary to play eight performances per week to meet the costs.

In between the matinee and evening performances the actors had a very short break. So we ordered dinners in. Then after eating, since all the dressing rooms had cots, the actors were able to rest until performance time. But this created a problem because there was only one cot and most of the dressing rooms had several actors. Nineteen actors for

James Earl Jones and Joseph Ragno in Eugene O'Neill's *The Iceman Cometh* (1973), directed by
Theodore Mann

ten dressing rooms, naturally they began to get on each others nerves,
not only because of the cot shortage but from the antagonisms inher-
ent in the play. This became extreme to the extent that dressing rooms
fights—both verbal and physical—broke out among the cast. They were
behaving with the same animosity that their characters displayed on
stage towards each other. This off-stage angst helped vitalize their por-
trayals. The play and the living conditions backstage were so intense that

I don't think anyone involved would ever forget the experience. The joy of performing O'Neill's play and the boiling tensions backstage—that is living life on the edge.

I had seen a production at Long Wharf directed by Arvin Brown where he had the indication of a staircase that went off stage left to the bar's unseen upstairs rooms. I decided for our production that the staircase and the doors to the rooms be visible to the audience. Interestingly, we did not have to change or delay cues for their longer staircase entrances and exits. The staircase enabled the audience to see the actors' forlorn faces as they frighteningly entered their cold elevator-size rooms. Also as the actors descended we could see their hesitant attempt at bravura in accepting Hickey's challenge to give up their pipe dream.

Jimmy as Hickey and his relationship to each of the characters was personal and made them feel that they were of the greatest importance to him, therefore you understood why the "inmates" responded to his pitch for salvation. Hickey has to be the ultimate winning convincing salesman and a Christ figure that they would follow anywhere, and the audience has to be just as enraptured.

As soon as Hickey enters, on his very first line, anything cold or methodical in his personality destroys his charisma. Jimmy has it all—the magic, the smile, the laugh, the warmth—a man you'd entrust your life to. And when that grin spreads over his face you just want to hug him. Hickey has found salvation by giving up drinking and he is bringing that key to salvation to his old friends living at the bottom of the barrel. "I finally had the guts to face myself and throw overboard the damned lying pipe dream that'd been making me miserable," he explains to them, "I didn't need booze any more. That's all there was to it" He believes that they too will be able to crawl out. Another great attribute of James Earl Jones is that he has size—expansiveness—and his warm laugh just rolls like thunder. You just loved the guy!

Some of the reviews were very good, others were tepid. Maybe they had trouble accepting Hickey as a black man. But for me I cast a great actor and he completely fulfilled the role. And for audiences, it was a memorable evening in the theatre and has been talked about for years.

Next we did a new play by Murray Schisgal, *An American Millionaire*. The director who started out, Gerald Freedman, didn't last. Remember, he was the director who replaced Word Baker years ago in my production *Smiling the Boy Fell Dead* off-Broadway. We were in previews and Murray and the actors were unhappy, so I had to step in. I worked with Murray to get script clarification. I work with so many playwrights who are no longer with us that sometimes it's a pleasure to work with a living one as affable and incisive as Murray. The play is about a spoiled rich man, Nathaniel Schwab, played by Paul Sorvino, who can't get along with his son, Josh Mostel (Zero's son), who is in his 20s.

Paul loves to sing and fancies himself an opera singer. At the drop of a hat whether requested or not he will break out into an aria. He does have a nice sound.

It was very difficult for me and the actors to get the play in shape. We worked very hard. On opening night we weren't sure that we had accomplished our goal. So when the reviews came out and they were all good we were pleasantly thrilled. Not long after, we were back down in our cups because the *Millionaire* business proved only so-so.

We were now in our second year on Broadway and although we had a great success the first year, expenses such as stagehands, postage, printing flyers, Con Edison, salaries, advertising had risen substantially, and consequently we were struggling financially. Speaking of advertising, we had long ago realized the only newspaper that drew audiences through our ads was *The New York Times*, so that's where all our advertising dollars went. We had tested this belief with ads in the *Daily News* and the *Post*, from which we got very little response.

Fortunately, good Fate was back waiting in the wings when Paul and I went to see the production of *Scapino* from London directed by Frank Dunlop with Jim Dale. It was playing at the Brooklyn Academy of Music in one of their unconventional theatres. Paul and I and our spouses liked it very much. It was a hoot, a modern-dress version of Molière's *Scapin*, now set in Italy. The language was Molière except for an occasional contemporary witticism.

The next day, after we saw the show, Paul went about securing the rights. Amazingly, no other Broadway producers were vying for them. They probably weren't interested because the play had been performed in a three-sided space in both London and Brooklyn. Paul got the go-ahead from the National Theatre of Great Britain to bring over their

Young Vic Theatre Company but we had to put up a $50,000 deposit which we didn't have. A couple of years before the Morgan Guaranty Foundation had contributed $3,000 to Circle in the Square so we went back to them to see if they could help with a larger donation. They demurred but suggested that we go see the managing officer of their branch at Rockefeller Center. The officer's name was Robert Taylor, a tall man, dark hair, as handsome as the movie actor with the same name. He asked why did we need $50,000. We told him about the production of *Scapino* which we wanted to bring to the Circle. The Young Vic Company had returned to London and we needed to provide transportation for their return. Mr. Taylor listened sympathetically and then asked if we would change our bank from Chemical to the Morgan Guaranty. We told him we couldn't do this because of our long and friendly relations with Chemical. Still being sympathetic and trying to help, he then asked us if we could provide him with a statement of our financial plan that afternoon. He must have thought "these scatterbrains will never be able to do it and that'll end the matter." We ran back to the theatre and re-read a financial statement we had provided to the Ford Foundation and realized that with omitting a couple of paragraphs and some rewriting of the proposal that was the exact information that he wanted. After Mr. Taylor read it he smiled broadly and said, "It is the most comprehensive report that I have ever received from any nonprofit or corporation." He said, "When do you need the money?" We responded "Immediately. We have to send it to London today." He said, "I'll arrange to wire it to the bank in London." Needless to say Mr. Taylor and his wife were our honored guests at the opening.

For some time we had been trying to get funding from the City but to no avail. Mayor Abe Beame was in office, having come out of the Madison Club in Brooklyn where my father had been a member and counsel to Erwin Steingut, the minority leader in the State Assembly, in the Thirties. His son Stanley was now the minority leader and Sheldon Atlas, both schoolboy friends, helped me to get the mayor's attention. After a very cordial and sympathetic meeting with the mayor he directed me to his Deputy, James Cavanaugh. We explained to Mr. Cavanaugh that we had been seeking money from the city for some time and now we needed it to help mount a British production at the Circle. Mr. Cavanaugh immedi-

Jim Dale in Molière's *Scapino* (1974), directed by Frank Dunlop

ately put into motion a series of events whereby we would receive $50,000 from the city! After we bid him goodbye, even though we didn't have the money in hand, we leapt for joy. It had taken us so long to get city help and then, just as quick as turning on a light switch or snapping your finger, we had the money we had been hoping for to put into *Scapino*.

It was a heart-stopping series of events. We had found a wonderful new interpretation of a classic and we thrust forward with the production.

Scapino offers audiences a ne'er-do-well son, sexy girls, bathing suits and a waterfront scene and two conservative fathers insisting that their way is the right way. It was performed with wild, fast-paced humor. Jim Dale, who is marvelously athletic, swung on a rope hanging from the ceiling from one side of the theatre to the other. Like a comic Tarzan. The production was extremely well received and Jim became a Broadway star. He floated over Broadway sprinkling stardust all around. The audiences stormed us and our coffers got filled up again! AHHH, the glory and magic of theatre! You're down down down into the hollowing depths of Broadway and suddenly you're rescued by the critics and audiences starved for good theatre. The world looks mighty good from that latter position. And my mistress the Circle was smiling again.

One night Dustin came to see *Scapino* and I tried to interest him in the role of a philandering husband in a Feydeau play but to no avail. What a great Feydeau character he would be—affably guilty but always landing on his two feet.

Next we brought in Peter Nichol's *The National Health* directed by Arvin Brown with Leonard Frey, Rita Moreno, and Paul Rudd. The play was critically well received but didn't appeal to audiences. It takes place in a British hospital which is under their welfare medical system and showed its coldness and indifference to the people's needs. A young man (Paul Rudd) had a serious head injury from a motorcycle accident and an elderly man (Emery Battis) who is failing in old age befriends him. The two of them find solace in each other's presence. It was a good evening of theatre, but the audience wouldn't sit for it. Hospitals and sick people don't usually appeal to them. Some of the rare exceptions were *Wit*, with Kathleen Chalfant; *Hospital* with George C. Scott; Tom Conti in *Whose Life Is it Anyway*; and the 1930s play by Sidney Kingsley, *Men in White* which became a great film success with Clark Gable. All these plays (and movie) take place in a hospital and became big hits.

Here we are in the second season. So far we have done three plays, but only one was a financial success. By this time, in our second year we needed to raise $350,000 in unearned income, which is people donating money to a nonprofit institution, as opposed to ticket buying and concession sales, which are earned income. Some of the contributions came from the board of directors and the rest we got from foundations, corporations, individuals, and subscribers. In future years, depending upon how ticket sales went, that figure began to inch up. Even though we had a development director, in all our years of existence, we always fell short of that annual necessity. We were constantly trying to play catch-up and were relying completely on the success of the next show. It was like a thermometer going up and down, cold and hot, and hot and cold. As the years rolled by, we proved to be extremely fortunate to have an influx of money through an average of at least two successful productions per season.

CHAPTER 35

THE RAUL FACTOR

For some time I had wanted to do a musical, so Patricia and I began listening to scores until we found Frank Loesser's *Where's Charley?* based on the English classic *Charley's Aunt*. Since it was first produced in the 1890s, *Charley's Aunt* had been an audience favorite. The musical version was directed and adapted by George Abbott, with Frank Loesser's music and lyrics. It was a Broadway success in 1948 with Ray Bolger. I thought it would benefit from a smaller production with strings prominent in the orchestration. Frank's widow, Jo Sullivan Loesser was delighted and told me that Frank had originally written it as a chamber piece but the Broadway necessities of the time required one brass number. So the orchestrations had been changed to accommodate that one number. I went ahead with the play using a chamber orchestra with strings and talked with the musical director and solved the problem of doing that number with just strings. Jo was in complete agreement with this concept which followed her husband's original orchestrations. Now I had to cast the lead, Charley.

I saw many Broadway musical performers for the role, but they didn't have the fun *savoir faire* that I was looking for. Eventually I found that charm and innocent joy of life in Raul Julia. Raul could sing but he couldn't dance and the legend of the show was centered on long-limbed Ray Bolger and his fantastic tap shoe ability. Raul told me right out he couldn't tap and I should find someone else. I wouldn't let him go and told him we'd find a way for him to tap and not look foolish.

Theodore Mann (director), Raul Julia, and Tom Aldredge in rehearsal for George Abbott and Frank Loesser's *Where's Charley?* (1974)

When the set was designed by the very talented Marge Kellogg, I requested that we have a swing center stage that would fly in when we needed it. So when Raul's tap number came up, "Once in Love with Amy," Raul sat on that swing and did the best sitting down tap you ever saw.

Raul was a very special human being. He exuded love. He was as warm as the Latin sun and made everyone laugh and feel comfortable. He was forever embracing the girls in the show and they adored his innocent affection and his flirting. He would put his hands on the women's waists and swing them towards him. It didn't mean anything sexual—it was like a child playing. Raul's optimism was infectious, he never sent out any negative vibrations.

One Sunday matinee, Raul spotted Ray Bolger in the audience and when he came to the Amy number as he was sitting in the swing and tapping he said in a loud voice, "Eat your heart out, Ray!" The audience didn't know what Raul meant until curtain call when he asked for Ray to come up and join the call. As he did the band broke into "Once in Love With Amy" and Ray took the actress playing Amy in his arms and tap-danced and waltzed all around the stage with her. The audience loved it. And the cast was in tears seeing this great artist dancing in their show.

On another day, George Abbott also came to see the show. At the end he came bounding up the stairs, all 6'3" of him calling out, "Where's Ted Mann?" The sight of him bounding up the steps shouting my name—well, I thought he was going to brain me because he hated the show. Instead he grabbed me, almost tackled me, with a big hug and told me how much he liked the show! That was a big thrill coming from one of the all-time great Broadway directors.

During the rehearsals lots of spontaneous things happened, which I call the positive "Raul Factor," like Mr. Spettigue, played by Tom Aldredge, running up and through the aisles so that the audiences had to pull their legs up so he could get through. Another time, when Peter Walker (Sir Walter Chesney), couldn't pronounce "Donna Anna's" full name in rehearsal, he would say the first part of her name clearly and when trying to pronounce her last name which is Spanish, he would put his hand over his mouth so that his mispronunciation would be disguised. We broke up every time that line was said in rehearsal. Happily, the same held true for the audience. Sometimes something that is so funny in rehearsal falls flat when presented to the audience. The other night, I saw our Spettigue, Tom Aldredge, in *Twelve Angry Men*, where he plays the role of Juror Number Nine. Aferwards, he and I talked about that Peter Walker pronunciation and had a good tear-filled laugh about it. *Charley* was one of my favorite directing experiences, in large part due to the inspired performances by the whole cast infected by the music, the book, and the "Raul Factor."

CHAPTER 36

A BANNED PLAY REACHES BROADWAY

In 1975, during our third season, I had been talking to George C. Scott about doing another play with us. He told me he wanted to do O'Neill's *All God's Chillun Got Wings*. It is mostly a black cast. I said, "But there is no role in it for you, George." And he said, "I want to direct it." My heart dropped to the floor—at that time George had never directed a stage production for us or anywhere else—as far as I knew. I said let me think about it. Paul and I read *Chillun'* and realized that it was a wonderful play but a tough go because of its controversial subject matter— a black and white marriage. We decided to roll the dice and go ahead with George's directorial debut.

In the beginning of the play, black and white kids are playing in the streets without prejudice. Later, as adults, two of these children—a black man aspiring to become an attorney and a white woman rejected by a boxer—agree to marry. His ambitions are thwarted and she gloats over his failure and in the end loses her sanity and calls out "nigger" to him.

All God's Chillun' Got Wings had been done off-Broadway at The Provincetown Playhouse in the Village in the twenties. It had caused a furor because it was the first play that presented a black man in love with and married to a white woman. The scene in which he kisses her on stage led to great public indignation. George had a special interest in it because he never could understand or tolerate white antagonism towards blacks. If you remember, he directed the television series *East Side West Side*, the first time black actors were hired for national television in prominent dramatic roles.

George's wife Trish Van Devere and Robert Christian played the lovers. The audience of 1975 proved to be almost as prejudiced as the one fifty-one years before in that they could not appreciate a play about black and white relations. The critics in 1975 also had a hard time with the play, unable to categorize it in the O'Neill canon. The play is about how love can lead to jealousy and can also kill.

It is interesting to compare the leading character of this play with Yank in *The Hairy Ape*, who is a coal stoker on board a ship when a beautiful white woman comes down into the hold of the ship. At the sight of him covered in coal dust, she whimpers and pleads, "Take me away from this filthy beast" and faints. Yank spends the rest of the play trying to overcome his humiliation. He is ignored by the Fifth Avenue rich as though he were invisible; and the I.W.W. (International Workers of the World) rejects his attempt to join them. The play ends with him being crushed by a gorilla in the zoo whose cage he attempts to enter. Both of these characters in *Ape* and *Chillun* have similarities— Jim in *Chillun*, a highly educated black man, and Yank, an ignorant worker both suffer from prejudice.

During O'Neill's bohemian time in the Village, mixed couples were a common circumstance. In his plays, O'Neill never made political comments but here was writing about the nature of man and how prejudice is a pervasive force of destruction. I'm sure that as society matures *Chillun'* will be recognized as the important play it is.

Chillun' fulfilled our subscription period and despite the small attendance we were proud for having presented another O'Neill play (our third in three seasons) and for giving George his first chance at directing on Broadway. Boy did that pay off, because in years to come he starred and directed in three more great plays for us, all wonderfully directed and acted by George. They were great successes.

For some time I had been trying to get the rights to Arthur Miller's *Death of a Salesman*. Paul had a very good relationship with Mr. Miller having produced the first revival of *The Crucible* at The Martinique. Paul originally had difficulty securing a lease from the Martinique Hotel landlord, so he invited Arthur Miller to come and see the potential theatre and to bring his wife. The landlord was introduced to Mr. Miller and then turned to say hello to his wife—his mouth fell open and babbled to Paul, "Of course you can have the lease." Mr. Miller's wife at the time was Marilyn Monroe. After the success of the *Crucible* Arthur was always very friendly with Paul which led him to giving us the rights to produce *Death of a Salesman* at the Circle on Broadway.

It was great having the rights but we didn't have a Willy Loman. Dear reader you might ask why I didn't ask George to play it? In retrospect it was an obvious choice. At the time George, right after he did *God's Chillun*, was directing Martin Balsam in *Salesman* in Philadelphia. Things fell apart and the production was canceled.

Vince Gardenia had agreed to do the role, with me directing, but before we started rehearsal or even any other casting Vince dropped out. George knew that we had *Salesman* on our schedule and expressed to me his interest in playing Willy. I heartily agreed. George had told me how unhappy he'd been about his experience in the recent Philadelphia. He also wanted to direct. Genuinely concerned, I had to ask him how he could do this most unusual combination of acting Willy and directing at the same time. He explained he'd rehearse all of the scenes of the play but when it came to Willy's scenes he would use an understudy for that purpose and step out into the empty theatre and become the director. I said yes and George gave me a most unusual bear hug.

George worked out his dual capacity with careful precision and made sure he himself delineated the actor from the director. He had the ability to compartmentalize his directing responsibilities as distinguished from his acting. While one of Willy's scenes was going on with his understudy he would be talking into a micro tape recorder giving notes for himself regarding the work of the other actors.

Another amazing gift George had was his photographic memory. He would read a play and, with very little study, knew not only his lines but all the other actors' as well. Despite this gift I never once heard him give a "lost" line to another actor while he was on stage. He was a Victorian man, very sensitive to his fellow workers—actors, stagehands, and designers. As a director he was specific. His explanations were brief and to the point. He completely trusted the actors, and in most cases he had worked with them before. George believed that a professional did not need to be taught how to act by the director. He also felt very strongly about an actor being comfortable in his costume; whatever adjustment the actor requested was paramount to George.

He also had a great eye for talent. In 1982 we did *Present Laughter* with George directing and starring again, and he cast two total unknowns, Nathan Lane and Kate Burton—both in their Broadway debuts. His knowledge of actors was vast because of the number of plays, films, and TV he had done. When I visited George at home, the TV was always on low volume and he would catch glimpses of actors he'd either worked with or observed for future projects.

From the beginning of casting *Salesman*, George had it in his mind that the next-door neighbors ought to be African-Americans as a way to express his positive feelings about white and black relations. Arthur was very much against this idea saying that in the thirties, in New York, such close proximity of the races didn't exist. He was adamant and he would not give us permission to do the play with that casting. Paul and I drove up to Greenwich, Connecticut, to George's house, to try and change his mind. George insisted that was the only way he would do the play. Once he had his mind made up it was like trying to split a rock with your bare hands. Well there Paul and I were, with no Willy and therefore no *Salesman*. We called Arthur to tell him of George's intransigence and he said he would think about it. There was nothing we could do unless one of these Mount Rushmore–like figures would relent.

The next day, Paul, myself, our wives, and other Broadway produc-ers, managers and other assorted theatre personnel had been invited to sail on the QE2 for three days to Bermuda with all expenses paid for by John Sheean. We didn't know whether to go or stay. But there was nothing to gain by staying, so we decided to go—not happy at all. After the boat sailed that night there was a cable to Paul from his son Charlie saying that Mr. Miller had called to say go ahead with George's idea. The next three days on the boat we were so happy! The problem had evaporated.

We notified George of Arthur's decision and when we returned George and I immediately began auditioning actors. He told me who he wanted—Teresa Wright for Willy's wife, Harvey Keitel for Happy, and James Farentino for Biff. I knew all of them and this was fine with me. George's approach to his own character was that Willy, through the defeats and pressures of his life, had lost his way—he was on the verge of madness, struggling to come through the fog that his life had become. For Willy the play is a remembrance of the happiness and joys of past years and how the guilt and humiliations he is now suffering are driving him to madness. George is a physically big man and his slow deterioration became a devastating experience for the audience. George gave every inch of himself in performance. He never held back. He played Willy as a powerful man with great potential ground down by society. George's direction was so acute and his performance so deep that even when Willy was in the ground you felt that he heard Linda saying, "Attention must be paid" at his grave site.

I have always felt very sad about Willy. My Uncle Tom (my mother's brother) was a traveling salesman, lugging suitcases with girdles and brassieres up and down the East Coast. Uncle Tom also always put on a happy face, but boy what a toll it took. He died in his early 6os.

The day we were going to have our first dress rehearsal, George strode out in full costume with a hat on his head. When he took his hat off he was completely bald—not a string of hair. He had shaved his head to make Willy look older. I was shocked—it was such a change but did make him look more tragic. It was right for the character. The production was a great success with a new appreciation of what a wonderful play it is. The actors were lauded as was George for his direction and acting.

Harvey left the show after a month and was replaced by Martin Sheen. Everything was very happy. One of the TV networks wanted to tape the show but George insisted that it be put on film not on tape so that the audience wouldn't see a flat version of the stage production as you would get on videotape. The network wouldn't go for the extra cost so a TV version of that monumental production was never preserved.

There have been other stage productions of *Salesman* since but none to equal George's direction or acting. I remember in one particular scene him walking upstage in silence, his back speaking louder and more poignantly than any words.

I also remember George's gentleness with Teresa Wright. He loved

George C. Scott in Arthur Miller's *Death of a Salesman*
(1975), directed by George C. Scott

her dearly and took seriously any suggestion she had, and used most of them.

But we had bad luck with the casting of the next-door neighbors. The first two actors were willing but didn't satisfy George. Finally we found Arthur French and he was perfect.

George was a very sensitive person and highly tuned to personal problems other members of the cast might be going through. He himself was very vulnerable. Underneath that tough exterior was a gentle passionate man or as one would say "He's a pussy cat." George loved to laugh, from a good joke or a good story and when he did his cheeks brightened and he laughed looking straight at the jokester. You can tell a lot about a person from the way they laugh. The truth of a person is in their laugh. One night at a cast party at the Village studio apartment of Julie Garfield (John Garfield's daughter), George sat down at the piano and played and sang popular songs. Everyone joined in singing along to his delight—and contrary to his serious public image. Often times when I talked to him about a mutual friend or a relative's hard time tears would gather in his eyes and he'd be sure to call and help them. Julie, by the way, played the Second Woman in *Salesman*, with whom Willie is having an affair in Boston, when Biff breaks in on them.

I'd walk to dinner with George after a matinee to his favorite haunt, Gallagher's Steak House. He always wore his Detroit Tigers jacket and he would sit in his self-appointed corner in the restaurant. He'd promptly order a whiskey with a beer chaser aptly known as a Boilermaker. He'd have a sip of the drink, order a steak dinner with French fries and vegetables, and when the meal was served it sat majestically waiting to be devoured. George would cut a slice and swallow it. To encourage him I'd chew my steak noisily and make mm-mm-mm sounds that George was totally oblivious to. He'd take another sip and he was mellow. He'd talk about the audience that day. How so and so's role went and talk more shop. All the while I'm looking at his plate and I say, "Have some vegetables, George, before they get cold." Then dinner was over. That first slice was the only taste George took, his glass was empty and then we'd walk back to the theatre and he'd take his nap and be as fit as a fiddle for the evening performance. Drinking for George was like another man having toast every morning for breakfast.

George enjoyed working with Marge Kellogg as his scenic designer. They'd have one preliminary talk and then he'd leave her alone to conceive the design they discussed. They had very successful collaborations in *Present Laughter* and later *On Borrowed Time*.

In *Salesman* when George walked out, feet heavy, carrying two suitcases, he dropped them down, tilted his hat up, leaned on top of the refrigerator, weary and exhausted with the disappointment and humiliation of every human being. It was a silent moment that set the mood of the play—this was going to be a story you had to listen to! Wow, that moment still hangs with me. *Salesman* was nominated for several Tony Awards: Best Actor, Director, and Revival. Actors did their best work when they played opposite George because they had to meet his standard. It was the joy of competing with this Olympian. George fulfilled his three-month commitment to us and we were on to our next production.

CHAPTER 37

HOW ONE THING LEADS US
TO ANOTHER

I had gone to New Haven, Long Wharf Theatre, to see O'Neill's *Ah, Wilderness!* with a board member, Sandra Payson. It was a very good production with Geraldine Fitzgerald and Swoosie Kurtz directed by Arvin Brown. I invited them to come to the Circle. It adapted well to our space and it was a success. There was a young actor, Paul Rudd, playing the older brother. I liked his work very much and began thinking about a play for him.

Around that time for our twenty-fifth anniversary celebration and fundraiser we did an evening of scenes. The material came from plays we'd produced, or would like to do. I had met Maureen Stapleton at Colleen's house—we became good friends. Maureen was always game for a challenge and I asked her if she'd do a scene from *Glass Menagerie* and she agreed. Now I had to find the right actor to play her son, Tom. He had to be someone tough whose personal appearance and face would tell us he'd lived roughly and deeply. Rip Torn was my choice. That night the reading went well and I got very excited and asked Rip and Maureen to do the play for us. I directed and chose Pamela Payton-Wright for Laura. We were very good friends—in fact Pamela convinced my wife and me to become vegetarians, which we followed for several years. Then for the gentleman caller role I asked Paul Rudd, who had the kind of cocky assurance and good looks I wanted.

The first day of rehearsal Tennessee Williams came and brought his sister, Rose who was in a nursing home—she had had a lobotomy when she was a teenager. That operation locked her mind at age 16 forever. At this time she was in fact 66 years old. At the rehearsal she was dressed very neatly wearing a cute little flowered hat. She watched very primly without making any comments although she did laugh several times. She was very shy and sweet—and behaved as a proper Southern Victorian young girl.

Maureen Stapleton and Pamela Payton-Wright in Tennessee Williams' *The Glass Menagerie* (1975), directed by Theodore Mann

Tennessee had written the play twenty-five years before but at the rehearsal he was listening intently and interjecting changes he wanted. I said to him, "Tenn, you wrote the play years ago." And he replied, "Yes, I know but I have some changes I want to add." And I put in those that he wanted. He was always like that—youthful and excited about his plays and forever wanting to improve them. From his point of view they were always works in progress and many of the scripts that you read today are not in some cases the actual dialogue that was spoken on Broadway but were the result of Tennessee's "improving" his plays.

As you may remember, Laura in the play has a limp. I asked Tennessee what was the cause of this and he said in his wonderful Southern drawl, "She has an affliction of the soul." I couldn't wait to work on that scene. He had given me the clue to it. I knew Laura could move naturally if the "affliction of her soul" could be removed. So in the scene when they are alone, the gentleman caller asks her to dance—she refuses so he takes her in his arms, the music is playing and they start to spin around the set, she feels love and her limp disappears. She moves gracefully

Tennessee Williams and Theodore Mann (1975)

without a limp. For the first time in her life she is complete. Her affliction is gone as she embraces love. In our production we achieved that miracle—every night and each time I saw it my heart skipped.

Maureen had done the play before but in her entire career she had only performed on proscenium stages never in a three-sided space like ours. I kept trying to persuade Maureen in our rehearsal space that she would have to fully use our stage but my words couldn't help. But once we left the rehearsal studio and began working in the theatre she immediately understood about the audience and their physical relationship to the actor and how she had to flow.

Maureen said, after several days of rehearsal at the Circle, "Now I know what you were bothering me about trying to move me around the stage!"

The role of Tom is usually played by a young actor of shall we say, gentle persuasion with poetic sensibilities. In the play, Tom describes the strike activities that he had gotten involved in and the rough life that he had led. So I wanted a lived-in face—not a pretty boy. Rip Torn has a weather-beaten face that you could believe had been a longshoreman's, an agitator's, a guy who'd hopped cross-county trains, who'd been kicked and shoved and beaten by the corporate policemen. In other words, a guy who had lived and fought for his rights. Rip is that kind of a man—always a rebel—outspoken—doing only plays, movies or television that he believes in. He is also from the South and that wonderful drawl was just right for Tom. Rip handled the narrator's monologues beautifully—the poetic language was natural to him with lyricism and bite. Because Rip was so outspoken he was always getting into trouble with directors and producers—he has quite a reputation. But I didn't hesitate—he was the actor for Tom.

The work in rehearsals was going well. At that time, Actors' Equity had a rule that before the end of three weeks rehearsal an actor could be replaced without cause. We were rehearsing in the theatre and after the run-through I went backstage to Rip's dressing room to give him some notes. As I walked in Rip said, "I know you're going to give me my notice." I said, "No, I'm here to give you notes." It took about fifteen minutes for me to convince Rip that I liked his work and had absolutely no intention of firing him. Tom smokes in the play but Rip didn't for health reasons. But I insisted that Tom smoke so he rolled his own grape leaves. They smelt like marijuana and members of the audience thought that was what "bad boy Rip" was smoking! It was a *very* strong smell.

Rip was married to Geraldine Page. Patricia and I went to dinner in their brownstone in the West 20s. The living room was filled with stacks of boxes that had been there since they moved in nine years earlier. It looked like the setting of the *Madwoman of Chaillot*. After a delicious dinner which Gerry concocted in her own improvisational style Rip insisted that Pat and I climb the ladder to his roof to the most beautiful vegetable garden and a fabulous view of the Manhattan skyline. Rip had had some run-ins with the FBI and he thought they didn't like him because of his opposition to Richard Nixon. Up on the roof Rip was sure that the FBI had him under surveillance and he laughed that they couldn't figure out what the hell he was growing up there.

During dinner Rip and Gerry told Patricia and I about their house in Mexico, which they generously offered to us with servants at our convenience. It had been the Governor's residence when Spain controlled the area. When we did visit, its walls still retained some of the old original wallpaper from those days as well as great heat-producing fireplaces, which we needed at night because it was so cold. Traveling to the bathroom which was outside was like walking barefoot through Siberia. We'd get up from the deliciously warm bed, run down to the bathroom and back to bed as fast as possible. The principle caretaker there was a man name Chimini. He took care of everything for us including wood for the fireplace which he went up into the hills to gather for us. The wood in that area is long-burning and superb in producing heat. Patricia and I would be lying in the iron frame bed with the light from the fireplace dancing across the wallpaper. It was very snuggly and romantic. There's nothing as nice as having a warm body next to you on a cold night.

We met other Americans who were retired and living in this small town. Most of them seemed like ex-government employees. I had the feeling they were retired military on the lookout for any activity dangerous to America. We did meet a wonderful couple from Tuscon who invited us to come and stay at their Arizona mountain retreat—which we took them up on the following year. AHHHH the life of a producer without money.

Our son Andrew was with us in Mexico and he and I would go play basketball in the outdoor court against the local kids. There was a jail in town that we went to visit. I was curious to see what the conditions were like. Most of the cell doors were open. The prisoners were cooking meals outdoors in the courtyard with family visitors stopping by at all times during the day. It was more like a small country hotel than a jail—the only restriction was that the prisoners couldn't go home but they could have visitors all day until sleep time.

There was a wonderful restaurant, the only one in town. We went there quite frequently, the service was calm and the waiters were patient. The most important thing in the restaurant was to have a good relaxing meal. There were no phones to answer, no appointments to run to. The only telephone in town was at the post office. On New Year's Eve we went to the Town Hall and celebrated with the local Mexicans and we danced our toes away.

Patricia would vocalize every morning and her extraordinary sound would draw the townspeople who stood outside our governor's hacienda. They were enchanted with her voice and with her long blonde hair—unusual in Mexico. The Mexicans treated her like a rare bird. Anything she needed people ran to get her. Patricia vocalized and did scales every morning of her life no matter where we were.

CHAPTER 38

"V"

While we were doing *Menagerie* I read in *The New York Times* that Vanessa Redgrave was visiting New York. She's a great actress. I had seen her perform in London, she had never been on Broadway and I thought how good it would be if she would appear at the Circle. So I sought her out and one afternoon we sat down to talk in the empty theatre. She was enchanted by it and wanted to work here. I had also seen Vanessa on film, where she was incandescent. Any scene she was in, even without dialogue, my eyes would be drawn to her. She said that she loved Ibsen and in particular *Lady from the Sea.*

I was excited about the possibility and realized what a demanding but perfect role it was for her. We quickly agreed to do it. Vanessa has become one of my favorite people and a dear friend. She is one of the most compassionate people I know, particularly where human or civil rights are involved. She has fought her battles for these causes with all the strength she has. "V" as her friends call her is a voluminous reader with great retentive ability. When she gets involved in a cause she becomes completely consumed and focused. For her, every living moment is consumed with achieving justice for people or persons who have been alienated from society.

When she is rehearsing she is a changed person, absorbing what the director tells her completely and trustingly. There is something child-like in her openness. As rehearsals begin she is like an empty canvas

Vanessa Redgrave in Henrik Ibsen's *The Lady from the Sea* (1976), directed by Tony Richardson

and as the work progresses she is meticulously painting in her tones and hues. She keeps growing and investigates the characters even after the play opens.

She and Patricia became very good friends. We've had many stimulating wonderful times with Vanessa. Her performance in *Lady from the Sea* was startling in its simplicity and strength. She also was supportive and loving to all the actors. Her ex-husband is Tony Richardson, the father of Natasha and Joely. His direction made *Lady* a memorable work.

Before Vanessa was to begin rehearsals for *Lady* the furor about her support of the Palestinians had already begun. That didn't stop us despite bomb threats and anonymous telephone calls that "you'll be picketed and Jews won't buy tickets." Paul and I felt fiercely she was entitled to the freedom to support whomever she wanted. None of these threats ever materialized and plenty of tickets were sold.

Vanessa was staying at our apartment and the threats extended there too. Pat and I didn't give it a thought. "V" was fearless and just went about her business without any paranoia. Vanessa went on about her work and just to be safe she did have a personal security guard. Patricia and I had many discussions with Vanessa in which she expressed her support for any oppressed people. At that time in her opinion the Palestinians were being denied their rights. She was just as fervent in her support for Jews when a human rights issue was involved. She, in fact, sought the opportunity to portray a Jewish woman in a Nazi camp in a script written by one of America's strongest advocates for human rights, Arthur Miller. Her performance in that TV play, *Playing for Time*, stirred your heart.

Years later she was involved in the struggles of the people of Bosnia. I helped do a fundraiser at the Marriot Marquis Theatre here in the city with all-star performers, which she gathered together. When Vanessa calls, actors come out of the woodwork to support her views. I also flew to England to participate in another of her fundraisers in support for the people of Kosovo with important actors, including Daniel Day-Lewis, and the leading actor from Kosovo. Towards the end of the evening two elderly Jewish women, holocaust survivors, spoke. They had never before revealed their experiences publicly but through their friendship with Vanessa, agreed to speak out. It was the highlight of the event and was further evidence of what drives Vanessa. These issues were not "political" to "V" but simply concerns for other human beings. She and her brother Corin have been outspoken critics of how prisoners of Guantanamo Bay have been treated. "V" will travel around the world at the drop of a hat to defend human and civil rights.

A few years after *Lady* she was engaged by the Boston Symphony to narrate a symphonic piece. The protests from Jewish organizations and individuals started up again. The symphony's board got frightened and rescinded her contract. She sued the orchestra for violation of her contract and her civil rights. She was fighting for those rights for herself and every American actor. I was a willing witness for her at her trial in Boston. I cited our experience with similar threats and my testimony confirmed the meaningless of the threats. Happily, she won the case and I was proud to be able to help Vanessa.

When she was performing in *Orpheus Descending* and of course working on one of her causes at the same time, we went to lunch at the Russian Tea Room with a friend of hers. While the friend and I were talking Vanessa's head went slowly down onto the table and she fell asleep—she was so exhausted! She had used up every ounce of her energy fighting all those windmills of the world's prejudices. My heart went out to her. I wanted to take her in my arms and let her know I would always support her and her causes.

After a performance of *Orpheus*, she and I had been talking in her dressing room; when we came out of the stage door the usual mobs of fans were waiting for "V," but what was not usual was the reception they got from Vanessa. Mind you it was drizzly. She not only greeted people, she asked their names so she could talk to them individually. They had a conversation, and then she signed their autographs. Afterwards, Vanessa and I went to the Russian Samovar and I asked her how she could stand there in the rain talking to people when she had a cold. She answered, "Well they were standing in the rain too, and, besides, they're so patient and so dear."

Paul and I bless Vanessa for helping us reopen Circle in the Square Theatre in February 1999 after we'd been dark for almost a year. In a library in Houston she had discovered an unproduced play by Tennessee Williams, one of his earliest works, *Not About Nightingales* which she brought to the attention of the National Theatre in London, where they had a successful run. Vanessa arranged for its premiere at a theatre in Houston—all this when there was no role for her to play. I called her and asked if it would be right for the Circle. She replied, with a smile in her voice, "It would be perfect." I said, "If you say so let's try and move it here." She immediately put the gears in motion. Under Trevor Nunn's direction, it enjoyed a very successful run at the Circle. It also thrust us back into the mainstream of Broadway. Her beloved brother, Corin, starred in it and gave a truly powerful performance. He, Trevor, and the play were nominated for Tony Awards.

CHAPTER 39

Cloudy Days

After the seriousness of the Ibsen play *Lady from the Sea* it was time for us to do a musical. One of my favorites is *Pal Joey* by Richard Rodgers and Lorenz Hart. It was rarely produced and I thought it was time for a revival. The first thing was to find a Joey who could dance and sing.

I asked Margo Sappington to do the choreography and we began the casting process, which went well, as did the search for the featured roles.

But we struggled to find a Joey. I offered the role to Eddie Valella, principal dancer with the New York City Ballet but he was reluctant. He is not a singer but a wonderful dancer, dark-haired, handsome with a mischievous smile.

At my suggestion, Eddie worked with our vocal coach and finally was confident enough to accept the role. But in performance, right at the first number, "I Could Write a Book," his vocal insecurity came across to the audience and made them fidgety. As the show progressed they forgave him because of his superb dancing, charm, and sex appeal.

Eleanor Parker was the female lead, Vera Simpson, a rich woman on the look out for a young guy. Eleanor was a film star and very nervous about singing and acting in a Broadway show. She requested that her husband be allowed to sit and watch rehearsals for the first few days, which I granted though he stayed more than a few days. As she was rehearsing, as usual the rest of the cast would be sitting around reading newspapers, knitting, studying their lines or whatever—all very casual and *not* being judgmental of the rehearsal going on. But Eleanor insisted that no one be in the rehearsal room while she was working. It got so bad that when she was working on a song with the accompanist she didn't want anyone in the room except her pianist—that included me. I thought she was so frightened maybe this would help calm her down. As the director I had to listen to her working through her song through the wall of the room next door! On top of this, Eddie became disenchanted with Margo's choreography and threatened to leave the show. Through the good offices of our attorney Floria Lasky, I asked Jerome Robbins if he would come in and help with the choreography. He of course had choreographed many ballets with Eddie. Jerry agreed and promptly went to work with Eleanor and Eddie.

Meantime I was doing scenes and songs with the other actors and would put in Jerry's choreography as we came to those scenes. It was an extremely difficult process. And we sometimes held our breath hoping a miracle would happen. After two weeks of working exclusively with Eddie and Eleanor, Jerry came to me and said, "I throw up my hands. I can't make it right. There is nothing I can do."

Eventually Eleanor stampeded across the line of propriety in the theatre, when during a preview she refused to wear a costume that had been designed for her and to which she had agreed. Just before the preview was to begin, Paul fired her based on her past behavior and the Actor's Equity rule that requires an actor to wear the costume designed for them. Joan Copeland, Eleanor's understudy, gloriously took over the role.

Shortly thereafter, Eddie left and there we were in previews with a fully mounted musical and still missing Joey. I replaced Eddie with Chris Chadman, a member of the chorus who could dance and sing. Suddenly this storm receded and the wonderful calm fell over the company and they all fulfilled their performance responsibilities. Chris did very well but the real victory was Joan Copeland as Vera Simpson. She was lauded by the critics and received a Tony nomination. I am eternally grateful to both of them for jumping in and saving the production and bringing high quality to the show. They helped us to narrowly avoid disaster. Richard Rodgers and his wife came to see the show and highly complimented myself and the cast, then he took the conductor quietly aside and told him to play softer so, "the lyrics can be heard."

The next play we chose was Marguerite Duras' *Days in the Trees*, one of the most beautiful plays we've ever done. It was brilliantly played by Mildred Dunnock. Joseph Maher played her ne'er-do-well bachelor son in his 50s, and it was sensitively directed by Stephen Porter.

Days in the Trees is a play about the relationship of an elderly mother and her mature son whom she is visiting. He's a gigolo living an indulgent life of booze and women made possible through the money his mother provides for him. He is still her child and she continues to treat him that way but at the same time wants to break his dependency on her. As much as he needs her, she also needs him. The selfish, vain son presents his monetary problems as temporary; he needs her assistance merely to tide him over. She knows better and refuses his requests.

Having denied him she is in fear that she might lose his love. So the night before her departure, Mildred stands alone on stage and says to her offstage son, "I'll leave a little something for you." She places a substantial amount of money on top of the refrigerator and quickly departs. That moment and their relationship rang a bell for parents with post-adolescent dependent children.

The critics didn't like the play much. I think they missed the kernel of what it was saying—no matter how old your child and how negligent his lifestyle is, we parents have great difficulty denying them their material requests, out of our own insecurities of how denial might affect our relationship. In audience seminars after the performance, people identified very strongly with the confusion of the grown child/parent relationship. And this is the kernel I think the critics missed. I have always felt that *Days in the Trees* was one of the most beautiful plays we have ever produced—unfortunately also one of the least successful.

CHAPTER 40

THE LADDIES OF THE CLUB

While *Trees* was running Paul and I also produced *The Club* at the downtown Circle.

I had heard about a production of the play, which was being performed in a small theatre in the Berkshires produced by Lynn Austin. So that summer, on one of my trips to visit Jonathan at school in Lenox, when I had a free afternoon I saw the show and had a wonderful surprise. The play with song and dance was a parody of a turn-of-the-century English gentlemen's club—their manners and interests—their little jokes about their wives, other women, and drinking. The dialogue was all about men's duplicitous feelings towards the female sex. We decided to bring it to the Circle that fall.

The delicious aspect of *The Club*, written by Eve Merriam, was that it was all performed by women with names like Algy, Bertie, Freddie, Bobby, Johnny, and Henry! Women were dressed in starched collars, tails, and top hats—even the male butlers were played by females. The women's hair was all cut short and combed in the style of the period. Under the brilliant direction and choreography of Tommy Tune, his first directorial job off-Broadway, the actresses assumed the manner of men physically and vocally. The men/women all sang beautifully and Tommy's tap dance choreography was sublime. All the songs performed were from 1894–1905.

The show made you happy to be alive! It was a play of perfect observations about male behavior. Even though the setting was the turn-of-the-century, the conduct of the "men" was as modern as today. (Which doesn't say much about the social progress of men!) The reviews were excellent.

Women loved it but men were very uncomfortable with the gender-switching. It was 1976 and the new women's lib movement was just beginning to bite into male security. A few years before I had attended a debate at Town Hall entitled *Sexual Freedom*. The participants were Norman Mailer and four women including Germaine Greer and Diana Trilling. Men and women were standing up shouting at the participants and at each other, throwing crumpled up programs and pens. It was a raucous event. It didn't help tempers that the air conditioning was malfunctioning that night. A documentary of the event was filmed by the great D. A. Pennebaker under the title, *Town Bloody Hall*.

When the audience came out of the *The Club* the men could be heard grumbling, "Were those men or women up there?"—their female mates would respond indignantly with variations of "they were women up there, you chauvinist pig!" The men would then say, "They look like faggots." The women shot back, "They are more butch than most of the men I know."

Paul and I strongly believed in the play and we fought to keep it alive, which we did for seven months, but unfortunately it never found a large audience.

After that, Tommy became a sought-after and successful director and choreographer of Broadway musicals and even played the lead in *My One and Only* with Twiggy. Tommy is one of the nicest, gentlest, but firmest directors I've ever worked with. The cast of *The Club* has remained friends. We had an anniversary party at my apartment twenty years after the opening. One of the women admired a photograph on our wall of Anna Magnani in the film *Orpheus Desending*. In her usual style my wife Patricia took it off the wall and gave it to her. The thirtieth is coming up and I look forward to seeing the women/men of *The Club*.

The Club was to be the last play Paul and I produced at Circle in the Square Downtown on Bleecker Street because our Board of Directors thought the expense of maintaining two theatres was beyond our

Richard Chamberlain and Dorothy McGuire in
Tennessee Williams' *The Night of the Iguana* (1976),
directed by Joseph Hardy

means. The board asked me to release them from their obligation to underwrite the space. I was hesitant because I still had a great sentimental attachment to our doing plays down there. I felt like I was losing a family member—so many friends and great plays were the fiber of that theatre. Paul convinced me to look to the future and I released the Board from their obligation. He said that I would make a lot of money just renting it. How right he was. Within a week after the Board's decision, Bob Kamlot working for Joe Papp called to ask if I'd rent the downtown Circle to Joe for his new musical, *I'm Getting My Act Together and Taking It on the Road* by Gretchen Cryer and Nancy Ford, directed by Word Baker. It ran for a year, and it kicked off a long string of many successful shows. Fifteen years later I rented it to The Actors' Studio training program of The New School for their exclusive use.

In 1976, back uptown, we did Tennessee Williams' *Night of the Iguana* with Richard Chamberlain, Dorothy McGuire and Sylvia Miles playing Maxine. This was a wonderful coup for us because Richard was an important actor based on his *Doctor Kildare, The Thorn Birds* and *Shogun* TV work, as well as his classical roles in England, and because Dorothy McGuire was such a respected movie star. Joseph Hardy directed. He had done it in Los Angeles with Richard and Dorothy. We cast New York actors in all the other roles and the set was redesigned for the

Circle. At this time, *Iguana* was not a favorite of the critics. Once again I thought they had missed the greatness. Our production was wonderfully received and very well attended. I felt proud to have helped resuscitate the reputation of another of Tennessee's plays.

Since our move uptown we had weekly, post-performance seminars with the actors participating. Richard resisted taking part in them. I finally convinced him that he might learn something about what the audience was thinking. After much more nudging, he finally agreed. After that first seminar, I couldn't keep him away from future ones. He loved hearing what the audience thought of the play and production. At one of the early seminars a young man stood up and asked, "Why do you use that funny accent?" referring to his Southern drawl which we all had been encouraging him to modify. At the next performance he quickly adjusted his speech. No one ever had to ask him that question again. It proves that criticism from outside the family is sometimes more easily accepted.

It was at this time that Patricia and I went to Rip Torn's old Governor's house in Mexico. We offered our home in Bedford to Richard and the cast members for the Christmas holiday. They had a wonderful white Christmas, sleds, snowballs, fireplace and all.

At one of the performances of *Iguana* the audience was in their seats, the house was full but the show was delayed because a woman was very drunk and talking loudly. The ushers tried to get her to the ladies room but she refused. The audience was annoyed and getting restless. Some were sympathetic but most were down-right hostile and shouting at her "to shut up" or "go home." At this point Dorothy walked out on stage — she was wearing a robe over her costume. Everyone quieted down as she went up to the lady, put her hand out in a friendly gesture and brought her to center stage. With her arm around the woman, she said to the audience in her soft-spoken voice, "Hello, I'm Dorothy McGuire." At Dorothy's request, the woman gave her name. The audience grew silent. Dorothy stood for a moment arm in arm with the woman by her side, looking at the audience. Then she said, "Ladies and Gentlemen, this is a human being." The subtext of which was: Don't shout at her; you should be ashamed. Dorothy embraced her and walked with the lady and her mate up the stairs into the lobby and into a waiting taxi.

The audience meanwhile sat in absolute silence. It had been a remarkable display of compassion for one person and done in front of a snarling cruel crowd of 600 people. Dorothy is a great soul. It was like a scene in the Colosseum in ancient Rome when the Christians were being offered up for slaughter and no one stood up to defend them. Here one brave soul demanded by her quiet grace and dignity that they stop the verbal abuse.

That night when Dorothy entered the stage she was received by a humbled audience with thunderous applause.

We had such a success with *Iguana* that twelve years later in 1988 we decided to do it again with me directing and Jane Alexander as Maxine Faulk, the bawdy owner of the Costa Verde hotel in the hills of Puerto Barrio, Mexico. I had called Jane and asked if she was interested in playing the role. I had always admired her work. I liked the idea of Jane challenging herself through Maxine who is low-down, lusty, mean, and dirty which is the opposite end of the acting spectrum from the patrician roles I had seen her perform in. It is always exciting when an actor wants to stretch herself which usually produces good results. In rehearsal she worked very hard to achieve the character. She is such a good actress the transition was very easy. Shannon says to Maxine in the play, "You

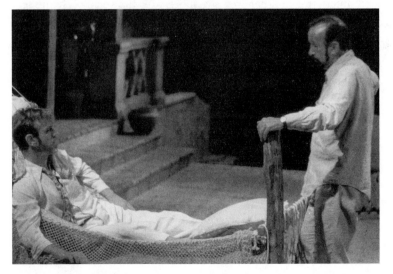

Vitali Solomin and Theodore Mann (director) in a rehearsal for *The Night of the Iguana* (1990), Maly Theatre, Moscow

are bigger than life and twice as ugly." That is Shannon pulling her leg because Maxine is actually very sexy and attractive. But Jane certainly was bigger than life.

The cast also included Nicolas Surovy as Reverend Shannon (the defrocked priest), Maria Tucci (Hannah Jelkes the poetess), William LeMassena (her grandfather Nano "the oldest poet alive"), Pamela Payton-Wright (Miss Fellowes, the leader of the group of Southern bible girls traveling in Mexico), Tom Brennan (Jake, the owner of the tour company), my son Jonathan Mann (Hank, the young bus driver), and Chandra Lee, my daughter-in-law as Hilda, the daughter of the German tourist family who are staying at the hotel. The time is 1940 just on the verge of the U.S. entering WWII and Shannon, as Tennessee's voice, mocks the Germans, their superior manners, and attempts at rigorous health routines. He never socializes with them at the hotel.

There was a tremendous amount of trouble during the casting period with Lady St. Just. She had been a great friend of Tennessee's in London and when he died she became his literary executrix. At one time in her career she had been an actress and probably married Lord St. Just. As far I know she was an American who had married an alleged Lord St. Just—but nobody knew whether he had really existed. She was opinionated, interfering and believed she spoke with the voice of Tennessee. Her behavior was completely opposite to the way Tennessee conducted himself when I directed *Glass Menagerie*. He was supportive and very adaptable. For example, when I chose Rip Torn it was completely against type for the role of Tom. Tennessee was delighted to go against the grain.

As rehearsals began and into previews, Lady St. Just continually gave notes to the actors and created a very unstable atmosphere. However, we all kept our eye on the ball to do the play as truthfully as we could. In the end, we persevered and received favorable reviews. To this day, I am unable to pass Lady St. Just's hotel on Central Park South—appropriately named The Ritz—without shuddering.

CHAPTER 41

MOSCOW MEETS TENNESSEE

It is interesting in life how many times one thing does lead to the other. In this case the work led to my being invited to direct *Night of the
Iguana* in Moscow, for Russia's National Theatre. Not long after our
1988 production of *Iguana*, the director of the Maly Theatre in Moscow,
Vladimir Andreov, came to visit me. The purpose was to discuss an exchange program between the Circle and the Maly. The idea was that I
would go and direct a play there and later we would invite one of their
directors to come and direct a play here. They would pay my transportation, hotel and food and we would do the same for them as part of the
exchange. So about a month or two later off I went to Russia, my family's
homeland. The Maly is right next door to the Bolshoi Theatre. Bolshoi,
which means big, presents ballet, opera, and symphonies. Maly, which
means small, presents theatre. The Maly itself is a gorgeous building
probably 150 years old.

At the Maly Theatre, I was allowed to sit in Stalin's chair—hidden
from the audience—from which he and I had an unencumbered view of
the stage. They had a company of 130 actors who were permanent members. It was exciting to see the variety of their plays and the excellence of
their actors—in particular, Yuri Solomin, who was now the head of the
company and whom I saw perform in many plays including Chekhov's
Ivanov and Pushkin's *Boris Godunov*. The quality of acting among the
company members varied widely from spectacular to ordinary.

While in Moscow, I saw several productions of Russian plays. Watching them perform Russain plays, it was like being in a Russian home. I could smell the samovar and the borscht.

I also attended a production of *Long Day's Journey*. At the end of Act One, James Tyrone was about to leave his house putting on his ten-gallon hat with his matching cowboy boots—he was as fat as a sausage—hardly the figure described by O'Neill of a matinee idol. Whenever Edmund was alone, he cuddled and talked to his teddy bear which he carried around with him throughout the play. In the upstage area was a series of steps leading to a representation of a small room, where James Tyrone had his desk, telephone, and coat hooks. On the back walls there weren't any windows to convey the sense of the outside, the sea, or the fog. When James Tyrone doled out money to Edmund he first calculated the amount on an abacus.

All of this was the Russian's interpretation of America, which they had obviously gathered from watching *Bonanza*. That production forewarned me of the misconceptions Russians have of America in body language, vocal intonations, costumes, hairstyles, furnishings, and props. Our body language, our haircuts and our clothing are simply different from theirs. I felt that when I directed an American play in Moscow, I would be an emissary. I was determined to present to the Russian audience all the elements of an American play, as though they were seeing it in New York. I chose Tennessee's *Iguana* because Williams is one of the best voices of our culture.

Zack Brown was the scenic designer and Jennifer Von Mayrhauser designed the costumes for our 1988 production of *Iguana*. These designs became the same ones I used in 1989 in Moscow.

The Maly agreed to use the same designs for the sets, costumes, and props by Zack Brown and Jennifer Von Mayrhauser from my Circle production, which made me feel very comfortable. The Circle has done many wonderful productions with great designers—I haven't given due credit to their work in this book. I am grateful to Zack and Jennifer in particular because their creation transferred easily to the Maly—a proscenium theatre—from their original concept for our three-sided space. I had enough problems on my mind with the language barrier and a rehearsal period of five weeks with actors accustomed to six months! I arranged that

Allen Moyer, Zack's assistant, be on hand in Moscow to supervise the painting and construction of the set, props, and costumes. Everything was made in the Maly theatre studios. The Maly and all other Russian theatre organizations are very poor but by ingenious substitution they were able to recreate our designs. Their technical staffs are on permanent salary and are true artists in their love of theatre which shows in their work. For *Iguana* they built Mexican bamboo chairs with leather straps—bamboo and leather were in short supply in Russia so they imitated it. The tables on Maxine's veranda looked Mexican to the audience, but on close inspection they were of Czechoslovakian design. Another small example of their improvisational skills was the screen door that Shannon comes out of. In the New York production, we had a metal spring to prevent the door from slamming. The Russians had never seen or heard of a door spring. I described its purpose to them and they constructed a spring out of a piece of cloth and rubber bands! All I had to say to them was "nyet" and clapped my hands together then point at the screen door. They understood. Sign language became more and more important. Thank god for my Indian sign language that I gathered from films—"Me Tonto."

The Russians use music in their productions to an extent similar to movie underscoring. Before I went to Russia, Patricia and I went through the script and chose pieces of popular songs from the period that would add emotional dimensions. Each character was introduced with a musical motif that I set at a low sound level so that it had a feeling of coming from a distance like memory. You would hear a small section of a character's music underneath their speech. For instance, when Shannon speaks about Maxine's dead husband, and the husband's love of baseball, Patricia and I selected a special piece that was sentimental and reminded you of baseball. The music I used was a powerful addition to the production. It adds another dimension to the play. Unfortunately, the use of music underscoring in a dramatic production in the United States is rare.

For productions done at the Maly the actors are assigned roles by the head of the theatre but I wanted to do this production the American way. I insisted that the company members audition.

In America, when you come to audition, you bring a head shot and resumé and then you do a monologue or scene. These repertory mem-

bers didn't have or need head shots and resumés because they were under lifetime contracts. They had in fact never auditioned before in their
career. They were shy at their first audition but at the call backs they had
gotten the hang of it. I cast the actors from what I saw that day.

Yuri strongly recommended his brother, Vitali, for the role of Shannon. Vitali was a movie star in his own right as I later observed when
we would be walking in the park or having dinner together—it was like
walking down Broadway with Al Pacino or like a king walking among
his peasants. I had gone to see him in a production at another theatre
and liked his work and met him afterwards and through my translator,
offered him the role. He is a very exuberant man and upon hearing the
news, embraced me like a bear and in the Russian style kissed me on
both cheeks.

We began rehearsals in a small room with a long table with the actors
sitting on either side. I placed the actors opposite the characters that
they would be playing scenes with.

The first day I spoke about the history of the play and its theme and
what the characters mean in American life. Then I stopped and said,
"Now take a break. And we will read the play." The actors' jaws dropped
and they began chattering amongst themselves. I asked the translator,
"What is going on?" and she told me that they were surprised at the
briefness of my remarks. In their traditional rehearsal period the director
talks and talks and talks for the first four months and *then* they read the
play and begin blocking.

The second day of rehearsal I told the actors through my two translators that if they felt like moving around to feel free to do so. So the reading began—within minutes they were on their feet. As they got more
into the play and more excited they climbed over the table to read the
scene with their play partner. They were exhilarated— they were set
free as though a huge weight had been lifted from them. Later they
told me of how frustrated and bored they became during the long Russian rehearsals where they listened while the Russian director talked
and talked.

At one point in the play Shannon asks Maxine, the hotel owner, to
cash a check for him. The Russian actors didn't know what that meant. I
asked Vitali, where he kept his money and he said, "Under the mattress

of course." I said, "what about banks?" And he said, "Well we don't trust them. We keep our money safe." And repeated, "Under the mattress." At that time there seemed to be very few banks in Moscow. So I had Shannon visibly wave the check to help the audience understand.

Shannon uses "Honey" repeatedly—a typical southern greeting. It turns out there is no Russian equivalent so we found a word of equal Russian tenderness. Of course they have honey in Russia but they don't use the word as a greeting.

The Russian actors performed the play wonderfully. They are people of big emotions and Tennessee's characters are bigger than life. They played his passions at full throttle. They and the audiences understood the significance of the religious and lustful aspects of the play. The Russian people have a deep love of religion and even though it had been suppressed and denied to them for so many years, they still longed for it like a lost love— It was in their bones. When they made the sign of the cross—Russian style—they did it with deep reverence. The audience loved and identified with this play because of the battle raging within Shannon, the defrocked minister, who is torn between his spiritual and physical selves.

The actors and the audience took me and the play into depths I never imagined but which Tennessee had obviously intended. For example, Shannon who is the tour guide for a busload of Southern Baptist women, bolts out of his room disheveled and sweating from the immediate negative circumstances pressing in on him. He is losing his already weakened grip on reality. In his mad fury he rips the cross from his neck and is about to hurl it into the jungle, when Hanna (the ethereal granddaughter of the poet Nanoo) extends her hand to him palm open in a spiritual gesture of compassion, understanding the chaos he is going through. At this moment, he realizes Hanna is his savior. Instead of throwing his cross into the jungle he places it a hair's breadth above her open palm and allows it to slip from his hand. And then he enfolds her hand and the cross in his palm. This was a moment of deep sensuality—as though their bodies had fused together for the first time and a spiritual lustful bond was consummated between them.

The production was filled with other fervent moments: Shannon with the young girl from the Bible tour recreating his thwarted seduction years before of a young parishioner, and Shannon with the bible school teacher using his charm in an attempt to overcome her fury, each of the women succumbing to his manliness.

I had a great time being there—living a monastic life of just directing with no other commitment, no checks to sign or telephone calls. Although I did call Patricia several times a week to enjoy with me the experiences I wished that she was there to share with me. I missed her deeply and wished she was with me. With an eight-hour time difference and their telephone system from 1925— it was no mean feat to make a call from Moscow to New York.

I would eat lunch in the theatre's commissary, located on the top floor where we had kasha and vegetables. I was surprised to find that kasha was eaten by other people besides Jews. When I was a kid my mother sent me around the corner to the A&P for kasha. And the Irish clerk in his lilting tone said, "Kasha? Don't know what that 'tis?" I went home to my mother embarrassed and crying. She wiped my tears with her handkerchief out of her apron pocket, hugged me and stroked the back of my neck and said, "Just go back and tell the man you want brown oats." So with a nickel in the pocket of my knickers I hesitantly went back to the A&P and my mother's advice worked. As I tell this story my ears still burn with the embarrassment of that incident.

After lunch we rehearsed until six o'clock. Then I would go to the theatre's restaurant, which is open to the public, for dinner with my translator. The restaurant was several blocks away. There was no sign on the building indicating it was a restaurant and the front door was locked. So I would knock on the wooden door. The peephole would open. The eye would appraise me and decide whether I was admissible or not —a hell of a way to run a restaurant! Once inside, there were almost never more than one or two customers. I wonder how many people were denied admittance by that eye.

After several meals there I realized that the entrées were not edible. One night I had ordered chicken Kiev which when it arrived was pink if not bloody. I sent it back. The next night I came, I was told that the chef no longer worked there; they had a new chef and I never ventured to order an entrée again. I didn't want to be responsible for the new chef losing his job. I would order soup and several appetizers; with the Russian black bread they were delicious. They also had a wonderful non-alcoholic drink, called Kav, which smelled like wood but was very tasty.

Then home to the hotel and watch one of the two stations on national television on which I saw some very interesting Russian films and plays. Before I had gone to Russia I studied the language at the Berlitz Institute at Rockefeller Center—but to no avail. I just couldn't get the hang of it. Russian language sounded heavy to me. But to prepare for the culture and the society of Russia I read a book by a *New York Times* writer, Hedrick Smith, about the country. And when I got there I tried very hard to learn at least one word a day. By the time I left I had accumulated 150 words. The most valuable of which for rehearsals was "paney mi," which means, "understand?"

I had a car and driver courtesy of the minister of culture to drive me wherever I wanted to go. I always felt that my drivers were KGB agents pretending they didn't understand English, while listening to every word I spoke. In the morning I went to play a game of tennis with whoever was in the park. The courts were soft, the tennis balls old, and the nets tattered and drooping. The bounce was very low to the ground which made the game even more difficult. The racquets were old and patched together. A can of new balls was unheard of in Moscow. My favorite weapon in tennis has always been a lob over the head of my opponent. This confused the Russians who are very rigid in their understanding. Rules are rules. In the Russian rule book on tennis there was no mention of lobs. Therefore it was an "Americansky" trick. I would warn them before I lobbed by shouting out, "lobofsky! lobofsky!" They didn't appreciate my humor. This general Russian rigidity did not extend to the artists and actors, who I found to be very curious and adaptable, as well as well-traveled and informed. They were not afraid of the unknown. I found the average Russian to be completely opposite to that. In fact, they could not understand anything that was even slightly off topic. Any variation scared them.

After tennis, it was back to a full day of rehearsal. The production was very well received and was televised throughout Russia. The play ran for five years in repertory!

The opening night party was memorable. It took place in the theatre's three large dressing rooms decorated by the actors with colored lights.

They sang, danced, and were lavish with their presents for me, including a Red Army shirt. The sweet Russian people love to give—both material things and of themselves. Caviar and champagne flowed. The U.S. Ambassador to Russia, Jack Matlock Jr., was present.

Rose and Pat Patek, good friends of the Circle came to the opening as did Paul and Florence. We all danced and joined in the spirit of the evening. The ambassador made a speech, saying that my production "was an important bridge of friendship between the Russian and American people." Yuri Solomin also made a speech expressing his gratitude for bringing this American play to the Russian people. The actors danced and sang and we all drank mucho champagne, and of course vodka.

While I was rehearsing, both the Libins and the Pateks traveled around Russia visiting relatives and ancient sites reuniting with their past. Pat and Rose are ardent Christians and they were determined to get all the churches that had been closed by the Communists reopened.

One day the Pateks came to see me rehearsing at the Maly. I took them to a small office in the theatre to meet the artistic director, Yuri Solomin, while the actors gathered together in the theatre to hear a speech by Boris Yeltsin. They were all members of the Communist Party, since the theatre was supported by the government. Yeltsin was not yet the world figure he became. In fact, I got the feeling he was trying to drum up political support with his speech. Afterwards, Mr. Yeltsin was introduced to us. We chatted with the help of a translator, and he told us of the problems the country was having. Pat Patek asked Yeltsin if he could have anything from the United States what would it be. Yeltsin responded quickly, housing!—modern housing was not plentiful in Moscow at this time.

In the early days of rehearsal when I started to block I asked, "Where is the stage manager?" I got a blank look from the actors and my translators, who didn't seem to know what I was talking about. I explained to Yuri that in American productions we have a man known as the stage manager who writes down the blocking and makes sure that all the substitute props are present for rehearsals. Yuri said, "We don't use stage managers; the actors remember the blocking." Mind you, these actors are performing four or five productions per week. Using the soft ap-

Pat and Rose Patek, Boris Yeltsin and aide, and Theodore Mann at the Maly Theatre (1990)

proach I said, "Yuri, I'm trying to do this just like an American production so I would like to have somebody serve as stage manager—I'll show
him what to do."

I was provided with an actor from their vast pool of 130, but he didn't
have any idea of what to do. Through my translator I asked him to sit
in rehearsals with the script and write down on the page where I tell
the actors to move. And if they have forgotten their lines they will call
to you with the word, "line." I told him to make a list of all the props
needed, then, when we got into the theatre, to write down my sound and
light cues. And I questioned him, "Paney mei?" He smiled and shook
his head up and down responding "Nyet," Over the rehearsal period I
taught him little by little what he had to do to become an Americansky
stage manager. Thank god we had the blocking because the Russian
actors love to improvise.

A truism that I discovered was that actors are the same the world
over—open to direction, willing to try new things and excited about
doing something risky.

I had brought over Mina Yakim, a mime performer and instructor at
the Circle School, to help the Russian actors achieve American body
language. She was very successful in her work with them. Amina grew

up speaking French, a second language for many Russians. Of course, mime, like music, is an international language.

I was directing as Gorbachev came to power with his policy of openness—Perestroika. The people were allowed to watch the Duma (the Russian Parliament) in session on television for the first time. At any break in rehearsals I'd find the actors glued to the TV. As we were putting the play together, communism was splitting apart! We were constructing a play and they were deconstructing a political system.

Russian audiences are scary—during performance they barely react but at the end, if they like the work, they let you know by clapping methodically like a metronome at low speed. This enthusiasm can go on through many curtain calls. They do not stand or shout bravo. They just sit in their seats stoically clapping, clapping, and clapping. I'm happy to say that with *Iguana* they clapped through many, many curtain calls. Tennessee is like Russia's adopted National Playwright. There's at least one production of his work somewhere in Russia every night. The Russian audiences lapped up our production like honey—because religion had been a taboo subject for so long. They were mesmerized by it.

The Maly Theatre trains young actors at the Schepkin School. I saw classes and did a critique of their scenes and I talked with Yuri about the possibility of doing an exchange program for four weeks between our two schools. The plan was that twenty-five of their students would come to study with us and the next year twenty-five of our students would go to them. I felt this would be a deepening experience for students from both countries and also a wonderful way for us to learn about them and vice versa.

In the summer of 1990, students from the Schepkin School came here and studied at the Circle accompanied by two of their faculty members and Yuri's wife Olga who was one of their top teachers and administrators. The Russians took classes in English (none of them spoke our language and I hired an interpreter to be with them in their classes and in their journeys around New York City). They also took acting technique, speech, voice, scene study, movement, and jazz dance. They loved all the classes, particularly the jazz—there was nothing like that in Russia. We arranged for them to stay at a New York University dorm and provided them with a per diem for food and entertainment. We set up for them theatre tickets, seminars, and shopping sprees. Russians love to find goods not available in their food or clothing stores. They were astonished by the abundance in all the stores. Russian stores at the time were almost completely empty.

In Moscow I had seen long lines of people standing patiently waiting outside a butcher shop. Peeking inside the store, there were some scrawny chickens. The stores that sold clothing did not have any displays in the windows and limited supplies of garments inside. There was a large department store near the Maly called Gums. I went inside to see if there was anything I could purchase, but the potential customers were shoving and pushing for what little merchandise there was. This paucity of goods was depressing and when I left Moscow and landed in Paris my eyes were opened with amazement simply by what was for sale in the airport terminal. I had this reaction after only a brief stay in Russia, so imagine how those kids, who'd spent their entire lives in deprivation, felt when they hit Macy's.

They also attended the classes we were giving for our own students. Before they came to the U.S. they had adapted a short story by O. Henry with music. After the four weeks of classes they presented it in Russian on our stage. This was a gesture of the students to show their interest and respect for things American. That same evening they also performed jazz routines choreographed by Nora Kasarda, our faculty member. The four weeks was a wonderfully enriching experience for the Russian students, and for us to have them in our midst. It was amazing to hear just how much English they had picked up in a month. The only negative was when one student defected and was never seen by us or the Russian embassy again.

The next summer we sent our students to Moscow to study at the Schepkin accompanied by two faculty members and Colin O'Leary, the school administrator. None of our students spoke Russian. So a translator was provided for them as well as classes in Russian, and in acting with Yuri and his wife Olga. They also learned Russian folksongs and took classes in ballet and improvisation. Our students stayed in dormitories and ate at an International Hotel. They went shopping, visited historical sites, including the Kremlin and many Russian theatres. They were treated royally as only the Russians are capable of.

At the end of the four weeks our students performed scenes from Chekhov, Russian folk songs, and dances. The Russians who had visited us and our students together sang "Anthem" from the musical *Chess*. It's a song in which the characters express their love of their country. Both Russians and Americans, to the delight of the audience, performed an ensemble jazz routine that Nora had put together.

The only defections we had were two female students who stayed and married Russian students. One has been divorced and has returned to the U.S. The other remained and I'm sure speaks fluent Russian.

The exchange was extremely valuable culturally and socially. But financially it proved too heavy a burden for both institutions, so unfortunately the exchange was not renewed.

Now as far as the original understanding of a directorial exchange between our two theatres was concerned, Boris Morozov of the Maly did come to America to do *Zoya's Apartment*. But more on this later.

When I returned home from the Russian *Iguana* production I was floating from the work experience, one of the best of my directing career. Everyone was pleased at the Circle with my success and especially with the coverage *The New York Times* gave to it.

CHAPTER 42

Productions Backwards and Forwards

Now, after that Russian interlude, I must jump back in time to 1977. We did a fine production of Oscar Wilde's *The Importance of Being Earnest* with Elizabeth Wilson (Lady Bracknell), John Glover (Algernon), Mary Louise Wilson (Miss Prism), Patricia Conolly (Gwendolyn Fairfax), Kathy Widdoes (Cecily Cardew), and G. Wood (Rev. Chasuble), directed by Stephen Porter. The critics carped about some of the performances not being as good as earlier English ones they'd seen or maybe they had been told about. It made me more determined than ever to do another Wilde, and twenty years later I got my wish with Al Pacino starring in *Salome*. More on this later too.

After directing *The Glass Menagerie* with Paul Rudd and Pamela Payton-Wright two years earlier, in which Pamela's character falls madly in love with the "gentleman caller," I kept thinking about what play we could do about love that would capitalize on their great romantic chemistry. I kept turning the thought over in my mind. One day Fate breathed the obvious answer into my ear: *"Romeo and Juliet."* Paul and Pamela would be perfect for this greatest love story ever written. Has a better play ever been written about two young lovers?

In several visits that famed British director Peter Brook had made to the Circle we had discussed the possibility of doing one of his productions. He had mentioned how the Circle's entrances and exits were similar to Shakespeare's requirements—noting the benefit of our additional exit, through the downstage vomitorium. This reassured me that a Shakespeare play could flow in the Circle space.

The set was designed by the great Ming Cho Lee and he beautifully solved the problem of "the imperatively necessary balcony." I wanted to perform the play without changing the scenery as they were able to do in Shakespeare's time. Ming's set provided a balcony upstage; the downstage was totally open to whatever we needed to create—a town square, ballroom, and all other scenes.

During rehearsals of *Romeo and Juliet* we studied with the Shakespearean expert Diana Maddox. Every morning we spent studying Shakespeare under Diana. The cast would read the script line-by-line and Diana would explain not only what was going on in the text, but how it related to Shakespeare's own time. She wasn't directing the actors, she was teaching. It was like the actors all went back to Elizabethan drama school for two weeks. Later in the afternoon we would have the actual rehearsals. The cast included: Armand Assante (Tybalt), John Shea (Paris), David Rounds (Mercutio), Jan Miner (the nurse), Jack Gwillim (Friar Lawrence), Lisa Pelican (Rosaline) and Lester Rawlins (Capulet). We rehearsed the play in Paul's Martinique Theatre.

Our most enthusiastic audiences were young people, who adored the play and would give us standing ovations. As a result of working so closely together, Pamela, Paul, and I have remained very good friends.

The joy of working with Shakespeare's characters and language made me want to do another of his plays. In 1982, I directed *Much Ado About Nothing* at SUNY Purchase New York with an amazing young student whose diction was impeccable and his mastery of Shakespeare's language and wit was superb: Stanley Tucci, playing Benedick. We performed in their black-box and converted it into an exact replica of the Globe. I wanted to have the challenge of directing the play in the exact confines of Shakespeare's own theatre to understand how the entrances and exits worked and how the minimal scenery was managed. It proved to be fluidly functional. I was very impressed with Stanley's capabilities and urged him to come to the city to seek his fortune and that I would help him move forward. A year later when we were casting *The Misanthrope* we hired him as Dubois.

Pamela Payton-Wright and Paul Rudd in Shakespeare's
Romeo and Juliet (1977), directed by Theodore Mann

Also in the SUNY Purchase production was actress Chandra Lee, a blonde thunderbolt from Virginia—with whom Patricia, assisting me on the production, fell in love. Shortly thereafter so did another member of my family, my son Jonathan.

One day on a rehearsal break during *Much Ado* Chandra was sitting in the hallway when a dark handsome young man approached her to ask her where the telephone booth was. She was so stunned by my son's persona that she couldn't speak but merely raised her arm and weakly pointed in the general direction. After he walked away, a friend of hers said, "Why didn't you go and show him where the phone is?" and Chandra replied, "I couldn't stand, my legs were too weak." Later that evening we all went to a cabaret performance on campus at which Chandra sang. Afterwards Chandra and Jonathan had a drink together and thus began in Shakespeare's hands a beautiful much ado romance. Ah, the magic of the theatre! They have since produced two explosions of life, Jackson Dylan and Dakota Brooks. Nowadays, Chandra is known as Drama Mamma teaching and directing young children in the art of theatre.

Around the same time my son Andrew, living in Paris and studying carpentry with a medieval guild, Les Compagnons, met a young painter on a nearly empty train. Andrew courageously walked up and asked if he could sit down next to her. She nodded her head yes. Correspondence ensued followed by romance which led to marriage which in turn led to three more grandchildren—*les petits enfants* —Samuel, who was born in Brooklyn (to be known forever in France as "the lad from Brooklyn");

Clementine, a beautiful pianist and painter; and Benjamin Theodore, a potential
guitarist. Andrew continues
to live in France. A couple of
times a year the families do
continental skipping. Much
ado about something.

I had been meeting with
the British actor John Wood
to interest him in working
here. He suggested various
plays and every time he

Theodore Mann with his sons Andrew and Jonathan

mentioned one I kept seeing him in another play. I told John the role
that he should be doing is the mischievous *Tartuffe* in Molière's great
play. He hadn't read it. After having done so, he agreed to do it. Stephen
Porter directed with Tammy Grimes, Stefan Gierasch, Mildred Dunnock, Swoosie Kurtz, Victor Garber, and Patricia Elliott.

In rehearsal, the usual problems took place: an actor can't remember
his lines; another can't get along with another actor; another feels the
director is not helping his scene and so on. This is where the producer
comes in to try to bring the team together and reignite the creative fervor
of cooperation. My meetings and chats with the actors worked and all
became harmonious. It even led to great reviews.

I tried to smooth the waters in many other stormy productions. Sometimes I've been successful and I have to admit other times my entreaties
went over like a lead balloon. As they say, you win some, you lose some.

At the end of 1978 we did our first production of George Bernard
Shaw. It was *St. Joan* with Lynn Redgrave. *St. Joan* and Lynn were well
received. The audience was enthralled. I realized anew what an important writer Shaw is. I love his wit and language and the complexity of
his dramatic situations and I began to think of what other Shaw plays
we could do. However, I put the idea on the back burner as I went on
to the next production.

During that period on a recent visit to London, I had seen a performance at the National Theatre of Feydeau's *A Flea in Her Ear* with Al-

Tammy Grimes and Stefan Gierasch in Molière's
Tartuffe (1977), directed by Stephen Porter

bert Finney. When I came back to New York, fate seemed to be tapping me on the shoulder because there in the *Times* was an article about a Feydeau production, *13 Rue de L'Amour* in Los Angeles starring Louis Jourdan and Leslie Caron—two people deliciously perfect for Feydeau.

I called Louis and asked him to come see me in New York. When he did, I immediately liked this charming Frenchman, who speaks English very well, having been in many American films. In our discussions I saw that he loved and was dedicated to Feydeau.

We agreed on dates and a director, Basil Langton, and began casting. Unfortunately, Ms. Caron could not be with us—she had a film commitment. But the role was played very well by Patricia Elliott.

Rehearsals and performances showed what a superb comic writer Feydeau is. His plays are almost always about married couples getting into embarrassing situations with third parties, and the husbands' excuses to their wives never seem to get them out of the trouble they have put themselves in.

He has written gem after gem and it is a pity more regional theatres don't perform them. The plays strongly resonate to our times of marital philandering—What would marriage be without that? *13 Rue de L'Amour* worked like gangbusters in our three-sided space. Our set had doors, which are essential to a Feydeau farce—the near discovery of the misbehavior. A character goes out one door as his nemesis comes in the other. But in our theatre the actors could also enter and exit through the downstage vomitorium. Which gives the actors three exits versus the two of a proscenium stage.

This was the only production of *13 Rue de L'Amour* that was ever performed on Broadway.

Around this time, I went to Washington D.C. to visit my dear friend Yolande Fox, former Miss America from Alabama. We went to see Kaufman and Hart's *Once in a Lifetime* at the Arena Stage with John Lithgow, Treat Williams, and Max Wright in the leading roles. I loved the satirical farce. That night I decided I wanted to bring it to New York, which we did with Tom Moore directing again. We recast several of the roles for Broadway.

The play is about a failed inept young man who through all of his mistakes becomes not only the head of a major movie studio but Hollywood's designated genius.

Lifetime was a success but the large cast made it just about break even. Incidentally, Jerry Zaks played one of the Schlepkin Brothers, Weisskopf, and has gone on to a very successful career as a Broadway director.

British playwright Alan Ayckbourn has continued the farce tradition of Feydeau, and Kaufman and Hart, brilliantly. Like Feydeau, his work should be seen more often. In 1991 we did another farce, Ayckbourn's *Taking Steps*, which requires two floors. Through Ayckbourn's creative playwrighting imagination we performed it on one floor. The second floor was created in the audience's mind by the magic of Mr. Ayckbourn. It was superbly performed by a cast of American actors and directed by Alan Strachan. More on this play later.

I'd seen a play called *Eminent Domain* in Princeton at the McCarter Theatre by a new playwright, Percy Granger, which I liked so much that I suspended my affectionate run of farcical plays. I mounted a production with Phil Bosco and Betty Miller, directed by Paul Austin. Paul Libin and I had many productive creative writing sessions with Percy. This was his first on Broadway and perhaps in New York. It is about a college professor, his long-suffering wife, and his young student. Percy's own father was a college professor so he had lots of insights. The play got quite good notices. Percy was an extremely promising young writer but tragically died at a young age, leaving a wife and children.

In my other wanderings to find plays I attended a performance at the Juilliard School of Franz Wedekind's *Spring Awakening* directed by Liviu Ciulei. His direction was very sensitive and the play was well acted by the graduating class. So I met with Liviu, a delightful man from Romania who had the impeccable manners and charm of an aristocrat. We talked about what play would be of mutual interest and finally settled on Gogol's *The Inspector General*, another delicious farce.

Liviu decided to use the theatre with the audience sitting on four sides. We have always referred to the fourth section as "the bleachers" even though the view from there was just as good as any other in the house. Above "the bleachers" we built a ramp which served as a balcony so the actors had an additional area for entrances and exits. Liviu used the theatre in an imaginative way, employing the exits as well as the aisles as entrances and exits.

Max Wright played Ivan Alexandrovich Khlestakov with a wonderful deadpan of perplexity as the townspeople persist in heaping gales of adoration on him. You see, the town has been nervously expecting the forbidding Inspector General when poor Max inadvertently stumbles in. He has not a single penny in his pocket but does have the clothing even though it was worn down. More importantly he had a bearing of nobility and through his mumbling and bumbling the townspeople mistake him for the inspector. Theodore Bikel and Helen Burns played the Mayor and his wife fawning over Max. They and Bob Balaban performed their roles to perfection. I consider this one of our best productions, but unfortunately New Yorkers do not swarm to see a play by Gogol or, for that matter, plays from any foreign country with the exception of England. The scenic designer was Karen Schulz. We were still in need of a costume designer and Karen recommended an unknown young man named William Ivey Long who designed several other shows for us and it is gratifying to me that he has become the most sought-after costume designer on Broadway.

There is also an odd shortage of American playwrights writing in the farce form. Why this is, I can't say. A farce with its furious slamming of doors and other comic action is not a "sit-down" comedy. It engages an audience in a very different way from a drama or musical. The farce form seems to have flourished only in American films. I think it is up to American writers to lead the way—if they write good farces, the American theatre audiences will come.

CHAPTER 43

AN ITALIAN GOES TO HELL
AS SHAW REVERBERATES

As you may remember, I had put Shaw on the back burner and now he leapt off the stove in his inimitable style. The *St. Joan* cast had included an important first for us, the then little-known but super-talented Philip Bosco, as well as Tom Aldredge. This was the first show Phil did with us and over the years he did nine more memorable roles. Phil has probably done more classic roles than any actor in New York. He loves the theatre and when given a theatre, movie, or TV offer he will always choose the stage even though it is less money. From the first day of rehearsal he is completely there, working on each scene as though he were in performance—he gives his all. He is a great actor whose ethic is about the work.

He agreed to perform in a workshop of *La Vie Parisienne* by Offenbach. This was a favorite piece of Patricia's that she and I adapted for a theatre performance. Phil for the first time sang in public and did very well. This workshop was very important for Patricia's emotional state. She was then in the early stages of multiple sclerosis and had had to stop singing, but she always had a creative drive and this was a perfect outlet for her. She sat by my side as co-director all through rehearsals making wonderful suggestions and providing insights. All the actors loved working with her. At one point Phil was offered a TV show but turned it down because of his affection for Patricia.

Lynn Redgrave in George Bernard Shaw's *Saint Joan* (1977), directed by John Clark

Phil Bosco kept talking to me about doing more Shaw. I wanted to produce as many of Shaw's great ones as possible, preferably with Phil in them. So I started with *Man and Superman* and asked Stephen Porter to direct. He had had a long successful career with Ellis Raab's Association of Performing Artists (APA).

Years earlier, I saw a production of Shaw's *Don Juan in Hell* done on Broadway directed by Charles Laughton, who also played the role of the Devil, with Claudette Colbert, Tyrone Power, and Agnes Moorehead. The actors stood behind lecterns that held their scripts. They were dressed in black tie. It was a staged reading of the *Don Juan* section from *Man and Superman.*

Stephen and I decided to do the full *Man and Superman* which includes *Don Juan in Hell.* It had not been produced in its complete form on Broadway since 1905 with Mr. Shaw supervising. Call us brave, call us mad—whichever—the play in its original form works.

Stephen did some judicious editing so that our 8 P.M. curtain would come down at 11.

Stephen is a very solid director who knows his plays inside and out and casts beautifully. We decided on George Grizzard for the role of John Tanner. I'd seen George's work in New York and Minneapolis. Phil Bosco was cast as Mendoza. Richard Woods played Roebuck Ramsden. Phil's dream of wanting to be in a repertory company came true as Richard and Philip became like a repertory company for us, gracing our stage in many plays. The cast was a wonderful group of New York actors that included Anne Sachs, George Hall, Bette Henritze, Laurie

Kennedy, Mark Lamos ("Markie" is my nickname for this now esteemed opera and stage director), Kate Wilkinson, and Nicholas Woodeson.

The design of the floor became the set of the play highlighted by the costumes and props. Paul miraculously found a repro- duction of an old-fashioned motor car which George bravely drove around the stage to the delight of the audience. So without ac-

George Grizzard and Philip Bosco in George Bernard Shaw's *Man and Superman* (1978), directed by Stephen Porter

tual scenery, Shaw's language was able to float freely through the audience's mind. Remember what Thornton Wilder said? "The eye is the enemy of the ear."

Shaw had been out of fashion for Broadway thanks to the critical deprecation of his work. I loved the challenge of bringing him back to his proper prominence as we did with O'Neill and Tennessee's *Summer and Smoke*. Even though Shaw had written his plays for proscenium they became even more vibrant on our open stage.

Audiences at this time were starved for literate and challenging lan- guage and *Man and Superman* was a big success as were all the Shaw plays we produced—nine in total. I think Phil's career really began to take off in his role of Mendoza.

Man and Superman played to sold out audiences, need I say more. We were a happy company and a happy producing staff.

Next we brought in Stewart Parker's *Spokesong* with John Lithgow, Rita Moreno, Maria Tucci, and the splendid Joseph Maher—another actor who could only perform at his best. Joe had come over from Ire- land years before and always retained his lovely Irish lilting sound and a happy attitude about life. We brought the Long Wharf production down intact. It was a modest success directed by Kenneth Frankel.

Roxanne Hart and Kevin Kline in Michael Weller's *Loose Ends* (1979), directed by Alan Schneider

Once again, I was in Washington visiting my friend Yolande and went to see a matinee performance of Michael Weller's *Loose Ends* at Arena Stage, directed by Alan Schneider. Alan and I had tried for years to find a play to do together and finally here it was. I was so excited after the matinee I went running around the confusing subterranean hallways of the Arena, trying to find Alan and to tell him that I finally found the play for us to do together. He asked, "Which one?" I responded, "The play upstairs."

When *Loose Ends* came to the Circle we had new scenic designs by Zack Brown. Alan had work to do with the actors and blocking adjustments. The production was an instant hit with the then unknown Kevin Kline, Roxanne Hart, and Jay Sanders.

While that was running we did a workshop of Bertolt Brecht's *Jungle of the Cities*, a fine early play of his, with Al Pacino. I'd been trying to interest Al in a play for a long time. We had read and read and read many plays and finally Al said yes to *Jungle*. Liviu Ciulei directed in a small off-off-Broadway theatre across from The Public. We performed it twelve times, which is the maximum number allowed by Actor's Equity Association for a workshop.

The play is about a poet who struggles against the pressures of society. It went very well, but Al did not feel comfortable. Paul and I urged him to go forward but he decided not to. Al is very much a solo thinker, he confers and likes to get lots of input but in all matters he makes the final decision. His choice of a play is based on what he feels he can contribute as an actor and also what he will learn from doing the play. Al is always a student, searching, analyzing and leaping into the unknown. He likens acting in the theatre to walking a tightrope; the balance has to be perfect for him to stay aloft. The play must seep into his bones and if it doesn't he just has to walk away from it. Al is a true artist. I think of him as Picasso working on a big canvas obsessed with the details of the play and character that he is working on. Twenty-four hours a day Al is thinking and behaving as the character. During the rehearsal period he lives in clothes similar to what he will be performing in.

In a genuine show of camaraderie with the actors he will say, "Let's have some coffee around four o'clock and talk before the show." So the company wanders in and conversations pop up about what has happened to them during the day. Out of that they begin talking about the play and their scenes. This prepared them for the night's performance. Generally, preparation for a performance takes place with the actor alone in his dressing room.

After *Man and Superman* we decided to do another Shaw play right away. The question was—what would be best for Phil? We decided on *Major Barbara*, which would provide him with back-to-back extreme contrasting roles—from the devil in *Don Juan* to the millionaire munitions maker in *Major Barbara*, Andrew Undershaft. Phil's presence lent assurance and enthusiasm to the company. Stephen directed again and Laurie Kennedy played his daughter Barbara. The cast also included Nicolas Surovy as Barbara's suitor Adolphus Cusins, Rachel Gurney as the manipulative matriarch, and Jon De Vries as the bruiser.

The play is about a munitions maker whose daughter, much to his consternation, works for the Salvation Army. Needless to say, father and daughter possess conflicting notions about humanity. *Major Barbara* was another Shaw success for us. Once again New York audiences, starved for sophisticated language, were able to luxuriate in his rich wit.

We've always been committed to new plays; in fact up to 1980 we had done thirty-three including classics which had never been done in New York.

I had found a new two-character play *Past Tense* by Jack Zeman about a young couple who had lost a child. *Past Tense* starred Barbara Feldon and Larry Luckinbill. I directed and we worked like hell to make

Philip Bosco in George Bernard Shaw's *Major Barbara*
(1980), directed by Stephen Porter

this play work. We felt it was a play that dealt truthfully with family emotions over the loss of a child. But the critics have the last word and so they did—Barbara, Larry, and I were crushed by the reception.

Every year Circle in the Square Theatre School auditions prospective students around the country. Edwin Howard, a critic for a paper in Memphis, had seen many of our plays and was very enthusiastic about them and the school. Edwin was on the board of Theatre Memphis, where I went with Lucille Rubin, our voice teacher, to audition young actors from the entire southeast area. Kids came from as far as Mississippi, Florida, and Kentucky. We did three days of auditioning to select one or two for a scholarship to our school. The scholarship funds were provided by Edwin's newspaper. I went to Memphis for the next eight years to continue this scholarship process. Two of the outstanding recipients were Alice Haining and Jane Wallace, who have gone on to have successful theatre and television careers. Alas, when the newspaper ran into financial trouble the program ended.

While in Memphis I met a native of that city, Ellis Raab, director, actor, and the founder of APA. APA had been a very important producing company in New York. I had seen and admired many of their productions but this was the first time I had met Ellis. We were at a party together and found two throbbing vital interests in common. One was the theatre and the second was my wife, Patricia. He had seen and heard my darling sing so we were on grounds of mutual admiration. Ellis had a classy educated Southern accent with the suaveness of Charles Boyer. Before leaving, I asked Ellis if he would be interested in doing a play for us. He said, "Of course, darling"—one of his favorite expressions. But the question of which one was left open.

On my plane trip back to New York, his beautiful speech kept swimming around in my head. And I kept thinking what is the role for that voice and persona? You know how you get that feeling—you remember something, it is on the tip of your tongue but you just can't quite pull it into focus? That's how I felt. Plays were running through my head trying to match the voice to the part. Then the plane hit the runway, hard, and all the seat-belted passengers popped up in their seats, me included. As I levitated, Sheridan Whiteside demanded my attention! That's it! *The Man Who Came to Dinner*—that's the play for Ellis.

I could hear his elegant mellow baritone saying those lines. Ellis had the wit, the intelligence, and the delicious ability to deliver the lines of the irrepressible Mr. Whiteside. I was so excited I called him and asked if he ever thought of doing the role. He responded by reciting several lines from the play, then added, "I've always wanted to play that role. You're the first one to ask me."

I jumped into action putting together a production team headed up by Stephen Porter as director. We gathered a wonderful cast with Leonard Frey playing Banjo, the Harpo Marx role; Anita Dangler as the beleaguered nurse, Richard Woods was Mr. Stanley (the indignant husband) and Patricia O'Connell his doting wife; their daughter was Amanda Carlin (Frances Sternhagen and Tom Carlin's daughter); Kate Wilkinson was Harriet Stanley (the grandmother); Bill McCutcheon played John with a wonderful deadpan; Maureen Anderman was Maggie Cutler; Roderick Cook as Beverly Carlton; Jamey Sheridan as Sandy; and topping the icing on the cake was Carrie Nye doing a wonderful turn as Lorraine Sheldon, the film star. Her Southern drawl was even deeper than Ellis's and matched his grandness.

The play by George Kaufman and Moss Hart is a side-splittingly funny farce if done right and we did! We had all the entrances and exits working perfectly and Ellis as Sheridan Whiteside was in charge of the chaos. Once again, Stephen's genius in casting was at work.

Through that production Patricia and I became very close friends with Ellis and Leonard. They would come up on the actors' weekends—Sunday evening through Monday night—to our home in Bedford. We laughed and gossiped and fell into a routine where Patricia and I were "Mom and Dad" and Ellis was "Bucky" and Leonard was "Chucky," our two new adopted sons. As "parents" we supervised their every move including washing their hands before eating, sitting properly at the table and clearing their dishes after eating. In their games they couldn't be abusive to each other. And when we read or told stories in front of the fireplace, each—as our good children—had to take their turn. We of course had adult theatre talk when we were outside the world of our adopted children. God we had wonderful times! Life was a play within a play. Patricia and I were stern parents and they were our irascible, lovable brats. As mom and dad, we would often argue in front of the children, saying, "How did they get this way—it's your fault," "No, it's your fault," "No, it's your crazy uncle." Every so often we commanded them to sit down for a moment of silence. Or what is known today as a time out. We had birthday cakes and special dishes that the children wanted. And to keep them quiet we gave them what they shrilly demanded. Oh, how Patricia and I looked forward to those delicious improvised weekends. In advance of their arrival, Patricia and I would run lines in anticipation of what our "children" would say.

Our next production was Euripides' *The Bacchae*. After the *Trojan Women* in 1963, Michael Cacoyannis, Irene, and I became very good friends, but then Michael and Irene had a cooling off period for a few years, during which Irene informed me that she had been working with Minos Volanakis and highly recommended his work on *Medea*. I had seen his production of Genet's *The Screens* at BAM and thought his work was good. Now seven years have gone by and Michael and Irene have become great friends again. Michael Cacoyannis called me from Athens to tell me that he wanted to direct *The Bacchae* with Irene playing Agave. And I said, "are you two talking again?" Michael in his Greek-English accent said, "Of course, we love each other dearly." Phil Bosco joined the cast as Cadmus. Irene (Agave) comes in in the last thirty-five minutes and I was sure that she would give what the script required—a tour de force performance. If the rest of the cast is up to her and Phil's quality, I thought, we will have a success.

Of the ancient writers, I am partial to Euripides because he deals with passions that contemporary audiences can identify with. The chorus expresses the point of view of the citizenry but the leading characters are all members of the ruling class and they suffer the same anguish, frustration, and fears that we all do.

In *The Bacchae*, a newcomer, Dionysus, arrives in Thebes. He has returned from the Orient bringing with him a cult of women devotees. He initiates orgiastic rites with the women of Thebes. *The Bacchae* portrays a conflict between reason and the irrational; civilized order and the disruptive forces of nature; the relationship between man (Pentheus) vs. god (Dionysus). Pentheus, Agave's son, becomes enthralled by the rites and despite his reluctance to do so he dresses as a woman to observe what is going on. Agave is a participant in the goings on and in her hedonistic madness unknowingly slays her own son. Agave arrives carrying Pentheus' head and moans with the pain and realization of what she has done and cries out to Dionysus for his mercy. He ignores her and she screams, "You are merciless." Dionysus responds that, "Mercy can never be demanded of a god" and he goes on that it is the nature of a god to exert power and man is responsible to the gods but the gods are not responsible to man.

To produce this play is to dare — so fools that we are we decided to jump in and do this great, but obviously very complex play that demands the very best kind of acting. Irene and Phil were wonderful but unfortunately the rest of the cast was not up to their level. I can still here the echo in my ear of the actor's voices reverberating through the hallways backstage down the stairs to my subterranean office. The actors were straining to achieve the passions of the play and to replicate Michael's pitch-perfect line readings. For me it became like hearing a competition between two scratching fingernails on a blackboard. On bad days the echoes still persist, swirling through the backstage hallways. The key reviews were bad and others were okay but on the strength of Irene and Phil's performance the show did pretty well.

Next was another difficult play, *John Gabriel Borkman* by Ibsen with Irene Worth, E.G. Marshall, and Rosemary Murphy, directed by Austin Pendleton.

This didn't pull together either. The play is about a failed banker, Borkman, who had been in prison for embezzlement. Downstairs are two sisters, one of whom he loves and the other to whom he's married. And they were both betrayed by him. The sisters are trying to come to terms with their failed lives. They must hear the endless restless pacing of Borkman upstairs, while they are talking. The audience must also feel from that sound his pain and anguish. We were never able to get that sound right and perhaps it was a contributing factor why the play was not fully experienced by the audience. Consequently, the reviews were not good.

Years later Vanessa invited me to see a production of this play at the Royal Shakespeare Company in London with herself, Eileen Atkins, and Paul Scofield. It was a stunning evening—rich with emotional reverberations. Borkman's pacing sounds were perfectly heard by the audience. I wanted very much to bring this production to New York but Mr. Scofield, who rarely performs in the United States, did not want to leave England at that time.

After our production of *Borkman* we followed with another tough play—boy, was I on a roll of great plays that weren't working—*The Father* by August Strindberg, with Frances Sternhagen and Ralph Waite, directed by Goran Graffman from the Royal Dramatic Theatre of Sweden.

What I was trying to do with these productions, *The Bacchae, John Gabriel Borkman*, and *The Father* was to push us. And to present to the audience great classic plays that were rarely if ever seen on Broadway. In each one of the productions one or more of the elements—actors, scenery, costumes, or sounds just didn't gel. After all the victories we'd had, I suddenly hit a dry spell. We were getting banged around pretty good by the critics with the sometimes added comment on our unusual space. As I noted earlier, audiences always loved our configuration but critics have had some reservations and rarely shall the twain meet.

Because of the bad times I tried to change our luck by doing a new play, *Scenes and Revelations,* that I had seen in a workshop off-off-Broadway. The literary agent was the eternally serene but tough Audrey Wood who was the champion of new young writers. Audrey had brought Tennessee Williams to center stage. She spoke enthusiastically about the virtues of this new play, so I went to see it and decided to do it at the Circle. *Scenes* starred Christine Lahti. I was hoping it would be a homerun, evening up the play-production score with one mighty swing. It got nice reviews but not enough to draw the audiences we needed and it ended up the fourth play in a row that tanked for us.

The Circle at this point was tottering. We desperately needed a hit. I felt these failures keenly but I always remembered what a wise sage had said to me when we first began, "If you have one success in five productions count yourself fortunate." On the other hand, Sophocles said, "Count no man fortunate, however happy, till the day he dies." But I am an eternal optimist—that around the next corner will be a wonderful surprise. And when Paul Newman asked me to come down to Ohio to see a production, I heard the unmistakable sound of Fate whispering in my ear.

The play was Shaw's *Candida* with Joanne Woodward at Kenyon College in Ohio, Paul's Alma Mater. I liked the production very much and invited the entire company to come to the Circle in the fall. It worked out very well. Joanne was the heart and spirit of the production. She kept everyone pointed in the right direction with her warmth and fierce determination to get the play perfect. She succeeded and the critics and audiences agreed. We were back on our feet! This was our fifth production and oh how right the sage was. Joanne was superb in the leading role with tenderness, intelligence and of course beauty. Joanne is much adored by theatre and motion picture–goers for her roles in, among others, *The Fugitive Kind* with Brando and Anna Magnani, *Suddenly Last Summer, The Three Faces of Eve,* and *The Long Hot Summer,* and *Mr. and Mrs. Bridges,* the latter two with her husband Paul Newman.

I was about to make another bad mistake. For our next production, I had approached Nicol Williamson about doing a play. He had been sensational in *Uncle Vanya* for us in 1972 and we'd kept in touch. Nicol is Scottish and his passion was to do the not-to-be-mentioned "Scottish Play." (That is, *Macbeth,* about which most thespians are astoundingly superstitious.) We couldn't come up with a director that was available and Nicol volunteered to direct it himself. I felt this whole thing was a gift from God—to have a great actor in this dangerous Shakespeare play. Sigourney Weaver agreed to play Lady Macbeth. I was in heaven! But after a short time in rehearsal, Nicol came to Paul and myself and said the play was not working. I asked, "why not" and he responded, "Sigourney and I can't continue."

I attended a rehearsal and thought: she's fine, she is going to be a great Lady Macbeth. But the director, Nicol, insisted.

So we had a choice: we could fire him as director and search for a new Macbeth, or abandon the production, or we could go along with

Joanne Woodward in George Bernard Shaw's *Candida*
(1981), directed by Michael Cristofer

him and hope for the best. It was a wrenchingly painful decision to let go of one of our most talented actresses. If we knew the folly that was to come, we should have followed our instinct and stuck with Sigourney and replaced the director and star. I am embarrassed to this day by this decision— she would have been a great Lady Macbeth. Perhaps the curse of the "Scottish play" was working after all. Laurie Kennedy stepped into the role—she was very good but I think Nicol had a third choice always in mind—a young untried actress who he said had the necessary innocence for the role. As the rehearsal proceeded we found she had the innocence all right but, alas, didn't have the technique or vocal skill to undertake Lady Macbeth. The production spun out of control and was slammed by the critics—we had to cut the run short.

It was a crushing defeat for us. We were hurting badly financially, just hanging on. Everybody was depressed. But, as the song goes, when you hit rock bottom, there's no place to go but up.

CHAPTER 44

GENERAL PATTON, MEET NOËL COWARD

I had to be very careful. We couldn't stand another failure. When I came upon Noël Coward's *Present Laughter* I knew this was it. It had never been truly appreciated by the critics. They considered it one of his lesser plays. The combination of these two opposite opinions—mine and the critics'—got my adrenaline going once more.

I asked Frank Langella to play the lead. He agreed and I began planning the production. One day he called to tell me he had a film and he couldn't do it. I heard the bells of doom ringing again. I felt Macbeth was haunting me.

That same day Paul and I had a scheduled lunch with George C. Scott to catch up and share family stories. During lunch G.C. said, "What's the matter Teedy? You look so down?" George always said my name as though there were two e's in the spelling. As briefly as possible I told him what had happened that very morning. He chewed his food, took a drink and then began reciting Garry Essendine's lines from *Present Laughter*. I asked, "George, how do you know these lines—why are you torturing us?" He chortled with his crocodile smile and then explained, "I played the young playwright at college." We all chatted some more and then went our separate ways.

The next morning, I woke up and my Circle mistress breathed into my ear, "Ask G.C. if he'll do the play now." He'd just come off a tremendous success in the film *Patton* and I thought what a wonderful change of pace it would be for him and how incredulous the critics and audience would be that "General Patton" could play this British, vain, self-absorbed matinee idol who madly chases after women. When I called George to ask him if he would do the play I was scared he wouldn't have the time but surprise of surprises he said "I'd love to play Garry. It's a 'hambone' role." I warned him we had to start right away—we're in bad shape. And George knew exactly what I meant—money. There were no agents, no contracts to be signed, George had given his word and that was as solid as any commitment could be.

He wanted to direct and that was fine with Paul and me—he'd done such a great job acting in and directing *Salesman* in 1975. So Paul got to work to secure the rights and called Noël Coward's agent in London, "We have the actor for Garry Essendine." The agent said "Who is that" and Paul responded "George C. Scott" and the agent said "That's General Patton. He's not right for the part." And Paul said, "He's a great actor. If you don't accept him we won't do the play." Several days later we got a cable from London saying go ahead with Mr. Scott.

George with his acute casting ability assembled a wonderful group of actors, including those two newcomers: Richard Burton's daughter Kate and a little urchin named Nathan Lane. Both of whom today, to put it mildly, have considerable careers. Anyone who was fortunate enough to see that production realizes the sheer joy of surprise to see a great actor turn your every preconception of him upside down. The shock of General Patton playing a gadfly paid off—the production was a great success and placed *Present Laughter* alongside Noël Coward's top plays.

George loved doing the play so much that he extended the run beyond our normal twelve weeks. We sent letters to our subscribers notifying them that we had a hit in *Present Laughter* and would extend the run and that the next production would be done at another theatre. We explained that hits don't come along very often and that we needed the infusion of *dinero* that *Laughter* was bringing in. Not a single subscriber complained about the change in schedule but we did get letters congratulating us on the success.

Throughout rehearsals, Nathan kept joking around by always making his entrances with one strange new prop on top of another. Finally, he came on in Dana Ivey's huge-plumed hat. This startled George so

Christine Lahti, Kate Burton, Dana Ivey, George C. Scott, and Elizabeth Hubbard in Noël Coward's *Present Laughter* (1983), directed by George C. Scott

much he went up in his lines. George blew his stack and yelled, "Nate! Stop screwing around with the props! You got that?" Nathan said he got it, walked away a few feet and stopped to turn back. George fixed him with a stare. "Is there anything else?" The whole cast froze with fear. Nathan said, "George, I have just one request. You've been calling me Nate since the first day of rehearsals. My name is Nathan." George offered a genuine apology. "And there's another thing," Nathan continued. "What's that?" George asked. Nathan smiled at him, "I loved your performance as General MacArthur." This broke George up. He fell to his knees laughing and Nathan kissed him on the head. Everybody relaxed. After that, the whole company came together. This was the turning point for the production. The cast had seen both sides of George in an instant—the worst and the best.

Waiting in the wings next was Colleen Dewhurst to do *The Queen and the Rebels* by Ugo Betti. What an irony. Here were two of the best and well known actors in the world—George happy in his success and agreeing to continue his run at the Circle, and Colleen—his twice-former wife—planning on coming into the Circle. I visited Colleen up at her farm where she and George had lived. They were divorced now, but still very good friends, being the parents of Campbell and Alex. I told her about the great success we were having with *Present Laughter* and that we needed to improve our financial resources so that we could continue to produce. The darling girl understood. Whenever I presented her with a problem in the past she would always say, "What do *you* want to do, Ted?" emphasizing the word "you." She would look deeply into my eyes and I knew that if I wavered I would either get across the top of Niagara Falls safely or go straight down. So when Colleen queried, "What do you want to do, Ted?" I told her that we would do *Rebels* at the Plymouth Theatre, one of the best dramatic houses on Broadway.

She agreed and invested all of her positive energy and anybody that knew her knows how monumental that was. They say that women are more positive than men, but Colleen left all other women in the dust with her superb attitudes about life, work, and friendship.

Paul took over the supervision of the load-in for *The Queen*: scenery, lights, and costumes. Since it was a Circle production, Paul was able to work out with the unions a deal similar to what we have at our own theatre. Without those concessions from the union we would not have been able to do the play. Paul has always handled all the union contracts since we moved to Broadway in 1972.

So now we had *Laughter* selling out and a new production with Colleen. We were proud to be working with two great actors and having two shows on Broadway at the same time. *Queen* played our scheduled twelve-week subscription run. *Laughter* kept going until George had to leave for a film. We had had a run of six months—thirty-two previews and one hundred seventy-five performances to sold-out houses! It was a great time. George loved playing the role and relished the audience's reaction to this great comedy. It was a joyous company!

I can still see George as Garry Essendine striding across the stage to answer the door bell for an anticipated female date. At center stage he would stop, look in the imaginary mirror, slick his pencil thin mustache, and smiling with debonair confidence in his handsomeness was ready to open the door. One night, the doorbell did not ring so ever-professional George stopped, looked in the imaginary mirror—preened himself and waited hoping the doorbell would ring. It didn't. So back to the mirror for more preening, which he kept up for several minutes. The Stage manager had missed his cue. George improvised Noël Coward-like language about his prospective amour for the night. Finally, George was now beginning to sweat. A handkerchief came out of his breast pocket to sop up the perspiration on his brow when the doorbell finally rang. George just continued on with Noël Coward's own dialogue without any hint of dissatisfaction. Afterwards, I took the stage manager to task for having missed the cue. I went backstage to George and explained what happened and he said with a laugh, "Well, that's the theatre."

Present Laughter opened on July 15, 1982 and closed on January 2, 1983. It was our first unqualified critical and audience success in a long time. Despite the brilliant performance and direction by George, unbelievably he did not receive a Tony nomination either as actor or director.

It would not be until 1996 when he would again receive a nomination. That year George played in Lawrence and Lee's *Inherit the Wind*. He was having physical difficulties at the time and missed several performances. Tony Randall, the producer of the National Actor's Theatre, called to ask if I could help. Over the next few days I saw George several times (as did George DiCenzio) and as gently as possible talked about the play. He confirmed how much he loved the Clarence Darrow role and he eventually agreed to go back into the show. He was nominated for a Tony for his incredible performance. At the same time George Grizzard was appearing in Edward Albee's *Delicate Balance* and he too received a Tony nomination. He and G.C. were very good friends and they used to kid each other about who would win the Tony. George, who didn't care about awards, said to me, "Old Grizzly will win it—I hope he does." And George Grizzard did win it.

CHAPTER 45

THE MISANTHROPE AND THE GRAVEDIGGER

After *Tartuffe*, I had been thinking about doing another Molière play. As we all know, Molière's plays are a centerpiece of French culture, but he's another example of a great playwright whose work is rarely if ever seen on Broadway. (Except for when the Comédie Française occasionally comes to town.)

Stephen and I were considering *The Misanthrope* but we had to a have the right actor to play the lead. A great actor of style who had played Broadway but never with us, Brian Bedford was the man! I called his agent, Clifford Stevens, and told him of our interest and he responded the next day affirmatively.

The Misanthrope is one of Molière's more difficult plays, it is quite cerebral. I chose it because of the danger in doing this almost forgotten play, and if we had Brian, an actor of wonderful wit and unusual ability with language, we might overcome the audience resistance to it. The cast included Mary Beth Hurt, Carole Shelley, and Stanley Tucci.

The Misanthrope was a superb production but Frank Rich's *Times* review was mildly approving and as a result we did "mildly" at the box office. Frank Rich found more wrong with a production than good as he had done with several other productions of ours. Which is the exact opposite of what his esteemed predecessor, Brooks Atkinson, would do.

Atkinson loved theatre so much he would concentrate more on the affirmative than the negative.

Rich drove audiences away and Broadway suffered a severe downturn in attendance because of his lack of intelligent enthusiasm. Of course, he has written many good reviews, and many which *he* may have considered good, but because of his qualified language audiences would understandably not respond.

A good motto for a critic would be "Put your enthusiasm first and your reservations last." Otherwise the reader moves on to another article without realizing that in the latter part of the review the critic was affirmative. Frank Rich certainly liked many plays, *Angels in America* was one I remember, but he buried a lot of good shows. We referred to him humorously as "the gravedigger." In other producing circles he was known as the "Butcher of Broadway"—perhaps a better image because there's lots of blood shed by a not-good review.

I was once commiserating with George about a mildly approving review that Rich had given a play we were doing. I told G.C. I'd heard a rumor that Rich would be leaving and I added optimistically, "So things will get better." George shook his great head very slowly, "No, Teedy. Behind every Frank Rich is another Frank Rich!"

Back in 1957 when we were doing the *Long Day's Journey into Night* national tour with Ruth Nelson and Anew McMaster, we were getting reviews in out-of-town cities that began by talking about how long the play was—over four hours. In the Cleveland newspaper the headline read, "A long long journey." In most cases the reviewer went on to praise the play *later* in their piece. But as a result, our business at the box office suffered and it would be impossible to continue the tour to the next city, Chicago. If we got the same reviews there we would have to terminate the tour. At the Chicago *Sun-Times* the drama critic Claudia Cassidy was the most esteemed and feared in America after Atkinson. If we got a review with a negative headline, or a negative first paragraph, we would be frozen in the snowstorm that was walloping the town the day we arrived. Ms. Cassidy had written admiringly in earlier columns about O'Neill so I called and asked if I could come and talk to her.

I had consistently avoided any personal contact with the critics except in the case of Brooks Atkinson, where he had sought me out. By calling on

Ms. Cassidy I was shattering one of my own cardinal rules: don't cross the line that separates the critic from the artists. I'd always felt that any overt move by me towards them would be interpreted as trying to curry favor and influence their review. But what the hell—*Long Day's Journey Into Night* was about to plummet like a giant icicle if I didn't stop this lethal mixed review motif that had greeted it in its previous stops.

We met in her office and talked about theatre and O'Neill and she said how much she liked his plays—and I thought, "Say it now, make your pitch." So I blurted out, "We've been having terrible problems at the box office in the previous towns we played." She asked, "Why?" and I replied, "Because the negative comments were in the front part of the review and the affirmative were in the latter." So I took a deep breath and cautiously proceeded as graciously as I could: "Ms. Cassidy, if you like the production and you have some reservations please write the good things first and if you didn't like some parts of our work, perhaps you could say it *later* in your review." She didn't say yes or no but she did say with a Cheshire cat smile, "I'll keep that in mind" and we parted. I walked out thinking I'd really slammed the door on us—she's going to hate the production.

We opened two days later in another heavy snowstorm—even in the subzero weather I was sweating through each day. I had trouble breathing—I didn't know whether my shortness of breath was caused by the freezing snow or my meeting Ms. Cassidy. But glory glory her review was glorious! There were some very minor negatives which didn't impinge on her enthusiasm for the production. We were a hit in Chicago and ran for several months! I was on the radio with Studs Terkel, a dream of a man—down home like Will Rogers and also Larry King, before the suspenders. I pushed very hard with our press agent for those interviews and many others. I was willing to go on any radio station however small the audience. Our press agent helped make the play a success there as well as in Denver, San Francisco, and Los Angeles.

The critics undoubtedly will take exception to what I've written. But I still maintain that *The Misanthrope* was a perfect production; it didn't deserve critical carping.

Next came *The Caine Mutiny Court-Martial* by Herman Wouk. It had started as a workshop at The Actors' Studio with Arthur Sherman directing. I knew Arthur from my afternoon basketball at the 47th Street YMCA. I had been playing there twice a week for fifteen years. We'd play full court games— the first team that got ten points stayed for the next opponents. As you can imagine, the games were fierce and physical because the winner got to stay on the court. But winning was everything and breeding and education went out the window. We were animals, primitive, shoving and fouling, doing anything to win then denying we'd done it. "I never touched him!" A couple of the guys were basketball rats—they played wherever they saw a game in progress on New York City public courts. One of our players, Charlie, was a rat who claimed to have played in over three thousand basketball games. He was counting streets, synagogues, schoolyards, YMCAs and peach baskets hanging from garages. He was about 50 years old, 5'10", balding with a slick of hair attempting to cover his pate.

I gave everyone a nickname. Phil Berger, sports novelist, was "Poncho" because of his long mustache. Burt Bacharach, composer, was "Johnny Stompano" because he ran up and down the court stomping his feet and holding his hands at chest level, wrists limp and flopping so as not to hurt his fingers. Johnny Mathis, singer, was "Batman" because he waved his arms like a bird. Ira Berkow, New York Times sports columnist, only shot from the corner and he was known as Mr. Corner. Bob Goldsholl, radio sports announcer, had a great outside shot—he was called "The Outsider." Arthur Sherman would twist and turn to drive to the basket—he was known as Curly. I was known as "Mr. One Arm" for my one-hander from the top of the Circle (where else?) above the foul line. We had many wonderful games but one day I decided all this screaming, shoving, and fouling was infantile and I really didn't care about winning anymore. I just stopped and switched to tennis—the alleged gentleman's game. But even there I found adolescent behavior, including my own, questioning whether the ball was in or out. I had terrific arguments, so childish, that I'm embarrassed to think about them now. My knees finally stopped me. I've always believed that you can tell everything about a person by the way he behaves on a tennis court. I get very low marks. Now my daily exercise is swimming ten laps or walking one mile. No competition, only the turmoil in my head.

Getting back to *Caine Mutiny*, Arthur talked to me about moving the workshop to the Circle with a cast including John Rubinstein as the forthright attorney, Lt. Barney Greenwald, and Michael Moriarty as the devious Lt. Commander Queeg. Both actors' work I've always admired. They were perfect. As was the rest of the cast: Sam Coppola, Jonathan Hogan, Geoffrey Horne, Stephen Joyce, Jay O. Sanders, and Brad Sullivan among them. Mr. Wouk came and saw our production and loved it, as did the public and critics.

When replacement time was coming around Paul had seen an actor interviewed by Johnny Carson on his television show. Paul had not been very impressed with two films he'd seen this actor in. But in his interview with Carson he was very relaxed, charming, and humorous—an impressive man. Paul called his agent Robbie Lantz and told him of our interest and after checking with the actor Robby reported in his sweet Viennese accent, "He is veddy veddy interested." So after an audition he was cast in the role of Lt. Stephen Maryk. His real life name is the famous football player Joe Namath. He brought a lot of energy to the role and blended well with the cast.

Our good luck continued. So much so that I worried what land mine was lying in wait for us.

Our next production was Shaw's *Heartbreak House*. I had read a review of a production in London with Rex Harrison and I thought: wouldn't it be great to have *My Fair Lady*'s Henry Higgins perform at our theatre? He was known as a debonair and witty actor. In other words Rex was a boulevard actor, deft but light. I thought any actor who can't sing but who took on Professor Higgins in the musical *My Fair Lady*, had to have "chutzpah" (a word Rex would never use let alone know the meaning of) to take on the role of Captain Shotover. Like George in *Present Laughter*, I thought Rex would surprise everyone by playing this old garrulous Captain who falls in love with a young girl. I talked to Paul about the idea and he said, "He'll never come because of the money we pay." Which was $1000 per week for a star. I said let's try. A week later Paul still hadn't made the call and I said as softly as possible and in a slow tight-jawed cadence, "Make the call. The worst that could happen is that you would be right and he won't come." So Paul picked up the phone and called Rex's attorney in New York to schmooze him, and convinced him how good it would be for Mr. Harrison to play this role in New York at Circle in the Square. Miracle of miracles the agent called back to say that Rex was interested.

We made arrangements for him and his wife to come to New York. We met with them both and went right to the problem of who would direct. I had recommended Stephen Porter, given the great work he had done for us in all of our Shaw productions. But Rex insisted that he had to have a British director. We finally agreed on Anthony Page, a Brit with good credits but not many classical ones. After getting good reports from our theatrical friends in London, we went with Anthony—and never, horrors of horrors, call him Tony.

Next was casting. We put together a fine company of classically trained Broadway actors: Phil Bosco, Rosemary Harris, Stephen McHattie, and Dana Ivey. But the role of the young girl, Ellie Dunn, eluded us. For Rex this was the key role for the whole production. If we didn't get the young lady he liked he wasn't going to do it. Rex had rejected all previous auditioners. Paul and I were getting really nervous. Then one day, Amy Irving showed up. Rex read with her and afterwards proclaimed, with his elegant English diction, "*I* have found *my* Ellie." He fell in love with Amy. I mean that literally. Nothing ever happened, but Amy allowed him to express his adoration. They only went so far as to hold hands. Amy was expert in both playing the part and Rex.

Rehearsals went well. Now we were about to start the first previews. Rex peeked out from backstage and was shocked to see the audience sitting so close. All of his life he had only performed on proscenium stages. "I can see their faces," he said. He was paralyzed for a few minutes. Rosemary and Amy were there and calmed him down with their warmth and love and they gently persuaded him to go on. But he was still so nervous that he insisted that an assistant stage manager sit in the first row, with script in hand, to cue him if he went up on his lines. He did the first performance without calling for a single line.

Anthony directed a superb production with a wonderful set by Marge Kellogg. We were so proud to present this masterpiece that is prophetic about World War I and the later nuclear power. Rex got the kind of reviews he must have dreamt about. The media praised him and the *Times* acclaimed him as, "A great classical actor." We sold out all the

Amy Irving, Rosemary Harris, and Rex Harrison in George Bernard Shaw's *Heartbreak House* (1983), directed by Anthony Page

performances and we were still flying high—Wow! Three hits in a row. Something bad *had* to happen on the next one.

Of course, Rex was himself at times a trial. He would summon Paul and myself to his dressing room to complain about this or that—an usher's stray flashlight beam or audience coughing or somebody rattling their *Playbill* or the theatre was too hot or the theatre was too cold. As any producers with a hit would do, we listened and agreed wholeheartedly and assured him that these atrocities would be rectified immediately.

It was now 1984 and a Clifford Odets' play was next on our agenda. He was *the* major playwright of the Group Theatre which flourished in the thirties and was the forerunner of companies presenting plays shunned by Broadway. The Group reached out for material that was new, different and challenging, and politically and socially significant. The Group Theatre was started by Cheryl Crawford, Lee Strasberg, and Harold Clurman.

Clifford Odets had been an actor and appeared with the Group Theatre in four plays, most notably *Men in White*. In 1935 he wrote his first play for the Group in which he also acted, *Waiting for Lefty* (the very first play I was ever in, playing the role of Sid at 14 at Erasmus High School). In the same year he wrote *Til the Day I Die* and *Awake and Sing*, neither of which he acted in.

Awake and Sing is about a Jewish family, the Bergers, in the Bronx and the economic turmoil they found themselves in as a result of the Depression. This is such an important play. As the director, I wanted to be sure the actors I chose were not stereotypical. So I went about selecting actors that I thought were right for the role whether they be Jewish or not. I knew I needed actors who would not be afraid of speaking in the staccato hard style of the play, much like the James Cagney movies of that time. I was lucky to find the right ones: Nancy Marchand as the mother, Bessie; Frances McDormand, Hennie; Harry Hamlin, the gangster Moe; Paul Sparer, the grandfather; Thomas Waites, the grandson; Dick Latessa as Myron Berger; Michael Lombard as Uncle Morty; and Benjamin Hendrickson as Sam Feinschreiber.

These actors were on the money. The only character whose voice was appropriately soft and dreamy was the grandfather—an immigrant who brought gentle European behavior, love of opera, and socialist teaching to the household. The grandfather is the voice of culture. He is the contrast to the tough manner of the natural born Americans. The family ignores him except for his grandson, Thomas.

Even though the play is set in the Bronx, I kept thinking of my own home and family life in Brooklyn. I used much of that experience in setting up the production—the set, costumes, and lighting. My input with the actors also came from that source.

Odets by this time had fallen out of favor and his works were rarely produced. I hoped our production would resurrect his reputation. I think we gave it a nudge in that direction.

CHAPTER 46

Big Hits and Little Misses

I kept after George C. Scott about doing another Coward play with us. On the phone from California, he said he was interested in doing the one-act plays *Tonight at 8:30*. With that in mind, I flew out to visit him at his home in Malibu to talk about the Coward possibility. Have you ever tried to find a house in Malibu off the main road? I started searching at noon and by around five o'clock I finally found it through the help of a local real estate agent. The hills and roads in Malibu were charming with discreetly hidden street signs which made it impossible for any stranger to find the home of a celebrity.

Meetings with George were always brief and to the point. We spent time talking about our families and about Patty, which is how he always referred to Patricia—as tears of true sentiment would always well up in his eyes—and he expressed his deep love for her. When he loved you he loved you for life. This can be attested to by Elizabeth Wilson, George Grizzard, Cicely Tyson, Paul Libin and many others. With George, his love and respect came with admiration for doing your work well.

In an hour we had covered all the pros and cons of the Coward plays and came to the conclusion that *Design for Living* was the one we most wanted to do—even though there wasn't a role for George. But he wanted to direct it. The last time the play had been done was its original engagement on Broadway in 1933 with Noël Coward, Alfred Lunt, and Lynn Fontaine.

Three months later we were in rehearsal and had decided on Jill Clayburgh, Raul Julia, and Frank Langella for the cast. There was laughter and happiness in the rehearsal and at performance time. I had known Frank since Williamstown and our 1965 production of John Webster's *The White Devil* at the Circle on Bleecker Street, and Raul from Frank Loesser's *Where's Charley?* Jill, I had never met before but we be-

Raul Julia, Jill Clayburgh, and Frank Langella in Noël Coward's *Design for Living* (1984), directed by George C. Scott

came friends and thereafter I have always referred to her as Jilly Poo. It was a huge hit and had a very successful run. The set was designed by Thomas Lynch.

For some time, I had been talking to Ellis Raab about directing a play for us. Gentle Fate was about to change into her heavy-footed Evil alter ego. We chose Arthur Schnitzler's *The Loves of Anatol.*

The cast was lovely including such major talents as Phil Bosco, Stephen Collins, and Michael Learned. The rehearsals went well until trouble started the first day of technical rehearsals. As a matter of fact, at the very first light cue! As you may know, when a play goes into technical rehearsal all the stagehands are on payroll until the light cues for the show are completed. So at the very first light cue, Ellis was not satisfied—roughly 250 attempts later, he was still not satisfied. So the whole day was spent on this one cue and there were probably seventy-five more still to be done! Needless to say, cue number one was costly or should I say, really costly. In addition, the actors became demoralized from having to hang around while Ellis was pondering.

The next day by two o'clock the first light cue was finally satisfactory to Ellis. Everybody unleashed a sigh of relief but we were all still panicky over how much longer the technical rehearsal would take. Actors get paid the same for the week of technical rehearsal whether it takes four hours or twelve — or more. Normally it is a day and a half or two days at the most, but at this rate it looked like it would be a week and a half. With the stagehands making mucho dinero. I pleaded with Ellis to hasten his selection because we were about to start and tickets had already been sold. But the light cue selection went on for the next three days. These delays definitely affected Ellis's work and the actors' enthusiasm. Evil Fate's big foot still sitting on my head, the reviews came back very mild.

While this unhappiness was going on I began putting together Shaw's *Arms and the Man*. I had several readings at my apartment with Raul Julia and Kevin Kline. At each reading they would switch roles — Captain Bluntschli and Major Sergius Saranoff — until they found which part they liked best. Both roles are delicious so I said, "Let's get on kids, and choose which ones you want to do." Frankly, I thought that Kevin — because of his precision of speech and the manner in which he holds himself physically — was properly suited to "Captain Bluntschli," and Raul who is jovial and phlegmatic was right for "Saranoff." I told Kevin and Raul about my choices and they accepted.

Everything was going along fine. We agreed on the play and on the roles but we couldn't agree on the director. Then Gentle Fate invited me to see a production off-Broadway that John Malkovich had directed. Watching the show, I realized that this was the man for us.

At lunch, John and I talked about our similar interests: his running of Steppenwolf in Chicago and me and the Circle. We also talked about our common interest in sports — particularly football. Later on during the run, we had a picnic for the company at my house and John displayed his quarterback passing capabilities to his receiver Louis Zorich, who played Major Paul Petkoff.

John met the cast and he agreed they were perfect for the roles and off we went. Glenne Headly, John's wife, auditioned for the role of Raina Petkoff along with many other women and we selected her as the best choice. Glenne is a beautiful blonde, devilishly coquettish, and a strong actress with great humor. In the *Playbill* biography Glenne did a very sweet thing; she thanked Paul and me for giving her her Broadway debut.

John was then famous for the films *The Killing Fields* and *Places in the Heart* as well as his performance in *True West* off-Broadway. Kevin and

Raul Julia, Glenne Headly, and Kevin Kline in the 1985 production of George Bernard Shaw's *Arms and the Man,* directed by John Malkovich

Raul of course were well known actors too, so there was a continuous "star banter" that went on in rehearsal. When they would be asked to do something, one would retort with, "I'm a star too." And John would respond, "I am asking you to do this because I am *the* star." He brought a wonderful self-effacing humor to rehearsals. But with all the jokes and jostling, John is very meticulous and definite and at the same time very open to actors' input. The whole rehearsal was a breeze of warmth and top workmanship by all concerned — designers, actors, crew, and director. John cooked up a perfect stew and liked the work so much that when we extended the run and Kevin had to leave for a film, John agreed to step in and perform Captain Bluntschli. *Arms* was another success with the press and the public.

We were flying again and next did *The Marriage of Figaro* by Pierre Augustin Beaumarchais. It was directed by Andrei Serban, whom I'd been wooing. I'd seen several of his productions, including Chekhov's *The Cherry Orchard* with the great Irene Worth and Raul playing Lopakhin. I had been after Christopher Reeve, too, having seen him on the stage in London with Vanessa Redgrave in Michael Redgrave's *The Aspern Papers.* He agreed to play Count Almaviva. He had made quite a reputation as *Superman* and was anxious to appear in a classical play. He immediately got into the spirit of the role as the required farcical elements came easily to him. The audience was surprised to see what a commanding presence

Christopher Reeve, Mary Elizabeth Mastrantonio, and
Anthony Heald in Beaumarchais' *The Marriage of Figaro*
(1985), directed by Andrei Serban

that Superman had on stage as the Count—the likable cad we dislike for his pursuit of women.

The rest of the company consisted of Anthony Heald, Dana Ivey, Caitlin Clarke, and Mary Elizabeth Mastrantonio playing Suzanne, the maid who is pursued by the Count. Beni Montresori did the set and costumes which was a series of beautifully fluid sliding panels that established different locales for the chase that is integral to the plot.

It was another happy time with positive results. *Figaro* completed its twelve-week run. The subscribers were satisfied.

We now needed something for Christmas—that wonderful time of year when people flock to the city hungry for theatre. Robert Klein had done his one-man show, entitled *The Annual Robert Klein Show*, at Carnegie Hall for the past two or three years. But this year, I didn't see any ads for that event. So I called Bobby on the phone and asked him if he would like to do his show at the Circle for not one night but from Christmas through New Year. He said yes and added that he would have a band and two singers accompany him. Paul worked out the financial details with his agent.

Robert was a star from his Johnny Carson appearances and his solo shows throughout the country. I felt confident he would draw big audiences, which turned out to be so.

This was just the beginning of the computer age, where we could get box office figures by just pressing a couple of buttons instead of the old-fashioned way where the box office treasurer slaved over an adding machine. Every night Paul would come down to Bobby's dressing room and every night Bobby would ask excitedly, "What are the receipts?" Paul would tease him a few minutes and say, "I don't know, we will have to wait until the treasurer adds it up." And then after a few beats he would give him a printout of the receipts for the day. Bobby would smile broadly in acknowledgement of the high revenue he was bringing in. I think Bobby still has those statements in his private file, or maybe on his wall.

Years before, I had directed him as Freddie in Shaw's *Pygmalion* for the Williamstown Summer Festival. The young girl who played Eliza Doolittle was very nervous. She felt she wasn't sufficiently endowed for the role and stuffed rubber pads into her bra. Upon her first entrance into Professor Higgins' home, as she sat down, one of the pads popped out of her bodice and bounced several times downstage. She was so nervous she didn't notice the bouncing pad. Professor Higgins, Anthony Zerbe, continued the dialogue as he calmly walked to the bouncing pad, caught it and put it blithely in the pocket of his swallow-tail coat—the scene went on as though nothing had happened. I've always been grateful to Anthony for this calm! Over the years, Bobby and I would have reminiscent laughs about the bouncing bra pad.

When I first directed Bobby in Williamstown in *Pygmalion*, Patricia's opera career was taking her all over the country to perform. Bobby would observe me walking into a telephone booth having long conversations with her. He would mock me for this telephonic devotion, but years later he himself was courting a young opera singer and ended up addicted to the same telephone booth routine. We both had to learn how to deal with a traveling opera singer/partner at ten cents a minute.

Back when Bobby was an undergraduate at Yale, he was obviously very talented, as well as very curious about New York theatre. In fact, he was roaring to get to New York. I don't usually encourage young people to leave college early. So I thoroughly questioned him about why he didn't want to stay in school. He convinced me it was past history for him. So I said come to New York and I will give you a job as an actor. If my memory serves me correctly, I think he started out as an usher and quickly graduated to a role in our production of Pirandello's *Six Characters in Search of an Author*.

When he opened his one-man show for us that Christmas, he started his routine by making fun of Circle in the Square's name and correlating it with different types of stages: proscenium, four-sided, theatre in the round, dinner theatre—"Where am I? In a box? In a square? In a circle?" Then he began striding around our three-sided stage saying "Will I have to keep moving so everyone can see me?" Then out of breath he began parodying scenes from our plays and making fun of the confusion the actor feels not knowing which way he should be looking: "Blow out your candles, Laura," "Romeo, oh, Romeo, wherefore art thou, Romeo?" "Attention must be paid." His band would play numbers to give Bobby some breathing time. The lead folk singer Kenny Rankin was superb. Bobby himself was a wonderful singer who could imitate any style—including a black singer backed up by two female singers. Business was great and went way beyond Paul's and my expectations and Bobby was a happy happy man.

I had been talking with John Malkovich about acting in another play. At a luncheon meeting he told me he had a movie commitment, but would love to direct a play. We decided on Harold Pinter's *The Caretaker* which he had done at the Steppenwolf Theatre. We invited the same actors that had performed it there, Gary Sinise, Jeff Perry, and Alan Wilder.

Gary and John, heads of Steppenwolf, had a long and warm relationship. It was an excellent production, wonderfully paced and beautifully acted. Unfortunately, the critics missed the richness of the production and we had to cut the run short.

We were preparing Bernard Sabath's *The Boys in Autumn* for a production with George C. Scott. A fable about Huck Finn and Tom Sawyer —now in their 60's—who meet accidentally and share with each other what their lives have been. There is still plenty of playfulness between the two as they slowly shed the years. George had agreed to play Huckleberry Finn but we had a lot of trouble finding the actor to play Tom Sawyer. I was directing and George and I were consulting daily. At one point in a meeting in my office he said, "What about Marlon?" And I said, "That would be great." He picked up the phone, dialed it and after a couple of rings, said, "Hello Bud? This is George." (Bud was Brando's nickname.) And proceeded to tell him the play that we were doing and Bud knew of it. There had been a production out in California with Kirk Douglas and Burt Lancaster. Brando said it would be fun, but . . . and my heart stopped. Then he added, "But I can't remember the lines and besides it is too much work." George said, "Thank you, Bud, and I'll see you next time I'm out there."

Like me, George had seen 1776 a few years before and we both agreed that John Cullum, who had played Edward Rutledge, would be perfect for the role of Tom with his down home, country Southern manner and his eternal boyish charm.

Off we went to rehearsals. On the first day George suggested we work only four hours a day and I said, "G.C., Actor's Equity says we can rehearse seven hours." George took a long draw on his cigarette and said, "Teedy, you gotta understand after four hours we're spinning wheels. We don't add or learn anything more." I thought about it and after a couple of days of rehearsal I realized that George was absolutely right. And if you think about it in your own lives—when we have creative work in reading, painting, photography or music—four hours is about the maximum creative time. So that became our daily schedule. Normally a play on Broadway rehearses seven out of eight hours six days a week. During that time, let's say it's a play with a cast of eight. So not every actor is rehearsing during the seven-hour period, their scenes are rehearsed separately. But with *Boys in Autumn* we had a two-character play that ran for an hour and twenty minutes without intermission. So four-hour rehearsals became our daily schedule.

Once George C. starts on a play he is completely focused and his life becomes absorbed in the character. Each night when he went home to Greenwich in his movie-career-supported limo and driver, he would be thinking about the play. When he got home—more thinking—when he was sleeping it was churning around in his head. George would never tell me this, of course, but I could just tell by looking at him when he came in the next day. Out of that twisting and turning, he always had a fresh idea about how to approach a particular moment or scene.

We felt we had something very special and meaningful about childhood buddies now grown up and how easily it was for them to resurrect their earlier camaraderie. When we had breaks in rehearsal George and John referred to each other as Huck and Tom. There was a lot of love and respect floating between the two of them. George loves to sing at parties and play the piano as well so I got him to sing a few lines from a period song but he would cut it short before the audience could applaud. He didn't want to interrupt the flow of the play. It was easy to get John with his background in musical comedy to do a little soft shoe.

John Cullum and George C. Scott in Bernard Sabath's
The Boys in Autumn (1986), directed by Theodore Mann

There is a memorable scene in the play. It is night, the cicadas are chirping and Tom is sitting on a rock center stage talking to Huck about the women in their lives. Huck (George) recalls an unnamed woman, talking about her with great tenderness and tears in his eyes. That scene always touched my heart because the way George did it said so much about the lost love of Huck's life. When the run was over, I asked him how he managed that same exact emotion every night and he said that there had been a girl in his life back in his college days that he saw at that moment. Or as Huck would say, "I conjures her up."

If you ever go backstage, never ask an actor how he achieved a particular moment. They hesitate to share that very personal information because the next time they do the scene, your comment would be in their head instead of what they had arrived at organically.

George, John and I all referred to the play as an "adventure." But, alas, the press didn't like it. We were terribly disappointed. It wasn't so bitter to take when you feel so good about the work.

Huck had become a recluse and George decided that the character living in a remote area of the country would have a beard. During rehearsal one day George was visited by two advertising executives. They had come to confirm a deal where George would appear in a television commercial. He would receive $1 million for lauding the virtues of a new model automobile. George asked me to stay with him. We all sat down in the front row seats and had a short friendly chat. One of the executives said that the shoot would be next week in the afternoon and would take just two days. "Oh," he added, "you will have to appear without a beard." All affability dropped from George's face. "I can't shave my beard!" he shot

back, "I grew it for the role. I have a play to do." With that the executives
said that they could not go ahead unless he shaved. And George said, "I
won't shave my beard." The executives left and George went right back
into rehearsal without the slightest sign of regret. His salary for *Autumn*
was $1000 a week. I was waiting for him to say something and he never
mentioned the incident to me again. My respect for George multiplied
tenfold that day.

Next we returned to Shaw. Since 1977 we had done one Shaw play
nearly every season. By and large they were his major plays and they had
all been successes: *St. Joan* (1977), *Man and Superman* (1979), *Major Barbara* (1980), *Candida* (1981), *Heartbreak House* (1983), and *Arms and the
Man* (1985). Now our problem was to find a top quality Shaw play that had
not been recently done in New York. So Stephen Porter, who had directed
three of the above perfectly, sat down in my office and we conferred and
read for several days those Shaw plays which we had not produced.

I always liked working with Stephen. He knows the text inside and
out and he is completely versed in the historical and social significance
of the time in which the play is set. He is capable of understanding and
explaining to the cast any obscure reference of the playwright.

He casts wonderfully and gives the actors lots of room and has complete faith in them. Some actors get very nervous about his silence, but
Stephen speaks when he feels his words are necessary to move the scene
ahead and when he does so, it is specific and to the point.

The first consideration for Paul, Stephen and myself in casting a
Shaw play was always to choose one with a role that would be right
for Phil Bosco. With that in mind, we selected *You Never Can Tell*,
in which Phil, after having played the millionaire munitions maker in
Major Barbara, would play a poor but aristocratic waiter. *You Never Can
Tell* had first been produced on Broadway at the turn of the century and
later was revived at the Martin Beck in 1948.

Stephen put together a tremendous company: Phil, Uta Hagen,
Amanda Plummer, Stephen McHattie, Victor Garber, John David Cullum (John's son), Stefan Gierasch, and Lise Hilboldt. Rehearsals and performances went extremely well—the public and most of the critics loved
the play. For the critics, it was a discovery of another rarely performed
Shaw work. Phil played the role of the waiter with high comedy and

Matthew Broderick in Horton Foote's *The Widow Claire* (1986), directed by Michael Lindsay-Hogg

subdued disdain for the wealthy family that he worked for, but also embarrassed to be the father of his son who has become an eminent barrister. Uta brought a down to earth immediacy to the role of Mrs. Clandon, the novelist. Stephen was joyfully superior to those beneath him, which he believed included everyone. Amanda and John were the perfect upper class adolescents and Victor and Lise fulfilled the romantic aspect of the show. Victor played a 19th century lothario now befuddled by the ladies of the 20th century. The play did well at the box office.

I've always admired Horton Foote's writing, one of America's finest playwrights and I had seen several of his plays done in workshop at the Bergoff-Hagen School in the Village. Horton is a wonderful Southern gentleman. And whenever we met at social occasions I would express my desire to do one of his new plays. It finally came to pass when he gave me *The Widow Claire* to read. The Circle on Bleecker Street was the right venue for this intimate play. So in 1986 we produced it there. We had a wonderful cast headed up by Matthew Broderick and Hallie Foote, Horton's daughter. It was directed by Michael Lindsay-Hogg, Geraldine Fitzgerald's son, who had extensive film and stage credits. The production went very smoothly and the play was honored by the critics. It was a happy time — Evil Fate was still being held at bay.

The Second Stage Company had opened off-Broadway Tina Howe's *Coastal Disturbances*. It had received very good reviews and I went to see it and admired it. Frank Rich loved it too. One day I received a call from Carole Rothman, the director and head of the company asking us if we would be interested in moving the show to the Circle. I discussed it with Paul and he agreed that we should go ahead on my say so.

When our first ad in *The New York Times* indicated that *Coastal* would be moving to the Circle we were swamped. Obviously the word of mouth for the short run of the play at Second Stage had been very good, but Frank Rich's unqualified fine review was an enormous help. (When Frank sang clear, beautiful notes, audiences flocked to the show.) Every day we kept selling more and more tickets. If my memory serves me correctly, I don't think we invited the critics back. They're reluctant to re-review a play they've

Timothy Daly and Annette Bening in Tina Howe's *Coastal Disturbances* (1978), directed by Carole Rothman *(Photo used with permission of Susan Cook Photography, and Susan Cook Photography © 1986)*

recently seen, so we reproduced the *Times* review in the arts section.

The play takes place on a New England beach where different groups of people come to enjoy its beauty and we learn about their lives overseen by a lifeguard. The cast was wonderful—this was Annette Bening's Broadway debut and also included Timothy Daly, Heather MacRae, Addison Powell and Rosemary Murphy. Tim played Leo Hart, the lifeguard yearning for, but in the end losing, Holly Dancer, played by Annette. Rosemary Murphy and Addison Powell as an elderly couple represented the stuffy conservatives of that region. Heather, as Mrs. Bigelow, the mother of two children, tries desperately with good cheer to teach them manners.

Moving this play from off-Broadway to Broadway was a heady bubbly champagne experience and bonded the company together like very few things can do. After a long run with the show Annette left to try her luck at Hollywood. When she got out there, she got some work and the sweetheart promptly sent a gift in support of the Circle—a gracious act of love and generosity.

Despite our success with *Coastal*, our deficit was still growing. In other words our costs were exceeding our fundraising efforts. This slow rise of the deficit was a great concern to Paul and myself and did not bode well for the future. The noose was tightening.

We put Tennessee Williams' A *Streetcar Named Desire* on with Blythe Danner, Aidan Quinn and Frances McDormand. Directed by Nikos Psacharopoulos, a longtime faculty member of Circle in the Square Theatre School and the Artistic Director of the Williamstown Summer Theatre.

The inevitable comparisons to the original *Streetcar* were voiced, but we came away pretty good and the play had a healthy twelve-week run. Nikos did good work. My son Jonathan was cast as the strolling musician and he wailed and wailed on the saxophone to set the mood for the scene changes. Jonathan has played music all his life—flute, guitar and sax. In addition, he can sing and act and has studied acting in London as well as a year at Juilliard. He tried acting in Los Angeles but after a year of rejection he gave it up. It's a shame; he has the talent and the good looks for theatre. He is now the director of the Westchester Arts Council Gallery and Performance Space in White Plains, New York.

Around this time Martin Segal, former Chairman of Lincoln Center—one of the finest human beings I've ever known—created New York's first International Theatre Festival. He had gathered together productions from companies all over the world and he invited us to present the Gate Theatre's production of Sean O'Casey's *Juno and the Paycock*.

Juno was directed by Joe Dowling and starred an incredible actor, Donal McCann (of The Gate's glorious company). Alex Scott, George and Colleen's son, was a great assistance to Paul and myself on the production. The play got the kind of reviews you dream about and sold out. Everyone wanted to see it and the company all agreed to stay past the engagement time except Donal—no amount of talking would convince him. He said he longed to go back home and missed his family. This was undoubtedly true but the real reason that he wanted to leave was that Donal was a drinker. He had promised Joe Dowling before they came to New York that he wouldn't touch a drop during rehearsal or the run. Not even a wee drop. The night the show closed he was released from his commitment of abstinence and he immediately tied one on so bad that the next morning he had to be carried onto the plane heading back to Ireland. It is a very sad thing when someone dear to you is afflicted with the disease of alcoholism.

I can still see the drunken pantomime scene that Donal as Captain Boyle, did with John Kavanagh (Joxer). They have just returned home

John Kavanagh and Donal McCann in Sean O'Casey's *Juno and the Paycock* (1988), directed by Joe Dowling

after an evening of Irish joviality in which Joxer has flattered and fawned on Captain Boyle announcing, "He's a darlin'man." As they come in the door they realize that the Captain's wife, Juno (Geraldine Plunkett), is sleeping; the two sots have to be silent so as not to wake her. She would be furious if she saw her husband drunk and Joxer the beneficiary of her husband's largesse. Drunk as they are they try to enter very quietly and cross the stage without falling, or bumping into each other, or laughing. The cross in our production took five minutes in complete silence—one of the most graceful, balletic scenes ever on Broadway. The audience relished every moment.

The production was the hit of the Festival and Paul and I were proud to be presenting such a mesmerizing play under the Circle banner.

The last play we did in the same season was Shaw's *The Devil's Disciple*, beginning in November. Once again Stephen Porter directed. Phil Bosco played General Burgoyne, Roxanne Hart (who had been

Philip Bosco in George Bernard Shaw's *The Devil's Disciple* (1988), directed by Stephen Porter

in our 1979 production of *Loose Ends*) starred as Judith Anderson, and Remak Ramsay, played her husband Anthony. The cast also included Victor Garber (Richard Dudgeon), Rosemary Murphy (Richard's mother, Mrs. Dudgeon), David Crier (Richard's father, William Dudgeon), Chandra Mann (Mrs. Titus Dudgeon), and Bill Moor (Major Swindon).

Disciple was written in 1879, a century after the American Revolution, and is the only play Shaw wrote that takes place in America. The play involves British officers reacting to the behavior of the Colonists. Many of the characters depicted in the play were familiar to the audience. For example, General Burgoyne, who in the play berates the British military and administration for their ineffectiveness—is taught in our history books as the British officer who lost the pivotal battle of the Revolution at Saratoga. Mr. Shaw's language, intricate plot and wit gave the audiences a wonderful time.

Phil was multifaceted as usual and played with a twinkle in his eye— another superb performance. Victor Garber was brilliant as Dick Dudgeon, a deliciously cynical young man adored by all women who offers his life to save that of a Colonist. Fortunately, Dudgeon, who is about to be hanged, is reprieved in the last moments of the play. Even Roxanne, not usually a comedic performer, was outrageously funny.

CHAPTER 47

TAKE ME OUT TO THE BALL GAME

Paul and I had gone to Israel at the invitation of Noam Semel the then head of the Haifa Municipal Theatre to see his work. We had a thrilling time visiting sites in Israel and came away excited by a new play by Joshua Sobol we saw at the Haifa entitled *Ghetto*.

The play involves the attempts of the remaining inhabitants of the Vilna Ghettos in Lithuania to preserve their library and their lives during the Nazi occupation in 1942–43, which they do by putting on scenes from plays and cabaret performances. They manage thereby to raise their own spirits and distract the Nazis. It was a powerful play that we felt critics and audiences would appreciate. The papers from the library that did survive are now at the Yivo Institute in New York City.

We brought over the Israeli director, Gedalia Besser, who worked very well with American actors. The title of the play, *Ghetto*, had a double connotation. In contemporary terms it means black housing areas and in the historical context of the play it referred to the sections the Nazis had confined Jews to. The cast was totally committed to the play and its honoring of the heroic survivors of Vilna. Unfortunately, Frank Rich's review in *The New York Times* was not good and others were mild, so business was weak. Each night after the performance Paul went out in front of the audience and made an impassioned speech urging them to spread the word and tell their friends about the play. I was proud of how Paul fought for the show. That's how he has always been — fighting with all his heart for what he loves.

The combination of poor reviews, small attendance, and the confusing title forced us to close the play before the end of the subscription period, one of the few plays we have ever had to close prematurely. It was a big punch in the stomach for us. Prior to our production, *Ghetto* had been acclaimed in Israel, several other countries on the continent, and Germany. Shortly after our production, *Ghetto* was lauded in England, which made us feel better about what we had attempted to do.

Then Stephen Sondheim's *Sweeney Todd* came into our lives! Paul and I had seen a production at the York Theatre and we liked it. It had to be remounted and reconceived for our space. But blocking our path to *Sweeney* was a bit of a chasm known as $350,000. Despite our recent successes we lacked that kind of money power. Now I have to tell about how we got the money to put on *Sweeney*. On to our good friends the Pateks.

One day, three or four years earlier, attorneys Bernard Berkowitz and Gene Korf, neither of whom I knew, had called and asked to meet about a couple from San Diego who were in the process of forming a new nonprofit foundation to support medical research and the arts.

Bernie is a tall man with graying hair and a friendly professorial manner whom you would love to be taught and represented by. Gene is jovial and sparkling with a solid awareness of the practical world and the law. Bernie is very reserved and Gene is effervescent. This couple wanted to know if I would be interested in serving on the board of the new foundation. If I was, Bernie and Gene would set up a meeting with them. I thought—giving money to the arts—I'm going to that meeting!

I met the couple a few days later, appropriately, at Café des Artistes, which has wonderful murals on the walls from the twenties. Pat and Rose Patek explained to me why this new foundation was being formed. Their friend and principal of the existing foundation, now deceased, had been involved in the arts and had also been generous in supporting medical research. The woman's father had accumulated great wealth in copper mines. They were eager to create this nonprofit entity to honor her memory and her interests.

I was so enchanted by them, the purposes of their foundation, and their lovely Texas accents that I agreed to join their board. One of the other members of the board would be Olympia Dukakis, who obviously I knew.

At that time, in addition to all of her acting chores, Olympia was running the Whole Theatre Company in New Jersey. So I knew we had simpatico interests, which further encouraged me to accept the invitation.

Getting back to *Sweeney*, as I said we needed a lot of money. I tried several individuals and foundations for funding but we were turned down. *Sweeney* was an important work of Sondheim's. It hadn't been seen in New York for ten years since the Hal Prince production at the Uris Theatre, now the Gershwin, but where would I get the money?

I decided that I would take a chance and ask the Pateks. I thought I might be jeopardizing our future relationship by asking for such a large amount of money. But I didn't have any choice. I particularly didn't want to make the request over the phone. I've always found that my requests for funding was always more successful when I did it face to face so I went to see the Pateks at their ranch south of San Diego.

When I arrived I was astonished to see how vast it was, extending to the Mexican border. They showed me around the property that stretched as far as the eye can see. I thought the ranch must be as large as the state of Israel. During the day I kept bringing up *Sweeney* but we never got down to a real discussion about it and the sun was setting in the West. My time was running out.

That night we went to dinner. Pat Patek said we had to hurry because, "we are going to the Padres game." That meant dinner was going to be short. I knew I had to bring up *Sweeney* now or never. My pitch had to be crystal clear. In other words, brief and to the point. So I told them about the musical. As anxious as I was, I managed to explain that it would cost $350,000 and quickly added that this was much cheaper than the usual cost of a Broadway musical. All this time we had been sitting over our T-bone steaks. I did not touch most of mine because I was too anxious to eat anything. I then asked, "Can we submit a proposal to the foundation for this loan which we would repay out of the surplus of the show?" There was silence for several minutes. Then they said they would think about it. I picked myself up heavily, completely depressed. I had lost my chance. I was trying to be affable but my brain crisscrossed with worries about how we would ever get *Sweeney* on.

We were sitting behind first base in the Pateks' season boxes. I was starving not having eaten my steak, so I excused myself to run out to find a hot dog. When I came back it was the beginning of the second inning. The first batter hit a high fly to left field—the Padre fielder ran and dove to catch the ball. As he slid into the rolled up tarpaulin, he struck his head and was carried off the field in a stretcher unconscious. The next batter swung at a 90-mile-an-hour pitch that missed the catcher's glove and hit the umpire in his mask. He passed out and was carried off the field too! The next batter, a lefty, fouled off the first pitch. As the pitcher began his wind up for the next pitch I turned to Pat Patek and said, "Watch out, the next ball is coming right at us!" Pat was in a seat in between Rose and me. The hitter took a mighty swing—the ball sailed high over first base and as it began its rapid descent towards us I thought to myself, "It *is* coming right at us!" and I lurched over to the left. Rose threw herself to the other side of Pat on the right. Pat, ever fearless sat straight up, totally erect, like a general defying the enemy. Then I heard a thud. Sure enough, the ball hit Pat smack on the left shoulder. Pat looked at me for a long moment and said with his Texas drawl and a smile on his face that seemed to be saying this guy knows something, "Ted, you got that $350,000."

I don't know what compelled me to make that prediction—It came out of my mouth without any pre-thought. It was pure intuition! I was sorry Pat got hit but it only grazed him and now the gods would sing for us and Sondheim!

But maybe Pat was kidding? For the next couple of weeks, I didn't hear anything from Pat and Rose. At the end of the third week, I got a message that Pat Patek had called. My heart was thumping pumping— what would he say? I got him on the phone and, in that sweet drawl, he asked, "When do you need it?" And I responded "right away." And he said, "I'll see what I can do." The next day a Federal Express envelope arrived with the check inside.

Susan H. Schulman directed. Bob Gunton played *Sweeney* the demon barber with a passion for revenge. His partner in crime and love, the pie baker Mrs. Lovett, was played by the incomparable Beth Fowler. Mrs. Lovett fantasizes about domestic bliss with Sweeney. The other characters relive the stereotype of the 1800s' sorrowful, exaggerated characters, several bordering on madness: David Barron's evil unforgiving Judge Turpin; a homeless woman harboring information; and the confused Beadle.

The simplicity of the set designed by the brilliant James Morgan allowed the audience to enjoy an unencumbered *Sweeney Todd* in a simplified setting. Many commented how they felt like they were sitting in Mrs. Lovett's bakery!

When *Sweeney* began previews, audiences loved the show and then we got great reviews from the critics. A critic or two saw fit to comment disdainfully about our space, which has been their perennial penchant since Circle began. Fortunately, actors, directors, and

Bob Gunton and Beth Fowler in Stephen Sondheim's *Sweeney Todd* (1989), directed by Susan Schulman

designers love to work at the theatre and most importantly audiences feel like they are part of the action. So these remarks go unnoticed by the public.

We were able to pay back in full the money that Pat and Rose had loaned us. *Sweeney* had a good healthy run and we were once again on the upside of the roller coaster life of a non-profit theatre producing on Broadway. My wife Patricia would always say, when I received a call from Gene Korf, "It's your 'Genee' on the phone." How right she was, and thereafter we always referred to him as my Genie.

CHAPTER 48

GLASNOST COMES TO BROADWAY

The time had finally come for me to fulfill our side of the bargain with Moscow's Maly Theatre and produce a Russian play in America. We chose a play by Mikhail Bulgakov, one of the most eminent Russian playwrights of the 20th century, *Zoya's Apartment*. A farce about the difficulties of living under Communist rule. The play had, of course, originally been banned in Russia under Stalin—even though Bulgakov was (and still is) the revered playwright of the Maly Theatre.

I had seen Boris Morozov's direction at the Maly and it was first-rate. I also thought a farce would interest New York theatregoers since it is about an overcrowded apartment under Stalin and all the problems that evolved from many different families and strangers living in one space.

One of the difficulties of *Zoya's Apartment* (written in 1926 and never produced in Russia before our New York production!) was that the normal rehearsal process pretty much went out the window. The cast and director spent most of the rehearsal weeks trying to get the script effective for an American audience. Work on character development was left for the last part of rehearsal and therefore the production never bloomed.

I thought American audiences would gain insight into life in the USSR under Communism. But, alas, critics and audiences didn't agree with me and we wobbled and stumbled like a Russian who's had too much vodka through our subscription period. After a couple of weeks into the run the diverse pieces of the production began to cohere. It became enjoyable but unfortunately the damage had been done by the poor critical reception and the audience's reaction in the first couple of weeks.

What to do next? We had done the best of the Greeks, Shaw, Williams and O'Neill. But we hadn't done a Molière in seven years, since *Misanthrope*.

I asked Stephen Porter to join us as director. We began reading Molière plays with Phil Bosco in mind for a lead role. Finally we chose *The Miser*. This was another happy time with Stephen casting and guiding a top-notch production. Philip Bosco played Harpagon and Carole Shelley his advisor, Frosine. Rounding out the cast: Thomas Gibson (Cleante), who went on to television fame with *Dharma and Greg*, Tracy Sallows (Marianne), Mia Dillon (Elise), John Christopher Jones (Maitre Jacques, Harpagon's cook and coachman), Adam Redfield (La Fleche), Joseph Jamrog (La Merluche), and Tom Brennan as the police officer.

They brought the house down every performance—the production was a sheer joy and a tour de force for the company. Harpagon is straggly haired and pot-bellied, eternally clutching his moneybox. He is enormously flattered when he is tricked into believing by Frosine that a young girl, Marianne, is in love with him when in fact she is in love with his vain, foppish, overdressed son Cléante. On learning of this great news Harpagon dances with delight. For a moment he forgets his age, holding himself like a young man, which catches up to him and causes him to break out into a coughing fit. From which he momentarily recovers only to break out into it again—his decrepit physique once more revealed to the audience. In the end, Harpagon has to choose between his lust or money. The more stable commodity wins out. Nothing grows old more graciously than money.

The delicious thing about this play is that nobody tells the truth—almost everyone wants Harpagon's money and will say or do anything to acquire it. Phil's coughing fits were three-to-four minutes in length and brought the house down every night.

Alan Ayckbourn's plays all start their runs in his arena-style theatre in Scarborough, which is similar to our space. I've seen many of his plays here in New York, which were always done on a proscenium stage and found them very intelligent and funny. But for some reason, the

Carole Shelley and Philip Bosco in Molière's *The Miser* (1990), directed by Stephen Porter

New York critics and public have not shown very much interest in them because the productions here are unfavorably compared to the English ones. I bravely hoped that we could change that reception by performing one of them in our space.

We chose *Taking Steps* to be directed by his longtime director and associate, Alan Strachan. The play takes place in a twenty-four-hour period in a haunted old English mansion. The sitting room, master bedroom and attic are all placed side by side at stage level. Carpets strategically placed represent the steps in which the actors feverishly traverse from "floor" to "floor" as three scenes happen simultaneously. It is like a round in music. The dialogue of one scene does not interfere with the dialogue going on in the other two scenes. Through Ayckbourn's magic you believe you're watching the play on three different floors.

Taking Steps was brilliantly directed with outstanding performances by Christopher Benjamin as the suffocating husband, Roland; Pippa Pearthree as the hilariously funny runaway fiancée Kitty; and Jane Summerhays as the former go-go dancer, Elizabeth. All the characters are literally "taking steps" to try and change their lives.

The critics didn't agree with my appraisal and the reviews ran from mixed to mild. But the people that did come found it to be ingeniously witty and an evening of "sheer froth" (according to one favorable review). The reviews affected the box office receipts, though, which in turn increased our deficit. We were taking in enough money to pay for the running expenses but nothing to help recover the cost of mounting the production, which probably at that time was $250,000. The hole was getting deeper even though we were having some pretty good successes.

We needed a winner. Shaw had been one of our most proven playwrights. We'd done most of his well-known plays, but Stephen and I unearthed one of his little known gems—*Getting Married*, which poses the question, "to wed or not to wed?" It is a play about the virtues, and as expressed by all the characters, the disadvantages of matrimony. Shaw through the voices of the bishop, the general, a gentleman, a snob, a greengrocer, a bridegroom and the women in their lives states his affirmation of polygamy. Lee Richardson, who was fine in all his roles for us, was a perfect Bishop, that most reasonable man; Elizabeth Franz was his wife, Mrs. Bridgenorth, whose sole purpose was to increase the race by encouraging the young people to produce more babies. Walter Bobbie, as the chaplain Soames, completely dislikes the institution of marriage; J.D. Cullum was Cecil, a young man about to be married and is very nervous about it; Jane Fleiss was his flighty unorthodox free-spirited bride to be, Edith; Patrick Tull was Collins, the ideal greengrocer—portly and opinionated; and Nicolas Coster was the prototypical empty-headed General. All these characters combine in a rollicking discussion of the famed institution called marriage.

This turned out to be the success we were looking for under Stephen's sure-handed direction, another example of the audience's delight in Shaw's wit.

George C. and I had been talking again about him doing another play, so back I flew to Malibu. The beautiful spacious house they lived in had French doors opening onto a garden and a tennis court beyond. The doors were kept wide open and the breeze blowing off the ocean made me feel like we were on a ship. It was very peaceful. While waiting in the library for George, I surveyed piles of plays and screenplays. George was a great researcher on any project that he worked on. There were books scattered all around the room on varied subjects. And of course there was a soundless television flickering in the corner. George's wife Trish was off riding her horse along the back trails of Malibu. George walked in to greet me.

He asked, "Do you know *On Borrowed Time*?" I replied that I'd seen the film but not the play. We discussed other possibilities and that night I read Paul Osborn's play and was sufficiently enthused to get to work on it with George the next morning. George was awake and ready to work. We sat in the living room right off the veranda having coffee and toast, tossing back and forth names of actors who could fill the roles.

On Borrowed Time had been produced on Broadway in 1938 in the

George C. Scott, Nathan Lane, Teresa Wright, and Matthew Porac in Paul Osborn's *On Borrowed Time* (1991), directed by George C. Scott

same season that *Our Town* had. In fact they opened within a day of each other. Both plays deal nostalgically with the charm of small town life in an earlier America, which is punctured by death. These scenes in both plays are handled with great gentility and compassion.

In 1938, America was just coming out of the depression and because WWII was looming on the horizon, there was a yearning for more happy peaceful times. In that same season on Broadway was an incredible list of plays, including: *Amphitryon 38, Golden Boy, The Playboy of the Western World, Of Mice and Men, Pins and Needles, The Cradle Will Rock, Tortilla Flat,* and O'Neill's one-act sea plays. God, wouldn't it be great to have that kind of a season on Broadway again? What a field day Brooks Atkinson must have had reviewing those plays!

To play the role of Granny opposite George as Gramps, we decided on the wonderful Teresa Wright who had played Linda Loman in our production of *Death of a Salesman*. We also cast Conrad Bain as Dr. Evans; and George DiCenzo as Mr. Grimes. There was still another role to be decided on. Who was going to play Mr. Brink? George and I always referred to this character as the devil because in the play he is always trying to push Gramps "over the brink" and into death. In the 1939 film, Mr. Brink had been performed by a very proper, stentorian bishop-like actor, Sir Cedric Hardwicke, who intoned the dialogue and made the character even scarier.

I thought it would be more interesting to go with an actor who would bring humor to the role rather than severity, someone who was funny and ingratiatingly charming. So of course Nathan Lane popped into my head and I suggested him to George. His face immediately brightened and he said to me, "do you think that he will do it, Teedy? His plate is pretty full." And I said, "Let's try." And so George, who is never one to waste time, picked up the phone and called him and told him what the project was. Nathan responded, "I will have to think about it." In a couple of hours Nathan called back and said, "Yes, I'll do it!" Years later, I asked Nathan why at that juncture in his career, when he was just blossoming into stardom, did he accept the secondary role of the devil? He answered, "When Pappy calls, I go." A real bond had developed among all of us, particularly George and Nathan, having worked together in *Present Laughter*.

When we were casting *On Borrowed Time* in New York, we had a lot of trouble finding a young boy to play Pud, George's orphaned grandson in the play. George read with many actors until he found Matthew Porac. He was sweet, gentle and in the play he really broke the audience's heart as well as George's. George really loved that kid who was adorable in the role. George, while working with him was very delicate, as he always is with actors, but with Matthew even more so.

On Borrowed Time is a very touching play about the distance between old age and youth. Finally the bridge is gapped when Gramps, played by George, makes a deal with the devil to save his grandson's life in exchange for his own.

There is a scene in the play where Teresa Wright, as Granny, is dying. She is sitting downstage as she gracefully extends her hand, with balletic beauty, to accept the inevitable. It was a moment in theatre which you never forget.

George as Gramps was very fine in the role, warm and memorable, as was Nathan, the devil, barricaded in the tree. At one point in rehearsal, a branch of the tree that Nathan was sitting on gave way and he fell. We were all horrified and there was silence for a minute. And then Nathan perked his head up with a reassuring smile on his face. George was furious that the limb broke and that there was no protective cushioning on the floor. Rehearsals stopped for a day and a half until the branch was secured so an accident like that would not reoccur. An event like this could throw the whole production into chaos. George was finally satisfied with the safety measures that Paul took and rehearsals resumed. When George gets mad, the walls shake. To him there is nothing more important than the dignity and protection of an actor. He also would not tolerate fussing by the designer about costumes. For him the costume that the actor was comfortable in was the right one.

The imaginary fly scene that went on for several minutes in which Conrad Bain, George DiCenzo, and George Scott try to swat and catch a fly was mime theatre at its best. The actors created the scene through improvisational rehearsals. The three actors knew each other's work so well that the scene very quickly jumped to life.

The audiences were moved by the play. Many nights I saw people wiping tears from their eyes. It was a popular play for us and we were able to make a dent in our own fat little devil, the deficit. This was the last play George ever did for us. Incredibly, George never received a Tony nomination for *Present Laughter*, *Salesman*, or *On Borrowed Time*, all of which he directed and starred in, and all of which are now acknowledged as not only good but great. Audiences and critics took his greatness too much for granted during his lifetime.

Having made that dent I was about to make a big mistake. I'd seen a new play at Yale that I'd liked entitled *Search and Destroy* by Howard Korder. We brought it to the Circle in 1992 but the dark cynicism and haplessness of the subject and their characters did not sit well with our audiences. Despite the fact that we cast fine actors, including Griffin Dunne, Paul Guilfoyle and Stephen McHattie, we still could not make the play tick. Also I think the title may have misled the prospective audience to think it was a war play and having lived through the Gulf War in 1990-1991, people did not want to be reminded of that time.

Who knows? It didn't work. Frank Rich liked it in New Haven but not in New York. You just never know. All you can do is just keep going and hope the press sees it like you do. Sometimes the vision of the play that you have and your achievement of that vision are looked upon by critics in a totally different way. As Groucho Marx may have said, "Who knows? It's all horse feathers!" But at any rate we were left in deep financial trouble with the failure of this play—our deficit had risen substantially. I realized now I had only one more chance to save my beloved mistress.

CHAPTER 49

THE LAST DANCE?

Riding to our rescue was Al Pacino to play in Oscar Wilde's beautifully articulate *Salome* with language as rich as precious jewels.

For years, I had been arranging readings of plays with Al to see if he would become interested in a new project. Al is one of those movie stars who needs the life of the stage. Al had done a workshop with Paul and I of Brecht's *Jungle of the Cities* and he had performed the New York premiere of *American Buffalo* at the downtown Circle. Our friendship had grown through all of this activity.

I had seen a production of *Coriolanus* at the Public Theatre directed by Stephen Berkoff and admired it. I met him and he told me about his production of *Salome* in London, which I went to see while visiting Vanessa Redgrave.

I fell in love with the startling language of the play. I spoke to Berkoff about Al doing the role and he liked that idea. So, I brought *Salome* to Al's attention. Al and I did a reading of the play and then a couple of workshops. But still Al wasn't convinced that he wanted to do it. Then he went to L.A. to do another film.

Through transatlantic conversations with Berkoff, I came to the conclusion that his ideas about the production were different than mine. When I told him I was not going to go ahead with him as a director he was understandably angry.

In the meantime, I still had not heard from Al. Then one day he called to say that he had done a reading of *Salome* in Los Angeles and said, "I want to do the play." So about a month later he came back to New York and we talked about directors and casting.

At the meeting, Al also brought with him a new play, *Chinese Coffee* by Ira Lewis and wanted to do it in repertory with him playing the lead in both plays. Both shows were to alternate nightly. Different directors, sets, and costumes were used for each show. Paul was rightfully concerned about the enormous expense of the stagehands changing the sets nightly. But Paul, in his usual brilliant way, was able to find cost effective means to accomplish this. Of course, it still turned out to be more costly than doing one show a week. Nonetheless, Paul and I were enthusiastic about a repertory performance like this with an opportunity for Al in two totally different roles.

In *Salome*, Al played King Herod bedecked in jewels with exaggerated white makeup, dark eye shadow and accentuated lips. Herod is a depraved despot who is quite content with the order of things. He can ask anybody in his kingdom to do what pleases him.

King Herod had one major problem: he was in love with his wife's daughter. He pleads with her to "Dance for me, Salome." She in turn is in love with Jokanaan, the Prophet, who has upset the entire society by prophesizing the arrival of the Son of God. In Roman society at that time the emperor was a god. In the Jewish society God was already ever present. So what Jokanaan was proposing was heresy to both sides. Salome adores Jokanaan but he ignores her advances by saying, "Back, daughter of Babylon."

Herod says repeatedly "Dance for me, Salome." If she acquiesces, he says, I will give you everything, "unto half of my kingdom." She remains silent and he continues to woo her with vivid descriptive language that makes one's head swirl with wonder.

With every urging to "Dance for me, Salome," Al used a different sensual intonation. Finally, she agrees and disrobes and dances for him. He then asks her, what she wants. And she replies, "The head of Jokanaan." Herod refuses and then continues to make other offers of treasures. But she persists and says, "You gave your word." At which point, Herod says with deep irony, "You are your mother's daughter." The head of Jokanaan is presented to Salome. She rhapsodizes over the beauty of

Al Pacino and Sheryl Lee in Oscar Wilde's *Salome* (1992), directed by Robert Allan Ackerman

his eyes and mouth. Herod in jealous exasperation says with his final vengeful command, "Kill her." Al's performance was deeply sensual and different from anything else he has ever done.

Sheryl Lee played Salome and Suzanne Bertish played Herodias, Herod's wife. They were both excellent.

It was an astonishing performance particularly in contrast to the character of Henry Levine that Al played in *Chinese Coffee*. *Chinese Coffee* is a contemporary play about a down and out novelist. Henry feels that he has the right to use the incidents and people of his life in his novels including those of his closest friend, Jake, played by Charles Cioffi.

Al was needy and intense as Henry and Charles was funny as Jake in his remonstrative denunciation of Henry's libelous actions. Both plays sold out for the run and audiences were enriched to see Al in two widely different roles—from Herod to Henry. He was mesmerizing in both! Moreover, the tilting financial keel of the Circle ship was straightening out. My mistress was again smiling.

We had been looking for a musical as part of our subscription series. Nancy Bosco, Phil's wife, who was our literary advisor, brought to my attention a new musical adapted from Leo Tolstoy's *Anna Karenina* by Peter Kellogg and Daniel Levine. The music was lovely, the book was fine, and the cast was good, including Ann Crumb, Scott Wentworth, and Melissa Errico in her Broadway debut. I directed and Patricia Birch did the choreography. We were nominated for a Tony Award for best musical and felt very good about that. It was a reaffirmation of our work.

However, we were rejected by the critics. Maybe because we had the audacity to attempt to adapt Tolstoy's literary masterpiece. As a general rule, critics don't like you to alter classics. Going into it, I knew that this aspect was a danger. But I thought the work of Peter and Daniel was so good that it would overcome that kind of critical resistance. But it didn't.

As a result, we were financially hit very hard by the failure of *Anna* and I have to say at this time, I was not functioning very well. I was especially distracted because around this time Patricia's multiple sclerosis had progressed and she was having more and more incidents. I had wanted desperately to make her happy by our having a success.

CHAPTER 50

MY LOVE

All of the time that I was directing *Anna*, Patricia was in our home in Carmel Valley. In September our son Jonathan had married his long-time love Chandra Lee. Patricia was so ill she had to go into the hospital and sadly, she could not attend the wedding, which took place on a ranch in Carmel Valley within eyesight of our home. The backdrop for the wedding ceremony was the Sierra Madre Mountains and the cloudless blue sky that rarely changes throughout the entire summer. Andrew came from Brooklyn and friends and relatives came from all over the country. The service was delivered by several "ministers"—Eve Tartar the wonderful artist/philosopher, Chandra's brother Faron who delivered traditional Bible material in the fashion of the Lee family and spiritual words by her father Jack, himself a former minister. During the services I was looking in the direction of our home which Patricia loved so much, speaking silently to her and praying for her recovery. After the wedding ceremony Jonathan, Chandra, her mother and father, Lily May and Jack, Andrew, and myself visited and shared with Patricia the joy of the occasion.

Patricia and I were scheduled to return to New York in the beginning of October. As the weeks went by while we were still in Carmel Valley, Patricia got stronger and better and better. She was making a miraculous but slow recovery. By the time we got on the plane to return to New York she was agile and effervescently happy. Back in Bedford her mobility was much improved. She was in great spirit and looked forward to her favorite time of the whole year, Christmas. She was never happier, busier, or more concentrated than at any other time or occasion during the whole year. For Patricia, Christmas was a rapturously joyous time for reuniting with friends and family, the grandest time of the year. She made lists of all the presents she wanted to give and went about methodically ordering the tree, the decorations, and all the presents. And then in mid-December as Christmas was approaching as so often happened for her at this time of the year, she had a relapse. She was completely depleted and had difficulty breathing, sleeping most of the day—her condition continued to deteriorate and she had to go to the hospital. My sons Jonathan and Andrew were with me on many of the daily visits with great love and kindness for their "little mommy" and tenderness and understanding for me. We realized that her illness was at an extreme point. When she could speak, she said, "I want to go home, I want to die, I don't want to live anymore." Which is something she had said on several occasions in the past but had always rebounded. This time there was a weariness in her voice, a finality and a plea. When the doctors advised us that all hope was gone Jonathan and I decided that we should take her home and remove her oxygen supports. I had always hoped and prayed for a miracle and never believed that Patricia would die. I rode home with her in the ambulance.

As we turned into our driveway in Bedford, I said to Patricia, as I had often said when we arrived at that spot, Eban's memorable line from *Desire Under the Elms* spoken by George C. Scott, "Har we be t' hum, Abbie," and Patricia, whose eyes had been closed for several days, opened them, looked up, and smiled at me.

I had had her bed moved downstairs to the living room and she rested there with Jonathan, Chandra, her mother Eda, Andrew and her two dogs, Carry and Lucky around her.

The previous Christmas while we were all unwrapping presents it began to snow. As we looked out the window we saw our neighbor riding on an old-fashioned sled pulled by her miniature horses. We all went out on the porch and reveled in the wondrous sight of the sled and the horses and the snow coming down against a blue-grey sky. Patricia was so happy.

However on this Christmas, with Patricia now back home from the hospital we talked with her about that scene the year before and she smiled, shook her head and said, "Yes." But on this day, January 20, 1993, she was able to have her final rest. After struggling and fighting for years, she just wanted to rest—my sweet darling was tired, exhausted—and I cried from deep down in my soul. I placed my hand on her heart which continued to beat for seven hours and because of that Andrew believed that she was still alive. I cried for days, months, I miss her so.

What an extraordinary human—I was blessed to have been with her for forty-one beautiful years. We rarely fought; we disagreed and argued. I don't remember a single time that we stopped talking, because of exasperation, for more than a few minutes.

Patricia always said that God had blessed her with her voice and that she had to share her gift with others. Her presence on stage was riveting. You couldn't take your eyes off this beautiful delicate creature who sang so gloriously and moved with such grace. She exuded love and vulnerability in her voice and in her whole being which endeared her to the audience.

At Patricia's memorial at the Circle, there were large performance photographs of her on the upstage wall. As friends came in they heard her singing one of her arias. They spoke, remembering her artistry, warmth, tenderness, and humor. It was the kind of event that Patricia would have wanted with her friends and family close by. As friends were leaving Patricia's voice rose in an aria which affirmed life!

Every time Patricia performed, she had a cassette recorder, slightly offstage or in a friend's lap in the audience, to record her voice so she could study and correct any mistakes. These recordings have been put on digital audio tape by our good friend Robert Israel, over a hundred hours of her singing. As I write this I am attempting to arrange with a small record company a CD of Patricia's finest arias. I derive great solace from these wonderful recordings of the woman I love and miss so much.

CHAPTER 51

A Dance That Didn't Happen

In April of 1993 we presented Ed Berkeley's Willow Cabin Company production of three one-acts by Thornton Wilder entitled *Wilder, Wilder, Wilder*. I was so distracted by my recent loss of Patricia that I had absolutely no input into this production only to the extent of seeing it off-off-Broadway and inviting the company to the Circle. I did manage to raise sufficient funds to get it on from several sources, including our good friends Pat and Rose Patek of the Stephen and Mary Birch Foundation, Gene Korf's The Blanche and Irving Laurie Foundation and Al Pacino's Foundation.

Most of the cast were Circle graduates, including Linda Powell, daughter of Secretary of State, Colin Powell. After *Wilder* closed I had neither the drive nor the means to put on another production. When the board asked me to bring in a new artistic director, I first resisted the notion, but then I came to realize that the Circle ship was in danger of going down. I would do anything to save my mistress.

Over the next few months, I interviewed prospective candidates and finally recommended Josephine Abady, who had been Artistic Director of the Cleveland Playhouse. John Russell (chairman of the Board of Directors of Circle in the Square), Paul, and I had heard rumblings about her departure from the Playhouse due to artistic differences. Josie said that she would support and continue our goals and tradition of doing classic American and European plays as well as new plays. She added that she admired our work and expressed her desire to bring in new board members, which we encouraged. Later we met with her potential board candidates and were happy with the possibility of increased financial support.

Josie and I agreed to hire Robert Bennett as Managing Director, who would serve under our control. He had worked at Brooklyn Academy of Music as General Manager and came with excellent credentials. For us he was to be solely responsible for financial affairs.

The first play Josie and I chose to do under our joint control was Michael Cristofer's *The Shadow Box* with Mercedes Ruehl, Estelle Parsons, Marlo Thomas, and Frankie Faison, a graduate of our school.

It was a good cast, well acted. The reviews were mild and the public was not in the mood to see a play about characters dying of an unspoken disease—which everyone concluded was AIDS. There was enough interest, however, to complete the twelve-week subscription run. During the rehearsals Mercedes reminded me that we had met before at Ford's Theatre. She was then a young college student whom I flirted with and took to lunch. She was so alarmed that she told her father, an FBI agent. He came to see me and told me to "Get lost!" Ha! As beautiful as Mercedes was then, she is just as beautiful now.

During this time, I had gone to Manchester, England, to participate with Vanessa Redgrave in a benefit for the people of Sarajevo at the four-sided Royal Exchange Theatre. I met the artistic director, Braham Murray, and talked to him about doing an exchange with the Circle. He suggested *Uncle Vanya* which he was anxious to direct with Tom Courtenay. I told him I would think about it and get back to him.

I discussed the possibility of *Uncle Vanya* with Josie and we agreed that this would be a good project.

We opened *Uncle Vanya* at the Circle in February of 1995 with Mr. Courtenay (Vanya), James Fox (Astrov), Amanda Donohoe (Yelena), Werner Klemperer (Serebryakov), and Elizabeth Franz (Maria). Regretfully, the production did not succeed. The worst of it was that it was completely devoid of humor. Almost all of Chekhov's plays are identified by him as comedies—including *Vanya*. You need the contrast of humor in order for the audience to experience the emotional truths of his plays. He, Tennessee and O'Neill were masters of humor to relieve intense moments. As

Mercedes Ruehl and Anthony LaPaglia in Tennessee Williams' *The Rose Tattoo* (1994), directed by Robert Falls

often happens with directors unaware of or unsympathetic to this chemistry, Chekhov suffers. The essential role of Vanya required an actor with a great comic sense but unfortunately comedy is not Mr. Courtenay's forte. It was neither mine nor Josie's fault, but as can happen so often in the theatre—despite a great play—the production still failed.

For our next play we embarked on one of my favorite playwrights, Tennessee Williams' *The Rose Tattoo*. Tennesee said it is a "celebration of the inebriate God." This would mark the first production since its last revival thirty-one years earlier in 1966 with Maureen Stapleton and Harry Guardino.

I had seen several of Robert Falls' productions at the Goodman Theatre in Chicago. Robert and I had been searching for something for him to direct at the Circle. Bingo—here was the right play! Bob selected a cast including Mercedes Ruehl as Serafina in an astonishing performance. Equally as good were Anthony LaPaglia as Mangiacavallo and Dominic Chianese as Father De Leo.

Tattoo is the story of a woman longing for her deceased partner and exuberant sexual mate. Into her life stumbles Mangiacavallo with a rose tattoo on his chest just like her husband's. She instantly falls dizzily in love with him and thanks the saints fervently believing him to be the reincarnation of her husband. Simultaneously her daughter, Rosa, has fallen in love with a sailor. Serafina strongly objects to this relationship and what it might lead to for her daughter's future.

The play is a humorous and optimistic view of carnal love and it ben-efitted from a wonderful romantic setting designed by Santo Loquasto. Bob did a great directorial job turning the coastal town filled with Italian immigrants into a fairytale idiosyncratic village that we would all like to visit.

Many of Tennessee's plays are about the suppressed eroticism of the leading characters. But in *Tattoo* there is an exception. Here the erotica bursts forth in a very funny scene between Serafina and Mangiacavallo as they awkwardly try to seduce each other.

Tattoo was a great success for all involved so we decided to keep rolling with Tennessee's two one-acts: *Something Unspoken* and *Suddenly Last Summer* under the title *Garden District*. *Something Unspoken*, which I directed, was performed by the ageless, wonderful Myra Carter as the wealthy older woman and Pamela Payton-Wright as her young assistant. Another example of Tennessee's elusively erotic plays, *Unspoken's* about an older lady who is in love with a young woman. I had happily worked with Pamela in *Streetcar*, *Menagerie* and *Romeo and Juliet*, all of which she was superb in. So the rehearsals with Pamela and myself were very convivial. But the experience with Myra was trying. Our rehearsals were simply not moving the play forward.

One night after rehearsals I asked Myra and Pamela to have a drink and something to eat with me. We went to the little restaurant on the corner. Pamela and I ordered dinner and drinks but Myra said she didn't want anything. I made a toast, but Myra refused to clink glasses. She said it was bad luck to toast with water. And then with some urging from Pamela and myself, she reluctantly ordered a drink and then said, "I'll only take a sip." We then toasted each other. Then the conversation started to flow. Sparks were flying. Ideas bounced around and communi-cations were perfect. We happily ate and voluminously conversed about the play. So every night this "eat-drink-speak" routine continued in the little restaurant on the corner. What we learned during those meals we put together the next day in the rehearsal studio. I came to love Myra as much I do Pamela. It was an offbeat way to rehearse but I'm sure Ten-nessee would have approved. And you know where we had our opening night party? The little restaurant on the corner. Unfortunately the eu-phoria we felt for our good work was not acknowledged by the critics.

Laura Linney and Tony Goldwyn in Phillip Barry's
Holiday (1995), directed by David Warren

From the time Bob Bennett was appointed managing director Josie began interfering in his financial management and ultimately ignored Bob's advice. Our financial situation was in disarray. Bob was being led instead of leading. After *Garden District*, Bob resigned and Josie, over my objections, hired an inexperienced flunky to replace him who withheld or made payments according to Josie's instructions. Josie's interference in management areas where she was totally out of her depth only made matters worse. We were sitting on a disaster waiting to happen.

Philip Barry's play *Holiday* had opened in 1928, eleven months before the stock market crash. Ironically, the play is about a super-rich New York family, the Setons, with three adult children. One of whom, Julia, the oldest daughter, falls madly in love with Johnnie, a young Wall Street financier played by Tony Goldwyn in our production. She later rebuffs him when he reveals to the family that he will retire when he accumulates $25,000, giving him enough funds to swim and have fun. After that glorious "retirement" and his funds expended, he will return to work. In other words he is reversing the pattern of retiring when you are old—he's going to do it when he's young.

Julia wants a house in the country and one in town and says like an echo of her father, "There is no such thrill in the world as making money." The other sister Linda, played by Laura Linney, who is very independent-minded, affirms Johnny's idea.

It was a superb production directed by David Warren with Tony, Laura, Reg Rogers, Tom Lacy, and Michael Countryman, with an ingenious set designed by Derek McLane in which the attic playroom was dropped in from our ceiling.

John Russell, Chairman, myself, and the Board of Directors, received notice from the IRS that payroll taxes had not been paid for the past several months. I hit the ceiling. I was furious and insisted that we immediately pay off the debt with our assets. So a procedure was set in place to make weekly payments and reduce the taxes. But lo and behold there was something amiss. The payments were not made.

I was fed up and wanted to end our relationship but the board wanted Josie to continue despite the dire financial situation we found ourselves in.

We were, however, having some successes, such as *Holiday*. Our next production was *Bus Stop* with Billy Crudup and Mary Louise Parker directed by Josie. The film had been very popular with Marilyn Monroe. Everyone knows the story about a young rodeo cowboy, Bo, in pursuit of a wayward, aimless beauty and sometime singer named Cherie. Bo is determined to take her back to his ranch in Montana and marry her. He is like a bull in a china shop in his pursuits and she is a scared mouse. After she rebuffs Bo many times, Cherie finally comes to the realization that she has fallen in love with him. Billy and Mary Louise were right on the money and joyful in their performances. The production didn't mesh in some of the smaller roles. As a result the reviews were mixed and business was mediocre.

Then Josie wanted to do Molière's *Tartuffe*. I was delighted to do this play again—one of the great works of literature. I thought perhaps Stephen Porter would come back and direct? We had had great success with his *Tartuffe* eighteen years earlier starring Tammy Grimes and John Wood. But no, Josie wanted to do a modern version of it, with a new young director. I read it and didn't like it and asked, "Why do this when the original with Richard Wilbur's glorious adaptation is a work of genius?"

But she insisted on doing the modern version. I thought, with the last success of *Holiday* that maybe she had some secret she didn't tell me, like Frank Rich had read the script and loved it! So I let *Tartuffe: Born Again*, reluctantly, happen. I had a terrible sinking feeling in the pit of my stomach. I should have stopped it. But we were partners — co-artistic directors, part of which is compromise.

The production failed badly and worse no payments had been made to the IRS to reduce our obligation. Several months before *Tartuffe*, Josie told me that she wanted to do an event honoring me and celebrating forty-five years of Circle in the Square. We would invite acting alumni to participate in the event and this would be a way for us to raise money. I agreed. But I made a very clear proviso to her: all the money above expenses would be used solely to reduce the debt to the IRS. She agreed.

Josie did a wonderful job for the evening selling the tickets and having alumni perform scenes, songs, and speeches in tribute to the theatre. Annette Bening was the host with Leslie Moonves, CEO of CBS Television. Presenters for the evening included Philip Bosco, Kate Burton, Myra Carter, John Cullum, Blythe Danner, Ruby Dee, Tony Goldwyn, Rosemary Harris, Salome Jens, Jane Krakowski, James Naughton, Christopher Reeve, Campbell Scott, Carole Shelley, and Teresa Wright. The evening was followed by a gala supper party. But not one penny made at the event went to the IRS.

Josie had made some good creative choices but her taking over the financial management of the company brought us to our knees.

CHAPTER 52

ENTER AL, EXIT JOSIE

Once again I turned to my good friend Al Pacino and asked him to consider doing Eugene O'Neill's masterpiece *Hughie*. Two years before I had directed a workshop at the downtown Circle of the fifty-five-minute play with Al. Al likes to keep his workshops secret so there was nothing in the newspapers about it, but when Pacino is in town and is acting, word gets around quickly. The house was filled up for all twelve performances. One of the audience members was Vanessa Redgrave and she told Al and me that it was the best acting and directing she had ever seen in New York. But Al was still not ready to go ahead.

After we had done *Salome*, whenever I would ask Al to do another play he would say, "Let's do Salome." I would respond, "We've already done that play, let's try to find something new." Obviously Al was not satisfied with what he had done in *Salome* and had not achieved the role as he envisioned it. After our production at the Circle Al took *Salome* on a national tour and three years ago he got his wish of performing *Salome* again under the wonderful direction of Estelle Parsons at another Broadway theatre with a fine cast that consisted mostly of Actor Studio members. In that production, Al completely realized the character of Herod. He obviously loves the play and the role. I'm now writing in 2006 and Al has just completed an engagement of *Salome* in Los Angeles, and also is filming the play for motion picture distribution in a style, I believe, similar to his earlier film *Looking for Richard*.

So now back to 1996—after many discussions with Al, I finally got his attention to talk about *Hughie*—which the Circle had done in 1964 on Broadway with Jason Robards. Al told me he had auditioned for the Actor's Studio when he was very young with the role of Erie Smith in *Hughie* and was accepted. He said, "I was a kid then, maybe I'm ready for it now."

Al did another reading of the play in Los Angeles and a couple of days later he called to say that he was now ready to do the play with Paul Benedict playing the Night Clerk and asked if he could direct it. I relented. Al knew of the discord between Josie and myself and said that he would do the play provided that I would be the producer in charge.

In preparation for the play I drove Al and Paul Benedict up to Saratoga to watch the horse races and absorb the atmosphere. We visited the paddock before each race to view the horses and then placed bets and cheered our choices. Al was dressed in a suit very similar to what he later wore as Erie. Being in that environment was valuable insight for our work on the play.

When Al is preparing for a play he always wants to do a tryout out of town to work out the wrinkles and decide whether he will bring the play into New York. So we arranged with Arvin Brown's Long Wharf Theatre in New Haven to put it on and then come to the Circle with the condition that no New York critics would be invited there. When I went to see it Al and I agreed that it was ready to come in. I got my wish of Al coming to play again at the Circle.

When *Hughie* came into the Circle, tickets went on sale and were snapped up by an audience eager to see one of our great actors on stage. His character Erie Smith is a low level gambler and hustler who would do anything for a buck. The play is set in the twenties in the lobby of a rundown hotel located in the 40s just west of Broadway. We meet Erie around 4 A.M. He is down at his heels—his good luck has abandoned him, which he attributes to the demise of the longtime night clerk, Hughie. Erie has been on a bender ever since, his gambling luck is down, clothes are disheveled, with several days growth of a beard and he moves like he hasn't slept in days. He is "moanin' low." He says to the new night clerk, "Hughie gave me confidence" by his interest and belief in Erie's gambling and female exploits. Hughie also provided empathy and admiration.

In an almost continuous dialogue Erie attempts to pique the interest and admiration of the current inaccessible nameless Night Clerk.

Erie tells his life story, which includes victories and defeats with women. Reliving an episode with a prostitute, he says, "Listen, Baby, I got an impediment in my speech. Maybe it sounded like ten, but it was two, and that's all you get." He also recalls his gambling victories and his missions for big-time gambler Arnold Rothstein and most importantly he rhapsodizes about his love of race horses and says, "I tell you, pal, I'd rather sleep in the same stall with old Man o' War than make the whole damn Follies." I'm sure that visit to Saratoga was always in Al's being when Erie talks about horses.

Al had the role down to his fingertips. Al, having been brought up in the Bronx, completely understood the street smarts of Erie and at the same time exposed the character's vulnerability.

As a result of our production and Al's work, the play is now recognized as one of O'Neill's masterpieces. All the tickets were sold and performances were Standing Room Only.

Every night after the performance people lined up behind police barricades and when Al came out they called out "Al! Al!" and strained forward trying to touch him. They would thrust their *Playbills* and photos for him to autograph, which patiently he did, and then he was off in his tinted-window jeep to rousing cheers. The Prince had come down to move amongst his people and then rode off in his chariot! There is a full-length photograph of Al in Erie's costume in the lobby of the Circle and I am so proud of Al's quote that accompanies the photograph, "I love this theatre."

With all this success Josie had still failed to pay the outstanding payroll taxes despite the specific instructions to do so from Chairman John Russell and the Board of Directors. Consequently in July of 1996 Paul, myself, John Russell, and our pre-Josie board all resigned. The remaining Board of Directors, those brought in by Josie, appealed to me to stay on as advisor through the run of *Hughie* because they knew that I was the only person Al would communicate with regarding any element of the production. I agreed to serve in that capacity because I wanted to be sure that Al's time with *Hughie* remained happy and trouble-free. (*Hughie* closed in November after a seventeen-week run after taking in over $2 million—enough dough to pull us clean out of our financial

Al Pacino in Eugene O'Neill's *Hughie* (1996), directed by Mr. Pacino

hole.) Shortly after our resignations, Josie's board fired her because of the company's disarray.

When I resigned I moved my staff and office to my downtown theatre on Bleecker Street. All I had to do was dust it out. I was depressed about this relocation, but the malaise lifted when I began working again in Greenwich Village where I had been involved in so many great productions and warm relationships. I am basically an optimist and I felt in my gut that Paul and I would be back in control of the Circle on Broadway since we were the holders of the lease. I didn't know how or when but I felt it in my bones. I was happy to be back down on secure ground in the Village at the downtown Circle in the Square. I was down the hall from a small room where my son Jonathan and daughter-in-law Chandra lived for a year; and alongside the studio where I had rehearsed so many plays. I enjoyed wandering around the theatre downstairs, which was filled with ghosts of many, many glorious theatrical events.

I also loved roaming the streets of the Village, dropping into cafes and restaurants. The charm of the Village is eternal—like Paris. I reveled again in being solely responsible for keeping the building in working order—taking care of roof and pipe leaks, boiler functioning, stage condition and lighting equipment as well as the overall security of the building. It was an old building that had originally been a nickelodeon at the turn of the century. I knew every inch of it and breathed it in deeply with satisfaction to be back. At this time there were no plays running at the theatre, off-Broadway was in decline, so I made a deal with the New School Actor's Studio to lease the theatre for classes and student productions.

My staff along with me included Michael Stapleton, and Susan Frankel, who had joined me many years before and as of this writing has been with us the past twenty-five years and is still 23 years old! Susan's responsibility was to keep the financial records for the school and the downtown theatre. She is a wonderfully efficient and dedicated colleague and extremely intelligent, a pleasure to be with, a beautiful woman. She is also my main source of recommendations for gifts for my grandchildren—French and American—and also for restaurants in the city, where she must take into account my penchant for tablecloths, decent food and quiet atmosphere, in that order.

In the evenings I would go uptown and visit Al and Paul Benedict and talk about our lives and the circumstances about the play. And whatever needed to be straightened out I took care of so the actors could do their work in peace and calm. At no time did I feel that I had lost the Circle since the school was also under Paul's and my guidance. The new board had failed to pay the rent and Paul and I met those expenses. The school was flourishing. I observed and critiqued classes, and continued a very active life.

CHAPTER 53

Hiatus

The new board appointed Greg Mosher to replace Josie. His first production was *Stanley*, a new British play that had received very good reviews in London. The critics here were mixed and the audiences didn't take to it at all. So the run had to be cut short. I was not there and I can only assume that the following took place:

They used the remaining *Hughie* money to produce *Stanley* and to help meet their weekly operating expenses. But when the *Hughie* money ran out, *Stanley* closed and they had no money to pay the actors or the staff. One day when I came in for some school activity, there was nobody in the theatre offices—just half-filled coffee cups on desks, cigarette butts in ash trays, scattered papers, and personal effects in the open desk drawers but no staff. It was as though a fire alarm had gone off. I was told by actors and staff that when they went to cash their last payroll checks the bank would not honor them.

The board of directors sought the protection of the United States Bankruptcy Court. The purpose of which was: one, to hold their creditors at bay until they could put a financial plan for the future in place; and two, to secure the lease, which has been in Paul's and my name for all these years. They wanted our lease rescinded and turned over to them.

Regarding the bankruptcy proceedings: on point one—which sought to protect them from their creditors—the judge ruled that they failed to provide the court with a practical financial plan for the future of their company. And on point two—regarding the lease—our landlord's attorney had appeared at the hearing and corroborated the fact that the landlord had insisted that they would only accept Paul and I as the signatories on the original lease. On this point, the court ruled that the lease between Paul, myself, and the landlord was still in effect. As a result of the court's negative findings on these two points the judge ruled against granting bankruptcy protection to the applicants.

Our counsel for this matter and its successful conclusion was the brilliant, articulate, and precise Arthur Olick, a man much honored in legal circles. When he spoke in our defense he spoke the truth. Mr. Olick had served on our board years before and knew the inner workings of the Circle very well.

All during this period—this bankruptcy proceeding and the collapse of Mosher and company, a time I refer to as "our hiatus"—Paul and I, with the able assistance of Colin O'Leary, School Director, continued to operate the Circle in the Square Theatre School in our classrooms and studios of the theatre.

With the court's ruling the theatre was now undeniably back in our hands, but we didn't have any money so we decided after forty-seven years of producing that we had to change direction. At this point there had not been a play in the theatre in twenty-one months! We began seeking productions that needed a Broadway home. We wanted to maintain Circle's reputation so from that point on we have chosen the plays very carefully.

CHAPTER 54

Rebirth

Sweet, beautiful, luscious Fate was back again tapping me gently on the shoulder, nudging me to open my eyes and read *The New York Times*. And there I found an article that Vanessa Redgrave, while doing research in the library of the University of Houston for her performance of Tennessee Williams' *Orpheus Descending*, had found his undiscovered play *Not About Nightingales*. This was Tennessee's first full-length play, and it had never been produced. Vanessa arranged for it to be performed in London at the Royal Shakespeare Theatre. Then some months later I read once again in the *Times* that it was now being performed at the Alley Theatre in Houston—a three-sided theatre similar to ours.

Sweet fate was working for Tennessee and us. My mistress would be so happy to have actors back in the Circle and another play by my beloved Tennessee with whom we had been so closely associated over the years—nine plays thus far.

I called Vanessa in Texas and told her that Paul and I were back running the Circle. She had seen the newspaper stories about our troubles and said in her beautiful English cadence, "Oh, Ted, that's wonderful! I'm so happy for you." And then I asked her if Tennessee's play and the staging would be right for the Circle. I could hear the smile in her voice, as she responded, "It would be perfect and I would do anything to help reopen the theatre." Then Vanessa got busy putting all the producing elements together with Carole Shorenstein Hays, Stuart Thompson, and the Royal Shakespeare Theatre to make this happen. Several months later after the run at the Alley, that company of actors, which included Corin Redgrave (as Boss Whalen, warden of the prison), Finbar Lynch (Jim Allison, his prisoner assistant and flunky) and Sherri Parker Lee (Boss's secretary, Eva Crane), all came to the Circle.

Trevor Nunn, Artistic Director of the Royal Shakespeare Company was the director for *Nightingale*, also his and Richard Hoover's concept for the set of the

Corin Redgrave in Tennessee Williams' *Not About Nightingales* (1999), directed by Trevor Nunn

prison was ingenious. We had trap doors from which steam heat floated that gave the illusion of real, high-degree heat into which uncooperative prisoners were thrown, called the "sweatboxes." There was another trap for the below-ground office for Boss Whalen, where he attempts to seduce his secretary, Eva Crane. Across the back wall were two levels of cell blocks. In two sections of the theatre, on either side of the stage, some seats were removed to allow for entrances and exits of the prisoners and their guards. With the guards and prisoners walking so close to the audience, it made them feel as though they too were helpless prisoners. The set and costumes were all gray and black, making the overall effect even more chilling. A "place in Hell" as Tennessee had originally entitled the play.

Nightingale kept you on the edge of your seat. It is about a struggle against inhuman conditions in an island prison. Was Tennessee thinking Alcatraz? The prisoners' hunger strike is caused by the warden's brutality and his ptomaine-inducing diet of spaghetti and meatballs. The play is multifaceted in its observations about the relationships between Boss

Whalen and Allison and Eva, the prisoners to each other and the guards to the prisoners. In other words, at 27, writing his first full length play, Tennessee was already exploring what was to be embodied in his future works—the complexity of human nature and the conflict between good and evil and lust and gentility. As far as I know, Tennessee had never been in prison. So it is astonishing that this young playwright was so intuitive of the customs and the relationships between the prisoners and their guards. It also reveals his knowledge of the technical limitations and possibilities of the stage. Where he got all of this knowledge I have no idea. I doubt he saw many plays living in St. Louis with his family. He loved movies, which was both his food and an escape from his family. Perhaps the prison films of the thirties influenced him.

If Tennessee had been an unknown writer when *Nightingale* came to the Circle, it probably would have been heralded as the arrival of a great new talent. Unfortunately, the critics, who have a penchant for comparing an author's current work with earlier ones, could not see it for its own merit. To some of them it had seeds of Blanche and Stanley in *Streetcar,* Biff in *Cat,* and Alma in *Summer and Smoke,* all of which is true, but each play should be judged on its own merit. Playwriting is not an assembly line.

One of the major critics said of the play, "A feverish, full-strength compassion for people in cages makes *Nightingales* fly toward a realm of pain and beauty that is the province of greatness." Unfortunately this was not written until the sixth paragraph. If it had appeared earlier it would have been of real value to the production. So based on good but not great business one can only assume that the readers of this major critic's review had lost interest before the "province of greatness" in the sixth paragraph.

Corin Redgrave was brilliant as the despotic warden reveling in his powerful position, disdainful of the sensitivities of the humans he is surrounded by, devious in his sexual pursuit and yet underneath concealing a secret insecurity. Jim Allison (Finbar), a stand-in for Tennessee, came through as a ray of torture, sunshine and hope. He falls in love with the secretary, Eva, and they plan to run away to a better life. Eventually he escapes by crashing through the window of the island prison. Whether he survives or not we don't know.

The production was nominated for six Tony Awards: Best New Play; Best Actor, Corin Redgrave; Best Featured Actor, Finbar Lynch; Best Lighting; Best Direction, Trevor Nunn; and Richard Hoover did win the Tony for Best Scenic Design.

We were ecstatic, the Circle was back on its feet and I was jumping for joy—doo daa, doo daa! I bless Tennessee, Corin, Trevor and Vanessa for making the magic happen! I remember standing in the back of the theatre at the first preview after twenty-one months of our being dark. The house lights were still on and audience members were filling the seats. Warm tears of happiness came to my eyes. My beautiful mistress was back on Broadway shaking her hips in happiness.

Next came Sam Shepard's *True West* directed by Matthew Warchus with Philip Seymour Hoffman (a former student at the Circle School), John C. Reilly, Celia Weston, and Robert LuPone produced by Ron Kastner, a play about two brothers and their latent jealousies. It was powerfully acted. For each performance John and Phillip would switch roles—a tour de force in acting and many people came back to see the actors in their opposite roles. This brought the audience great joy and insight into the art of acting. The production was nominated for Best Play and Best Director and John and Philip were both nominated for best leading actor. The production was a big success. Young people were sleeping on the streets outside the box office hoping to get canceled tickets. Paul and I knew Sam Shepard from the days long ago when we had produced *Six from La Mama*. *True West* was a lovely reunion for us.

HBO then did *The Chris Rock Show* for a four-month run. It was taped at the theatre for HBO viewing. He is one very funny guy with big eyes, which are capable of moving in several directions at the same time. This was followed by *The Rocky Horror Show* directed by Christopher Ashley and produced by Jordan Roth.

All three shows brought in very young audiences, which is a healthy thing for theatre—get them while they are young, so when they grow up they've got the habit.

Next, Paul and I got a call from Carole Rothman, the Artistic director of the Second Stage Theatre to come and see *Metamorphoses*. She wasn't sure if it would work well at the Circle, she wanted our opinion. The Second Stage Theatre is a proscenium, so we were curious to see

John C. Reilly and Philip Seymour Hoffman in Sam Shepard's *True West* (2000), directed by Matthew Warchus

how this production might work in our space. Paul, Florence, my assistant Holly Ricciuti and I saw the play and loved it. The subject matter is based on the poems of Ovid. The action of the play takes place in and around a swimming pool. Watching the play at Second Stage's proscenium theatre, the action was at a distance, and it was difficult for me to connect with the material. Paul and I thought that the subject matter and direction would be enhanced by being in the center of our audience thereby making the material immediate. The swimming pool would in effect be in the audience's lap. Seeing it there at Second Stage, I thought it would only run for about eight weeks because the material seemed too esoteric but in the Circle Ovid's stories splashed up onto the audience like the water in the pool and towels were provided to keep them dry. People laughed and cried at the contemporaneity of these ancient stories.

Roy Gabay, Robyn Goodman, and others produced the play at our theatre. It was very well-received and had a sustained run for a year. Mary Zimmerman won a well-deserved Tony Award for Best Director, and nominees were Daniel Ostling for best scenic design and the entire production for Best Play.

Next Matthew Warchus was back again directing *Life (X) 3* by Yasmina Reza (who wrote *Art*) with Helen Hunt and John Turturro, Linda Edmond, and Brent Spiner. Ron Kastner was the producer. The action takes place between two couples. Each scene is a variation on their relationships. Audiences ate it up for its insight into the relationship of married couples but not the critics. We sold out for practically the whole run.

And then we were dark again for eleven months. I spent much of the time seeing off-Broadway shows in the city and traveling to wherever else I heard there was a good production.

Swoosie Kurtz, who had worked for us in *Tartuffe*, was performing in an off-Broadway show entitled *Frozen*, by Bryony Lavery. So I went to see it and I was just knocked out. Swoosie and the other actors were great. It was directed by Doug Hughes, the son of Barnard Hughes and Helen Stenborg.

I invited the producers from the Manhattan Classic Company (MCC) theatre, to bring the show to the Circle. I knew it would work even better at the Circle because of our seating configuration; better lighting equipment and the stage could be made higher and therefore more accessible to the audience.

The producers agonized over which theatre should bring it to Broadway—a proscenium or a three-sided space like us? After many visits they finally came to the conclusion that the play would work best in our space. Sweet fate and some big bucks made it happen. The central figure in the decision to move to the Circle was Doug Hughes who with a sure hand guided every aspect of the play with his brilliant direction.

Co-starring with Swoosie were Laila Robins and Brían F. O'Byrne. *Frozen* received four Tony nominations for Best Play, Director, Actor, and Featured Actor, which Brían won.

After *Frozen*, we were dark for several months. Believe it or not, I was getting nervous again because the expenses of maintaining an empty house are high. But Paul kept saying, "Don't worry, something'll come along." I am an optimist but Paul does me one better by being a pragmatic optimist. The pragmatic optimist wins out! Paul and his wife Florence, had been invited to see the off-Broadway production of *The 25th Annual Putnam County Spelling Bee*. Paul was hesitant to see it and complained to Florence that he did not want to see adults performing the roles of youngsters. Florence responded very patiently, "But it's your granddaughter who called and said it was a wonderful musical." He relented, "All right, I'll go." And the next night Paul and Florence, as dutiful grandparents, went to the opening night. After five minutes

Paul turned to Florence and said, "I love it." I felt the same way when I saw it.

Paul called David Stone, the producer, after the opening night to encourage him to move *Spelling Bee* to the Circle. In that conversation David said he "knew who wore the pants in the family!" Paul queried him as to what that meant and David Stone said he had met his granddaughter, Milah, at a preview and she had told him that *Spelling Bee* was a terrific musical and it should be on Broadway.

We invited James Lapine, the director, to see the Circle; he brought his designers along to discuss how he could restage the production. James commented to Paul and myself that he thought the play would work well here. Paul was in Florida at an industry conference which David Stone also attended. Paul talked and talked and talked to David whenever he had a chance and in his most persuasive way convinced him that it was a good idea for the show to move to the Circle. As I write this it is July 2006 and the play has been running over a year. Milah, if she chooses, will become a very successful producer, she's already batting a thousand!

There is now a national tour of *Spelling Bee*. Recently the New York City *Daily News*'s 42nd Annual Citywide Spelling Bee for middle school students was held here on the set of *The 25th Annual Putnam County Spelling Bee*. The two winners have appeared in a performance of Circle's *Spelling Bee* and were also featured on the nationally syndicated television show *Live with Regis and Kelly*. So the "Queen Bee" is doing as nature requires—bringing forth many other bees. However, it is time now to print this book. If it has closed, you'll have to read *The New York Times* to find out what's playing here, as this is certainly not the end of our journey.

CHAPTER 55

COMING FULL CIRCLE

Since *Nightingales* in 1997, all the plays at the Circle have been produced by other individuals, but Paul and I have been producing in other
enriching ways.

Way back in 1963 I started the Circle in the Square Theatre School
which has evolved into a comprehensive two-year training program for
college graduates interested in pursuing a career in the professional theatre. I wanted to play a part in training the actors who in future would
be working at our theatre and others. A couple of years later we added
classes in other disciplines to make for a rounded education in theatre
work: scene study, dance, voice and speech, combat, script interpretation,
etc. At the time we created this school we were providing something quite
different than what was being offered for actor training in New York City,
which were individual teachers providing a class that was not in any way
connected to any other theatre discipline. In 1995, we started an Outreach
program to introduce the K-6 school kids of New York City to the theatre.
Our graduates perform multicultural plays for the children—many of
which I have directed. I try to make productions as participatory as possible and it thrills me to see the children interacting with the play. There
is nothing more joyful in the world than asking a child a question that
evokes a rousing answer. Their tumultuous responses stop the show and
only when the actors raise their arms for silence can they proceed. I think
of those happy children as the stand-ins for my own five grandchildren.

Nine years ago, with the help of my son Jonathan, in our efforts to fill the gap of Arts Education in New York City, Jonathan initiated a program where we teach the third and fourth graders of Public School No. 11 how to write a play. At the end of the semester their plays are performed by our Artists in Residence (Circle graduates) on our Broadway stage. In attendance are their astonished parents observing the transformation that has taken place with their children through their successful struggle to write a play. Our work at P.S. 11 has proven to be a literary and socially expanding experience for the children. So, with these activities Paul and I do continue to produce at the Circle but in a different way.

The 1990s were a roller coaster ride, with Paul joining Jujamcyn Theaters (Rocco Landsman, the president of the company, made him an offer he couldn't refuse). He has made great contributions to the company and has become one of the most important and respected men in the theatre and with Jujamcyn is involved in all of their outstanding productions. Fortunately for the Circle, our partnership has continued for forty-three years. We've come through tremendous traps which seemed at the time to be a bottomless pit. But thanks to Sweet Fate my mistress is smiling and we're still standing.

Recently, I was asked to write a play for a one-act festival at the First Stage in Los Angeles. I said, "I've never written a play and I just can't do it." I tried to put it out of my mind. I then went to France to visit my son Andrew and *mes petits enfants*, Samuel, Clementine, and Benjamin Theodore. Still the challenge was swirling around in my head and I thought, "Why don't I try? Don't be afraid to do something new." Then one night while sleeping in a medieval house the play suddenly came to me—complete with exposition, crisis and resolution. The next day I called my beautiful trusted assistant Holly and told her I had written a play, and she said, "You? No!" And I said, "Listen" and I proceeded to dictate the dialogue that just poured out of me.

The play is about an incident that occurred between George C. Scott and me. I didn't know what title it should have. Colleen and his close friends always lovingly referred to him as "G.C." so I decided that that should be the title because of the love that I felt for George and besides it would make the potential viewer curious about what "G.C." means.

I believe the title of a play should never be on-the-nose of its subject matter. Look, for example, at *Cat on a Hot Tin Roof, Who's Afraid of Virginia Woolf?*, and *The Iceman Cometh.*

In May of the same year, GC was performed. I directed it at the festival and it was very well received. I can tell you it was one strange experience directing an actor playing Theodore Mann. I knew exactly what he was thinking every moment. As a result of the good reception, I have been invited to bring the play and do seminars with students at several universities around the country. In September of 2005 I directed GC at the University of Louisville. While in Louisville, I did what every good grandfather would do, I bought "Louisville Slugger" bats for my French grandchildren with their signatures embossed on each one. They are revolutionizing France's interest in baseball.

People always ask me how theatre has changed since I began. When I look back and think of all the plays that we have done, I realize that nothing but everything has changed, such as laser lighting, computerized box offices, digitized light and sound cues, the sale and acquisition of tickets, the internet both for research and for ticket sales. The pattern of theatre ticket sales has also changed dramatically. July was always a bad month, as were the two weeks before Christmas and the whole month of January after it. All of that is different now. I believe that this is because there is more interest throughout the country in theatre. Obviously the cost of producing has increased tremendously. Off-Broadway shows that used to cost four thousand now need almost a million to put them on—and ticket prices both on and off have gone up! When we started in 1951 they were $1.50 and now prices range from $85 to over $100 for a dramatic play. But a meaningful play that touches the heart will still draw an audience on and off-Broadway, and a new innovative musical will do the same. The hunger for good theatre continues due in part to the tremendous influx of tourists.

As far as the actual process of preparing a play for production however, nothing has changed in the fifty-plus years I've been involved in theatre. On the first day of rehearsal in a semi-darkened studio or theatre a group of actors gather together around a table, scripts in hand, and are introduced. Many know each other from previous productions. Then the director talks about his understanding of the play and what he would like the group to accomplish. Then the actors read the play to the end of Act One. After lunch, they return and read the rest of the play. Then they are dismissed for the day. That night, thoughts and emotions about the play swirl about in the heads and hearts of the actors. On the second day, actors are encouraged to speak of their impression of the play and of their characters. And then they read through the play again. On the third day, the director, more than likely, will start blocking. Rehearsal period for Broadway plays is three-and-a-half weeks with very few exceptions and musicals are for six weeks, but these first three days lay the foundation for the work ahead. And so it goes, the enduring tradition of doing a play.

The process is slow but with hard work, the play begins to materialize through the actors, who transform into the characters. Every actor is a chameleon with multiple characters deep within.

The Circle's reputation is worldwide and when I travel to a theatre I'm gratified that the Circle is so well respected. Recently, I redid my Who's Who biography for *Playbill* and was amused and amazed at how much Paul and I had accomplished, most of which I hope I have conveyed in this book. Through the generous contribution of the Stephen and Mary Birch Foundation headed by Patrick and Rose Patek, the Circle has been able to donate its entire archive—over 400 cram-filled boxes—to the New York Public Library at Lincoln Center.

For the future, dramatic theatre has to find a way to reenter each Broadway season through the efforts and the energy of new young producers, directors and playwrights. Which I firmly believe will come to pass. After all, if the Circle can come back from many near extinctions, certainly Broadway drama can too.

Circle's unique stage and audience closeness is very much in the tradition of Greek theatre, which has survived for over two thousand years through many changing fashions. The resurgence of three-sided and four-sided theatres throughout the county seems to be signaling a change away from proscenium stages, in which the audience sits at a distance looking at a picture frame. Perhaps as our culture evolves our young people will want to see more substantial, emotionally moving drama, plays that deal with the truths of our lives, as any of the great classics do, that have survived through the ages.

To you, the reader, thank you one and all for your kind attention. Writing this book has been an interesting journey for me. Recalling the incidents of my life, have in many cases been painful and difficult and sometimes even wrenching to write about. At times, I didn't want to continue because I was thinking to myself this is all about the past. Around three years ago the past became very interesting and rich to me and recalling it became energizing. The past became like a play with many acts. Even though I knew the ending of each act I wanted to tell it as accurately as possible. Some of the remembrances have been dizzyingly happy like fine champagne. I've often thought that even the smallest incidents of my life were like short scenes from a play. I'm glad I haven't missed a minute of it.

Conflict, however sad, is part of life and an essential ingredient in theatre. And my beloved mistress keeps the circle of theatrical life moving round and round. As Shakespeare wrote, "All the world's a stage and the men and women merely players; they have their exits and their entrances; and one man in his time plays many parts." Which is, if you'll excuse me, my exit line.

Curtain.

Q&A with Circle School Students

Every September, at the beginning of the term, since the Circle school moved uptown I do a seminar with the first-year students. I tell them the history of the Circle and then ask for questions from the group. It is fascinating every year to find out what is in the minds of the young actors:

When and why was the school at Circle in the Square started?

We were operating down on Bleecker Street and I had a large unused studio and at that time there were all kinds of ads in show business newspapers about schools and classes offered. I thought we should be involved in this because we will be hiring the actors as they come along so we need to be part of the training process. So I decided to start acting classes in a large empty studio.

What are the challenges facing actors today as opposed to when you started?

How to get the job. The only place that I know of where you don't have to run around trying to find work is in Russia because there they have repertory companies funded by the government. When you are hired it's for life.

The challenge for actors here is always the same. You gotta hustle around, make yourself known. Take opportunities that come even though they may not be for money. Continue to study and practice your craft. And what you will learn here at Circle and in life will prepare you for your career.

What is the process by which you choose the plays?

As always, myself and the staff read everything that comes to us—and if something grabs us, I do a reading of the play first, and then a workshop. If it still has promise, I arrange for a regional theatre production and then, ultimately, a Broadway one. Or I see something in a regional theatre or off-off-Broadway and I invite it to come here. We also read very carefully the submissions of producers who want to do plays at the Circle. Obviously, we choose the ones we like the most.

What type of an actor do you find the most engaging to work with?

First of all I like to be surprised by an actor's audition. When I chose actors for a play I often cast against type. I admire actors who do research and have a point of view about what it is they want to accomplish with their role. And who are open to the rehearsal process, which I've always considered a period of give and take. I have my opinions; the actor has his and somewhere we have to find the truth of the play and how the playwright intended the play to be performed. This process is a very engaging and creative one. I try to find an actor who speaks to me as though they are the character.

Is there a certain acting technique that is taught here at Circle?

The faculty presents many styles and the actor chooses over the two-year period of their training what is most beneficial. The Method, Stella Adler, Stanislavski, Uta Hagen, and Meisner Technique are all presented here. An eclectic selection of acting methods.

How has the philosophy of Circle changed over the years?

It hasn't really changed. I think the same elements are still there. I always choose a play from a personal point of view and I go with my gut feeling. You can't try to analyze what the general public might like. You have to be attuned to your own response and be as honest to that as possible. When I read a play I like that others don't, I become intrigued. It tells me that there is something provocative. For example, *Trojan Women*, most of my associates thought it was a terrible idea and that there would not be a public for this. They proved to be totally wrong. *Trojan Women* was a huge success and we are very proud to have done that and other Greek classics. When I wanted to do Shaw, for example, he had been discredited by the critics as much as O'Neill had been; both of them considered old-fashioned. We did nine Shaw plays and all of them were extremely well received by the critics and public. And eighteen productions of O'Neill, for which we received our highest honors.

When you decide to go ahead and produce a play you are putting yourself on the line. You are risking your reputation as well as that of the actors and also risking a lot of money. So you want to choose well and meaningfully. I haven't been right all the time but I have a pretty good batting average.

What are the opportunities for Latin actors?

We have had very few Latin actors come to us to audition. I don't know why that is. Benicio Del Toro was a student here and he has a great career. So it is possible to break through. We don't restrict. As a producer I am trying to find the best actor for a role. I don't care what color or what ethnic background he or she is. I directed Raul Julia (a Puerto Rican with a strong Latin accent) as an Englishman in *Where's Charley?* without hesitation.

What production of yours stands out most of all?

I am very proud of *Hughie* because it took a lot of effort to get Al Pacino to agree to it—a three-year pursuit.

Why are you not producing anymore?

Well, after producing for fifty years and going through all the stress we just decided to have an easier time of it. But we are involved in the productions, attending rehearsals, and providing our input. We just got tired of gambling so long. My wife always used to say you are a gambler—you love to gamble—and I would respond, "We are the longest floating crap game in New York," and that response is still true today. Because when we select a play to come in here it is a roll of the dice.

What keeps you coming back to the theatre? What advice can you give to us?

I direct one production a year with graduating students and I direct Opera. I've also been directing Irish classics and new plays for a small theatre company, Hamm and Clov, in Westchester. And I help friends and students with scenes that they're preparing. I love the theatre and the creative juices that you have to have in directing. Rehearsal is such an exhilarating and difficult time and then to come out with the finished product with the actors doing the performance that you had hoped for and the play being realized and appreciated by an audience—it's a wonderful process and satisfaction for me. But I do get frightened every time I do one.

Have you ever had participation in film or TV?

Trumpets of the Lord, with James Earl Jones, which I directed for Canadian Broadcasting as a film. We taped several of our productions for Pat Weaver's Pay Television, a company that came into existence before you were born and before there was cable television. Pat, by the way, is Sigourney's father. I have long had a desire to make a film of a Lanford Wilson short play, *Eukia,* and I still hope it comes to be. I'm a photographer as well, so my visual training will come in handy.

Sources

Gelb, Arthur and Barbara, *O'Neill*. New York: Harper & Row, 1973.

Gelb, Arthur and Barbara, *O'Neill: Life With Monte Cristo*. New York: Applause, 2000.

Sheaffer, Louis: *O'Neill: Son and Playwright*: Boston: Little, Brown and Company, 1973. Sheaffer, Louis: *O'Neill: Son and Playwright*: *Vol.1*: Boston: Cooper Square Press, 2002.

Scovell, Jane, *Oona: Living in the Shadows: A Biography of Oona O'Neill Chaplin*. New York: Warner Books, 1998.

Tao House, Eugene O'Neill National Historic Site, National Park Service, Danville, CA.

Researchers

Paul Libin
Holly Ricciuti
Cody Perret
E. Colin O'Leary
Susan Frankel
Patricia Michael
Arthur Goldman
Susannah Conn
Joey Stocks
Kevin Jones

Photographers

Bert Andrews   pp. 193, 205, 207

Susan Cook   p. 346

Bettina Crone   p. 306

Peter Cunningham   p. 333

Jerry Danzig   p. 43

T. Charles Erickson   p. 379

Elliot Erwitt   p. 161

Friedman-Abeles   pp. 82, 164, 187 (both), 246, 249

Gerry Goodstein   p. 371

Henry Grossman   p. 221

Tom Lawlor   p. 348

Theodore Mann   p. 15

Joan Marcus   pp. 384, 387

Mary Ellen Marks from Lee Gross, Inc.   pp. 252, 253

Gjon Mili   pp. 100, 103 (both), 104, 106, 143, 148 (all), 151

Inge Morath   pp. 271, 274

Nickolas Muray   p. 109

Carol Rosegg   p. 373

Roy Schatt   p. 58

Sheldon Secunda   p. 170

Anita & Steve Shevett   p. 364

Anisim Sorkin   p. 289

Martha Swope   pp. 165, 226, 261, 264, 279, 287, 305, 307, 311, 312, 315,
    324, 336, 339, 343, 349, 354, 357, 359

George D. Vincent   p. 313

Zodiac Photographers   p. 240

INDEX